TEEN LIFE IN
AFRICA

**Recent Titles in
Teen Life around the World**

Teen Life in the Middle East
Ali Akbar Mahdi, editor

Teen Life in Asia
Judith J. Slater, editor

TEEN LIFE IN AFRICA

Edited by Toyin Falola

Foreword by Richard M. Lerner

Teen Life around the World
Jeffrey S. Kaplan, Series Editor

GREENWOOD PRESS
Westport, Connecticut • London

Library of Congress Cataloging-in-Publication Data

Teen life in Africa / edited by Toyin Falola; foreword by Richard M. Lerner.
     p. cm.—(Teen life around the world, ISSN 1540–4897)
  Includes bibliographical references and index.
  ISBN 0–313–32194–9 (alk. paper)
  1. Teenagers—Africa—Social conditions. 2. Teenagers—Africa—Conduct
of life. 3. Teenagers—Education—Africa. 4. Self-esteem in adolescence—Africa.
I. Falola, Toyin. II. Series.

HQ799.8.A35 T44 2004
305.235′096—dc21   2002192765

British Library Cataloguing in Publication Data is available.

Copyright © 2004 by Toyin Falola

Library of Congress Catalog Card Number: 2002192765
ISBN: 0–313–32194–9
ISSN: 1540–4897

First published in 2004

Greenwood Press, 88 Post Road West, Westport, CT 06881
An imprint of Greenwood Publishing Group, Inc.
www.greenwood.com

Printed in the United States of America

The paper used in this book complies with the
Permanent Paper Standard issued by the National
Information Standards Organization (Z39.48–1984).

10 9 8 7 6 5 4 3 2 1

For Professor Bayo Oyebade, Oko Sade Omo 'Badan

CONTENTS

FOREWORD: TOWARD A WORLD OF POSITIVE YOUTH DEVELOPMENT

In these early years of the twenty-first century a new vision and vocabulary for discussing young people has emerged. Propelled by the increasingly more collaborative contributions of scholars, practitioners, advocates, and policy makers, youth are viewed as resources to be developed. The new vocabulary is legitimated by scholarly efforts at advancing what are termed "developmental systems theories." These models emphasize the plasticity of human development, that is, the potential for systematic change in behavior that exists as a consequence of mutually influential relationships between the developing person and his or her biology, psychological characteristics, family, community, culture, physical and designed ecology, and historical niche.

The plasticity of development legitimizes an optimistic view of potential for promoting positive changes in human life and directs emphasis to the strengths for positive development that are present within all young people. Accordingly, concepts such as developmental assets, positive youth development, moral development, civic engagement, well-being, and thriving have been used increasingly in research and applications associated with adolescents and their world. All concepts are predicated on the ideas that *every* young person has the potential for successful, healthy development and that *all* youth possess the capacity for positive development.

This vision for and vocabulary about youth has evolved over the course of a scientifically arduous path. Complicating this new, positive conceptualization of the character of youth as resources for the healthy development of self, families, and communities was an antithetical theoretical approach to the nature and development of young people. Dating within science to, at least, the publication in 1904 of G. Stanley Hall's two-volume work on adolescence, youth have been characterized by a deficit view, one that conceptualizes their behaviors as deviations from normative development. Understanding such deviations was not seen as being of direct relevance to scholarship aimed at discovering the principles of basic developmental processes. Accordingly, the characteristics of youth were regarded as issues of "only" applied concern—and thus of secondary scientific interest. Not only did this model separate basic science from application but, as well, it disembedded the adolescent from the study of normal or healthy development. It also often separated the young person from among those members of society that could be relied on to produce valued outcomes for family, community, and civic life. In short, the deficit view of youth as problems to be managed split the study of young people from the study of health and positive individual and social development.

The current scholarly and applied work that counters the historical, deficit view of adolescence, and in turn builds upon developmental systems theory to advance the new, positive vocabulary about young people and the growing research evidence for the potential of all youth to develop in positive ways, is both represented and advanced significantly by the *Teen Life around the World* series. More so than any other set of resources currently available to young people, parents, and teachers, the volumes in this series offer rich and engaging depictions about the diverse ways in which young people pursue positive lives in their families, communities, and nations. The volumes provide vivid reflections of the energy, passion, and skills that young people possess—even under challenging ecological or economic conditions—and the impressive ways in which adolescents capitalize on their strengths to pursue positive lives during their teenage years and to prepare themselves to be productive adult members of their families and communities.

Across the volumes in this series a compelling story of the common humanity of all people emerges, one that justifies a great deal of hope that, in today's adolescents, there exist the resources for a humane, peaceful, tolerant, and global civil society. To attain such a world, all people must begin by appreciating the diversity of young people and their cultures and that, through such diversity, the world possesses multiple, potentially productive paths to human well-being and accomplishment. Readers of the *Teen Life around the World* series will be rewarded with just this information.

Ultimately, we must all continue to educate ourselves about the best means available to promote enhanced life chances among all of the world's youth, but especially among those whose potential for positive contributions to civil society is most in danger of being wasted. The books in this series constitute vital assets in pursuit of this knowledge. Given the enormous, indeed historically unprecedented, challenges facing all nations, perhaps especially as they strive to raise healthy and successful young people capable of leading civil society productively, responsibly, and morally across the twenty-first century, there is no time to lose in the development of such assets. The *Teen Life around the World* series is, then, a most timely and markedly important resource.

Richard M. Lerner
Eliot-Pearson Department of Child Development
Tufts University
Medford, Massachusetts

SERIES FOREWORD

Have you ever imagined what it would be like to live in a different country? What would it be like to speak a different language? Eat different foods? Wear different clothes? Attend a different school? Listen to different music, or maybe, the same music, in a different language? How about practicing new customs? Or, better yet, a different religion? Simply, how different would your life be if you were born and raised in another region of the world? Would you be different? And if so, how?

As we begin the twenty-first century, young people around the world face enormous challenges. Those born to wealth or relative comfort enjoy technological miracles and can click a button or move a mouse and discover a world of opportunity and pleasure. Those born without means struggle just to survive.

Education, though, remains a way out of poverty and for many privileged young people it is the ultimate goal. As more and more jobs, including those in the manufacturing and service sectors, require literacy, numeracy, and computer skills, brains are increasingly valued over brawn: In the United States, entry-level wages for people with only a high-school education have fallen by more than 20 percent since the 1970s. Job prospects are bleaker than ever for youths who do not continue their education after high school. And, to be sure, while there are exceptions—like the teenager who starts a basement computer business and becomes a multimillionaire—working a string of low-paying service jobs with no medical insurance is a much more common scenario for those with limited education. And this seems to be true for adolescents in most post-industrialist countries around the world.

Adolescent girls, in particular, are at a disadvantage in many nations, facing sex discrimination as an obstacle to obtaining even basic education and social skills. In the Middle East and South Asia, girls are more likely to be pulled from school at an early age, and are thus less likely to develop critical literacy skills. Across most of the world, girls face more demands for work in the home and restrictions on movement that constrain their opportunities to gain direct experience with diverse social worlds. Similarly, as rates of divorce and abandonment rise worldwide, so do the chances in the workplace lessen for young women who fail to obtain skills to function independently. And as adults, they are increasingly vulnerable to poverty and exploitation.

ADOLESCENCE AROUND THE GLOBE

Adolescent life is truly plagued by difficulties and determined by context and circumstance. Anthropologist Margaret Mead (1901–78) may have been the first social scientist to question the universality of the adolescent experience. When Mead contrasted the experience of North American and South Pacific young people in terms of sexuality, she found their experiences and attitudes toward sexuality dramatically different (South Pacific adolescents were more tolerant), and, she contended, adolescence should be seen in the contexts in which people live and dwell. In fact, for Mead and other social scientists, the only definition that can best describe adolescence is at best, restricted to a "period of transition," in which young people are no longer considered children, but not yet considered an adult.

Adolescence is generally understood as the period between the ages of 15 to 19, with some scholars referring to it as up to age 24. The term *young adult* is the most apt term for this age group, and without doubt, the many biological, psychological, and behavioral changes which mark this age, make this a concept that is continually dynamic and fluid in its change. Depending on which region of the world, the concept of adolescence or young adult is either emerging, or already well established. Most Western European societies use legal markers to underline the passage to adulthood, commonly set at age 16, 18, or 21. Thus, from country to country, there are minimum legal ages for marriage, for consensual intercourse, and also for access to sexual and reproductive health services without parental consent.

In many developing countries, though, the concept of adolescence has either been non-existent or is relatively new in concept and understanding. Rather than define adulthood by age or biology, children become adults through well-established rites of passage—for example, religious ceremony, or marriage. In India, for example, especially in rural areas, many girls enter into arranged marriages before the onset of their first menstruation cycle, and then, have their first child at around 16 years of age. For these young Indian girls, there is no adolescence, as they shift so quickly from childhood to motherhood. Similarly, in traditional Sri Lankan society, young people—once they enter puberty—are expected to get married, or in the case of a male, wear the yellow robe of a monk. To remain single is not held in high esteem because it is considered "neither here nor there."

Yet, the world is changing. Traditional patterns of behavior for young people, and what is expected of them by the adults, are in a state of flux, and in more open societies, adolescents are emerging as a powerful force for influence and growth in Africa, Asia, and Latin America. In these regions, massive economic, institutional and social changes have been brought about by Western colonial expansion and by the move toward a global society and economy. With more young people working in non-agricultural jobs, attending school longer, delaying marriage, adolescents are holding their own with adults.

In Indonesia, for example, young boys in urban areas are no longer tied to the farm and have started forming peer groups, as an alternative to life spent entirely inside the immediacy of their family. Similarly, in the urban areas of India, many girls attend single-sex schools, thus spending more time with peer groups, eroding the traditional practice of arranged marriages at an early age. In Nigeria, young people attend school for longer periods of time, thus preparing for jobs in their now modern economy. And in many Latin American countries, where young girls were once also hurried into pre-arranged marriages, now, young girls are staying in school so, they too can prepare for non-agricultural jobs.

And yet, those without means can only fantasize about what they see of mainstream material culture. As always, money is the societal divide that cruelly demarcates and is unrelenting in its effects on social, cultural, and psychological behavior. Young people living in poverty struggle daily with the pressures of survival in a seemingly indifferent, and often dangerous world. And access to wealth, or the simple conveniences of modern society, makes a considerable difference in the development of the young people. In rural areas in Zimbabwe and Papua New Guinea, for example, simple changes such as building of a road or highway—enabling the bringing in of supplies and expertise—has had profound effects on young people's lifestyles

When young people must leave their homes—either because of poverty, or increasingly, due to civil war—the result is often unprecedented numbers forced into bonded labor and commercial sex. For example, in the Indian cities of New Delhi, Mumbai, and Calcutta, thousands of young people take on menial jobs such as washing cars, pushing hand carts, collecting edibles from garbage dumps, or simply, begging. In Thailand, still more thousands of young girls earn their living as prostitutes. And in many countries of Eastern Europe, tens of thousands of young people are believed to be not attending school or formally employed, but instead, engaging in drug trafficking. Worldwide, the streets and temporary shelters are home to between 100 and 200 million children and adolescents, who are cut off from their parents and extended families (World Health Organization, 2000). What is it like to be them? What is it like to be young, scared, and poor?

Since the 1980s political and civil rights have improved substantially throughout the world, and 81 countries have taken significant steps in democratization, with 33 military regimes replaced by civilian governments. But of these fledgling democracies, only 47 are considered full democracies today. Only 82 countries, representing 57 percent of the world's population, are fully democratic.

Economically speaking, the proportion of the world's extremely poor fell from 29 percent in 1990 to 23 percent in 1999. Still, in 1999, 2.8 billion people lived on less than $2 a day, with 1.2 billion of them surviving on the margins of subsistence with less than $1 a day. In 2000, 1.1 billion people lacked access to safe water, and 2.4 billion did not have access to any form of improved sanitation services.

And armed conflict continues to blight the lives of millions: since 1990, 3.6 million people have died as a result of civil wars and ethnic violence, more than 16 times the number killed in wars between states. Civilians have accounted for more than 90 percent of the casualties—either injured or killed—in post–Cold War conflicts. Ninety countries are affected by landmines and live explosives, with rough estimates of 15,000 to 20,000 mine victims each year.

TEEN LIFE AROUND THE WORLD—THE SERIES

The Greenwood series *Teen Life around the World* examines what life is like for teens in different regions of the world. These volumes describe in detail the lives of young people in places both familiar and unfamiliar. How do teens spend their days? What makes their lives special? What difficulties and special burdens do they bear? And what will be their future as they make their way in their world?

Each volume is devoted to a region or regions of the world. For the purpose of this series, the volumes are divided as follows:

- Teen Life in Africa
- Teen Life in the Middle East
- Teen Life in Europe
- Teen Life in Central and South America and the Caribbean
- Teen Life in Asia

Readers can see similarities and differences in areas of the world that are relatively close in proximity, customs, and practices. Comparisons can be made between various countries in a region and across regions. American teens will perhaps be struck by the influence of American pop culture—music, fashion, food—around the world.

All volumes follow the same general format. The standardized format highlights information that all young people would most like to know. Each volume has up to fifteen chapters that describe teen life in a specific country in that region of the world. The countries chosen generally are representative of that region, and attempts were made to write about countries that young people would be most curious to learn more about.

Each chapter begins with a profile of the particular country. Basic political, economic, social, and cultural issues are discussed and a brief history of the country is provided. After this brief introduction to the specific country, an overview of teen life in that country is given, with a discussion of a teenager's typical day, family life, traditional and nontraditional foods, schooling, social life, recreation, entertainment, and religious practices and cultural practices. Finally, each chapter concludes with a list of resources that will help readers learn more about this country. These resources include nonfiction and fiction, Web sites, other sources to find information on the country, such as embassies, and pen pal addresses.

Although these chapters cannot tell the complete story of what it means to be a teenager in that region of the world and recognizing that perhaps there is no one typical lifestyle in any country, they provide a good starting point for insight into others' lives.

The contributors to this series present an informative and engaging look at the life of young people around the world and write in a straightforward manner. The volumes are edited by noted experts. They have an intimate understanding of their chosen region of the world—having either lived there, and/or they have devoted their professional lives to studying, teaching about, and researching the place. Also, an attempt was made to have each chapter written by an expert on teen life in that country. Above all, what these authors reveal is that young people everywhere—no matter where they live—have much in common. Although they might observe different social customs, rituals, and habits, they still long for the same basic things—security, respect, and love. They still live in that state of the half child/half adult, as they wait anxiously to become fully functioning members of their societies.

As series editor, it is my hope that these volumes, which are unique in publishing in both content and style, will increase your knowledge of teen life around the world.

Jeffrey S. Kaplan
Series Editor

REFERENCES

Baru, R. (1995). The social milieu of the adolescent girl. In S. Mehra (ed.) *Adolescent Girls in India: An Indian Perspective.* Saket, New Delhi. MAMTA, Health Institute for Mother and Child.

Caldwell, J. C., Caldwell, P., & Caldwell, B. K. (1998). The construction of adolescence in a changing world: Implications for sexuality, reproduction, and marriage. *Studies in Family Planning.* 29(2), 137–53.

Dehne, K. L., & Reidner, G. (2001). Adolescence: A dynamic concept. *Reproductive Health Matters.* 9 (17), 11–16.

Deutsche Gesellschaft fur Technische Zusammenarbeit (1997). *Youth in development cooperation: approaches and prospects in the multisectoral planning group "Youth."* Eschborn: GTZ.

Disanyake, J. B. (1998). *Understanding the sinhalese.* Columbo: Chatura Printers.

Larson, Reed. (2002). The Future of Adolescence: Lengthening the Ladders to Adulthood. *The Futurist.* 36(6), 16–21.

McCauley, A. P., & Salter, C. (1995). Meeting the needs of young adults. *Population Report*, Series J. 41:1–39.

UNAIDS (1999). *Sex and youth: contextual factors affecting risk for HIV/AIDS.* Geneva: UNAIDS.

UN Development Report (2002).

World Health Organization (2000).

PREFACE

Teen Life in Africa is intended for students and general readers interested in learning about teenagers in Africa. The need for a book of this kind is evident in view of the growing awareness of the need to understand other cultures, to make sense of and appreciate the lifestyles of teenagers, and to interpret the wide-ranging impact of globalization on teenagers in various parts of the world.

The contributors to this volume write in a straightforward, accessible manner, covering the important issues relating to teen lives in various African countries.

ACKNOWLEDGMENTS

The completion of the volume is testimony to the commitment and co-operation of all the authors. This is the first volume on African teenagers, and I sincerely hope that it will instigate additional works on the subject.

My indebtedness to others is considerable: special thanks to Wendi Schnaufer of Greenwood, who asked me to edit the book. To Dr. Sarah Freligh, my able copyeditor, I give my thanks. And to all the authors and countless scholars whose ideas make the book possible, I offer my gratitude. For the photographs, thanks are due to Segun Fayemi and my student from Uganda, Catherine Agnes Nantongo.

Finally, I continue to be appreciative of the love and kindness of my graduate students (Joel, Christian, Steve, Ward, Kirsten, and Ann) as well as of my friends and family.

INTRODUCTION

Toyin Falola

Teen Life in Africa presents the various aspects of teen life in 15 African countries. This introductory chapter offers a broad perspective, drawing examples that are applicable to most countries on the African continent. The 15 chapters that follow focus on one country each.

The book's scope covers all the regions of Africa—north, west, central, east, and south. The rationale for the coverage is to reflect the various cultural differences among African teens, as in the areas dominated by Islam in the north, by Christianity in the south, and by both religions in other countries. The chapters show the impact of modernization on African teenagers, as well as the survival of traditional practices among them.

The authors use a variety of sources, both oral and written, as well as extensive first-hand observations of various teen practices in the context of the country's culture and history. Each chapter provides a brief history of the country and offers valuable information on all the leading aspects of teen life, covering the typical day for a teenager, family life, food dishes, schooling, social life, recreation, entertainment, religious practices, and cultural ceremonies. A list of additional reading materials as well as Internet resources is offered at the end of each chapter, in order to facilitate additional research and the exploration of other areas of interest about a country and its teenagers in the modern world.

Africa provides opportunities for teens to live their lives in stable environments, while also offering great challenges in places with limited economic resources. Where teenagers live under strong religious and patriarchal values, the common tendency is to obey authorities. Where opportunities and amenities are severely limited, many families must migrate to cities. Millions of teenagers are in school, and they have a positive self-image. They dream of a great future for themselves, but they often join protest movements if they think government policies and inaction affect them in negative ways. Because of Africa's population growth rate, it has one of the highest numbers of teenagers in the world. Thus, one of the challenges of development is to raise them to be productive and better prepared for the responsibilities of adulthood.

Africa is a huge continent, comprising 52 different countries. In comparison, the United States, as big as it is, is less than a third the size of Africa. The African continent is diverse in its geography and cultures. Almost half of the land mass is located in the savanna, noted for its tall grass and scattered wooded areas. Next is the desert, especially the Sahara, which is the largest desert in the world. The areas covered by desert comprise almost 40 percent of the continent. Together the desert and the savanna comprise almost 90 percent of the continent. Where, then, is the jungle? This is a false image of Africa popularized in the Western media. Humid rain forests, about 8 percent of the land area, can be found in Central and West Africa.

Vegetation and climate affect economic production and ways of life. In the savanna, animals play a prominent role, notably cattle and horses. Thus, there are large pastoral communities among the Fulani of West Africa, the Xhosa of South Africa, and the Dinka of the Sudan. In these and other areas, teenagers can be seen taking care of animals, keeping an eye on herds, milking cows, and riding horses. Teenagers in the desert, as among the Berbers, are very adept at horse riding. In the forest areas, teenagers will join their parents to work on farms. One can also see regional variations. The countries in the north—Morocco, Tunisia, Algeria, Libya, and Egypt—are predominantly Arab and Muslim. In all five countries, the orientation of their politics is toward the Middle East, while their cultures tend to be Middle Eastern and Islamic. As the chapters on Algeria and Egypt show, the impact of Islam is substantial.

Teenagers are involved in most traditional occupations, in addition to all new ones. Agriculture is the dominant occupation in Africa, with the majority of teenagers living in rural areas with their parents. Teenagers help their parents produce food crops to feed their families and to sell surpluses in the markets. The teenagers understand the rules guiding family land, the production system, the exchange of goods and services, and the tools for various farm tasks. Traditional occupations are organized by gender: girls do domestic work in addition to other tasks, and boys engage in farm work.

Traditional occupations are not limited to farm work. Training in crafts industries and a host of services are provided. Thus, teenagers can be seen learning how to become blacksmiths, traditional healers, traders, barbers, masons, weavers, shoemakers, jewelry makers, carpenters, potters, wood-workers, and textile makers, among other occupations. Some of these jobs are highly specialized and require long periods of training. Learning to be-come a priest or a smith is prestigious in many communities. In rural areas where the people depend on local smiths to make and repair tools, the teenagers are respected for their help in turning raw iron into metal. The forge is treated with respect as well. Although those with a modern edu-cation are better paid, teenagers involved in one craft or another are praised for being focused, spending their time wisely. One big change in traditional occupations is that recruitment is now open to everybody, un-like in the past when it was controlled by families and guilds.

Teenagers are involved in trade, and they can be seen hawking goods from house to house, inside buses, motor garages, open markets, and other places where their wares may sell. They trade to help their parents, but there are many cases where they actually trade independently. Trading provides an opportunity to learn how to transact business, manage time and money, and interact with others. Teenagers who trade on a full-time basis can be seen in the regular markets, in intercity trade systems, in banks depositing cash, and in stores and farms buying goods for resale.

Of course, there are many new, modern occupations which involve teenagers, from bicycle repair to Internet service. These require either learning from masters in an apprenticeship system or going to modern schools where the skills are imparted. Both opportunities exist. To learn a craft or a modern industry, a teenager may serve as an apprentice for a number of years. A formal graduation ceremony marks the beginning of independence, which enables graduates to start their own businesses. There are trade and technical schools in which to acquire a variety of modern manufacturing and industrial skills. Modern education may delay the age of graduation beyond the teenage years.

There are more than two thousand different languages in various parts of Africa. Many teenagers can speak at least two languages. First is their mother tongue, that is, the indigenous language spoken in areas where they are born. They then can use any of the more widely spoken languages such as Arabic, Fulani, Hausa, Yoruba, English, Portuguese, French, or Swahili, depending on where they live. There is no barrier to communi-cation in Africa. In North Africa, for instance, Arabic is used by millions of people. The same is true of Swahili in East Africa and Hausa in West

Africa. Local languages are combined with European ones to offer a variety of creole languages which are also widely used by teenagers and others.

FAMILY LIFE AND VALUES

African teenagers are part of large family and kinship networks. Unlike American teenagers, they may have direct contact with a great many family members, dating back three generations, all living in close proximity. Very early, they are brought up to be closely attached to their mothers. As babies, their mothers would have carried them on their backs for many hours each day. As they become teenagers, the females among them will also carry on their backs babies born to other family members. Teenagers must respect members of the extended family and others in the community older than them. Respect is demonstrated through respectful language, greeting codes, obeying commands, and performing errands. Teenagers know their cousins, uncles, aunts, and other relatives and socialize with them, even when they live in small nuclear families.

Kinship rules promote sharing and community participation. In many places, ideas of property do not promote individuality, thereby encouraging teenagers to share, to regard land and other assets as collective, and to be aware that sins committed by one person can affect others. Economic activities, such as farming and herding, can be done on a group basis, and a teenager is part of a team or a cooperative work group.

Parents exercise control over teenagers. The widespread belief is that a teenager's bad behavior may damage the family's name and reputation. Parents tend to be harder on girls, always warning them to avoid premarital sex and manners that could cost them prospective husbands. Children are not expected to move out of their homes when they turn 18. In many parts of Africa, the transition to adulthood comes not at 18, but when one gets married. A college degree may be needed to begin the process of minimizing parental control.

Religious views and worldviews teach respect for ancestors, elders (both living and deceased), parents, and others. Teenagers are told to take care of their elderly parents and to seek the consent of their parents in the choice of marriage partners. Religious freedom is allowed in most African countries, and teenagers, like their parents, may belong to either main or fringe religions. The majority of teenagers follow the religious practices of their parents. Teenagers are active in Islamic and Christian worship, as well as in traditional religions, all depending on what is prevalent in a place. Many teenagers are able to recite historical traditions and history. In many instances, teenagers tend to avoid customs that they associate with "primitive traditions," which partly explains why many are less active in the worship of local gods.

Teenagers participate in communal activities and in all religious festivals and holidays. The schools adjust their calendars and schedules to allow them to participate in religious activities. In Muslim areas, schools close early on Fridays. During Ramadan, teenagers are expected to fast, which involves the avoidance of food and liquids during daylight hours for 30 days. Ceremonies and festivals promote the habits of sharing, and teenagers participate in feasting and the entertainment of relations and friends. Teenagers can be devout, and many use religion to explain why they do not drink, smoke, watch certain kinds of movies, or visit nightclubs.

Western education is the top priority in most families, as it ensures jobs in the professions. University education is highly valued, and parents can pressure their children to study law, medicine, or engineering. Most schools are public, financed by the governments. Private and religious schools exist in many countries, thus providing various options. The majority of schools are coeducational, although single-sex schools exist in some places, in part because of religious beliefs. One of the reasons behind single-sex schools, especially in Islamic areas, is to minimize interaction between boys and girls so that situations will not arise for them to hold hands, kiss in public, and attend the same parties, all practices believed to be immoral and irreligious.

Schools tend to be strict, with rules to regulate habits and behavior. The majority of schools insist on the wearing of uniforms, and the laws in many countries do not prohibit punishing teenagers when they violate school rules. Languages of instruction include indigenous ones such as Arabic, Swahili, and Hausa (in areas where they are spoken), as well as established European languages such as English and French. Teachers are usually Africans, drawn from the same communities as the students. A high number of teenagers are in schools which are open from early morning to the afternoon. They may walk to school, be driven to school by their parents, or live in boarding houses. Back home, they have lunch and do their homework. Then, play with friends can follow in addition to errands for their parents.

In general, teenagers in school do not work for wages, in part because their parents may not have financial needs or there may be no jobs for them. There are exceptions. Parents with farms and businesses may expect their teenagers to assist them. Thus, one can see teens working as clerks, hawkers, salespeople, farmers, and so on. There are generally a number of domestic chores for them to do. Most homes do not have vacuum cleaners, dryers, washers, or dishwashers, and teenagers join their parents in doing many things manually. They are expected to clean, cut grass, and do a host of other domestic tasks. Indeed, it is regarded as good parenting to insist that teenagers learn how to cook and do other things. It is not regarded as demeaning for teenagers to work, and it is not regarded as child abuse to punish them if they refuse to. Rich parents have housemaids who do most of the work. Teenagers in rich households are often looked upon as "lazy and spoiled," and it is the responsibility of their parents to create chores for them, as part of their parental duties. In particular, teenage girls must learn how to cook as part of their preparation to get married. In most of Africa, women cook for the household.

Sports and indoor games are popular among teens. Traditional sports and games such as wrestling and board games are common, and soccer, swimming, and Ping-Pong are among the most common sports for teens. The most popular sport is soccer, although it involves mainly boys. Tennis, basketball, and volleyball are played by boys and girls in schools. While swimming is well known, pools are not accessible to the majority of the population, and swimsuits are expected not to expose the body.

Social life is active, as teenagers meet one another to play and share experiences. Not all cultures encourage dating. Boys have more freedom than girls, and tend to socialize more outside of their homes and with many more people. Parents are always anxious to know the friends with whom their daughters socialize. In cultures where virginity is much valued, socialization that can lead to premarital sex is condemned. Local and Western music are popular, as are films and homemade videos. Preferences vary from one region to another, but Western and Indian films circulate widely in cities. Although society frowns upon them, there are teenagers who smoke and drink alcohol.

Teenagers eat the same food as their parents. Those in cities can add imported food items to local ones. Food dishes vary from one place to another, but are generally dependent on established cuisines based on root crops, grains, and vegetables. One-course meals are common. In most areas, picnics are not common, except during festivals and holidays. Teenagers can eat in restaurants or buy foods and carry them home.

MODERNITY AND YOUTH

African teenagers are much attracted to modern cultures and economies. Indeed, teenagers constitute a large number of those who migrate to the cities. Bored with farm work and with the lack of amenities and modern recreational facilities in villages, millions run to the cities, even if they have no jobs or schools to attend. In various African cities, teenagers can be found in markets, high-rise buildings, luxurious homes, and other places where they have access to televisions, cell phones, computers, satellite dishes, and other modern imported items.

If teenagers in rural areas establish connections with nature, those in the cities have to deal with telephones, computers, cars, and other objects of technology. They have to deal with objects and change that they cannot fully manipulate or control. They even change the way they dress, preferring Western-style to traditional attire. It is not uncommon to see an African teenager in jeans, a T-shirt, and a baseball cap worn backwards. Traditional attire has not been completely abandoned, but teenagers in the cities choose imported styles, comprising American and European fashions. Essentially, teenagers simply choose what they like in African and Western attire and use them for various occasions. Teenagers who are attracted to modern culture may criticize others as "too conservative" or "too religious" in order to emphasize their own distinction.

Teenagers can be developed or destroyed by cities and modern technologies. They can creatively use cities and technologies to acquire skills, education, jobs, and friends. However, because access to modern objects is competitive and the majority of parents do not have the means to buy them for their children, there are cases when teenagers take to crime primarily to obtain the resources to enjoy modern objects. As in many other countries, there are dangerous gangs, the use of drugs (notably marijuana), and increasing cases of prostitution, motivated by the desire to acquire independence, power, and money.

African teenagers are fascinated by Western cultural practices and ideas, and they follow the major sports, songs, movies, and news. African teenagers know about Michael Jordan and Michael Jackson, and one can see their posters in many teenage bedrooms. Western popular cultures have spread among African teenagers, sometimes annoying those who believe in traditional values. The Western values imbibed by the teenagers may threaten older values. In Islamic areas, there is fear that such acquired external values may destroy Islamic societies and cultures. When Islamic leaders are afraid, they see the teenagers as enemies who require conversion. In general, there is a pervasive fear that modernized teenagers lack morality, a sense of direction, and respect for local traditions.

Teenagers are known to protest conditions that affect them. Where economies are undeveloped and politics unstable, the teenagers join protest movements to demand changes. They participate in armed conflicts, street conflicts, and antigovernment rebellions. There is a strong belief, especially among teenagers in high schools and universities, that political leaders do not care about them, their needs, and their future careers.

Where Western influence is large, as in many cities, the ambition of teenagers is to acquire Western education and imported objects, drive cars, and travel abroad. As most countries lack the resources to provide all of what they seek, teenagers often ask for too much and make unrealistic demands on their parents and governments.

Dating, friendship, and marriage are being affected by modern changes and exposure to Western influence. Members of the older generations complain that teenagers have low moral values when it comes to matters relating to sex, and that they often ignore their parents and extended families in preference to their friends.

Some of the problems experienced by African teenagers—gang membership, petty theft, burglary, drug use, and other difficulties—derive from the widespread poverty in many areas. The majority of teenagers are not from middle- or upper-class families, but often seek objects of modernity that their parents cannot afford. Unlike in the United States, the rate of traffic accidents is rather low, as the majority of teenagers have no access to cars. A number of teenagers, based in cities, who are products of nuclear families complain of anomie—that is, a belief that they have identity problems or that they are seeking to define themselves. They wonder about who they are, what they should do with their lives, what careers to pursue, and what values to uphold. They are concerned about their image and self-esteem. Other than in their families, the opportunities for counseling are limited in many countries.

Teenagers will always be important in Africa. They represent the bridge between generations, old and new cultures, traditional and modern occupations, and Africa and the rest of the world. As they seek to enjoy mobile phones, cars, computers, and other imported items, teenagers will contribute to the impact of globalization in Africa, and possibly invent alternatives to what their countries cannot produce or import. Their desire for prestige, survival, success, progress, and a better future will pressure political leaders to seek ways to prevent violence, provide more amenities, and build more schools. Many of the teenagers' visions and ideas will survive and will surely become part of the development package of the twenty-first century.

ADDITIONAL READING

Davidson, Basil. Modern Africa: A Social and Political History, 3rd ed. London: Longman, 1995.

Falola, Toyin, ed. *Africa, vols. 1–5*. Durham: Carolina Academic Press, 2000.
———. *Key Events in African History: A Reference Guide*. Westport, Conn.: Greenwood, 2002.
Fredland, Richard A. *Understanding Africa: A Political Economy Perspective*. Chicago: Burnham Inc., 2001.
Khapoya, Vincent B. *The African Experience: An Introduction*. Englewood Cliffs, N.J.: Prentice Hall, 1994.

Chapter 1

ALGERIA

Ann Cooper

INTRODUCTION

Algeria in North Africa shares its borders with Morocco and Mauritania on the west, Mali and Niger on the south, and Libya and Tunisia on the east. It is the second-largest country in Africa, being roughly the same size as western Europe. Despite Algeria's vastness, about 90 percent of its people live near the northern coast, on and around the fraction of arable land that exists in this country that is about 80 percent desert.

The lives of Algerian teens are powerfully shaped by the area in which they live, the ethnic affiliation of their family, and their country's history and politics. Before discussing the daily life of a typical teenager in Algeria, this introduction will provide background information to some of these important factors. Algeria's geography and the distribution of its population are important to teens because their way of life and social behavior vary according to whether they live in an urban or rural area. Algeria's geography can be grouped into three different regions: the coastal hills and plains, the Atlas Mountains, and the Sahara Desert. The hilly northern coast with its scattered plains is home to most of Algeria's population. It is on these plains that some of Algeria's biggest cities, such as Annaba and the capital, Algiers, can be found. About 50 percent of Algeria's 31 million citizens (California has about 33 million people) live in cities, most of which are on or near the Mediterranean coast. Algiers itself is home to 2.6 million people.

The ancient Atlas Mountains can, in turn, be divided into three groups: the Tell Atlas, the High Plateaus, and the Saharan Atlas. The Tell

Atlas region provides some of Algeria's most fertile farmland. The High Plateaus are dry and severe, while the Saharan Atlas Mountains enjoy more rainfall and house large ranches. The third region, the Sahara Desert, is the southernmost region of Algeria. It is composed of two Ergs, like seas of sand, called the Great Western Erg and the Great Eastern Erg. In the center of the desert is the Hoggar Massif, a mountainous area whose highest peak is Mount Tahat, at 2,918 meters.

Algeria's regional climates vary widely. On the coast and in the northern mountains, summer temperatures are in the mid-80s, and winter temperatures, in the 50s or 60s. Temperatures in the High Plateaus range from 100 degrees or more in the daytime to 50 degrees at night in the summer, and from 60 degrees in the day to 30 at night in the winter. In the Sahara, the temperature ranges are similar to the High Plateaus, but more severe. The greatest amount of rain falls in the eastern mountains and in the northern coastal zone. Algiers gets about 30 inches of rain annually. In the Sahara, rainfall measures less than four inches annually, with some regions going for three to five years straight without rain.

Teenagers are an important group in Algerian society, as people between the ages of 10 and 19 constitute about one-fourth of the population. Approximately 80 percent of Algeria's population is ethnically Arab, and the remaining 20 percent are Berber. Berbers were the original inhabitants of Algeria, and they still live throughout North Africa. Algeria's population is now largely Arab, as over the centuries Arab traders and soldiers migrated to and settled in Algeria, usually in the process of spreading Islam. Teenagers belonging to different ethnic groups accordingly have different cultural traditions regarding food, the wearing of veils, and their first language. Berber subgroups include the Kalbylie and Chaouia, who traditionally live in the Kabylia and Aures Mountains in the Tell Atlas, respectively.

The Tuareg are a Berber population and speak Tamershak. The Tuareg of the northern Sahara and the Mozabites from the Hoggar region of the desert are two distinct groups of Algerian Berbers. The Tuareg were historically a nomadic people, traveling across the Sahara to trade in luxury items from North Africa, the Middle East, and West Africa. The Tuareg are also known as the "blue men" because of the distinctive deep blue dyes they use on the fabric that the men wrap around their heads and faces to protect them from the harsh desert conditions. This "veil" covers the entire face except for the eyes, and men usually begin to wear it at age 25. Contrary to practices among most other Algerians, Tuareg women do not wear veils, although the Tuareg are Muslims. Historically, women did not wear veils because they usually did not participate in the trans-Saharan trade, which required long trips through the desert. Tuareg women also have a tradition of being very strong and independent. Heritage among the Tuareg is matrilineal—nobility and inheritance follow the mother's line.

Islam among the Tuareg is not as strict as it is throughout most of the rest of Algeria's population. Daily prayers are usually observed, but other tenets of Islam are not as commonly practiced. An example is Ramadan, the month of fasting during daylight hours. Extended fasting is not practical for a people historically engaged in constant travel. Islam for the Tuareg has absorbed many aspects of traditional African religion, some of them being a belief in spirits and the importance of divination. Today, the Tuareg mostly live in permanent villages in the Hoggar region in southern Algeria.

The M'zab is a valley in the Great Western Erg that is home to the Mozabites, a group of people belonging to a tradition in Islam that began in 656, regarded by some to be heretical. Originally Arabic, the Mozabites are mostly Berber today and speak a Berber dialect closely related to Kabyle, the language of Berbers who live in Algeria's northern mountains. The population of the M'zab is around 100,000. Islam among the Mozabites is particularly strict, women are secluded, and outward signs of wealth are forbidden. Traditionally, women wear a head-to-foot robe and a veil that leaves only one eye exposed.

The most commonly spoken languages in Algeria are Arabic and French. Algeria's ethnic Berbers speak regional dialects of Berber as well as Arabic or French. French was the official language of government and education under French colonial rule and is still widely used. However, since independence in 1962, a policy of Arabization has called for Arabic in schools and in public life. On July 5, 1998, the Algerian government promulgated a law making Arabic the official public language. The Berber community, which had been fighting for recognition of their culture and language, took political action against this law. After a Berber youth died while in police custody in April 2001, a fresh series of protests broke out in Kabylia. Activists' goals included recognition of Tamazight, the Berber language, and an end to the cultural discrimination they identified as inherent to the 1998 law. Although President Abdelaziz Bouteflicka has announced his wish to ameliorate the Berbers' situation, negotiations have so far been unsuccessful.

COLONIAL HISTORY

With Algeria having been independent for only 40 years, its colonial history is still relevant to its people. The French landed in Algeria in 1830 with the goal of taking over the country to expand their empire. By 1847 they had succeeded, and French settlers flocked to Algeria. French colonialism often operated on the system sometimes known as direct rule. One of the most important aspects of direct rule was assimilation. To that end, all interactions were conducted in French. One of the chief objectives was to create an extension of France in North Africa. Algeria was governed more like a French province than a colony. Most government functionaries, high-level managers, and technical workers were French. Algerians were typically not trained for these types of jobs. As a result, when the French left Algeria, they took most of those experts with them. Algeria had difficulty filling these positions, due to its lack of experienced or trained people. While Algeria's colonial experience was marked by violence, its struggle for independence was particularly brutal. Rebel Algerians used guerilla warfare techniques in fighting the French, who violently suppressed rebel activity and tortured Algerian captives. Algeria's struggle for independence lasted from 1954 to 1962. The Front de Liberation Nationale (FLN) led the Algerian independence effort and later became Algeria's national political party.

POLITICS

Algerian teenagers are necessarily aware of Algeria's difficult political and economic reality, because it has shaped their view of their place in society. Teenagers have historically been, and continue to be, important participants in Algeria's political life. Algeria is a republic led by a popularly elected president with a five-year renewable term. The president then appoints a prime minister, who in turn appoints the cabinet. Algeria's first president after independence was Ben Bella, who had been involved in the provisional Algerian government during the War for Independence. In 1965 Colonel Houari Boumidienne, who had control of the army, carried out a successful coup d'etat against Ben Bella. Boumidienne was president until his death in 1978, and Colonel Chadli Benjedid was nominated by the FLN to succeed him. Boumidienne's regime ushered in an era of military control of politics. The military's presence in Algerian politics only started to become less obvious in the 1990s.

In 1988 a new constitution established multiple political parties; previously the only legal party had been the FLN. The period of 1989 to 1991 is considered Algeria's experiment in democratization. Unfortunately, it was not successful. The first of two rounds of voting for the National Assembly in December 1991 showed a landslide in favor of an Islamic fundamentalist group, the *Front Islamique du Salut* (FIS). The FIS was established along the lines of Iranian fundamentalist groups, and aimed to institute a theocratic government. The FLN panicked and intervened with the army to cancel the elections just days before the final round of voting for the National Assembly. President Benjedid resigned in January 1992, and the FLN nominated and swore in his successor, Mohammed Boudiaf.

These events sparked a violent reaction from armed Islamic groups, some of the most active of which were the *Armée Islamique du Salut* (AIS, the armed wing of the FIS) and the *Groupe Islamique Armée* (GIA). However, there were many different groups operating, and some were splinter groups of the aforementioned. These Islamist insurgent groups, seeking to overturn the Algerian government and institute a government of Islamic law, began a campaign of terror and violence. Their main targets included government workers (29 percent of the population), teachers, journalists, students, artists and intellectuals, and foreigners. Women believed to have inappropriate lifestyles (defined as anything from going to the hairstylist to wearing jeans to not wearing a veil) were also targets of violence. The worst of the violence lasted from 1991 to 1998, but sporadic incidences of violence continue to occur.

Internationally, Algeria has been active in facilitating the resolution of disputes, such as the U.S. hostage situation in Iran in 1981 and the Ethiopia/Eritrea border war in 1998. Since his election in April 1999, President (and former foreign minister) Bouteflicka has made more than 40 trips abroad, to the consternation of Algerians who think he should be at home. Algeria's almost entirely Muslim population and historically anti-West orientation facilitated the formation of relationships with other Arab and Muslim countries. It became a member of the Organization of Petroleum Exporting Countries in 1960, and the Organization for African Unity in 1963.

ECONOMICS

Although the government of independent Algeria started out with a socialist orientation, a centrally planned economy, and no foreign relations with the West, it has since shifted to privatize some of its industries and businesses, and has formed diplomatic and commercial relationships with Western countries. The economy is largely based on exporting petroleum products and natural gas. Algeria's most significant trading partners are Italy, the United States, France, Spain, Brazil, and the Netherlands. Other exports include citrus fruit, dates, fertilizer, and wine (although the Islamic ban against drinking alcohol is leading to a decrease in production). Some of the food crops grown in Algeria include olives, dates, citrus fruits, wheat, barley, and oats. Algerian farmers also raise livestock like sheep and goats. The country imports consumer goods, iron, steel, and three-fourths of its food from France, Italy, Germany, Spain, the United States, and Turkey.

One of Algeria's most significant problems is its extremely high rate of unemployment, and those that suffer most from this are young people. Algeria currently has 30 percent unemployment; compare this with the U.S. unemployment rate of 4 percent. Consider also that 23 percent of Algerians live below the poverty line, as opposed to 12.7 percent of Americans. Many Algerian teens want to go to France to find work, but it is becoming increasingly difficult for them to do so, as French immigration laws are becoming stricter, and racism against North Africans in France is widespread. However, there is a large and long-established Algerian community in France that includes Algerian artists and intellectuals who sought political asylum, and those who work to send money home to relatives.

Housing has also become a severe problem for Algeria, as there is a shortage of about 2 million housing units. Housing is difficult to acquire and some of it is too crowded, or has substandard sanitation or unsafe drinking water. Difficult housing conditions have made diseases like tuberculosis, trachoma, malaria, measles, typhoid fever, and dysentery more common.

TYPICAL DAY

When an Algerian teenager wakes up in the morning to go to school or work, his or her mother is usually already awake and making breakfast for the family. Typically, the mother of the family cooks three meals a day, each of which is an important family event. Because so many young people, especially young men, are unemployed, they may not rise with the rest of the family, but go to meet friends later. Groups of young men can be observed gathering and talking outside cafés or in their neighborhoods, leaning against the buildings. This is called "hittisme" in Algeria, which means "holding up the walls." This phenomenon is widely interpreted as a sign of the youth's disaffection and alienation.

School usually begins at 8:00 A.M. and ends at 5:00 P.M., with a lunch and rest break midday. Everybody comes home for lunch, which the mother also cooks, and rests before going back to school or work. Afternoon rest breaks are particularly important in desert regions, where midday temperatures are extreme. Almost everyone in Algeria is Muslim, and says five daily prayers. One of these prayers falls during instructional time, but classes do not stop for it; everyone makes up for the missed prayer at home.

In 1997, almost 88 percent of children 6 to 15 were enrolled in primary education. About 850,000 of 2.7 million total children aged 16 to 19 were enrolled in secondary education. However, 1994 statistics from UNESCO show 66 percent of males of the appropriate age and 58 percent of females attend secondary school. About 73 percent of Algerian males are literate, as opposed to 49 percent of females. Some young people quit school early to help in their parents' business or to find work themselves.

FAMILY LIFE

Family, both immediate and extended, is very important in an Algerian teenager's life. After independence, Algeria's economy went through a rapid process of industrialization and modernization with the increased importance of oil and gas production for export. During that period, Algeria's population also became more urban. There has been a shift in family structure as well, with nuclear families replacing extended families. Islam shapes Algerian family life. Algerian society is patriarchal, and men are socially more powerful than women and are usually the head of the family. A woman's primary role is to take care of the household and obey her husband. Women usually marry soon after they finish school, around their late teens or early twenties, and it is not unusual for families to arrange marriages. Around the house, daughters are expected to help with chores but sons are not, as men and boys traditionally do not do housework.

Women's roles in Islamic culture have historically been subservient, and women have generally been powerless. In Algeria, this is slowly beginning to change as more women are entering the workforce and young women in urban areas can choose to not wear a veil. Veiling is meant to preserve the honor of a woman and her family by preventing men who are not related to her from seeing her. Women in different areas of Algeria practice different styles of veiling. In the capital city, Algiers, women wear a *haik* (loose-fitting clothing that covers the head and body) in white silk or rayon, which stops above the knee. They also usually wear an *a'djar* (a kind of veil), which covers the lower part of the face, made of finely embroidered tulle. In Algeria's central region women wear much more conservative veils, which usually consist of a large piece of white wool in which the woman wraps herself. This veil covers her face as well, and only lets one eye show. In Constantine, women wear a veil called a *melia*, which is close-fitting and made of a lightweight black cloth. The *melia* reaches all the way to the woman's feet, and she wears a black *a'djar* to cover the lower half of her face. In Oran, women veil themselves in the

Moroccan style; they wear a long, loose-fitting robe called a *djellaba*, which has long sleeves and is typically dark in color. The *djellaba* has a hood attached, and women usually also veil the lower half of their faces. In southern Algeria women usually wear a veil of white wool in the same style as the women from the M'zab. Approaching the borders with Mali and Niger, the veil becomes less restrictive, and Tuareg women do not wear veils at all.

TRADITIONAL AND NONTRADITIONAL FOOD DISHES

Algerian teenagers, like most other Algerians, eat traditional North African food, a blend of Middle Eastern, Mediterranean, Turkish, and Berber cuisines. Some of the most commonly eaten dishes include tajine, chorba, tabouli, and couscous. Both tajine and chorba are meat-and-vegetable stews. Tabouli is a salad made with bulgur wheat, parsley, tomatoes, and lemon. Couscous is a kind of pasta made from cracked wheat and can be served sweet or savory, with vegetables or meat. There are many different ways to prepare couscous, and different regions of Algeria have their own signature way of preparing it. In Algiers, couscous is typically prepared with either a red sauce and lamb, or a white sauce and chicken. Couscous from Kabylie has only a white sauce, and couscous from Constantine has red sauce with either spicy beef or salted meat. One way to prepare sweet couscous is with raisins, butter, and sugar. Other popular sweets include baklava (a dessert made with thin sheets of dough, honey, and nuts) and macaroons.

Certain foods and beverages are forbidden to Muslims. Among them are alcohol, pork, animals slaughtered by non-Muslims or without a blessing, animals with claws, reptiles, birds of prey, and carnivorous animals. The only proscriptions that are closely followed in Algeria are those pertaining to pork and alcohol; all else is interpreted on an individual basis.

Shopping for food is typically done by women or girls at open-air markets. Traditional dishes show up on the dinner table often, as the ingredients are relatively inexpensive and most Algerians have to economize. Meals are family events and are eaten together off a common platter. In some very traditional households, women still wait to eat until after the men have finished, but in most households, everyone eats together.

SCHOOLING

The state encourages young people to pursue their education and spends as much as 25 percent of its annual budget on the educational system. The Algerian government has allotted this extraordinary percentage of the budget for education in a continuing effort to reorganize the schools to fit Algeria's national needs as an independent country. Since independence, the Algerian government has implemented a policy of "Arabization" in school, which includes Arabic language instruction in primary and secondary schools. French was the primary language of instruction from colonial times until independence. French is still used at higher levels of education and in government.

The school week runs from Saturday to Wednesday, and the weekend falls on Thursday and Friday, with Friday being the day of worship. Algerian schools from primary through university levels are state-run, state-supported, and coeducational. Sometimes advanced students will take classes together, or schools will allow students to use their rooms or library for study after hours. There are no "magnet" or private schools in Algeria. Most students attend state schools, but some wealthy people send their children to private schools abroad (usually in France). Mandatory education lasts from age 6 to age 15, although there is a significant portion of Algerian teens that leave school early to help at home or to work. Approximately 90 percent of primary school-age children are enrolled in school (6 to 15 years old). About 66 percent of secondary school-age boys and 58 percent of secondary school-age girls are enrolled. Only a very small percentage of Algerians continue on to the college level. The illiteracy rate for males above the age of 15 is 26.1 percent; for females, 51 percent.

There is a tracking system in Algerian schools, which is similar to the French school system. Students follow a course of study organized around an academic strength such as math, science, or literature. At the end of their secondary education, Algerian students have to take the baccalaureate exam, which is extremely difficult. Many students who pass do not do so until the second or third time they take the exam. In order to go on to university, a student must have very good grades and a passing baccalaureate score.

Much as in French schools, most of the work in Algerian schools is done in the classroom, and homework is not given regularly. However, teachers expect the students to apply themselves in class and to prepare for classes. Students are encouraged to speak in class, but there are certain subjects that are taboo, like religion and sex. Education is a rite of passage in Algeria. While almost everyone has some education, many young people despair for a lack of opportunities to use their education after they graduate.

SOCIAL LIFE

School is one of the primary places where Algerian teenagers meet and interact with one another. Unlike American schools, Algerian schools do not usually host dances or social events. Also, many of the places where American and European kids go to hang out or go on dates, like discos and dance clubs, are not available to Algerian teens. They do exist, but many parents do not approve of clubs, because they often serve alcohol. Though Islam forbids drinking alcohol, clubs and bars often serve it. The legal drinking age is 21.

Algerian teens have romantic relationships with people of their own choosing, but these relationships are often kept secret from their parents. Boys have much more freedom than girls as to where they go with their friends and what they do in their spare time. If girls want to socialize, their option is to go to a female friend's house. Boys can go to cafés or concerts, but girls' parents are usually very restrictive of their activities. Boys also have more freedom choosing what kind of clothes they want to wear, so it is easier for them to adopt popular Western fashions.

If a young couple wants to see each other, the girl usually has to tell her parents she's going to a female friend's house and then meet up with the boy at someone else's house. They cannot go somewhere public like a café to hang out because of the possibility of being seen by somebody's father or brother. Not surprisingly, premarital sex is strongly discouraged. Abortions, however, are legal under restricted circumstances, such as to save the life or health of the woman. Contraceptives are available and the government supports their use to help control the rate of population growth. The rate of HIV infection in Algeria is very low, at a mere 0.07 percent.

American music, movies, and television shows are popular with teenagers. Similarly, fashions in Algeria generally follow trends in France and Europe in general, and teenagers wear them as much as possible. The driving age is 18, but teenagers generally do not own cars unless their families are very rich, because cars are too expensive.

RECREATION AND ENTERTAINMENT

The most popular sport in Algeria is soccer, which is enthusiastically followed and which both males and females play. Both Algerian and foreign teams are popular with teenagers. Some favorites include Olympique de Marseille, Real de Madrid, M. C. Alger, and J. S. Kabylie. The neighborhood is the primary arena for social activities for young people. Sports matches, music, and concerts all take place in the neighborhood. Movies

Algerian soccer fans. © Stephane Mantey/CORBIS Tempsport.

are popular, and Algerian cinema has a long history. However, during the recent civil war, filmmaking decreased due to attacks on filmmakers and other artists, censorship, and the scarcity of funds, facilities, and theaters. During the civil war, the *Groupe Islamique Armee* was allegedly responsible for the deaths of more than one hundred artists, writers, and intellectuals. Production is returning to normal now, and both Algerian and foreign films are popular and accessible. Algerian teens like foreign and Algerian movies, and American actors like Bruce Willis and Julia Roberts are very popular.

Algerian youth have a tradition of political involvement. Political action in Algeria is often violent, but not necessarily so. Algerian youth comprised an important sector of political party membership during the democratization era, when opposition political parties were legalized (from about 1989 to 1991). The FIS was one of the parties that had significant support among young Algerians. In the aftermath of the civil war, political apathy and feelings of alienation were more widespread among youth. By 1995, youth involvement in political associations had already dropped significantly from levels in the early 1990s.

Popular music has responded to these problems. Both Rai and rap artists express political and social ideas in response to profound political, social, and economic problems. Rai is a specifically North African form of music whose origins lie in a traditional form of poetry called *malhun*. Modern Rai started to develop in the 1930s, and it has constantly incorporated elements from both traditional and Western music. Because of its often rebellious or "improper" content (Rai musicians sing about politics, love, sex, drinking, and freedom), fundamentalists succeeded in passing a law to ban it in the early 1980s. This ban was lifted in 1985, and Rai has remained a form of protest music.

Rap is a relatively new style of music in Algeria and is extremely popular with teenagers there. Young rap artists use their music to speak to the problems that Algeria's youth face today, like poverty, unemployment, and violence. Both rap and Rai artists from Algeria have moved to France for more security. In 1994 one of Algeria's most popular Rai musicians, Cheb Hasni, was shot and killed in a café in Oran.

RELIGIOUS PRACTICES AND CULTURAL CEREMONIES

The population of Algeria is 99 percent Muslim. Islam is the official religion, and 95 percent of Algerians are Sunni Muslims. Basic to Islam are its five pillars: accepting Mohammed as God's prophet and the seal of the faith, prayer five times daily, giving to the poor, fasting for Ramadan, and pilgrimage to Mecca. Muslims pray five times daily facing Mecca, and these prayers can be roughly described as falling during the morning, at noon, afternoon, dusk, and nighttime. Because the morning prayer can be very early, children do not usually say all five prayers until they are around 10 or 11 years old. Islam began in the sixth century in modern-day Saudi Arabia and spread to Africa through military conquest and trade. It reached Algeria in the eighth century, after Muslim Arabs militarily subdued the native Berbers, who had previously been Christian. The Berbers, in turn, converted to Islam and continued to spread the religion through West Africa.

Religious festivals and holidays are determined by phases of the moon, so their dates vary. March 7 is Eid al-adha, or the Feast of the Sacrifice, which celebrates Abraham's sacrifice of his son Isaac. April 8 is Ashoura, which is a festival to celebrate one's ancestors, and an occasion where the children receive gifts. June 6 is Mouloud, the birth of the prophet Mohammed. From mid-November to mid-December is Ramadan; this is a time of fasting during daylight hours and it lasts for one lunar month. After Ramadan ends, the Eid al-Fitr feast and celebration occur.

Islam has served as a powerful unifying force in Algerian society, especially since the struggle for independence in the 1950s. It is a complete social, legal, and religious system. The Sharia, Islamic law, sets rules for economic exchange, inheritance, and marriage practices, among other things. Although Algeria is officially Muslim, its government is not theocratic, but secular. This is an issue that displeases many fundamentalist Muslim groups that typically advocate instituting the Sharia as national law. The Iranian revolution of 1979, during which Islamic fundamentalist leaders took over the Iranian government, reverberated throughout the entire Muslim world. One of its important effects on Algeria was the rise of fundamentalism in the 1980s and 1990s. Teenage participation in religious life varies among Algeria's different populations of Arabs and Berbers. It also varies between urban and rural dwellers. Algerian teenagers have opportunities to participate in Muslim youth organizations for student and political activities. Islam also heavily informs social activity and relationships, as elaborated above in the section pertaining to social life. Algerian society and Islam are inextricably entwined, and most teenagers are Muslim. As we would expect, degrees of orthodoxy vary throughout the adult and teenage populations.

CONCLUSION

Islam, their families, and their country's turbulent political history are all forces that significantly affect the lives of Algerian teenagers. Islam is a force that both unites and divides Algerians; it is the basis of culture and of nationalism, but it is also an object of contention. The role of religious law in Algeria's government was an important issue in the tragic civil war of the 1990s. Islam is so significant to Algerian society that it is a major force in politics. Because the FIS was prohibited from taking the seats they had won in the National Assembly, armed Islamic groups with similar goals of instituting the Sharia as national law attacked the government. The ensuing decade of violence had an understandably profound effect upon all Algerians. Islam is not just an issue of contention in Algeria, but also serves to unify the Algerian people. Islam was especially important in binding Algerians together as a nation during and after their struggle for independence from France. Islam also serves as a bridge with the wider Muslim world and as the center of family life.

The family is essential to an Algerian teenager's life. Teenagers spend a lot of time with their families and are strongly influenced by their parents' opinions and rules. Although men are still far more powerful in the family and in society, Algerian women and girls are making strides in gaining equality. More and more women are entering the workforce and getting involved in government. Girls, especially those who live in big cities, are gaining more independence by deciding whether they want to wear a veil or not. The language and culture that Algerian teenagers learn from their families are also important to their identities. A Berber teenager might speak Tamazight as her first language and Arabic or French as her second, while an Arab teenager might speak Arabic as her first language, French as her second, and not speak Tamazight at all. However, all Algerians speak Arabic, and it is a requirement for Muslims to be able to read the Koran in Arabic.

In some ways, Algerian teenagers are like teenagers in the United States or Europe. They like to watch movies, hang out with their friends, and keep up with the latest fashion. However, Algerian teenagers cope with violence and political turmoil unlike anything that most American or European teenagers encounter. They are also more politically aware than the typical Western teenager. The cultural implications of living in an Islamic country also introduce important differences in the experiences and outlook of Algerian teenagers versus Western teenagers.

ACKNOWLEDGMENTS

I would like to thank Ryad Djahnine and Halim Bouzelboudjen for all their help.

RESOURCE GUIDE

Books and Articles

Alexander, Caroline. "Algerian Rap" [electronic newspaper]. ABC News.com. Cited October 1, 2001. http://abcnews.go.com/sections/world/Daily News/algeria000509_rappers.html

Art and Life in Africa Online. "Tuareg Information" [Web site]. Cited November 20, 2001. www.uiowa.edu/~africart/toc/people/Tuareg.html

Azzi, Mohamed Fardi. "Maghrebi Youth: Between Alienation and Integration." In *North Africa in Transition: State, Society, and Economic Transformation in the 1990s,* ed. Yahia H. Zoubir. Gainesville: University Press of Florida, 1999.

BBC News. "Algerian Berbers Stage Peaceful March" November 1, 2001 [online newspaper]. Cited December 1, 2001. http://news.bbc.co.uk/hi/english /world/middle_east/newsid_1632880.stm

BBC News Online, "Berbers Quit Algeria Government," May 1, 2001. Cited June 18, 2001. http://news.bbc.co.uk/hi/english/world/middle_east /newsid_1307282.stm

Boujedra, Rachid. *La vie quotidienne en Algerie.* Paris: Hachette, 1971.

Bouzelboudjen, Halim. Interview by Ann Cooper. E-mail. August-November 2001. College De Bone, Algiers, Algeria.

Center for Middle Eastern Studies, University of Texas, Austin. "Introduction to Rai Music of Algeria" [Web site]. Middle East Network Information Center. Cited May 28, 2001. http://menic.utexas.edu/menic/rai

Central Intelligence Agency. *The World Factbook 2001*. Cited December 3, 2001. www.cia.gov/cia/publications/factbook

The Economist [electronic version], "Identity Crisis," July 9, 1998. Cited 2001. http://Economist.com

Electionworld.org. "Elections in Algeria" [Web site]. Cited June 18, 2001. www.agora.stm.it/elections/election/algeria.htm

Encyclopedia Britannica. "History of Algeria." Cited August 15, 2001. www.britannica.com

Foukara, Abderrahim. "Algeria in the Grip of Massive Protests." allAfrica.com, May 22, 2001. [electronic news source]. Cited May 28, 2001. http://allafrica.com/stories/200105220375.html

Global IDR Database. "Algeria: Physical Security and Freedom of Movement" [Web site]. Norwegian Refugee Council. May 28, 2001. www.idpproject.org

Heggoy, Alf Andrew, and Phillip Chiviges Naylor. *Historical Dictionary of Algeria*. 2nd ed. African Historical Dictionaries, Number 66. Lanham, Md.: The Scarecrow Press, 1994.

Inter-Parliamentary Union. "Algeria" [Web site]. Cited August 12, 2001. www.ipu.org/parline-e/reports/2003.htm

Kjeilen, Tore. *Encylopaedia of the Orient* [Web site]. Lexicorient.com. Cited May 28, 2001. http://i-cias.com

Lafer, Latefa. "Algeria, 'Revolt in Prose'" (Number 4) [electronic newsletter]. Cited September 14, 2001. www.echo.org/caravan/en/4/algeria.htm

Library of Congress. "Algeria—A Country Study" [Web site]. Cited June 8, 2001. http://lcweb2.loc.gov/frd/cs/

Martinez, Luis. *The Algerian Civil War 1990–1998*. New York: Columbia University Press, 2000.

Marzahn, Michelle A. "Killing the Singer." *Aljadid* 24 (1998): 3, 24.

McLauchlan, Anne, and Keith McLauchlan, eds. *North African Handbook with Moorish Southern Spain*. Bath, England: Trade & Travel Publication Limited, 1993.

Messaoudi, Michele. "The Cultural and Artistic Heritage of Algeria." In *Algeria: Revolution Revisited*, ed. Reza Shah-Kazemi. London, England: Islamic World Report, 1997.

National Office of Statistics. "Statistics of Algeria" [Web site]. Cited June 18, 2001. www.ons.dz

Naylor, Phillip C., and John P. Entelis, eds. *State and Society in Algeria*. Boulder, Colo.: Westview Press, 1992.

Nour, Ines, and Imache Djedjiga. *Algeriennes Entre Islam Et Islamisme*. Aix-en-Provence, France: Edisud, 1994.

Oxfam Internet Team. "Virtual Journey through Algeria" [Web site]. Ontheline.org. Cited December 2001. www.ontheline.org.uk/index.htm

Rarrbo, Kamel. *L'algerie Et Sa Jeunesse: Marginalisations Social Et Dessaroi Culturel*. Paris: L'Harmattan, 1995.

Sanson, Henri. "Peuple Algerien, Peuple Arabe." In *Le Maghreb Dans Le Monde Arabe Ou Les Affinites Selectives*, eds. Hubert Michel and Jean-Claude Santucci. Paris: Editions du Centre National de la Recherche Scientifique, 1985.

Summer Institute of Linguistics, Inc. "Ethnologue: Algeria (13)" [Web site]. Cited June 8, 2001. www.sil.org/ethnologue/countries/Alge.html

Taleb, Dalila. "Hopes and Dreams of Algeria's Youth." In *Unesco Courier* (September, 1998). Archives at www.unesco.org/courier/archives/1998uk.htm

United Nations. "Youth at the United Nations" [Web site]. Cited December 2001. http://esa.un.org/socdev/unyin/

United States Department of State. "Algeria-Consular Information Sheet" [Web site]. Cited June 1, 2001. http://travel.state.gov/algeria.html

Vinckx, Yael. "Rai under Siege." *World Press Review* 44 (November, 1997): 30.

World Algeria Action Coalition. "Algeria's Armed Islamist Groups" [Web Site]. Cited July 11, 2001. www.waac.org

WorldTravelGuide.net. "World Travel Guide-Algeria (2001)" [Web site]. Cited June 18, 2001. www.travel-guide.com/navigate/world.htm

Zaoui, Mohamed. *Algerie: Des Voix Dans La Tourmente: Temoignages De 40 Ecrivains, Artistes, Et Intellectuels*. Pantin, France: Le Temps des Cerises, 1998.

Zouari, Fawzia. "The Death of Algerian Culture." *World Press Review* 44 (November, 1997): 30.

Zoubir, Yahia H. "State and Civil Society in Algeria." In *North Africa in Transition: State, Society, and Economic Transformation in the 1990s*, ed. Yahia H. Zoubir. Gainesville: University Press of Florida, 1999.

Nonfiction

Entelis, John P., and Phillip C. Naylor, eds. *State and Society in Algeria*. Boulder, Colo.: Westview Press, 1992.

Nelson, Harold D. *Algeria: A Country Study*. Washington: Department of the Army, 1985.

Said, Edward W. *Orientalism*. New York: Vintage Books, 1994.

Stora, Benjamin. *Algeria 1830–2000, A Short History*. Ithaca, N.Y.: Cornell University Press, 2001.

Fiction

Camus, Albert. *The First Man*. New York: Knopf, 1995.

———. *The Stranger*. Washington: University Press of America, 1982.

Djebar, Assia. *A Sister to Scheherazade*. Portsmouth, N.H.: Heinemann, 1993.

Web Sites

Algerian embassy: http://www.algeria-us.org/

Algerian government: http://www.gksoft.com/govt/en/dz.html. Part of a Web site called "Governments on the World Wide Web," it provides links to Algerian government institutions.

Encyclopedia of the Orient: http://i-cias.com/e.o/index.htm

www.jumhur.com. Contains links and information about the Arab world, including Algeria.

Belgourmet.com/cooking/links/alger.html; 1st-spot.net/topic_africancooking.html; www.ivu.org/recipes/african. All provide recipes and tips for cooking Algerian food.

Africoco.com has links for children and teenagers about Africa and the Caribbean. It is also a forum and discussion area.

Learn about African music at http://www.afropop.com/

Take a "Virtual Journey through Algeria" on http://www.ontheline.org.uk /index.htm

Pen Pal/Chat

Find a pen pal at www.penpal-pinboard.de

Chapter 2

CAMEROON

John Mukum Mbaku and Nicodemus Fru Awasom

INTRODUCTION

Modern Cameroon is a colonial creation with Germany as its first colonizer, followed by both Britain and France. In 1884 Germany signed "agreements" with several chiefs on the Cameroon River District and founded a colony called Kamerun along the Gulf of Biafra. German authorities eventually undertook additional explorations inland, and the size of Kamerun was extended as far as Lake Chad. During the summer of 1914, war broke out in Europe and by 1916, Germany had lost all of its African colonies, including Kamerun, to the Allied Expeditionary Forces. The colony of Kamerun eventually became a League of Nations mandate and was administered by both France and Great Britain. The League granted Britain the power to control two discontinuous portions of the former German colony along the eastern border with Nigeria—these were named British Southern Cameroons and British Northern Cameroons. The French received nearly four-fifths of Kamerun. In 1945 most of what had been Kamerun became the UN Trust Territory of Cameroons under French administration, the UN Trust Territory of Southern Cameroons, and the UN Trust Territory of Northern Cameroons under British administration. On January 1, 1960, the UN Trust Territory of Cameroons under French administration was granted independence and took the name *République du Cameroun* (Republic of Cameroon), with Ahmadou Ahidjo as the new country's first president.

In plebiscites organized and administered by the UN in 1961, British Northern Cameroons chose to gain independence by joining the Federation of Nigeria, and British Southern Cameroons opted for reunification with the now-independent *République du Cameroun* to form a federation. That union took place on October 1, 1961, and created a bilingual federation called the Federal Republic of Cameroon. The latter consisted of two nominally autonomous federated states called West Cameroon (the former British Southern Cameroons) and East Cameroon (the former *République du Cameroun*). Ahmadou Ahidjo became the first president of the new federation. In the federation, West Cameroonians came to be known as Anglophones and East Cameroonians as Francophones. English and French were made the country's official languages and this qualified it as a bilingual state.

In May 1972, Ahidjo abolished the federation and adopted a unitary form of government. The process to get rid of the federation in favor of a highly centralized form of government had started in 1966 with the adoption of the one-party political system. Then, Ahidjo had successfully co-opted all the nation's political parties in favor of a single political party called the Cameroon National Union (CNU). Thus, in 1972, when the federation was abolished and unitarism adopted, Cameroon effectively became a one-party authoritarian system under the tutelage of the CNU and Ahidjo. On November 6, 1982, Ahidjo's long reign as Cameroon's head of state came to an end when he voluntarily resigned his office and handed the government to his prime minister, Paul Biya.

In 1988, Cameroon held its first competitive elections since the multiparty system was abolished in 1966. However, to qualify to participate in the elections, each candidate had to be approved by the leadership of the country's only legal political party, the Cameroon People's Democratic Movement (CPDM), which had succeeded the CNU in 1985. In response to criticisms of his government and its political practices, especially by Anglophone elites, and also because of a general dissatisfaction with his heavy-handed approach to governance and extremely high levels of corruption in the government, Biya announced his commitment to the reestablishment, in Cameroon, of a multiparty political system. He argued at the time that multipartyism would mark the beginning of his government's efforts to bring about a more democratic governance system to the country. Despite this alleged commitment to democracy and democratization, Biya appeared unwilling to share power with the opposition. In 1991, opposition groups made several demands of the president, including the dissolution of the CPDM-controlled national assembly and an improvement in press freedom, especially with respect to the public-broadcast media, which since independence have been controlled and monopolized by the government and the ruling party. In addition, members of the opposition demanded that the government convene a Sovereign National Conference to draw up political principles for writing the country's permanent constitution. Biya rejected the demands and shortly after that the country was plunged into severe and debilitating strikes and protests, organized and promoted by the opposition. On November 13, 1991, after meetings with leaders of the opposition, a compromise agreement was reached. The government lifted martial law in the provinces, permitted public meetings, and called for an end to the demonstrations.

On March 1, 1992, Cameroon held its first multiparty elections in more than 25 years. Of 60 registered political parties in the country, only 32 were able to participate in the elections. Most of the important opposition parties in the country decided to boycott the legislative elections because they believed that the exercise would be marred by government-sponsored fraud and corruption. The CPDM won the elections and together with the *Mouvement pour la défense de la république* (MDR) and the *Union des populations du Cameroun* (UPC) formed a coalition government. Although the opposition complained that the government had engaged in fraudulent practices during the election, international observers reported that they did not find widespread vote-rigging.

After the March 1992 legislative elections, opposition groups continued to demand that the government convene a Sovereign National Conference to create a transitional government whose job would be to engage the people in designing a new constitution, clearing the road for the democratization of the country's political system. In addition, opposition parties struggled to secure a unified candidate to run against Biya in the presidential elections that were scheduled for the early part of 1993. Before the opposition could agree on a unified candidate, however, Biya moved the presidential elections to October 1992 and rejected demands by the people that the elections be conducted under an independent electoral commission and that election rolls be opened to people who had boycotted the March legislative elections. The latter action on the part of the government effectively disenfranchised many people, especially supporters of opposition parties, who had not participated in the previous elections.

In the presidential elections held on October 11, 1992, the main challengers to Paul Biya were Ni John Fru Ndi of the Social Democratic Front (SDF) and Bello Bouba Maïgari of the *Union nationale pour la démocratie et progrès* (UNDP). Before the results were released, the opposition presented a petition requesting that the election be annulled because of compelling evidence of massive fraud and vote-rigging. The petition was rejected by the government. When the official results were released, Biya finished with 39.9 percent of the votes, while Fru Ndi received 35.9 percent. Although international observers announced that the election was marred with significant levels of fraud and thus had not been fair, Biya proclaimed himself the winner and proceeded to form a government.

When it became clear that Biya did not intend to cancel the elections and schedule new ones, violence erupted in most major urban areas throughout the country, and the government subsequently sent police and paramilitary forces to gain control of the streets and maintain law and order. A state of emergency was declared in the Anglophone North West province of the country. Many people were imprisoned and the province was effectively placed under military rule. At the end of 1992, the human rights organization Amnesty International revealed that it had uncovered evidence of the systematic torture of prisoners by Cameroon's security forces. The government, however, argued that the detainees were routine criminals and not individuals imprisoned for their political views.

As Cameroonians enter the year 2001, Cameroon remains a de facto one-party authoritarian system under the leadership of Paul Biya and the CPDM. In the 1970s and 1980s, Anglophone Cameroonians decried their marginalization by the Francophone-dominated central government. Then, many of them called for either a return to the 1961 federation or the institution of a more decentralized governance system in which the Anglophones would be granted significant levels of political and economic autonomy. Today, especially after the brutal suppression of pro-democracy movements by central government troops, many Anglophones are now seeking secession to form an independent Republic of Southern Cameroons.

The Republic of Cameroon—the official name—is located on the west coast of Africa, with Nigeria to the west, Chad and the Central African Republic to the east, and the Republic of Congo (Congo-Brazzaville), Gabon, and Equatorial Guinea to the south. Climate differs significantly throughout the country. It is hot and humid in the south and west, with average temperatures of 26 degrees Celsius (80 degrees Fahrenheit). Cameroon is located slightly north of the equator and has an area of 183,567 square miles or 475,440 square kilometers, an area slightly larger than the state of California in the United States. The northern part of the country is characterized by a dry plain with Sahara winds and hot temperatures which are quite standard from October to May. Cooler winds and rain come between June and September, allowing for large irrigated farms and the grazing of several varieties of animals. Much of the central, southern, and eastern parts of the country are covered by a plateau of 2,000 to 4,000 feet (600 to 1,2000 meters). In this part of the country, the daily heat of the dry season is relieved at night and by occasional rainfall. From May to October, rains—some of them often quite heavy—bring significant amounts of water to the plateau's cities, villages, and towns. Rich volcanic soils at the base of Mount Cameroon provide for extensive agriculture. The most important network of plantations in this area are those of the Cameroon Development Corporation. The country's coastal areas are hot and humid all year; for example, Douala's average high temperature is 32 degrees Celsius (90 degrees Fahrenheit). These areas support large plantations of rubber, cocoa, oil palms, bananas, and timber. Logging is an important activity, although excessive exploitation is threatening the country's fragile ecosystem. The main highland, Mount Cameroon, is the highest point in west and central Africa (4,100 meters) and is an active volcano. The most recent volcanic eruptions took place in 1982, 1999, and 2000.

Cameroon has a population of about 15.5 million people with a population growth rate that is currently 2.5 percent. More than 50 percent of Cameroonians reside in the rural areas. However, the country's big cities (e.g., Douala, Yaoundé) are growing rapidly. Douala, the country's economic capital, has a population of 2 million and Yaoundé, the political and administrative capital, boasts a population of 1.2 million people. Because of its more than 250 ethnic groups, Cameroon is known as "Africa's crossroads." Major ethnic groups include the Bamiléké (in the west), the Fulani (in the north), and the Beti (in the south). However, no single ethnic group comprises more than 20 percent of the population, and many of them make up less than 1 percent of the population. For many years, these groups have managed to coexist peacefully. Each has its own culture, and political and economic system.

Cameroonians speak many languages. An educated Cameroonian will usually speak a variety of local languages, as well as French and English, the country's official languages. Although French is used predominantly in the eight Francophone provinces colonized by France, and English in the two English-speaking provinces colonized by Britain, many Cameroonians are fluent in both French and English. It is important to note that most of the people who live in the rural areas are not fluent in either English or French. Some languages dominate communications in certain regions of the country, such as Duala on the coast, Ewondo in and around Yaoundé, and Fulfulde in the north. Pidgin English, a language with its roots in English and other European languages, emerged during the colonial period to enhance communications between those members of ethnic groups who had migrated to the colonial economic and political centers. Today, pidgin English remains an important medium for trade and communication in the urban centers. It is quite common for a highly educated Cameroonian to speak French and English at work, his tribal language at home, and pidgin English when he socializes with friends in a bar (night club) or interacts with traders in the market. During the presidential elections of October 1992, Ni John Fru Ndi of the opposition Social Democratic Front, who is not fluent in French, conducted his campaign in pidgin English.

Cameroon has a president as its chief of state and a prime minister as its head of government. Under the 1996 constitution, the president is elected by universal suffrage for a term of seven years and can serve a maximum of two terms in office. The legislature is the National Assembly, which is made up of 180 members, with each elected to serve a term of five years. Allowance was made, through a recent constitutional amendment, for the establishment of an upper legislative chamber to be called the Senate. The president appoints the Cabinet, as well as governors for the country's 10 provinces. Cameroon's branches of government include the executive, legislative, and judicial branches.

The end of the Cold War and the cessation of superpower rivalry changed politics in Cameroon significantly. The legalization of political competition and the introduction of a multiparty political system in the early 1990s have significantly enhanced the ability of teens to participate in domestic politics. Since then, Cameroon's teens have become quite well informed and politically astute. Most of them know the major political parties in the country and their leaders, as well as the goals and objectives of these organizations. In fact, in many cases, young Cameroonians have become active "foot soldiers" for these political organizations. During the opposition-led demonstrations of the early and mid-1990s, which eventually forced President Paul Biya to legalize multiparty politics in the country, teens performed very important roles.

Cameroonians are very serious about education. In fact, since reunification in 1961, Cameroon has recorded one of the highest rates of school attendance in Africa. Provision of educational facilities, however, differs by region. Providers of education include missionary societies, private entrepreneurs, and the government. Attendance in public schools is almost free of charge, while the government provides subsidies to private schools and financial assistance for a few outstanding students to attend private schools. Primary school begins at the age of six and lasts for six years for children in Francophone Cameroon (where it is compulsory); in Anglophone Cameroon, it lasts for seven years. Secondary education begins at the age of 12 or 13 and lasts for an additional seven years: in Francophone Cameroon, secondary school is divided into cycles of four years and three years, whereas in Anglophone Cameroon, it is divided into cycles of five years and two years. Enrollment in primary school is higher in the southern part of the country than in the north. Boys are more likely than girls to complete primary school and proceed to secondary school. Throughout the country, Muslim children attend Koranic schools in the evening and memorize passages from the Koran. UNESCO estimates show that the average rate of adult illiteracy in Cameroon is 30.7 percent (males 22.8 percent, females 38.4 percent). The central government spends about 10.0 percent of its budget on education. During the last fifty years, Cameroonians have contributed significantly to African culture through the areas of literature (especially the novel), music, arts, science, and sports. Cameroon won the gold medal for soccer in the 2000 Olympic Summer Games in Sydney, Australia. Many Cameroon intellectuals, because of their fluency in both French and English, currently serve in many regional and international organizations around the world, including the United Nations and its several agencies.

According to the World Bank's *World Development Report, 2002,* Cameroon had a per-capita income (average income per person) of U.S. $570 in 2000, compared to $34,260 for the United States. Although Cameroon has an active petroleum subsector, agriculture remains the backbone of the economy. In recent years, agriculture has contributed as much as 43.5 percent of the gross domestic product and has employed 60.6 percent of the country's labor force. Cameroon's most important cash crops are cocoa beans, coffee, and cotton. Although Cameroon has a lot of natural resources, sustainable development in the country is constrained by high external debt levels, poor physical infrastructure, and fraud and corruption in government. Many Cameroon teens believe that the government is not making a concerted effort to clean up corruption and improve conditions for them. As a result, many of the country's teens have become very interested in politics (as a way to change domestic economic conditions) or migration to foreign economies that offer them greater opportunities for self-improvement. Although France, Germany, Nigeria, and Britain remain the most desired destinations for these teens, the United States, Canada, the Netherlands, South Africa, several countries in the Middle East, Korea (South) and other west European countries have become quite attractive. During the Cold War, a significant number of Cameroon teens went to the Eastern bloc (notably, the USSR and its satellite states, as well as the People's Republic of China) to study. Today, the United States has actually emerged as the most important and desired destination for Cameroon teens.

Cameroonians produce incredibly beautiful crafts, including embroidered clothing and household items (for example, stools, baskets, handbags, house shoes, and ceremonial clothes). Wood carving is a very important occupation in many ethnic groups. In fact, Cameroon is famous for its carved art, some of which can be found at famous museums in the United States and the United Kingdom. Cameroonians also produce some of the best palm wine on earth. A lot of these items can be purchased at street markets and in stores.

Cameroonians are very religious. More than 50 percent of Cameroonians consider themselves Christians, 25 percent adhere to traditional religious beliefs, and about 22 percent, most of them located in the northern part of the country, are Muslims (mostly Sunni). Even after converting to a nontraditional religion (e.g., Islam or Christianity), many Cameroon believers continue to practice and respect several of their local beliefs. This merging of religions, however, actually enhances their overall faith. Indigenous beliefs are very important in burial and marriage ceremonies, family relationships, the rearing of children, medical practice, and other social activities.

In the early 1980s, the "born-again" religious movement came to Cameroon and captured the imagination of many teens. Many of them, especially those in high school and college (university), joined these charismatic religious movements, most of which were affiliated with U.S. churches. Evidence shows that there was a certain level of opportunism on the part of the teens who flocked to these organizations—many of them were hoping to use their membership in these religious groups to enhance their ability to study abroad. In fact, many of these churches did offer generous scholarships for members to study either at universities in Africa or at church-owned colleges and universities in the United States.

Cameroonians are a peaceful people and do not like wars. In the 1960s, Cameroonians witnessed the destructive effects of the Nigerian civil war and promised themselves that they would never resort to war to resolve their differences. Yet, in Cameroon today, many English speakers believe that war may be the only way for them to prevent the Francophone-led central government from continuing to push them to the political and economic periphery. Although several English-speaking teens have openly supported the secessionist movement in that part of the country, many of them hope that the issue can be resolved peacefully. Most teens see military service as a way to improve themselves economically and socially and usually do not anticipate becoming engaged in prolonged and brutal military campaigns. Today's teens, much more than earlier ones, know about Cameroon history. They love their country; however, they are also angry at national leaders who remain unable or unwilling to deal effectively with high levels of corruption and to significantly improve the domestic economic environment. Many teens complain that corruption continues to deprive those of them who are not politically connected or do not have the money to pay the bribes required by officials from attending national institutions of higher learning. Many of them must seek entrance to foreign universities, often without any assistance from their own government.

TYPICAL DAY

Most Cameroon teens do not have any special morning ritual, although those who live in the rural areas may be required to feed the animals (pigs, goats, cattle, chickens, and so forth) very early in the morning before they proceed to other duties. In the palm wine-producing areas, boys may have to assist their fathers with the wine collecting duties in the early morning. The girls are usually required to help their mothers with household duties. Teens in the villages must travel relatively long distances to get to school. Thus, the starting time for school and the distance the teen has to travel to get to school will determine how early the boy or girl must get up. If the teen is required to assist his or her parents in some activity prior to school, that will also have an impact on the wake-up time. In the urban areas, some children ride buses to school, others are driven by their parents, and others walk to school. In some high schools, all students must reside in a dormitory and go home only on holidays. Those students who live in dormitories follow a strict daily routine which is administered by the principal of the school. Penalties are usually allotted for failure to follow the rules, and students who accumulate a certain amount of penalty points may be subject to expulsion from school.

Not all students who live at home live with their parents. Quite often, teens travel from the village to urban centers to live with relatives so that they can attend school. Usually, the urban-based relative provides the teen with a place to live, contributes to the teen's educational expenses, and generally assumes parental responsibility for the teen. In exchange, the teen is expected to perform well in school and assist the family in the performance of several chores, including taking care of younger children, gathering firewood, washing clothes and dishes, and cooking.

Most school lessons begin around 8:00 A.M. and run until 3:00 P.M. in both primary and secondary schools. In secondary schools in which students must live in the dormitory, the schedule may be slightly different, since all activities are monitored. Thus, even after classes are completed at, say, 3:00 P.M., students still can engage only in activities that are sanctioned by the school. Universities have more flexible schedules, with some holding classes during the day as well as during the evening. Most schools do not supply students with food. However, in those schools where students reside in dormitories, food is included in the fees charged each student. Usually, three meals a day, including Saturday and Sunday, are provided. Such schools usually have dining facilities.

Schools do offer breaks to their students. During such breaks, many students can be found playing soccer or engaged in conversation with their classmates. In schools with dormitories, students usually have mandated times during which they are expected to study and do their homework. Typically, students return to the classroom from 7:00 P.M. to 9:00 P.M., when they sit quietly, usually under supervision, and work on their assignments. In secondary schools owned by churches, students end each day by a short worship service at the chapel (with attendance being compulsory) between 9:00 and 9:30 P.M., with "lights-out" at 10:00 P.M. A typical weekday for students at a church-owned secondary boarding school in Cameroon goes something like this: 5:00 to 5:30 A.M.—bell rings and students wake up, make their beds, clean their rooms, and engage in light manual labor; 5:30 A.M. to 6:00 A.M.—students take a shower and dress for breakfast; 6:00 A.M. to 6:30 A.M.—breakfast; 7:00 A.M. to 8:00 A.M.— chapel for morning worship (all students, regardless of religious affiliation); 8:15 A.M.—classes begin; 12:00 noon—lunch; 1:00 P.M. to 2:00 P.M.—siesta, rest time during which students are actually required to return to their dormitory rooms and lie in bed; 2:30 P.M.—students return to class; 5:30 P.M.—classes over, students return to their dormitories and prepare for light manual labor; on alternate days, students engage in physical training; 6:00 P.M.—dinner; 7:00 P.M. to 9:00 P.M.—study/homework time. Students must attend all activities unless excused by the school nurse for medical reasons. Most of Saturday is devoted to cleaning the dormitory, washing and ironing clothes, completing homework assignments, sports, manual labor, and, of course, chapel attendance in the morning and evening. On Sunday, attendance at chapel occupies most of the day for students at such a school. Some students, especially those in the higher grades, leave campus on Sunday to serve as missionaries (Sunday school teachers) in neighboring villages. Although they would rather spend time listening to music and watching television, participation in these activities is determined by the type of school they attend. Most religious schools strictly regulate student access to popular music and TV programs. Religious music and programming are usually preferred.

Teens who live at home usually do not have such a well-structured daily program. However, Cameroon teens usually obey their parents and abide by the rules set for them. The majority of them go to bed between 10:00

P.M. and 11:00 P.M. On Saturday, they do their homework, study, wash clothes, and perform other tasks assigned by their parents or guardians. On Sunday, many go to church with the family, participate in church activities, and return home to play. Many of them would prefer to watch TV, listen to popular music, and go to movies. However, their ability to engage in these activities is determined by their family circumstances. For one thing, many Cameroon families do not have TV sets or access to stereos. In addition, going to the movies is relatively expensive.

American TV programs, as well as country, rap, and rock music, are quite popular in Cameroon. Young Cameroon teens like to watch such American programs as cartoons and sports on TV. Older teens prefer action or police films (e.g., James Bond), science fiction (e.g., *Star Trek*), karate films, and war movies. The girls prefer soap operas and films about romance. In recent years, talk shows have become quite popular among teens. Both boys and girls follow domestic as well as foreign singers and bands. Rap has come to dominate the music tastes of most teens in the country.

Despite the participation of many Cameroon women in the worldwide movement to liberate women, girls are still expected to do most of the housework. However, many adults now believe that involving boys in household activities will actually improve their ability to grow up to be responsible adults. Most Cameroon teens help their parents or guardians with household work, especially on weekends.

Most Cameroon teens do not engage in paid employment during the school year. Those who attend school and live in the dormitory do not have the opportunity to engage in activities outside those required by the school. Students who live at home and commute to school often do not have the extra time to engage in such employment. Occasionally, students might be able to engage in trading activities during the holidays. Secondary school students often travel to the urban areas during the summer in search of jobs to earn some spending money. Teens who already live in urban areas may also be interested in securing employment so that they can earn some spending money; however, their ability to do so is constrained by what their parents or guardians have in mind for them. Usually, parents have specific tasks for the teens to perform, including sending them back to the village to deliver gifts and visit with family members. On weekends during the summer, teens enjoy dancing, visiting with friends, having "dates," watching movies, and going to discos. It is important to note that participation in these activities is determined by the nature of the teen's family. Many traditional Cameroon families do not allow their children, especially the girls, to date in the American

Teen boys hanging out in Cameroon. © S. Mead/Trip Archive.

sense of the word. Going to discos is usually discouraged by many families, as young girls who engage in such activities may develop a reputation that could ruin their chances of securing a good husband.

FAMILY LIFE

The size of a family in Cameroon depends on whether the family lives in an urban or rural area, and whether the head of household is Christian, Muslim, or adheres to a traditional religion. A Christian family will usually consist of a mother, father, and the children. Rural families often have as many as 10 children. Both boys and girls are desired, with boys expected to carry on the family name and the traditions and customs of the ethnic group. At marriage, girls bring significant wealth into the family since the husband has to pay the parents of the bride what is usually referred to as the "bride price." In the rural areas, parents tend to have more children for economic reasons—the children are expected to help out on the farm, as agriculture is the main occupation of most rural inhabitants. Also, since the infant mortality rate is higher in rural areas, most families have more children in order to increase the chances that some of them will survive to adulthood.

Urban families are smaller, usually for economic reasons. The cost of having a child is usually higher in the urban areas. In both situations, young children remain under the care of their mothers until they are weaned; after that, they are reared by older female siblings and relatives. Breast-feeding is the most preferred method of feeding children, although some educated urban mothers have in recent years begun to experiment with formula. Cameroon fathers are usually not active in the care of infants, although they take an active part in teaching the boys the traditions and customs of the village/ethnic group and helping them make choices regarding marriage, careers, and the acquisition of property. Grandparents, especially those who live in rural areas, are quite important in the raising of children. Quite often, parents who live in the urban areas may actually send some of their children to live with their grandparents in the rural areas. By age 10, children who live in rural areas are already involved in farming, goat- and/or sheepherding, helping their parents "tap" palm wine, and performing other domestic work. In the Muslim north, where many fathers raise cattle, teens help their parents in the fields with the cattle. Some teens travel long distances with their fathers when the latter take the cattle to the market.

The extended family is very important in Cameroon. Hence, cousins, nephews, nieces, uncles, and aunts are as close as siblings. However, the order of birth and the degree of relatedness are still maintained and considered, especially at the time when inheritance issues are being decided. The elderly are not placed in nursing or retirement homes, but are cared for instead by their children or other relatives, usually within the family compound. Ancestors are revered and honored through several ceremonies.

In the urban areas, men usually work for wages, either for the government or within the private sector, or own and manage their own businesses. In the rural areas, most men raise cash crops such as coffee, cocoa, palm kernel, and bananas. Producing palm wine is the occupation of many men in the southern part of the country. Urban women either engage in wage employment or stay at home to take care of their children. In the rural areas, most women are engaged in farming food crops. What the women cannot produce, the men are expected to provide. Thus, in most parts of Cameroon, the men are responsible for providing housing for the family, buying clothes and most of the household items, and paying fees for the education of the children. In Cameroon society, women are expected to be fertile, maintain the family home, cook food for the family, raise the children, and meet the needs of the husband. A wife can be sent back to her parents if the husband is generally dissatisfied with her. Generally, urban women are better educated and more likely than their rural counterparts to work outside the home in wage employment.

Families in rural areas usually live in compounds, each consisting of several houses. The husband has his own house and each wife (in the case where a husband has multiple wives) has her own house and lives in it with her children. Home ownership is more difficult in urban areas and many couples often end up living in rented apartments.

Teens usually stay with their parents until they get married. In recent years, however, young, unmarried, educated girls can be found living on their own in the cities. These young women are usually gainfully employed either in the public or private sector. It is rare to find young women living on their own in rural areas—such girls usually live with their parents or a relative such as a grandparent until they marry.

In Cameroon, marriage is considered a very important institution. However, marriage is often viewed as a contract between two families and not necessarily as an affectionate relationship between two people in love. Arranged marriages, which often involve many months of negotiations between families, remain quite popular. It is quite common, however, for young people living in the urban areas to fall in love and get married. On the average, women marry by age 20 and men, by the time they reach 27. In the rural areas, girls tend to marry at an earlier age. In addition, less-educated girls also tend to marry early. Three types of weddings can be found in Cameroon: traditional, civil, and religious. Quite often, couples will engage in all three of them. Couples who meet in an urban area may first marry in a civil ceremony, then in a religious ceremony at their church, and finally in a traditional ceremony when they return to the village. The traditional ceremony may be delayed substantially by the high bride price required of the bridegroom. Usually, the future husband's family is expected to compensate the girl's family for raising her. Payment can be made in cash or goods—cattle, pigs, and goats are considered a favorable alternative form of payment.

Polygamy, the practice of having multiple spouses, is legal in Cameroon. It is quite common for men to have several wives. Cameroon civil law permits up to four wives; however, many ethnic groups allow husbands to have more than four wives, especially if the man is a member of the royal family. Men who live in urban areas are less likely than their rural counterparts to have multiple wives. Married men may have girlfriends, some of whom are known to their wives. In some instances, such girlfriends may cultivate friendly relations with the man's wife or wives and engage in social activities with the family. In the case where such girl-friends become pregnant, the children from such encounters can be in-vited to join the family or placed in the care of the extended family. Cameroon women are expected to be mothers first and wives second.

Globalization has had a significant impact on teen attitudes in Cam-eroon. Unlike their parents, Cameroon teens, including girls, are fast be-coming relatively more liberal and place greater emphasis on education. Girls no longer consider education as a way to enhance their chances of marrying well. Instead, they see education as providing them with the skills they need to secure employment and enhance their ability to sup-port themselves. In fact, today in Cameroon, teens have become more in-volved in politics in an effort to improve governance and economic structures.

TRADITIONAL AND NONTRADITIONAL FOOD DISHES

The foods that Cameroonians eat differ by region. However, the fol-lowing are quite common: corn (maize); millet; cassava root, including the grated form called *garri*; yams; peanuts (groundnuts); rice; potatoes; cocoyams (staple food, especially in the southern region, they are starchy underground tubers, and often after cooking they are pounded and eaten with stew); and plantains. Fufu is a common dish and is usually produced by boiling and pounding corn, millet, cassava, and sometimes rice. Most dishes include stewed vegetables seasoned with salt, red pepper, and palm oil. Chicken is considered a delicacy consumed primarily by rich families. Meat is considered a luxury, especially in the rural areas. However, "bush meat" (e.g., snake, monkey, crocodile, porcupine, squirrel) is widely con-sumed. Sauces or stews are present in virtually all Cameroon meals. In the urban areas, breakfast may include tea or coffee, fruit, and bread. In the rural areas, breakfast usually consists of leftovers from meals eaten the pre-vious evening. Eating between meals or snacking is quite common in Cameroon, especially in the urban areas where individuals may purchase snacks from street vendors who sell everything from raw sugarcane to fried fish. At meals, most Cameroonians drink water, although beer is quite popular in social settings. In recent years, soft drinks such as Coca-Cola, Pepsi Cola, and locally made sodas such as Champagne soda have become very popular among teens. These drinks are usually taken at room tem-perature and without ice. In the northern part of the country, Muslims usually prefer tea to coffee and occasionally eat beef but not pork. The lat-ter is quite popular in the southern part of the country, where the fat is used as a popular form of seasoning.

As mentioned earlier, women and girls do most of the cooking in the home. Some men cook as well, although they usually make light and easy dishes. Grilling of meat, especially game meat, is quite common among rural men. Although families rarely eat in restaurants, it is not uncommon for unmarried men to frequent restaurants. A type of restaurant called the "chicken house" is quite common in urban areas. These establishments sell baked fish and chicken, along with beer, and men—including married ones—often take their girlfriends to these establishments, even after having eaten dinner at home. The chicken houses are considered places where people go to socialize, drink beer, and discuss anything from politics to soccer games.

Globalization has brought American fast food to Cameroon. Today, pizzas, hamburgers, French fries, and hot dogs are becoming quite popular among teens. Young people in Cameroon tend to think that anything that comes from the United States is good and fashionable. In their parents' day, the obsession was with things originating from France and Britain. While their parents drank bottled water from France and French wines during meals, teens in Cameroon are likely to opt for Sprite, Fanta, Coke, and Pepsi. Sweets have also become quite popular among teens, an unfortunate development, since access to dental care is still quite difficult.

The older generation does not seem to be very keen on junk food. Most of them remain quite committed to traditional cuisine. However, a faster lifestyle, the demands of urban life, and increasing affluence continue to make fast foods quite attractive. Poor eating habits continue to plague Cameroonians, as reflected in the fact that a lot of people suffer from high blood pressure and diabetes.

DEVELOPMENTS IN SECONDARY SCHOOL EDUCATION

There has been a phenomenal development in secondary education since the 1960s, but only a little over 30 percent of primary-school graduates are able to proceed to the secondary level. The starting age is 12 or 13 years (some students are known to have started at 11 years) and students are expected to stay in school for seven years. Attendance by girls has increased tremendously during the last twenty years. The academic program in secondary schools is about 5.5 hours and is divided into three terms which last a total of 35 weeks per year. Cameroon's secondary school system remains dominated by the French and British system, with the "grammar type of general education" remaining dominant. The goal is for students to work towards passing a General Certificate of Education (Anglophone) and the baccalauréat (Francophone). Since reunification in

1961, the central government has tried to harmonize the two systems but has received a lot of opposition from Anglophone elites and parents who fear an erosion of their identity.

The most important innovation in secondary school education in Cameroon has been the introduction in the early 1960s of the bilingual school, where students receive instruction in both French and English. Most secondary schools in Cameroon have been able to keep abreast of changes and developments in subject matter introduced in the UK and France through textbooks supplied by publishers in both countries and also through study abroad by relevant faculty.

SOCIAL LIFE

Teens in Cameroon can meet other teens at social events, programs run by the schools they attend (for example, soccer matches), church programs, cultural and social programs (such as a marriage or birth celebration), and places of amusement. Older teens in the urban areas are more likely than their rural counterparts to go to a disco. In rural areas, teens sometimes organize dances with entertainment provided either by a record player or a local band. Quite often, such dances may be organized around an important family event (such as the marriage of a relative or the celebration of the birth of a child). The rural marketplace, where people from several villages meet once a week to sell and buy goods and services, is also a popular place for teens to meet each other.

Cameroonians consider marriage a very important institution. While dating is gaining ground in the country, arranged marriages are still very popular. Regardless of how the couple meets, marriage still is considered a union between two families, as opposed to one between two individuals.

Rich and poor teens mix freely with each other in school; however, the rich tend to look down on the poor kids. As a consequence, permanent relationships rarely develop between economic classes. Since independence, however, education—especially at the higher level—has continued to serve as a major equalizer. The more educated teens are, the less likely they are to let economic background determine their relationships.

Many teens in Cameroon enjoy having pen pals in other countries. Since the advent of the Internet, this activity has become very popular as teens can easily communicate with their pen pals without having to wait to receive a letter every month or so.

Teen fashions differ by region and the extent of parental influence. Teens who attend religious-based schools are most likely to wear uniforms and dress relatively conservatively after school. Dress, of course, can also be influenced by the nature of the climate. In the southern part of the country, loose and sporty fashions are preferred because of the high heat and humidity. In the north, fashions for teens are dictated by the Islamic religion and harsh climate. Teens in the urban areas are more likely than their rural counterparts to be influenced by European and American fashions. Thus, one is more likely to find blue jeans on an urban, rather than a rural, teenager. Girls, even those residing in urban areas, are still expected by their families to dress modestly and avoid outlandish costumes that may be common to teens in Western Europe and North America. However, CNN, MTV, and American and European fashion magazines continue to have a significant influence on fashions preferred by Cameroon teens.

The type of clothes that teens wear is often determined by the economic status of the family. Richer teens have more access to so-called designer fashions. While poorer urban students may also wear jeans, they are more likely to have only a single pair and restrict their purchases either to used ones or those that are not considered "designer." Richer teens are more likely to have several pairs, with most of them being of the designer type.

Traditionally, many Cameroon parents have tended to be more lenient on boys who engage in sex before marriage than on girls who engage in the same activity. Girls have always been expected to wait until they get married before engaging in any sexual activity, especially since men in many ethnic groups prefer to marry virgins. For girls in school, the fear of pregnancy has been one of the reasons why many parents have traditionally been against sexual experimentation by unmarried girls. However, in recent years the HIV/AIDS pandemic has changed the minds of many parents, and most of them now view sex out of marriage as a dangerous practice for both boys and girls. Homosexuality and lesbianism are largely unknown and are perceived as taboo practices. Throughout the country, parents now discourage their teens (both boys and girls) from engaging in any kind of sexual experimentation, as this could turn deadly.

RECREATION

The most important sports and recreation activity for boys in Cameroon is soccer. Boys also like to swim, although most do not have access to swimming pools. Most swimming is done in rivers, lakes, and streams and only rarely in swimming pools. In rural areas, hunting for birds, squirrels, possums, and other small game is quite attractive to teens. Since it was introduced by missionaries, scouting remains one of the most important recreational and social activities for teens. Basketball and tennis are gaining in popularity as some schools now include these activities in their athletic curriculum. In urban areas, companies and urban social clubs sponsor team sports. Soccer, of course, remains the most popular team sport. The country's national team won the Africa Nations Cup in 2000 and the gold medal at the 2000 Olympic Summer Games in Sydney. Boys and girls in schools play team handball, volleyball, and basketball. A yearly marathon is traditionally run up Cameroon Mountain in January.

Girls play netball, volleyball, tennis, and other sports that do not involve boys. Unfortunately, recreational opportunities for girls still lag behind that for boys as society continues to consider it unladylike for girls to play sports. Other sports and recreational activities enjoyed by Cameroon teens include running, jogging, aerobics, bodybuilding, hiking, tennis, table tennis (Ping-Pong), and checkers. Movies (at the cinema), videos, and television are quite popular in urban areas. Live music is popular in the country. Cameroonians are quite famous for the musical instruments they create, including drums and lutes made out of gourds and wood. Modern music in Cameroon has been influenced by European and African traditions. Popular are *makossa* and *bikutsi*, which have become globally famous.

RELIGIOUS PRACTICES AND CULTURAL CEREMONIES

As mentioned earlier, more than 50 percent of the Cameroon population is Christian, 25 percent is Muslim, and most of the rest follow indigenous beliefs. Cameroonians are free to practice the religion of their choice. Most teens follow the religion of their parents and go to church with them. During the 1980s, when the born-again movement swept Cameroon, a lot of teens joined the movement despite the fact that some parents who belonged to mainstream religious organizations opposed the switch. The dominant church in Cameroon is the Catholic Church, with bishops wielding significant religious, social, and political power. Other important churches include the Presbyterian Church in Cameroon (Buea), *Fédération des Eglises et missions évangéliques du Cameroun* (Yaoundé), *Eglise évangélique du Cameroun* (Douala), *Eglise présbyterienne camerounaise* (Yaoundé), *Eglise protestante africaine* (Lolodorf), and the *Union des Eglises baptistes au Cameroun* (New Bell, Douala), as well as the Cameroon Baptist Church, the Cameroon Baptist Convention, the

Church of the Lutheran Brethren of Cameroon, the Evangelical Lutheran Church of Cameroon, and the Union of Evangelical Churches of North Cameroon. The Bahá'í Faith also has a significant presence in Cameroon. A large Muslim population is present in the northern part of the country.

Most teens in Cameroon are often opportunistic in the way they view religion, easily switching faiths in order to take advantage of opportunities for education and economic and social advancement offered by "newer" religions. In fact, during the Ahidjo years, when Muslim teens were the preferred recipients of national scholarships to study abroad, a lot of teens became Muslims, gained scholarships to study abroad, primarily in the Middle East, and later returned to their family faith after obtaining their education. In the early 1980s, when the born-again movement swept the country, a lot of young people also switched sides in order to take advantage of the opportunities available for study abroad. Many of these teens came to the United States to study at universities and colleges maintained by these evangelical missions.

Muslim teens spend a significant amount of their time, especially in the evenings, memorizing passages from the Koran. Many Christian teens also are required by their parents to attend Sunday school and learn many passages from the Holy Bible. Among many ethnic groups, teens must study the customs and traditions of their ancestors. These often include learning traditional dances, ways to cure certain diseases, religious practices, and different types of ceremonies. Girls are often required to learn how to cook, care for children, and be good mothers. In the village, girls also learn to do traditional dances, which are performed at important ceremonies, including weddings, funerals, coronations, entertainment of important visitors, and so on.

National holidays in Cameroon include New Year's Day, Youth Day (February 11), Labor Day (May 1), and Unitary State Day (May 20). A few religious holidays have national recognition, including Assumption Day (August 15) and Christmas (December 25). The most important holiday for Muslims is the *fête du Ramadan* at the end of the holy month of fasting, and the *fête de mouton*, which is held 40 days later to honor Abraham's willingness to sacrifice his son to please God. Throughout the country, many villages hold festivals and dances to honor their ancestors. Quite often, people who live in urban areas return to their villages during the holidays (usually with gifts for their kinfolk) to celebrate.

While many Cameroon teens continue to be affected by new influences from France, Britain, and the United States, many of them are still interested in learning about their cultures and the traditions of their ancestors.

Teens, however, are becoming more liberal than their parents and hence are more likely to be open to foreign influences.

CONCLUSION

Teens in Cameroon are very hardworking, well educated, and may know more about the world than their counterparts in other African nations. The Cameroon educational system requires teens to learn a lot about the world. For example, in secondary schools, students must learn American and English literature (Anglophone students) or French literature (Francophone students), as well as world history, European history and geography, African history and geography, literature, and so on. Cameroon teens have come to understand that even if one is not born rich, one can still make a good living through education and training. They know that "knowledge is power." They know that there are a lot of highly educated and skilled Cameroonian scientists, engineers, professors, accountants, and other professionals working all over the world. Many of these people were born poor, but through education and hard work, they have been able to achieve a relatively high standard of living. Hence, Cameroon teens consider education the most important way to improve themselves.

Cameroon teens are interested in freedom and have become very active in politics. They like to read books and magazines about struggles for freedom in other parts of the world. They are aware of the struggles of people of African descent in the United States, the UK, and other places around the world. In the past, Cameroon teens were active in the anti-apartheid movement.

Despite the serious economic problems Cameroon has suffered since the mid-1980s, the high levels of corruption and financial mismanagement in the public sector, and the inadequate school facilities, Cameroon teens are very optimistic and continue to seek all available opportunities to educate themselves. They utilize facilities such as the cultural centers provided by foreign embassies to educate themselves about other countries and cultures. In recent years, the Internet has become a very important source of information for Cameroon teens.

Cameroon teens love and respect their parents and their families and remain quite family-centered. The majority of teens are neat, ambitious, and open to new ideas, at least much more so than their parents. Parental influence on teens seems to have been much greater in the past than today, as teens have become more economically independent. However, the family unit remains the most important feature in the life of Cameroon teens. During the Christmas holidays, for example, many teens who live in the urban areas are eager to visit their grandparents and other relatives in the villages.

Teens in secondary schools are especially ambitious. They study very hard and by the time they graduate, they have already decided what profession they want to pursue. Some of them have already corresponded with several universities abroad, seeking opportunities for further study.

Teens in Cameroon are very competitive and are not afraid to sit for scholarship examinations offered to them by different embassies. Through such examinations, many Cameroon teens have secured scholarships to study in Western Europe, North America, Australia, New Zealand, and other countries. Such a competitive spirit has allowed Cameroon teens to be quite successful when they study at foreign universities.

Cameroon teens are very interested in teens in other parts of the world, how they live, and what their interests are. In addition to gaining information through foreign embassies, the Internet, and foreign newspapers, many teens also have several pen pals. They feel that teens in other countries, especially those in the developed West, do not know much about the way they live and the problems they face on a daily basis. They believe that the world would be a much better place if teens in other parts of the world took an active interest in learning not only about their own environment but also about people in other countries. Cameroon teens are quite concerned that foreigners may not have the appropriate information about them.

Poor economic conditions continue to make it difficult for Cameroon teens to achieve their goals. Many teens in Cameroon would like to have some of the opportunities available to U.S. teens, especially in the area of education and career development. Unfortunately, Cameroon's deteriorating economic conditions and the country's underdeveloped status make it quite difficult for teens to function to their full potential.

RESOURCE GUIDE

Books

CultureGrams and Brigham Young University. *2002 CultureGrams, Standard Edition, Vol. II: Africa, Asia, and Oceania*. Provo, Utah: Brigham Young University and Millennial Star Network, 2002.

DeLancey, Mark W. *Cameroon: Dependence and Independence*. Boulder, Colo.: Westview, 1989.

Europa Publications Limited. *The Europa World Year Book, 2001*. London: Europa, 2001.

———. *The World of Learning, 2002*. London: Europa, 2001.

Fonge, F. P. *Modernization without Development in Africa: Patterns of Change and Continuity in Post-Independence Cameroonian Public Service*. Lawrenceville, N.J.: Africa World Press, 1998.

Husén, T., and T.N. Postlethwaite, eds. *The International Encyclopedia of Education*. 2nd ed. Vol. 2. New York: Elsevier Science, 1994.

LeVine, Victor T. *The Cameroons: From Mandate to Independence*. Berkeley, Calif.: University of California Press, 1964.

Mbaku, John M., and Joseph Takougang, eds. *The Leadership Challenge in Africa: Cameroon under Paul Biya*. Trenton, N.J.: Africa World Press, 2003.

Njeuma, Martin, ed. *Introduction to the History of Cameroon: The Nineteenth and Twentieth Centuries*. New York: St. Martin's Press, 1989.

Takougang, Joseph, and Milton Krieger. *African State and Society in the 1990s: Cameroon's Political Crossroads*. Boulder, Colo.: Westview, 1998.

Turner, B., ed. *The Statesman's Yearbook: The Politics, Cultures and Economies of the World, 2002*. New York: Palgrave, 2002.

World Bank. *World Development Report, 2002*. Washington: The World Bank, 2002.

Fiction

Beti, Mongo. *Mission to Kala*. London: Heinemann, 1958. Translated from the French by Peter Green.

———. *The Poor Christ of Bomba*. London: Heinemann, 1977. Translated from the French by Gerald Moore.

Bognomo, J.E. *Madoulina: A Girl Who Wanted to Go to School: A Story from West Africa*. Honesdale, Pa.: Boyds Mills Press, 1996.

Matalon, R. *The One Facing Us*. New York: Henry Holt, 1999.

Mollel, Tololwa M., and Kathy Blankley. *The King and the Tortoise*. Toronto: Lester Publications, 1993.

Oyono, Ferdinand. *Houseboy*. London: Heinemann, 1966. Translated from the French by John Reed.

———. *The Old Man and the Medal*. London: Heinemann, 1989. Translated from the French by John Reed.

Philombe, René, and Richard Bjornson. *Tales from Cameroon*. Washington, D.C.: Three Continents Press, 1984.

Tchana, Katrin, and Trina Schart Hyman. *Sense Pass King*. New York: Holiday House, 2001.

Web Sites

Official Cameroon home page, in French: http://www.camnet.cm

Africa Online has a significant amount of news and resources about Africa, in-
    cluding Cameroon: http://www.africaonline.com

Republic of Cameroon: http://www.compufix.demon.co.uk/camweb

http://www.sas.upenn.edu/African_Studies/Country_Specific/Cameroon.html

http://travel.state.gov/cameroon.html

Cameroon Tribune (newspaper): http://www.cameroon-tribune.cm/index2.html

Cameroon Football Federation: http://www.cameroon.fifa.com/cda/cda_
    container/0,1503,countryCode%3Dcmr_localeID%3D104_siteCategory
    ID%3D2044_siteID%3D1001,00.html

Travel Guide on Cameroon: http://www.travel-guide.com/data/cmr/cmr.asp

Information on Cameroon from the publishers of *Africa South of the Sahara*:
    http://www-sul.stanford.edu/depts/ssrg/africa/camer.html

Mount Cameroon (West Africa's highest mountain): http://web.ukonline.co.uk/
    mountains/cam.htm

Cameroon Chamber of Commerce: http://www.g77tin.org/ccimhp.html

Information on Cameroon from the African Studies Center at Columbia Uni-
    versity, New York: http://www.columbia.edu/cu/lweb/indiv/africa/cuvl/
    Cameroon.html

Information on Cameroon from Europa Publications Limited, London: http://
    europa.eu.int/comm/development/country/cm_en.htm

U.S. State Department Annual Report on Human Rights in Cameroon:
    http://www.state.gov/www/global/human_rights/1999_hrp_report/camero
    on.html

Recent Developments in the Cameroon Economy: http://www.newafrica.com/
    economy/cameroon.asp

Organizations

Embassy of the Republic of Cameroon in the United States
2349 Massachusetts Avenue, NW
Washington, DC 20008
(202) 265-8790 phone
(202) 387-3826 fax
http://www.embassy.org/embassies/cm.html

Ministry of Youth and Sports
(Ministère de la Jeunesse et de Sports)
Yaoundé, Cameroon
237 23 12 01 phone
237 23 26 10 fax

United States Embassy in Cameroon
Rue Nachtigal

P.O. Box 817
Yaoundé, Cameroon
(237) 223-05-12 phone
(237) 222-25-89 phone
(237) 222-17-94 phone
(237) 223-40-14 phone
(237) 223-07-53 fax
http://usembassy.state.gov/yaounde/

Youth-Related Organizations

AIESEC—Cameroon
B.P. 337 (DOU-DASA)
Université de Yaoundé
Yaoundé, Cameroon

Association des Guides du Cameroun (AGC)
B.P. 185
Yaoundé, Cameroon

Association des Jeunes Filles du Cameroun (AJFC)
B.P. 5081
Nkwen-Bamenda
Cameroon

Croix Rouge Camerounaise
Division de la Jeunesse
B.P. 631
Yaoundé, Cameroon

Les Scouts du Cameroun
B.P. 6031
Douala, Cameroon

United Nations Development Programme (UNDP)
UNDP Resident Representative
B.P. 836
Yaoundé, Cameroon
237 225 035 phone
237 224 199 phone
237 224 369 fax

Volunteer Center/Youthlink & IT Services
Association of UNESCO Volunteers
B.P. 255
Limbe, Cameroon
237 333 25 09 phone
237 333 23 76 fax

Youth Organization of the Democratic Union of Cameroon (YODUC)
ABS Ministère de la Jeunesse et Sports
Yaoundé, Cameroon

Youth and Sustainable Consumption
Tamaifo Nkom Marie
Jeunesse Verte du Cameroun
B.P. 7814
Yaoundé, Cameroon

Youth & Development
B.P. 5213
Douala, Cameroon
237 422 970 phone

Youth Outreach Program (YOP)
Suite 105, NWCA Building
Box 5185
Bamenda, Cameroon
237 361 080 phone
237 363 195 fax

Chapter 3

EGYPT

Ann Genova

INTRODUCTION

Egypt, located in the northeast corner of Africa, is one of the most important countries in the world because of its geography and history. Within its borders are the Sinai Peninsula, the only land bridge between Africa and Asia, and the Suez Canal, which is the only access from the Indian Ocean to the Mediterranean Sea. Since the emergence of the great civilization of Ancient Egypt around 3100 B.C., several waves of groups such as the Arabs, Greeks, and Romans have conquered Egypt. With these groups came the introduction of different languages, cultures, and religions. The Romans introduced Coptic Christianity and the Arabs introduced Islam, Arab culture, and Arabic (the official language). The Coptic religion is a form of Christianity that arrived in Egypt in the third century and used an ancient Egyptian written language called Coptic. British colonization of Egypt from the late 1800s to the mid-1900s not only introduced British culture, language, and political systems, but also started a wave of economic and social instability that has lasted well after independence. While Egypt's government seeks to improve the economy and pushes for development in Egypt, its population still suffers from a growing economic gap between the wealthy and the poor, and the urban and rural population.

Egypt has a population of almost seventy million, with 15 percent of it living in Cairo, the capital. A majority of the population lives in Alexandria, located on the Mediterranean coast, and Luxor and Aswan, which are situated along the Nile River. The Nile is Egypt's major source of fresh water, and its banks have fertile soil suitable for agriculture in an otherwise desert landscape. Beyond the banks of the Nile River, Egypt is sparsely inhabited because parts of it receive rain less than once a year, allowing little vegetation to survive. In these areas, staples of urban life such as electricity are not always present.

In large cities such as Cairo and Alexandria, teenagers represent a wide range of economic and social backgrounds. The cities offer a wide range of opportunities for education, entertainment, and socializing that may not exist in the rural areas. Cairo attracts people from all over Egypt and the world because it is the financial and cultural capital of the country. Teens often interact on a daily basis with other teens from around the world in and out of school.

For Egyptian teenagers, where they live within the country plays a significant role when talking about what life is like for them. Egyptian teens share a common citizenship, yet they may not share social, religious, or economic backgrounds. Teenagers in the rural areas and villages tend to experience a more conservative or traditional upbringing than in the cities. A small number of Egyptian teens come from wealthy families while the majority come from middle-class or poor families. In 2000, 22 percent of Egypt's population was estimated to live below the poverty line.

Even today some Egyptian teenagers live a nomadic life with their families, such as the Bedouins, who travel throughout rural Egypt in an annual pattern that allows the briefly occupied land to rejuvenate. Over the years, however, roads into the desert and urban expansion have changed some of their nomadic ways. Some families were given land to farm by the government and have settled, or they continue to travel but with the use of modern items like trucks. The Nubians are another group that has changed because of the Egyptian government's push for modernity. They live in southern Egypt near the city of Aswan, which is situated near the Aswan Dam on Lake Nasser. While the Nubians have faced extensive hardships such as forced relocation and flooding because of the Aswan Dam, they have retained much of their culture and language. Nubian teenagers help their families work in agriculture, fishing, and jobs within the city. Many young adults from both groups have moved into the major cities in search of new employment and educational opportunities.

In Egypt there are political issues that affect Egyptian teens whether or not they are directly involved. These issues often affect both the urban and the rural-dwelling Egyptians. The widely criticized practice of female circumcision affects many female teens. This issue has received substantial media attention, particularly in Europe and the United States, and represents a growing tension between traditional and contemporary social practices. The practice raises questions in Egypt regarding the government's concern for the health and treatment of young females. Another issue that teens may face is the influx of people from Sudan. Sudan's civil war between the Muslim north and the non-Muslim south has displaced many families and destroyed schools. Wealthy Sudanese families may move to Egypt together, while less fortunate teens move by themselves and become poor refugees in Egypt.

Egyptian teens who support the Islamic fundamentalist movement face strong resistance from the Egyptian government. While the government supports the Islamic culture and customs of its people and uses Islamic law as part of its judicial system, it has banned religion-based political parties from forming and running in elections. The Egyptian government has also been criticized for discriminating against Coptic Christians based on their religious affiliation. Many Coptic Christians argue that Christian issues are ignored by the media and that the Coptic era of Egypt's history has been omitted from secondary school textbooks. While Coptic Christians make up a small percentage of the Egyptian population, this treatment negatively affects these teenagers.

Within the last twenty years Egypt has focused funding and efforts on building up tourism in the country. With the beauty and mystery of the Nile River, the ancient Egyptian ruins, and the Pyramids, the attraction to visiting Egypt cannot be denied. However, Egyptians have struggled against the negative image created by the United States and Europe of Egypt as an unstable country of terrorism and Islamic fundamentalism. This stems largely from a misunderstanding of Islam, as well as the unfortunate attacks on tourists in Luxor and Cairo during the 1990s in a country often described as having significantly less crime than the United States. This kind of negative portrayal negatively affects teenagers in Egypt; it particularly affects those who enjoy numerous goods from Europe and the United States because many feel conflicted over buying from a country that does not truly respect them.

TYPICAL DAY

While teenagers in Egypt have diverse backgrounds and interests, the daily routine and activities in their lives can be largely summarized by whether they attend secondary school or not and their religious affiliation.

Like teenagers in the United States, the Egyptian teen's typical day generally centers on attendance at school because that is where much of his or her day takes place. For teens who do not attend school, their day revolves around their formal or informal occupation. Also, Muslim and Christian teenagers add a religious aspect to their typical day.

For teenagers who attend school, their day starts as early as 6:00 in the morning, regardless of whether the school is in a city or a village. School generally starts around 8:00 but may vary depending on the grade and whether the school has adopted a split-shift system to handle the high volume of students. Teens get up in the morning generally an hour or two before school starts in order to allow enough time to get ready, eat breakfast, and travel to school. During the day they attend classes, study, and socialize with friends. The school day concludes between 2:00 and 5:00 in the afternoon, again, depending on the grade or if the school is on a split-shift system.

After school, Egyptian teenagers go home to eat or to a restaurant, depending on the student's family customs and economic situation. After lunch teens do a variety of activities until dinnertime; however, they tend to devote a significant amount of this time to studying because they take their education seriously. Besides studying, teens may socialize with friends through playing sports or just hanging out. Some teens find time after lunch to watch television or surf the Internet. According to the CIA, 300,000 Egyptians use the Internet and almost 8 million have televisions. For many Egyptian teens this is also a time to help around the house; generally girls are expected to do so more than boys. These teens help prepare meals and do general chores around the house. Dinnertime is much later in Egypt than in the United States; Egyptians usually eat around 10:00 in the evening, and shortly after that they go to sleep.

For Egyptian teenagers who do not attend school, the typical day depends on the kind of work they do and the time of year. An Egyptian teenager who lives in a rural area along the Nile River may do unpaid agricultural work for the family. The hours that teens work every day depends on the agricultural season. Farmers in Egypt often grow cotton, rice, corn, wheat, beans, fruits, and vegetables. They also raise sheep, goats, and cattle. Egyptian families in rural areas often expect their teenage daughters to help with the household duties, sometimes more than in the cities, since rural families tend to retain the traditional role of females. A teen living in a city such as Aswan or Cairo who does not attend secondary school may either work for the family or have his or her own paid job. In many cases, teens learn a skill from their parents or the everyday functions of their family's business in the hope of inheriting it.

For Muslim teenagers, regardless of where they live and whether they attend school, the typical day includes praying five times a day, starting with the first call to prayer early in the morning. For Christian teenagers, religious activities throughout a typical day vary depending on personal preferences.

FAMILY LIFE

Family life in Egypt acts as an essential component of Egyptian culture. Whether teens practice Islam or Christianity or live in urban or rural areas, family connections and gatherings hold great importance. As much as possible, Egyptian families eat meals together and enjoy each other's company, especially during holidays. Some families own a lake house or vacation home as a way to spend time together as a family away from work and school. The average Egyptian household includes immediate family members, with an average of three children. In many cases these families also include grandparents, aunts and uncles, and cousins. Egyptian teens generally live with their parents until they marry. In Egypt, older family members such as grandparents receive a great deal of respect and often live with, or in close proximity to, their grandchildren. They often act as caretakers or work to contribute to the household income.

After-school supervision, just as in the United States, provides a constant challenge for parents. While some Egyptian parents work in the home or have older relatives to help, others do not. Also, since the 1970s, many Egyptians have migrated to the Middle East in search of better-paying jobs. An estimated 2.5 million Egyptians have moved abroad for work. This often means that the father goes overseas, temporarily leaving his family in Egypt. A similar migration happens to families in the rural areas whose members migrate to cities in search of work. In these cases, the oldest or female sibling in the family helps take care of the younger ones. These teens prepare meals, clean the house, and often run errands for their parents.

Egypt has a high unemployment rate, and an increasing number of adults from the rural areas are migrating to the cities. Because of the large number of adults looking for work, teenagers generally do not take on part-time jobs. To give a sense of comparison, in 2000 the United States had an unemployment rate of 4 percent and Egypt had a rate of 11.5 percent. Egyptian business owners will often hire an adult in need of a job before hiring a teenager because they know an adult has more financial responsibilities. Also, because Egyptians value education so highly, some families discourage activities that would distract the student from it.

Egyptian parents generally have a strong role in their teenagers' lives. Most parents set curfews and rules on dating and socializing. One teen described Egyptian parents as seldom liberal and mostly moderate to strict in their rules. The challenge that most Egyptian families face is dealing with outside influences that go against Egyptian culture and Islam, which is the case with much of the music, movies, and culture from Europe and the United States that teenagers enjoy. Just as in the United States, teenagers in Egypt often resist or challenge their parents' authority, particularly the teenage girls whose parents do not treat their sons and daughters the same in regard to education and socializing with friends. This kind of family dynamic tends to occur less in the cities than in the rural areas. Some people attribute this to Europe's and the United States' influence on Egypt, which is most evident in urban centers such as Cairo.

Unlike teenagers in the United States, Egyptian teenagers do not view their 16th birthday as particularly special because the legal driving age in Egypt is 18. The test to get a license is quite difficult and driving around cities such as Cairo is not easy. Most Egyptian families do not own a car, and very few teenagers have their own. It has been estimated that Egypt has over 2 million cars. Besides economic constraints, driving in Cairo does not appeal to many Egyptians because of the immense traffic, limited parking, and overall congestion. People in Cairo get around the city by using the subway system, taxicabs, buses, or by foot.

TRADITIONAL AND NONTRADITIONAL FOOD DISHES

The teen diet displays an integrated combination of Islamic, Egyptian, and Western food. The type of food most largely consumed depends on where teenagers live and their social backgrounds. A majority of teens continue to eat most of their meals at home with their family. They eat three times a day and in most cases the mother and daughter prepare the meals. They buy their ingredients in supermarkets, open-air markets, and specialty shops. In Cairo, small supermarkets that sell canned goods, cheese, and other items are located on almost every street corner. Most urban Egyptians have refrigerators, so they are purchasing more frozen foods, but only the upper classes have microwaves. The trend toward frozen foods and processed foods is growing as the number of supermarkets increases.

Typically, Egyptians start the day with a light breakfast of bean cakes, cheeses, or eggs. Lunch occurs later in Egypt than in the United States, usually around 3:00 or 4:00 in the afternoon. Lunch is the largest meal, with time allotted for a siesta. Dinner generally occurs later than in the United States as well. Egyptians will often eat as late as 10:00 or 11:00 at night and the meal consists of something light, perhaps leftovers from lunch.

The basic diet in Egypt includes *ful*, which are feva beans cooked with spices and a variety of vegetables. *Ful* is also mixed with eggs when served at breakfast. *Taameya* is a deep-fried patty of ground beans, parsley, coriander leaves, and other spices. These patties are stuffed into bread, making a sandwich. The bread, or *aysh*, comes in a variety of forms. *Aysh shami* is made in a pita shape out of refined white flour, while *aysh baladi* is made out of whole wheat. Egyptians also make *aysh* in the form of long French-style loaves. Other common dishes are *hummus*, which is mashed chickpeas with lemon, garlic, and *tahini* (sesame seed paste); and *baba ganoush*, which is similar to *hummus* with eggplant. A mixture of lentils and rice called *koshary* is a common dish in Egypt but varies in taste depending on whether it is the country or urban style.

Numerous fruits and vegetables are an everyday part of Egyptian dining. *Molokhyyia* is a green leafy vegetable that is unique to Egypt. It can be made into soup or into a thick sauce over rice. Egyptians often add yogurt or beans to their salads of greens and tomatoes. Depending on the season, a variety of oranges, dates, bananas, and grapes are available throughout Egypt. While fruit and vegetables are widely available, not all Egyptians can afford them.

Accompanying Egypt's rice, bread, and vegetables are a variety of meats such as chicken, beef, and lamb, which are often made into *kabobs*.

Teenage boys at a bazaar in Luxor, Egypt. © H. Rogers/Trip Archives.

Seafood and fish from the Red and Mediterranean Seas are also an important part of the Egyptian diet. For most Egyptians, meat is a luxury served in small portions. Although pork is available in Egypt, it is not widely consumed. The basic practices of Islam forbid the consumption of pork or products with pork by-products, such as lard, in them. Because such a large percentage of Egypt is Muslim, the demand for pork is low; only a few shops sell it to the expatriate and Coptic communities. Even fast food chains from the United States like McDonald's do not have pork on their menus. Although fast food restaurants have sprung up all over Cairo and Alexandria, they mainly appeal to upper-class families and teenagers because of the high cost.

During the holy month of Ramadan, Muslims throughout the world abstain from eating or drinking during the day and eat a large meal at night during Ramadan festivities. After a month of fasting, Egyptians celebrate a three-day-long holiday called *Eid Al-Fitr*; like Ramadan, it is dated according to the Arabic calendar. Celebrants will often eat *kahk*, which is similar to shortbread and is served between meals with tea.

Egyptians also celebrate *Eid Al Adha*, which starts on the tenth day of the last month in the Arabic calendar and lasts four days. They are celebrating the slaughtering of a sheep by Abraham, as ordered by God. During this celebration a cow or sheep is slaughtered and divided into thirds to be given to family, the poor, and the owner of the animal. At lunch the celebrants eat *fattah*, which is beef or sheep cooked with rice.

Although most Egyptians are Muslim, a small percentage are Coptic Christians and have their own traditional holiday meals. For example, on Christmas Eve they prepare *fattah* and on Christmas Day they eat *kahk* and *shorbat* (lentil soup).

SCHOOLING

Egyptian teens have a variety of schools they may attend based on their economic situation and religious affiliation. Borrowing from the British, high school is referred to as secondary school. Egypt's government offers youth free, but not compulsory, public education, which former President Abdul Nasser enacted in the 1950s. The secondary school system includes several types of education: general, religious, and vocational. These schools vary in whether they are government- or privately funded. Countries such as England and Indonesia have established schools in Cairo for international students and wealthy Egyptians to attend. In 1999, the World Bank determined that the general secondary schools represented only 30 percent of total enrollment as compared to vocational schools, which had 70 percent.

The general secondary school system includes public and private schools throughout Egypt that provide a three-year educational program. The Egyptian educational system stresses vocational and technical training and admits about one-third of general primary school graduates into the general secondary schools. The average age for these students ranges from 14 to 17 years old, just as in the United States. To enter secondary school, students in the eighth grade take an entrance exam. When they are in secondary school, they must pass a test every year to move up a grade. They receive a *Thanaweya a' Amma,* or general secondary education certificate, upon completion of their schoolwork.

The typical school day for an Egyptian teen in the general system starts around 8:00 A.M. Throughout the morning and afternoon, teens take eight or nine courses, with a half-hour break in the middle of the day. With the exception of religion classes, they stay in one room for the duration of the day, and teachers from the various disciplines go to the classroom. In the public schools the language of instruction is Arabic, with the requirement of one or two other languages. In Egypt, teenagers speak using colloquial Arabic in everyday conversation, while in school they learn classic Arabic for their formal papers. The popular choices for students are English or French. In private schools, the language of instruction may not be Arabic, but English or French. Depending on the school, the first year may include a variety of required courses such as math, science, government, history, and geography. After that year, the students have an option of three tracks in which to focus their studies, depending on their plans for college: mathematics, sciences, or arts. The school day often ends between 2:00 and 5:00 P.M. Egyptian students do not have a lunch break because they typically eat a large meal after school.

While the general secondary school system offers religion courses in either Islam or Christianity, teenagers also attend religious schools that are privately funded. For example, the *Al-Azhar* school system runs several secondary school facilities throughout Egypt's 26 regions in which students devote their studies to Islam as well as to the general curriculum. Egyptian teens may also attend private Christian schools organized by such groups as the Coptic Christians or Catholics. Students may also attend vocational/technical schools. These options include three-year and five-year technical schools that train students generally between the ages of 14 and 19 in industrial or agricultural skills. Egyptians also have the choice of attending a single-sex school or a mixed-sex school. While some teenagers say they prefer mixed-sex schools, parents often prefer that their children attend the single-sex schools.

In the rural areas, schooling often depends on the flexibility of the family. Since the primary occupation in these areas is agriculture, teens are often busy helping their families with the farms; as a result, attendance may vary. Some teenagers in the rural areas finish secondary school and move on to a university, while others attend irregularly or not at all. In the rural areas, students have fewer choices of where they can attend school. Most schools in the rural areas are publicly funded and less money goes into enriching the quality of the education.

In both the rural and urban areas of Egypt, the educational system suffers from overcrowding and inadequate facilities. Some classrooms lack learning aids that students in other countries take for granted, such as enough textbooks for the students. Also, in many schools the books and audio-visual aids are often significantly out of date. The adequately funded schools tend to be privately funded and provide their students with up-to-date science laboratories and learning aids.

Despite the variety of schools available and the government's efforts to extend educational possibilities to the remote regions of Egypt, a disconcerting number of teenagers do not attend school, even at the compulsory primary level. One reason, as mentioned earlier, is because of the need for teenage sons and daughters to financially contribute to the family, particularly in the agricultural/rural areas. Another reason, one that has prompted European and North American groups to organize, is because of a bias toward only the male children of a family receiving an education. Religious and nonprofit organizations have set up schools geared toward educating young females. While this idea is changing in Egypt, it still exists. The literacy rate among females lags behind that of males by about 20 percent.

SOCIAL LIFE

Egyptian teens meet and socialize much the same way as teens in the United States do. They establish friends through classmates and family members. In areas where teens may not attend school, they often socialize with members of their extended family or neighbors their age. In most cases, teens develop close friendships within their gender because of social customs. For example, a teenage boy may have a male friend over to his house without parental supervision but a female friend is generally not allowed. Egyptian teens tend to socialize in groups of boys and girls instead of in pairs. Also, boys are often allowed to stay out until midnight or later with their friends while girls may stay out until around 10:00 at night. Of course, these curfews depend on the family.

In Egypt dating is not acceptable for teens, unless there is a strong possibility of marriage, but many teens find ways around this custom by dating secretly. Quite often couples will meet in a public place to spend time together. In the cities, such as Cairo and Alexandria, they meet at the cinema or the mall to hang out together. With these social rules, premarital sex is definitely out of the question. Whether the couple is planning to marry or is dating secretly, public displays of affection toward each other are not acceptable. Even married couples do not hold hands or show affection in public. While few formally arranged marriages exist, families do hold a strong opinion on the prospective partner. In general, teenagers in rural areas tend to marry at an earlier age than in urban settings.

Since most Egyptian teens wear uniforms to school, the weekends and hours after school are their time to wear clothes that express their taste and style. Most Egyptian teens take great pride in their clothing, and will spend a large amount of their money on it. The style of dress largely depends on their financial situation and social clique. In general, Egyptian teens do not dress as casually as teens in the United States. For example, sneakers are reserved for sporting activities, not everyday wear, and shorts and tank tops are not worn. Just as in the United States, their clothing often expresses the subculture of the music with which they associate themselves. Heavy metal or hip-hop fans in Egypt, for example, may wear the same band T-shirts and style of shoes or pants as those in the United States. In the case of Egypt, however, males tend to subscribe to this more than females.

Most females do not wear short skirts, shorts, or tank tops as everyday wear. Some females may choose to cover their heads and bodies, which is referred to as *hijab*. Veils can be covered with bright and colorful designs or can be the more traditional black. While veils are often perceived in the West as oppressive, many Islamic women view them as a symbol of self-expression regarding their class, nation, and religion.

RECREATION

Egyptian teens enjoy much of the same sports as teens in the United States. They follow their favorite teams or players on television or in stadiums. Because the weather is hot in the summer and warm in the winter, there are many months during the year for outdoor activities. Teenagers enjoy playing on teams that are both club- and school-affiliated. As with teenagers around the world, a large part of their recreation also includes informal games with friends after school or on weekends.

The most popular sport for teenagers to play and follow is soccer. Egypt has one national team that plays in the World Cup and several leagues that compete on the national and local levels. Because of the numerous teams, teens have a variety of games to attend and teams to follow. Egypt, like the United States, has national sports heroes that teenagers admire. Handball, which has similar rules to soccer, is also popular. Like soccer, handball is organized into national and local teams that compete within and outside of Egypt. Teenagers in Egypt also enjoy playing sports such as squash, tennis, basketball, volleyball, and swimming in lakes and pools.

Egyptian teenagers in the urban areas often join sporting or social clubs which include athletic facilities and maybe a little restaurant or cyber café. The more expensive the club, the greater the variety of activities and facilities that are offered. In general, the athletic facilities often include swimming pools, squash courts, basketball courts, and soccer fields. In addition to organizing teams that play against other clubs, these clubs host parties and social events that teens may attend. Because of the high price of membership, teenagers usually join the clubs with their parents. Teens may join more than one club or go to different clubs with friends.

The secondary schools also provide teenagers with an opportunity to engage in sports. Some schools have organized teams that play against other schools in contests, which family and friends may attend. At mixed-sex schools, boys and girls may play sports together, but school teams are divided by sex.

As in the United States, not all teenagers engage in athletic activities, but spend their recreational time doing other activities such as playing an instrument on their own or through school-organized programs. Working on computers and playing video games are also quite popular. The video game systems in the United States are also available in Egypt.

ENTERTAINMENT

Egyptian teens in the big cities, such as Cairo or Alexandria, have a variety of choices for entertainment. Their weekend starts on Thursday after school and lasts until Saturday evening. With the exception of going to pray at the mosque on Friday afternoon, their days are open to socialize, do homework, and just relax. They can watch a movie in a theater, watch television at home, attend a sporting event or music concert, dance at the discotheque, go to a café, or just hang out with friends. Teens also enjoy family gatherings and celebrations with their friends during religious and national holidays. For those in the rural areas where cafés, television, and movie theaters are not available, teens will socialize at meals or gatherings within their community.

No matter where an Egyptian teen lives, he or she often follows the same religious and cultural views regarding the issue of alcohol consumption. Alcohol is not widely sold or consumed in Egypt by teens or adults. Religious and cultural customs in Egypt have little tolerance for alcohol consumption. The legal drinking age in Egypt is 21, except in areas where a voluntary ban has been implemented. While teens in the United States begin to experiment with alcohol, Egyptian teens for the most part do not have the same interest. Yet, as in the United States, some teens in Egypt experiment with drugs such as marijuana. Most Egyptian teens, however, do not experiment with drugs or consume alcohol; this is reflected in the type of parties they host.

An Egyptian teen will often host a party for a birthday or other special occasion. The parents are present and sometimes relatives also join in the celebration. For birthday parties Egyptians serve cake with candles and decorate their houses with paper garlands. They offer soda to drink with a variety of snacks, such as chips or popcorn, throughout the evening. The parties often involve a lot of dancing, with friends and relatives joining in the fun. Egyptian teens play a variety of music during the parties, including songs in Arabic that are popular in the Middle East and songs in English that are popular in the United States and Europe.

Much of the music from the United States and Europe, as well as the culture behind it, reaches Egypt. An Egyptian teen's preference may range from popular to heavy metal. They may choose a style of music based on enjoyment or as a form of personal expression. Heavy metal music in Egypt received international attention in the late 1990s when police raided homes in order to arrest teenage metal fans and confiscate their CDs and T-shirts. This small group of heavy metal fans had been accused of practicing Satanism, which goes against Islamic law. Some Egyptian teens choose not to listen to music from the United States as an expression of their dislike for the United States' international policies. Whatever the reason for listening to a specific type of music, teens experience a wide range of indoor and outdoor concerts. Arab musicians are quite popular to hear in concert, particularly Egyptian groups. Famous musicians from the United States have also stopped in Egypt. The ticket prices for these acts range dramatically from just a couple of dollars to close to 50 dollars. Throughout the rural areas of Egypt, local musicians often play for their community. As in much of Africa, music is an intrinsic part of life and many teens are raised learning how to sing, dance, and play music. In urban centers such as Cairo, teens can go to dance clubs or discotheques to enjoy their favorite kind of music, but many clubs are too expensive for the average Egyptian.

Another very popular source of entertainment for Egyptian teens is going to a movie. In Egypt's urban centers, several cinemas have opened (including a drive-in theater), offering a variety of new releases using a surround-sound system. The cinemas often receive movies at the same time as Europe and are receiving more movies from the United States all the time. Egypt has an international reputation for producing quality films that not only provide entertainment, but also confront social issues such as teen pregnancy.

In addition to hanging out at the movie theater as a weekend activity, teens enjoy walking around the mall with their friends. Malls give Egyptian teens an opportunity to socialize with their friends while enjoying a variety of activities. The malls in Egypt are quite similar to the malls in the United States, with multiple levels, many clothing stores, and food courts. Movie theaters are often a part of the mall as well as Internet cafés and pool tables. While a large city in the United States may have a couple of malls, cities like Cairo have more than 20.

RELIGIOUS PRACTICES AND CULTURAL CEREMONIES

Most teenagers in Egypt practice the Islamic faith. In fact, only 10 percent of all Egyptians are of another faith. Islam is not only the major religion of Egypt, but also the prevailing determinant of its culture. This is evident in the high school calendar as well as how Egyptian teens dress. Islam is the world's youngest religion and also has the fourth-highest number of followers.

Islam started in A.D. 610 when God spoke to a man named Mohammed in Mecca, Saudi Arabia. Mohammed spread the word of God and through many challenges and much persecution became the leader of a great religious movement. Through Mohammed's recordings of God's words, the Koran was introduced to people as the divine thought and law which all Muslims should follow. In addition to the Koran are the fundamental beliefs, practices, and duties that are referred to as the "five pillars" of Islam. The five pillars are the professions of faith (shahada), the praying five times a day, the alms-tax (zakat) or giving to the poor, fasting during the month of Ramadan, and the pilgrimage to Mecca (hajj). The profession of faith is a declaration that there is only one God who is known in Arabic as Allah. This profession is a major part of every Muslim's prayer.

Throughout the day Muslims are called to prayer from a nearby mosque's loudspeaker. At this time, a Muslim stops whatever he is doing to face Mecca and pray. On Fridays Muslims go to the mosque for a group prayer, similar to how Christians go to church on Sunday. Because Mecca has such historical and religious significance in Islam, a Muslim is expected to go to Mecca at least once in his or her life.

While Muslims throughout the world agree on the history of Mohammed and the words of the Koran, they do not agree on everything. After Mohammed's death in A.D. 632, Muslims looked to a successor for leadership and did not agree on who it should be. As a result, over half of all Muslims are Sunnis and live throughout the world, including in Egypt, while the Shi'ites mainly live in and around the country of Iran. While a majority of Egypt's population is Sunni Muslim, they respect the practice and presence of the small number of Coptic Christians. A Roman saint brought the Coptic Church to Alexandria, Egypt, during Rome's rule, around A.D. 200. While only a few continue to study and practice this form of Christianity, Coptics feel a strong sense of pride for having continued the Christian tradition in Egypt for more than 19 centuries.

Both religions have many rituals and holidays in which Egyptian teens are actively engaged. The biggest holiday for Muslim teens takes place during Ramadan, a month-long time for fasting during the day and feasting during the night. Muslims are expected to refrain from eating, smoking, and drinking from the first light of the sun to the last. During this month, the hustle and bustle of life slows down significantly. The purpose of Ramadan is to unify and strengthen Muslims' dedication to God and to each other. During this time, family and friends spend time preparing and eating the evening meals together. With the festivities in the air, non-Muslims also enjoy this time of celebration. For Coptic Christians, their holidays and practices are much like Christians in other parts of the world, except they celebrate Christmas on the seventh of December instead of the twenty-fifth. During Advent, Coptic Christians are expected to refrain from eating meat and dairy products. On Christmas Eve, they go to church wearing new outfits and the service ends at midnight. At this time, they go home to enjoy their Christmas meal.

Religion is an important part of an Egyptian teen's life and in many cases religion and culture are one and the same. Many teens today are discovering for themselves the importance of Islam as a cultural tradition in their lives. While most teens are simply embracing a religion passed down from their parents, some are taking a more fundamentalist approach to ensure that Islam remains a part of Egyptian culture. This explains why

Islam is the youngest, but fastest-growing, religion in the world. A part of this movement is in response to the increasing influence from Europe and the United States.

CONCLUSION

While Egyptian teens comprise a variety of young men and women, they share the commonality of simply being teenagers. Teen life in Egypt resembles teen life throughout the world in that teenagers strive to find a balance between childhood and adulthood. They attempt to both challenge and respect their parents while developing into independent people. Teenagers often find themselves playing an important role in the family as babysitters for the younger siblings and wage earners. Like teenagers in the United States, the Egyptian teen's typical day generally centers on attendance at school, because that is where much of his or her day takes place. For teens who do not attend school, their day revolves around their formal or informal occupation. They fill their daily schedule with socializing and working toward a future career, whether in school or in a job.

Like teenagers everywhere, Egyptian teens also face questions of spirituality and the future of their country and ethnic group. The cultural distinctions of ethnic groups in Egypt disappear bit by bit every year as teenagers leave the villages for jobs in the cities and do not return. As with the Nubians and Bedouins, they are forced by Egypt's development of dams and roads to change the way they live. At the same time, as people from neighboring countries such as Sudan and Libya settle and become part of Egypt, new aspects of ethnic culture are introduced.

Egyptian teens share a common citizenship, yet they may not share similar social, religious, or economic backgrounds. For Egyptian teenagers, where they live within the country plays a significant role when talking about what life is like for them. Teen life in Egypt's urban areas resembles that in the United States in regard to recreation and entertainment. Egyptian teens, particularly those who live in the big cities like Cairo or Alexandria, have a variety of choices for entertainment. Sports, music, and movies provide numerous social activities in both countries.

Teenagers in Egypt know a great deal about life in the United States through news, music, and movies. While they enjoy many aspects of U.S. culture, they hold great pride in being Egyptian. Yet they conclude that teens in the United States do not know much about them. Egyptians have struggled against the negative image created by the United States and Europe of Egypt as an unstable country characterized by terrorism and Islamic fundamentalism. Egyptian teenagers realize the importance of education as the fundamental way of building an understanding and eliminating these misperceptions between the United States and Egypt.

RESOURCE GUIDE

Books

Cochran, Judith. *Education in Egypt*. London: Croom Helm Ltd., 1986.

Diamond, Arthur. *Egypt: Gift of the Nile*. New York: Dillon Press, 1992.

Fernea, Robert A. *Nubians of Egypt: Peaceful People*. Austin, Tex.: University of Texas Press, 1973.

Fluehr-Lobban, Carolyn. *Modern Egypt and Its Heritage*. Pittsburgh, Pa.: Carnegie Museum of Natural History, 1990.

Hopkins, Nicolas, Sohair Mehanna, and Salah El-Haggar. *People and Pollution: Cultural Constructions and Social Action in Egypt*. Cairo: The American University in Cairo Press, 2001.

Hvidt, Martin. *Water, Technology, and Development: Upgrading Egypt's Irrigation System*. New York: Tauris Academic Studies, 1998.

Hyde, Georgie D.M. *Education in Modern Egypt: Ideals and Realities*. London: Routledge and Kegan Paul Ltd., 1978.

Inhorn, Marcia C. *Infertility and Patriarchy: The Cultural Politics of Gender and Family Life in Egypt*. Philadelphia: University of Pennsylvania Press, 1996.

Kamil, Jill. *Coptic Egypt: A History and Guide*. Cairo: American University in Cairo Press, 1987. This is a useful introduction to the Coptic Christians in Egypt.

Lengyel, Emil. *Modern Egypt*. 2nd ed. New York: Franklin Watts, 1978.

Lippman, Thomas. *Understanding Islam*. New York: New American Library, 1982. This is a short and useful guide to the beliefs, history, and practices of Islam.

———. *Understanding Islam: An Introduction to the Muslim World*. 2nd ed. New York: Penguin Books, 1995.

Wilson, Susan L. *Culture Shock! Egypt*. Portland: Graphic Arts Center Publishing, 2001. This book offers the author's personal observations on the culture and customs of Egyptians for North Americans planning to travel to Egypt.

Web Sites

Al-Ahram Weekly Online. http://www.ahram.org.eg/weekly. January 2001.

Belail, Ali. "Growing Up Away from Home." In *Civil Society: Democratization in the Arab World* 8, 92 (August 1999). http://www.ibnkhaldun.org/newsletter/1999/aug/essay1.html. January 2001.

Central Intelligence Agency, *World Factbook*, Egypt. http://www.cia.gov. January 2001.

Embassy of the Arab Republic of Egypt: http://www.embassyofegyptwashing tondc.org. January 2001.

Labeeb, Nermeen lauz. *Egyptian Attitudes and Habits*. http://www.sogang.ac.kr/ ~burns/auc-cult/auc-attitudes.html. August 2001.

Microsoft Encarta Online Encyclopedia 2001. "Egypt." http://encarta.msn.com. January 2001.

Microsoft Encarta Online Encyclopedia 2001. "Cairo." http://encarta.msn.com. January 2001.

Ossama, Karim. Home page. http://www.geocities.com/kimo_the_maniac/ main.html. January 2001.

Sidahmed, Abubakr. "Nubians." In *Encyclopedia of the Orient*. http://icias. com/e.o/nubians.html. August 2001.

UNESCO/International Associations of Universities. "Egypt." In *Higher Education Systems*. http://www.usc.edu/dept/education/globaled/wwcu/background/ Egypt.html. January 2001.

World Bank. "Egyptian Secondary Education Enhancement Project." 1999. http://www1.worldbank.org/education/secondary/wbprojects/eGYPT2.htm. January 2001.

Zayed, Mayye. Home page. http://www.mayye.4t.com. December 2001.

TeenStuff Online is an online magazine geared to young Arabs. It features articles written for teens by teens. They also have a bulletin board where teens can chat about music, politics, and relationships. http://www.teenstuffonline.net

The Ministry of Tourism and the Egyptian Tourist Authority Web site offers an abundance of information on Egypt, particularly for those interested in visiting. http://www.touregypt.net/

For a wonderful and in-depth look at life in Cairo, check out Karim Ossama's Web site: http://www.geocities.com/kimo_the_maniac/main.html

To get statistical information on Egypt's people, economy, and geography, check out the CIA's World Factbook: http://www.cia.gov

To learn a little Arabic, check out the language section of a Web site entitled "The Egyptian Castle." http://www.egyptiancastle.com/main/culture/ language/alphabet.htm

For a Web site devoted to Egyptian soccer, check out Egypt Soccer Online: http://www.egyptiansoccer.com/

For information on Islamic beliefs, practices, and dress, check out: http://www. islamicgarden.com/article1016.html

For current news from Cairo, check out Classic Cairo Live: http://www.cairolive. com/

Videos

Turning 16 by Adobe Foundations.

In this eight-part television series, teens from Egypt, Niger, Brazil, Thailand, India, and Jamaica talk about the concerns and issues they face.

Young Voices from the Arab World: The Lives and Times of Five Teenagers by Leslie S. Nucho.

> In this video, five middle-class teenagers from Egypt, Jordan, Lebanon, Kuwait, and Morocco talk about their families, interests, and hopes.

Teens around the World by In the Mix.

> In this video, teenagers from Egypt, the Philippines, Russia, Korea, and Namibia talk about their interests, families, and the issues they face.

Africa Close-Up. Egypt, Tanzania as part of the *Children of the Earth Series* by Maryknoll World Productions.

> In this video, a 15-year-old girl from Cairo shows the viewer what life is like in her neighborhood and some of Cairo's major attractions, such as the Nile River and the Pyramids.

Cairo by International Video Network.

> This video offers a tour of Cairo with information about its history.

Organization

Egyptian Embassy
Embassy of the Arab Republic of Egypt
3521 International Ct., NW
Washington, DC 20008
http://www.embassyofegyptwashingtondc.org

Pen Pal/Chat

Check out *TeenStuff Online*'s bulletin board for a pen pal from Egypt or another Arab country.

Check out Mayye Zayed's Web page for Egyptian pen pals: http://www.penpalsworld.4t.com

Chapter 4

ETHIOPIA

Edmund Abaka

INTRODUCTION

Teens in Ethiopia, like teens everywhere, have a zest for life. Many aspire to get a good education and a good job, to make a lot of money and start their own families. They love sports, games, and fun. However, a chronicle of teen life in Ethiopia is a story of hopes and aspirations shattered and rebuilt; one of famine, war, and political dictatorship. Many teens have experienced displacement, starvation, and conscription to fight in Ethiopia's wars. They have lost a parent or both parents to HIV/AIDS, or have been forced to become adults overnight to look after younger siblings. This chapter examines the varying facets of teen life in Ethiopia. It puts in perspective the complex history of the oldest state in Africa, and examines the daily life of teens, family life, schooling, and social life and recreation, among other things. It also asserts that in spite of all difficulties, life, for Ethiopian teens, goes on.

Ethiopia is located in the often inaccessible mountains between the Red Sea and the Blue Nile. It has long been acclaimed as a complex and mysterious country. For one thing, the Nile, which brought life to ancient Egypt, partly took its source from Ethiopia. For another, an ancient international trade route through the Red Sea and the Gulf of Aden linked the Mediterranean with India, China, and other countries.[1]

Ethiopia is bounded in the west and north by Sudan, in the south by Kenya, in the southeast by Somalia, in the east by Djibouti, and in the north and east by the Red Sea. Its rugged topography consists of the Ethiopian Plateau, many rivers, deep valleys and mountains. The highest mountain, Ras Dashan, is about 4,620 meters (15,157 feet).[2]

Ethiopia is primarily agricultural; its soils, climate, and vegetation permit the cultivation of a wide range of agricultural products. At the same time, Ethiopia is affected by periodic droughts which, coupled with the war against Eritrea and Somalia, led to severe famine in the 1970s and 1980s.

A 1995 population census put Ethiopia's population at 55.9 million. Some of the major ethnic groups in Ethiopia include the Amhara,[3] Tigrayans (who occupy large parts of the Ethiopian highlands), the Galla, the Shanqall, the Somali and others. Scholars believe that the Ethiopian Plateau was occupied by Cushitic speakers who developed one of the earliest centers of agriculture (based on grain) in Africa.[4] The North Cushites concentrated on agriculture and produced an indigenous cereal, teff, and imported grains like barley and millet (possibly from Egypt).[5]

Ethiopia was home to the powerful Christian Aksumite kingdom in the first century A.D. Aksum fostered a distinctive civilization that formed the nexus for medieval and premodern Ethiopian civilization.[6] By the second century A.D., the Aksumite kingdom was ruled by the Solomonid dynasty, but in the early seventh century, the Solomonids lost control of parts of the kingdom, and were replaced in the early tenth century by the Zagwe dynasty, based at Lasta. The Solomonids regained control of the country around 1260, although Muslims retained control of the coastal area and the southeast.

King Ezana, who ruled in the mid-fourteenth century, subdued the Beja and Kush, who had rebelled against Aksumite overlordship. Ezana, attributing his victories to the "Lord of Heaven," converted to Christianity.[7] However, Christianity was possibly introduced into Aksum through mercantile relations with Byzantium, but became official after Ezana's conversion, supposedly through the work of a Syrian Christian tutor, Frumentius.[8]

Zara Yakub, who reigned from 1434 to 1468, streamlined the administration of the Ethiopian Church and codified its religious doctrines to curtail sectarianism and factionalism. He also introduced political reforms that instituted an absolutist monarchical system, which lasted in one form or another until the middle of the twentieth century. Ethiopia resisted the Muslim invasion from Harar around 1527, albeit with Portuguese assistance. After the Muslim defeat in 1542, Jesuit missionaries arrived in Ethiopia in 1557, and later in 1603. They converted Emperor Za Dengel (r. 1603–4),[9] whose subsequent attempts to convert the country by force provoked a revolt in which he perished.[10]

Ethiopian civilization flourished, and commerce thrived under Emperors Sussenyos (1572–1632), Fasiladas (r. 1632–67), Yohannes I (r.

1667–82), and Yasus the Great (1662–1706). The construction of grand structures, especially at Gondar, started the creation of an extensive imperial compound.[11] Yasus was the last strong ruler before a prolonged period of strife, confusion, and decline, known as Zamana Masafint, or era of the princes, led to the disintegration of the state into separate regions.[12] However, during this period, the Ethiopian Orthodox Church became the fulcrum around which the state rallied. With the support of church officials, a successful brigand from the northwestern frontier, Ras Kassa (1818–68), was crowned as Emperor Tewodros II in 1855.

When Tewodros imprisoned some British officials in 1868, a British expedition under Robert Napier fought its way to Maqdala. Faced with defeat, Emperor Tewodros committed suicide rather than be taken prisoner. After a four-year struggle, Dejaz Kassai, governor of Tigray province, succeeded, with British aid, in being crowned Emperor Yohannes (John IV) of Ethiopia.[13] In the 1870s Ismail Pasha of Egypt, after extending Egyptian protection to the Muslim ruler of Harar, attacked Ethiopia from both the north and the east. Yohannes IV successfully halted the Egyptian invasion, but Egypt's control of the Red Sea and Somali ports curtailed the arms supply to Ethiopia. Yohannes was killed defending his western frontier against the Mahdist state of Sudan in 1889.[14] Menelik II, who established a new capital at Addis Ababa and united Tigray and Amhara with Shoa, succeeded Yohannes.[15]

With the opening of the Suez Canal in 1869, European powers tried to outdo each other on the Red Sea coast in a scramble for Ethiopia. Italy became particularly fixated on Ethiopia, and seized Assab in 1872 and Massawa in 1885. In 1889 Menelik and the Italians signed a treaty of friendship and cooperation, the Treaty of Wichale (Ucciali). But furious at the discovery that the Amharic and Italian texts of the treaty were different, Menelik repudiated the treaty and mobilized against Italy in 1895. The Italians were decisively defeated at Adwa (Adowa) in 1896 and forced to recognize Ethiopian independence.[16] Menelik's conquest of non-Ethiopian areas in the south and west shaped the present-day boundaries of Ethiopia. Menelik's successor, Lij Iyasu (r. 1913–16), was deposed in favor of his aunt, crowned Empress Zauditu (1876–1930). Ras Tafari Makonnen, her cousin and heir apparent, later ascended the throne as Haile Selassie I.

Under the fascist dictator Benito Mussolini, Italy revived its designs toward Ethiopia and invaded that country in October 1935. Due to inaction by the League of Nations, Italy captured Addis Ababa in May 1936. Haile Selassie fled to Europe and despite his address to the General Assembly of the League of Nations, nothing was done until Italian forces invaded

British-controlled Egypt and threatened the Suez Canal route to India. British forces pushed the Italians back to Libya in January 1941. Finally, British and African troops took the Ethiopian capital in May 1941 and restored Haile Selassie.

The Allied peace treaty signed after World War II stipulated that the powers should reach agreement within a year about the disposition of the former Italian colonies of Eritrea, Italian Somaliland, and Libya. UN General Assembly members could not agree, and voted for the federation of Eritrea with Ethiopia, to be completed by September 1952. In 1963 Haile Selassie became one of the major architects of the Organization of Africa Unity, which was headquartered in the Ethiopian capital, Addis Ababa.

Border disputes between Ethiopia and the Somali Republic in 1964 led to war between the two states and in 1965, another war broke out with Sudan after Ethiopia accused Sudan of abetting an Eritrean independence movement. In December 1970 Ethiopia laid siege to parts of Eritrea.

In the early 1970s Haile Selassie, an influential head of state on the continent, mediated in disputes between Senegal and Guinea, and between Tanzania and Uganda. But while his international stature grew, he neglected domestic problems—unequal wealth distribution, rural underdevelopment, government corruption, inflation, unemployment, and a severe drought in the north from 1972 to 1975. These conditions were exacerbated by secession problems. In the absence of any reform programs, students, workers, and soldiers resorted to strikes and demonstrations in February 1974 that culminated in Haile Selassie's deposition on September 12, 1974. A Provisional Military Administrative Council (PMAC), or the Derg, led by Lt. Col. Mengistu Haile Mariam, eventually took over the country. In late 1974 it issued a program calling for the establishment of a state-controlled socialist economy and the formation of workers' committees in work places. It nationalized all agricultural land in 1975, some of which was parceled out in small plots to individuals. In March 1975 the monarchy was abolished, and Ethiopia became a republic.

The period of 1976–77 was a time of consolidation for Col. Mengistu as the PMAC was purged in 1977. All the same, the government faced strong opposition from students, political leaders, and especially two secessionist movements in the Ogaden region of southwestern Ethiopia and in Eritrea. In the Ogaden, Somali-speaking inhabitants sought to unite with adjacent Somalia. The conflict escalated in mid-1977, and with considerable Somali help the secessionists soon won control of most of the Ogaden.[17]

The Ethiopian government relied on Soviet and Cuban support in the form of Russian advisors and Cuban troops. It embarked on poverty alleviation and economic development plans, but recurring drought and the attendant famine of the 1980s negated any achievements in that direction.[18] In September 1984, Ethiopia became a communist state, with Mengistu as secretary-general of the newly established Workers party. The nation changed its name to the People's Democratic Republic of Ethiopia in 1987. In 1991 two allied rebel movements, the Ethiopian People's Revolutionary Democratic Front and the Eritrean People's Liberation Front, ousted the Marxist government of Ethiopia and Mengistu Haile Mariam fled to Zimbabwe. Under a provisional charter, the 87-member elected Council of Representatives chose a president to govern Ethiopia, pending general elections in 1993. A separate government was established in Eritrea, and the province was recognized as an independent republic in May 1993.

Ethiopia has a large teenage population and the conditions and role of teens in Ethiopia should be outlined in the context of the political and social events in the country. In 1997 the youth population of 15-to-24-year-olds stood at 18.6 percent of a population of 56 million. Ethiopia has a large peasant population and a large teenage component that has been at the mercy of natural disasters such as failure of seasonal rains, occasional heavy rains, and widespread flooding. Drought recurrence, which intensified in the late 1960s, was exacerbated in the 1970s and 1980s by armed conflict and political repression. These have put untold hardship on Ethiopian teens. The Ogaden War of 1977–78 and the drought of 1978 in eastern Ethiopia, followed by an Ethiopian counteroffensive against Eritrean guerillas, and more famines in 1984–85 and in 1990, created even greater problems of displacement. Food aid, while not adequate, suffered from bad roads, and the war raging in the country and the politics of food aid bedeviled distribution of much-needed food to many starving families, including teens. This resulted in the massive displacement and migration of Ethiopians to neighboring countries such as Sudan.

Ethiopian teens have been affected in no small measure by the recent events chronicled above. In Yabello Woreda in southern Ethiopia, over 24 percent of children and teens were acutely malnourished. According to the UNICEF Ethiopian Senior Program Officer, "we are talking of over 1 million children at high risk of acute malnutrition...their very weak status makes them extremely vulnerable to disease and death."[19] Teens constituted some of the vulnerable groups that succumbed to disease, famine, and war from the 1970s onward. In a region devastated by years of war and recurring droughts, teens help their parents in the fields, fetch water and firewood for cooking, and perform many domestic chores. By the same token, Ethiopian teens have been scarred by the war in another major way. Faced with dwindling conscripts for the war in the Ogaden and against Eritrea, the Ethiopian government set the age of conscription on paper at 18 to 70 years, but boys as young as 12 were also conscripted. Ethiopian teens were therefore part of a generation of African youth known as "child soldiers."[20] Many teens live in refugee camps in neighboring countries and others have resettled in North America, especially in Toronto, Canada. Ethiopian teens do not like the idea of war, population displacement, family break-ups, and the death of siblings, but they have been caught up in a whirlwind of events that have devastated their country.

Ethiopian teens know a lot about their country and are very proud of their homeland, but they cannot understand leaders who plunge their country into war even in times of famine and scarcity.

TYPICAL DAY

While Ethiopian teens may not have special morning rituals, the conditions of war, devastation, and poverty mean that the typical day starts very early for many teens, whether they attend school or not. Ethiopia has the second-largest population in Africa but is one of the poorest countries on the continent. Malnutrition is high (about 64 percent) and enrollment in primary schools in 1999 hovered around 24.9 percent. The illiteracy rate for people over 15 was 64.5 percent in 1996.[21] Therefore, Ethiopia has a large teen population that is not enrolled in school due to poverty and paucity of resources.

Teens usually start the day with early-morning chores, which involve fetching water, washing pots and pans, or sweeping the compound. Those who go to school usually leave around 8:30 A.M. and remain in school until around 4:00 to 4:30 P.M. Colleges and universities have evening and night classes as well.

Because Ethiopia has a large rural population, many teens walk to school, as is done in many parts of Africa. Many schools tend to be neighborhood schools, even in small villages, and children commute on foot to and from school all year long. In the urban centers, such as Addis Ababa, urban teens have to fight the rush-hour traffic of the cities—buses, cars, and bicycles—to reach school.

Some of the villages in rural Ethiopia are small, with a collection of houses, a store or shop, a marketplace, and usually a primary school and a church building. Such villages usually have a main street and a few side

Ethiopian girl with a large jar. © Liba Taylor/CORBIS.

streets. Some of the compounds are surrounded by bamboo or wooden fences, with wooden gates to keep out domestic animals such as sheep, goats, and fowls. In such places, there are no high schools, and teens who want to continue their education after primary school, assuming the parents can afford it, have to go to towns that have high schools.

After school, teens go home to be with family members. Teenagers in urban centers visit friends, play together, watch television, and play soccer or even computer games (affluent families), while their counterparts from poor families help parents at home, play in the neighborhood with other teens, or go to work for a few hours to make some money to supplement family income. In the rural areas, teens tend to go to the farm after school to carry home food or firewood. Others do odd jobs, such as running errands or fetching water from wells and sometimes streams for a small fee, or in some cases even a meal. What is usually considered leisure time is often spent doing something that will add to family income.

Ethiopians, like other Africans, generally eat a big evening meal anywhere from 6:00 P.M. to 9:30 P.M. Teenagers and even small children often stay up quite late playing games or swapping stories.

Children in communal societies make contributions to the family welfare earlier than their counterparts elsewhere. In many parts of Ethiopia that have seen long periods of drought and extreme poverty, teenagers are often looking for odd jobs to supplement the meager wages of their parents. They weed other people's farms, fetch firewood for cooking, and run other errands. Ethiopian teens generally rely on their parents for spending money, and whatever money they make in part-time jobs or odd jobs is usually given to their parents for safekeeping and family use.

Some urban families have servants, mansions, and plots of land, and might employ several housemaids, cooks, drivers, and even nannies for their smaller children if they cannot find any family member to do that job. Sometimes, poor people may send their teenage children to live with rich relatives and perform the tasks typical of nannies or cooks. Many teen domestic workers are often poor people with no skills who go to work in affluent homes. In many cases, they return to their own homes after the day's work. In other instances, they live with their employers in small, separate quarters outside the main building. African families, both rich and poor, are generally large and highly valued. Family sizes have dwindled across the continent from an average of eight to four or five children. Teens have household responsibilities: sweeping or mopping rooms; washing pots and pans; fetching water, sometimes over very long distances (especially in parts of drought-prone Ethiopia); fetching firewood; and working on the farm both on weekdays and weekends. In Africa, a gender division of labor exists, and many Ethiopian girls assist their mothers with cooking and housework while the boys fetch water or firewood. In some cases, whole families go to fetch water at particular times, either in the morning or evening.

FAMILY LIFE

Most Ethiopians, like other Africans, live in extended families, often in compounds containing several rooms in which several generations of the same family live: grandparents, parents, brothers and sisters, aunts, uncles, and cousins. Where families live apart, there is a sense of obligation to visit members as often as possible, on weekends, or during Christian and Muslim holidays. Ethiopian children socialize with their aunts, uncles, cousins, and other relatives.

Early and universal marriage, kinship and religious beliefs that generally encourage large families, a resistance to contraceptive practices, and the absence of family planning services for most of the population have led to the existence of large families. Many Ethiopians believe that families with many children have greater financial security and are better situated to provide for their elderly members.

Teenagers of families displaced by war and famine may occasionally visit their grandparents, aunts, and uncles living in another part of the country if it is feasible. Similarly, the lucky ones may visit family members living in other parts of the world, such as Canada or the United States, usually at the invitation of the relatives overseas. Family members in North America arrange for teenagers back home in Ethiopia to visit them, and oftentimes sponsor them to live in North America and go to school. Various Ethiopian community groups in North America help newcomers through this process of adjustment and naturalization. Family members who live in Europe and North America also visit relatives back in Ethiopia from time to time.

Ethiopian teenagers of today are more likely to be educated as compared to their parents and grandparents. Today, there are schools in both urban and rural areas, though rural areas have mostly primary schools. The destruction of schools and educational facilities in Eritrea, Tigray, Gonder, and other parts of the country in the early 1990s means that money that should have been put to use improving schools has been used to restore educational facilities. In spite of this, Ethiopian teenagers today, especially those living in urban centers, have far greater educational opportunities than any previous generation.[22] The value of education is widely recognized and even when parents have very little education or none at all, they want their children to take advantage of the opportunity to go to school.

Many Ethiopians still live in fairly poor rural areas. But the urban Ethiopian teen of today is growing up in an era full of global opportunities. Those in the urban areas have access to the Internet and other technological appliances that were not possible in their parents' time. While access is restricted by the paucity of computers and telephone infrastructure outside the major urban centers, teens have access to information, music, movies, and material things, including trips to other countries.

The changes of the present decade have undoubtedly given teenage girls greater opportunities in public and private employment than their mothers and grandmothers, even if they still have a very long way to go. Some educated Ethiopian women hold important, albeit limited, positions both at home and in the international arena, but the opportunities can only multiply in the future. Due to the extended family system, some women can leave their children with parents, uncles, aunts, and nieces and go to school and to work.

Religious inscription dating back to the medieval period shows that medieval Ethiopian children remained frequently seen but rarely heard.[23] Not much has changed even today. Parents make all decisions, including financial decisions, at home. Teens live with their parents or their mothers. Others live with relatives such as uncles, aunts, and grandparents. The mean age of first childbirth for women is in the teens, but it is slightly higher for men. Many women in their teens have children. Some have children when they are still in school, though the pattern is changing slightly.

Teenage marriage in Ethiopia has always been the norm. It still is today in the rural areas of the country. According to one observer, "Women had no say in the choice of the man they had to marry. If they were divorced, they had no rights to half of the property."[24] Since the war against the Mengistu regime, the rights of women have begun to change, in part due to the preponderant role of women in the war. Before the armed struggle, women "had to serve their husbands, but could not get educated, and they were expected to marry at 8, 9, or 10 years."[25] After the overthrow of Mengistu, the Women's Association of Tigray, a partner of Oxfam Community Aid Abroad, organized workshops attended by religious leaders, lawyers, and doctors, and the marriage age of women was raised to 18.

Children after ages four and five are given low status until they reach adulthood. They are taught to show deep respect for their elders, to be obedient and unquestioning toward authority. Children must not interrupt adults engaged in conversation or call adults by their first names. Respect is demonstrated by their behavior, and by the tone of voice and the language they use with elders. It is common for children to stay at home until marriage.

Discipline is taught through common values. Fathers are traditionally the authority figures who make most of the rules; mothers enforce the rules for children. Whole communities further reinforce discipline. The norms of good behavior are traditionally very clear, so anybody, even a stranger, can correct a child's bad behavior. A child protects family pride by trying to behave well. Self-identity is regarded as being based on strong group identity and goes from the group to the individual, rather than the other way around.

Due to societal perceptions of dating, relationships between teenage boys and girls may be conducted in secret until they are ready for marriage. There is very little information on sex. It appears to be a taboo subject and mention of anatomical parts in biology classes is carefully made. Women's virginity is cherished, and the whole family may be shamed if the bride is not a virgin at marriage. Female genital mutilation or female circumcision was practiced to ensure virginity. It is still practiced by some groups, although there have been successful attempts in different parts of Ethiopia to discontinue the practice after the recent outcry against it, especially in North America and Europe. Inter-religious marriage is not usually encouraged. In the past, arranged marriages were common, but the practice is not rigidly enforced today, though it is usually important to marry someone the family approves of so there will be peace and harmony between the different families. Rural women, in particular, tend to marry at a young age and may be 6 to 10 years younger than their husbands. Since the Koran (the holy book of Islam) permits Muslim men to marry more than one wife, large families and large numbers of children are traditionally considered to be a sign of status. If the husband of a Muslim woman dies, it is the responsibility of the husband's brother to take care of the wife and family. He may be required to marry her.

TRADITIONAL AND NONTRADITIONAL FOOD DISHES

Ethiopian food is based on a staple grain called teff, which grows only in Ethiopia. Teff is made into dough, which is allowed to ferment before it is cooked into a flat, pancake-like, thin broad-bread called *injera*, one of the oldest types of food in Ethiopia. This is then eaten with various kinds of stew called *wot*. *Wots* can be made of meat, vegetables, peas, lentils, and so on, and can be very highly spiced. *Doro wot*, a stew of chicken marinated in chili, spices, butter, and hardboiled eggs, which is eaten with *injera*, is the most popular one. Orthodox Christians and Muslims do not eat pork.

Dinner in an Ethiopian restaurant or at home is quite an experience. Guests sit on low, comfortable divans with a handmade wicker table in front of them. A woman carries a long-spouted copper pitcher and a copper basin into the room, pours warm water over the fingers of the right hand, and catches the excess water in the basin while the guest wipes his hand with a towel. When the woman returns a second time, she comes in with a domed cover. When the dome is removed, the table will be covered with an "edible tablecloth"—*injera*—overlapping a huge tray. Food is brought to the table in enamel bowls, portioned on the *injera*, and guests tear off pieces in which they roll the food and eat. After dinner, amber-colored honey wine (*Tej*) or homemade beer may be served.

One popular Ethiopian tradition in both cities and countryside is serving Ethiopian coffee. Kaffa Region, Ethiopia's premier coffee-growing area and quite possibly the birthplace of coffee, was the region where wild coffee trees were cultivated and then shipped to Yemen, eventually to become a part of world culture.

Sometimes coffee is served in a special ceremony which can take up to a few hours. The beans are roasted by hand, ground in a special way, prepared in a special pot, and poured into a special cup.[26] In many parts of Ethiopia, this ceremony takes place three times a day, and food is served with it.

SCHOOLING

As late as 1985, only about 2.5 million (42 percent) of the 6 million primary school-age children were in school in Ethiopia. At the senior secondary school level (grades 9 through 12), 292,385 (5.3 percent) out of a total of 5.5 million children were going to school. The junior secondary school to primary school ratio of one to eight meant that many Ethiopian children could attend only primary school.[27]

Children, primarily boys, start school between ages five and seven. In the Christian areas of Ethiopia, education was vested in the church, and until 1950 the government left education to missionaries.[28] After the overthrow of imperial rule in Ethiopia, the provisional military government embarked on educational reforms. After closing Haile Selassie I University and all senior secondary schools in early 1975, the government mobilized about 60,000 students and teachers to the rural areas for the Development through Cooperation project, which aimed at land reform, improved agricultural production, health, local administration, and educating peasants about the new political and social order.[29] In the same year, the military government nationalized all private schools and made them part of the state school system. Curricula reforms were initiated based on the socialist orientation of the government. A new educational policy put emphasis on education in the rural areas as a means to increase productivity. The government attempted to change the structure of education from the primary, secondary, and higher educational models that existed in the imperial period and replace it with an eight-year unified curriculum system. Committees drawn from peasant associations and augmented with teachers and student members from each school administered the public schools.[30]

The government also worked to redistribute the number of schools, focusing on the rural areas and small towns that lagged behind in educational facilities. Individual communities were assisted by the Ministry of Education in building schools. The community involvement made the project a resounding success. The number of primary schools grew from 3,196 in 1974–75 to 7,900 in 1985–86, and the number of primary schools increased throughout the country, except in Eritrea and Tigray, where fighting was going on.[31] This means that many teenagers were able to go to school, some for the first time.

The number of junior and senior secondary schools also doubled. Whereas the prerevolutionary distribution of schools had focused on a few urban areas, schools were now redistributed across the country. The number of female students, while still low, increased from 32 percent in 1974–75 to 39 percent in 1985–86. Similarly, the number of teachers, especially in senior secondary schools, increased.[32]

While these statistics are impressive, universal education is nowhere near attainment. Many children and teenagers do not go to school. Only 2.5 million, or 42 percent, of primary school-age children were enrolled in school in 1985–86. Their prospects for continuing education were slim because there was still an imbalance between the number of primary schools and the number of junior secondary schools. Shortages of schools and overcrowding were further worsened by the rural-urban migration of the 1980s. Fighting in Eritrea, Tigray, and other places disrupted school attendance; school infrastructure was destroyed and even looted.[33] Therefore, many primary-school pupils who cannot continue education will end up on the job market. The situation has improved, but not by a whole lot. The number of children and teenagers with no education is still very high, despite the help of the United Nations Educational Scientific and Cultural Organization (UNESCO) and other international agencies.

At the higher education level, the revolutionary government created a Commission for Higher Education to improve the quality of education and strengthen and expand the tertiary-level institutions. Enrollment in higher education also grew modestly. Eleven percent of the growth was in female enrollment. However, in aggregate terms enrollments were low. Admission standards were raised because of limitations at the colleges and universities, and some students were sponsored for further education abroad on scholarships and fellowships.[34] The government also encouraged the creation of technical and vocational schools.

A 1979 National Literacy Campaign Coordinating Committee was charged with the task of raising literacy levels nationwide. Operating in five languages—Amharic, Oromo, Tigrinya, Welamo, and Somali—it registered about 17 million people by the end of round 12 in the late 1980s. Follow-up courses for participants were introduced, after which they could enroll in public schools. For its efforts, UNESCO awarded Ethiopia the International Reading Association Literacy Award.[35]

SOCIAL LIFE

Ethiopia, as already indicated, is made up of many ethnic groups. However, most teens socialize with other Ethiopians. They generally shake hands when they meet and friends usually kiss three times on opposite cheeks. All Ethiopians see themselves as part of a larger community, and closest neighbors often get together for coffee and fried chickpeas or bread. This provides opportunities for teens to meet and interact. In addition, teens meet at school, at restaurants in the cities, at friends, and neighbors' houses in towns or villages, at community events, or in self-help associations. On these occasions, they meet the classmates of their friends, brothers, or sisters.

Rural inhabitants constitute a little over 80 percent of Ethiopia's population. In that context, they live in fairly close proximity, since the rural towns and villages tend to be small. In the large cities, it is not uncommon to find families from disparate economic and social classes living side by side. The result is that teenagers from families with disparate wealth and social status do meet and socialize.

In the urban areas, schools bring together teens from different locales, classes, and religious affiliations. While historically rooted antagonism has created a barrier between Christians and Muslims,[36] schools and urbanization have tended to break down the barrier between teens in Ethiopia. In short, education in Ethiopia, especially after 1950, has tended to break down some of the old barriers and bring teens from different religious and class backgrounds together. The new educated elite have often married across ethnic lines.

Ethiopians belong to larger social groups that have particular significance for rites of passage ceremonies—birth, marriage, and death. All of these events, which are accompanied by feasting and drink, become avenues for meeting and socializing for teenagers. In additions, teens also socialize during the many religious festivals such as Timkat or Epiphany (Ethiopian Orthodox Church), or Id-al-fitr (Muslim).

Dating among teens, more often than not, is conducted discreetly, since the society frowns on sex before marriage and talking about sex appears to be taboo. Ethiopian society values women's virginity and parents are stricter with their teenage daughters than with teenage sons. Many rural women tend to marry in their teenage years.

HIV/AIDS infection among teenagers in Ethiopia is fairly high. Ethiopian President Negasso Gidada has asserted that Ethiopia is one of the countries hardest hit by the AIDS pandemic. And according to the United States Agency for International Development and the Ministry of Health, 460 persons between the ages of 15 and 45 will die daily of the virus after three years. About 9.3 percent of the population aged 15 to 45 is HIV-positive.[37] Sexually active teens between the ages of 13 and 15, especially those in urban areas and those who are in school, have only gradually come to accept the importance of condoms in preventing HIV/AIDS and sexually transmitted disease, as the number of AIDS cases in Ethiopia has continued to increase since the first cases were reported in 1985.[38] At the same time, a large number of teenagers do not use condoms, and very few have been tested for HIV, due to shortages in the health delivery system. Infection rates are higher in urban than in rural areas.

ENTERTAINMENT

Ethiopian teenagers love to hang out in the village square, at neighbors' houses, or in restaurants and cafés in the large urban centers. These provide meeting grounds for teenagers to meet and chat or argue about the vicissitudes of life.

Many Ethiopian teens enjoy music. While they enjoy Ethiopian music, they also appreciate music from other parts of Africa and from North America, especially the United States. The "global village" effect accounts for the worldwide appeal of hip-hop and Ethiopian teenagers' love for the music, especially in the urban areas. But more importantly, Ethiopian teens love sports—especially athletics and soccer. Ethiopia has some of the best middle- and long-distance runners in the world.

Ethiopia has produced a number of world-class athletes who are revered as heroes. They include, among others, Abebe Bikila, M, Mamo Wolde, Miruts Yifter, Haile Gebre Selassie, and 23-year-old Derartu Tulu, who won the 10,000-meter race at the 1992 Barcelona Olympics. These men and women have won medals at Olympic and other international competitions, and teenagers see them as heroes for carrying the name of the country aloft throughout the world. Soccer is another popular sport in Ethiopia. Both the junior and national soccer teams have won continental honors in the past.

For a small fee at the Family Guidance Association of Ethiopia, set up in 1990 to provide youth reproductive health education and services, teenagers enjoy Ping-Pong, volleyball, soccer, and several other games. Similarly, a Youth Activities Council supports year-round activities for youth, but most especially throughout the summer. These summer activities include archery, carpentry, arts and crafts, cooking, first aid, bowling, tennis, miniature golf, basketball, dramatics, baseball training, and various levels of swimming classes.[39]

RELIGIOUS PRACTICES AND CULTURAL CEREMONIES

Teenagers follow the established religions of Ethiopia. Like Egypt, Ethiopia is one of the few countries in Africa with a very ancient Christian tradition. Headed by a patriarch, the Ethiopian Orthodox Church is closely related to the Egyptian Coptic Church. It was an integral part of the state apparatus and supported the monarchy through trying times until it was disestablished in 1974. About 50 percent of Ethiopians are members of the Ethiopian Orthodox Church, though orthodoxy was identified mainly with Amhara and Tigray peoples, who constitute close to 40 percent of the population. About 2 percent are Protestant and Roman Catholic, and about 40 percent are Muslim. The rest of the population follows African religions. Sometimes there are tensions between the groups but many African societies tolerate plurality of religion.

The introduction of Christianity into Ethiopia is credited to the Aksumite king, Ezana, around the middle of the fourth century. Subsequently, the Bible was translated into the old literary language, Ge'ez, and in the fourteenth century the *Kebra Negast* (Glory of Kings), which chronicled the visit of the Queen of Sheba to Solomon, clearly identified the term "Ethiopia" with the country and the place. The military revolution of 1974 brought major changes to religious life in Ethiopia. Beginning in 1974, the Mengistu regime disestablished the church and declared all religions equal; it removed the patriarch of the Orthodox Church in 1976. The government also made Muslim holy days official holidays in addition to the Christian holidays.

Whereas Christianity is predominant in the northern regions, the southern regions have Muslim majorities. The Gamu-Gofa, Sidamo, and Arusi regions contain large numbers of practitioners of African religions. The Somali and the Oromo constitute the two largest Muslim groups. Several other much smaller Islamic groups include the Afar, Argobba, Hareri, and Saho. The Oromo also constitute a large proportion of the Muslim population. There are Muslims in other important ethnic categories, such as Sidamo speakers and the Gurage. Islam spread among ethnically diverse and geographically dispersed groups at different times and therefore failed to provide the same degree of political unity to its adherents.

Prior to the nineteenth and twentieth centuries, the imperial regime officially tolerated Muslims. The government retained Muslim courts, which dealt with family and personal law according to Islamic law. However, the imperial authorities gradually took over Muslim schools and discouraged the teaching of Arabic. Additionally, the behavior of Amhara administrators in the local communities and the general pattern of Christian dominance tended to alienate Muslims.

Traditional belief systems are strongest in the lowland regions, but elements of the systems characterized much of the popular religion of Christians and Muslims as well. Beliefs and rituals varied widely, but fear of the evil eye, for example, was widespread among followers of all religions. The evil eye was believed to bring evil to anything it surveyed.

Another distinct and identifiable religious group in Ethiopia is the Falashas or Black Jews (or Beta Israel). The earliest reference to Ethiopian Jews appears in the chronicles of the emperor Amda Seyon, who ruled in the first half of the fourteenth century.[40] While it is possible that there were Jews in Ethiopia at an earlier date, the Aksumite kings did not display the fascination with Israelite customs that became pervasive during the Solomonid emperors. The literature of the Falashas appears to be Christian in origin, and they preserved customs such as monasticism that were definitely Christian. Consequently, some scholars dispute their ancient origins.

A number of reasons account for Hebrews in Ethiopia. First, the expanding Hebrew kingdom in the days of King Solomon and his successors introduced Jewish immigrants into southern Arabia, Yemen, and eventually into Ethiopia via the Red Sea ports. The *Kebra Negast*, the famous Ethiopian epic, asserts that the royal Ethiopian line stemmed from the liaison between the Queen of Sheba and Solomon. It also claims that Menelik, son of Solomon and Sheba, brought the Ark of the Covenant to Ethiopia.[41] Judaic beliefs and ceremonies of the Cushitic Falashas, and other Hebraic practices such as dietary requirements and observance of the Jewish Sabbath, closely mirror those of the Jews of Israel, even though the Falashas had no contact with the larger Jewish society.

In the fifteenth century, the Christian emperors persecuted the Falashas, and they became increasingly estranged from the Christian state. The sixteenth-century chronicle of Emperor Sarsa Dengel describes the resistance of the Falashas against the emperor in the Semien Mountains. The early seventeenth-century emperor, Susneyos, continued the policy of persecution of the Falashas who lived in the region between Lake Tana and the Semien mountains. Susneyos's son, Fasiladas, was less hostile, but the position of the Falashas continued to be precarious in the following centuries. They were persecuted in part for not being members of the Orthodox faith. In response to persecution, the Falashas developed and strengthened their unique sense of identity, and became artisans, weavers, and traders.

From 1904 onward, and especially in the 1920s, the Falashas came into increasing contact with other Jews around the world. A Polish Jew, Jacques Faitlovitch, opened a Jewish school in Addis Ababa.[42] This led to dramatic changes, especially the disappearance of monasticism, the introduction of a calendar of festivals observed by Jews elsewhere, and an increasing use of Hebrew. In late 1984 and 1985, Operation Moses brought thousands of Beta Israel to Israel.[43] Consequently, Ethiopian teens (Jews) are attending schools in Israel. They listen to American radio stations, watch American television programs, and wear designer jeans, but are increasingly decrying the lack of educational opportunities and the racial slurs they endure from time to time.[44]

Some Ethiopians are also practitioners of indigenous religious systems of deities and spirits. They recognize the existence of a supreme god, identified with the sky and relatively remote from the everyday concerns of the people, addressed through spirits. The configuration of the accepted roster of spirits, the rituals addressed to them, and the nature and functions of religious specialists are different from one ethnic group to another. The Oromo, for example, believe in a supreme god called Waka, represented by spirits known as *ayana*, who are mediators between the high god and human beings. Through the *kallu*, a ritual specialist, the individual can communicate with the spirits and indirectly with Waka.

Due to the multiplicity of religious beliefs, Ethiopians celebrate a number of religious festivals. Teenagers love these festivals because they constitute occasions for revelry, feasting, music, and dance. Timkat, or the Epiphany, which takes place on January 18 and 19, is the most important celebration of the Ethiopian Orthodox Church. Christians also celebrate Easter, usually a week later than the Easter date of the Gregorian calendar. For Muslims, Ramadan, which takes place in the ninth month of the lunar year according to the Islamic calendar, is the most important festival. It marks the end of a month-long fast and is characterized by feasting and celebration, the Id-al-fitir. The Islamic New Year celebrates Mohammed's flight from Mecca and follows the fast of Ramadan. Similarly, the birthday of the prophet Mohammed is celebrated. These celebrations bring together friends and families all over the country. Teens socialize and visit with friends and relatives on these occasions, and enjoy every bit of it.

CONCLUSION

In a country dominated by war, recurring drought, and famine over the past 30 or so years, teenagers have become as indispensable as ever as members of the family. Since the larger segment of the Ethiopian population lives in rural settings, teenagers help weed farms, water seedlings, fetch water from wells and streams, clean compounds, and care for families. In some cases, they have suddenly become adults with the death of parents and older siblings. Some endured life in the military due to the conscription of teenagers to fight in the secession wars of the 1970s and 1980s. But the life of teenagers in Ethiopia is not all war and famine. They enjoy soccer, basketball, athletics, music, and Ping-Pong. They dream of education and good jobs, trips abroad to visit family, and going to school. They study hard in school and work in the hope of making the most out of their education and providing for their family in the future.

NOTES

1. Richard Pankhurst and Denis Gérard, *Ethiopia Photographed. Historic Photographs of the Country and Its People Taken between 1867 and 1935* (London: Kegan Paul International, 1996): 7.

2. Many mountains and valleys dot the landscape in northern Ethiopia. The northeastern edge of the Ethiopian Plateau is covered by the coastal plain and the Danakil desert, while Lake Turkana lies on the south and southeastern edges of the plateau. For the role of geography in Ethiopia's history, see Teshale Tibebu, "Ethiopia: The 'Anomaly' and 'Paradox' of Africa," *Journal of Black Studies* 26, 4 (March 1996): 414–17.

3. In the first millennium B.C., the Amhara, a partly Semitic highland people believed to be founders of the original Ethiopian nation, migrated to Ethiopia in search of trade but were encouraged by the mountain climate to settle among local Kushitic speakers as farmers. They were reinforced by a continuous stream of migrants over the next thousand years. Sabaean (Semitic), the language of these Yemeni Semites, combined with local Kushitic forms to produce Ge'ez, the classical language of Ethiopia (believed to derive from Agaziyan, a southern Arabian tribal name). Robert July, *A History of the African People*, 5th ed. (Prospect Heights, Ill.: Waveland Press, 1998), 42.

4. Ibid., 41.

5. Ibid., 41.

6. S. C. Munro-Hay, *Excavations at Aksum: An Account of Research at the Ancient Ethiopian Capital Directed in 1972–4 by the Late Dr. Neville Chittick* (London:

British Institute in Eastern Africa, 1989). For more information on Aksum, see Kevin Shillington, *History of Africa* (New York: St. Martin's Press, 1995): 69–71; Pankhurst and Gérard, 8–9.

7. July, 43.

8. July, 43; Pankhurst and Gérard; Richard Caulk, "Bad Men of the Borders: Shum and Shefta in Northern Ethiopia in the 19th Century," *The International Journal of African Historical Studies* 17, 2 (1984): 201–2.

9. Pankhurst and Gérard, 13–14.

10. Ibid., 14.

11. Ibid., 14.

12. Ibid., 16.

13. Pankhurst and Gérard, 17; Getachew Haile, "The Unity and Territorial Integrity of Ethiopia," *The Journal of Modern African Studies* 24, 3 (September 1986): 466–67; Caulk, 209–10, 213.

14. P. J. Vatikiotis, *The History of Egypt* (Baltimore: Johns Hopkins University Press, 1986); Pankhurst and Gérard, 7; Caulk, 214–16; Haile, 467.

15. Haile, 468–69.

16. The Italian version of the treaty claimed that it made all of Ethiopia their protectorate.

17. Bereket Habte Selassie, *Conflict and Intervention in the Horn of Africa* (New York: Monthly Review Press, 1980).

18. Louise A. Tilly, "Food Entitlement, Famine and Conflict," *Journal of Interdisciplinary History* 14, 12 (Autumn 1983): 333–49.

19. http://www.unicef.org/newsline./06pr27.html. Cited February 17, 2002. (3 pp.).

20. This phenomenon of using children as soldiers has been prevalent in Sierra Leone, Liberia, the Democratic Republic of Congo, Rwanda, Burundi, and other places where there is civil war.

21. http://www.esa.un.org/socdev/unyin/country3b.asp?countrycode=et. Cited February 17, 2002 (1 p.).

22. "Ethiopia. Education," http://lcweb2.loc.gov/cgi-bin/query/r?frd/cstdy: @field(DOCID+et0080. Cited January 25, 2002 (3 pp.).

23. Steven Kaplan, "Seen But Not Heard: Children and Childhood in Medieval Ethiopian Hagiographies," *The International Journal of African Historical Studies* 30, 3 (1997): 541.

24. "Ethiopian Women Say No to Early Marriage," http://www.caa.org.au/horizons/may_2001/ethiopia.html. Cited February 17, 2002 (92 pp.).

25. Ibid.

26. http://missions.itu.int/~ethiopia/culture.html. Cited January 25, 2002 (2 pp.).

27. "Ethiopia. Education," http://lcweb2.loc.gov/cgi-bin/query/r?frd/cstdy:@ field(DOCID+et0080.et0080. Cited January 25, 2002 (3 pp.).

28. Richard Pankhurst, *A Social History of Ethiopia: The Northern and Central Highlands from Early Medieval Times to the Rise of Emperor Tewodros II.* (Trenton, N.J.: Red Sea Press, 1992), 3.

29. http://lcweb2.loc.gov/cgi-bin/query/r?frd/cstudy:@field(DOCID+et0082). Cited January 25, 2002 (3 pp.).

30. Ibid.

31. Ibid.

32. Ibid.

33. Ibid.

34. http://lcweb2.loc.gov/cgi-bin/query/r?frd/cstudy:@field(DOCID+et0083). Cited January 25, 2002 (3 pp.).

35. http://lcweb2.loc.gov/cgi-bin/query/r?frd/cstudy:@field(DOCID+et0084). Cited January 25, 2002 (2 pp.).

36. Muslims live largely in Bale, Eritrea, Harerge, and Welo, but smaller communities are scattered across the country.

37. Agence France-Presse, "Ethiopia-AIDS: Ethiopia among Hardest Hit by AIDS—President," Friday April 23, 2000, http://www.aegis.com/news/afp/2000/AF000475.html. Cited May 7, 2002 (91 pp.).

38. http://www.geocities.com/healthinfo_ethiopia/page38.htm. Cited May 7, 2002 5/7/2002 (2 pp.); http://www.mesob.org/hivaids/docs/briefing.htm. Cited May 7, 2002 (6 pp.).

39. http://www.asa.npoint.net/youth-act.ht m. Cited February 17, 2002 (2 pp.).

40. G. W. B. Huntingford, trans., *The Glorious Victories of 'Ámda Seyon, King of Ethiopia* (Oxford: Clarendon, 1965).

41. The story is preserved in an epic titled the *Kebra Neghast*.

42. http://www.africana.com/Daily Articles/index_19990907.htm. Cited February 17, 2002 (4 pp.). www.rac.org/issues/issuewj.html

43. Teshome G. Wagaw, "The Political Ramifications of the Falasha Emigration," *Journal of Modern African Studies* 29, 4 (December 1991): 560.

44. http://www.hadassah.org/news/feb98/rap.htm. Cited February 17, 2002 (2 pp.).

RESOURCE GUIDE
Books

Appleyard, David L., A. K. Irvine, and Richard K. P. Pankhurst, trans. *Letters from Ethiopian Rulers (Early and Mid-Nineteenth Century)*. London: Oxford University Press, 1985.

Harris, Joseph E., ed. *Pillars in Ethiopian History*. Washington: Howard University Press, 1974.

Ullendorf, Edward. *The Ethiopians—An Introduction to Country and People*. Stuttgart: F. Steiner, 1990.

Organizations

Embassy of Ethiopia
3506 International Drive, NW
Washington, DC 20008
(202) 274-4566, -4550, -4551; (202) 364-1200.

UN Information Service
Economic Commission for Africa
P.O. Box 3001
Addis Ababa, Ethiopia

United Nations System Focal Points on Youth in Ethiopia
United Nations Development Program (UNDP)
UNDP Resident Representative
P.O. Box 5580
Addis Ababa, Ethiopia

Nongovernmental Organizations Working on HIV/AIDS and Related Issues

Christian Relief and Development Association
P.O. Box 5674
Addis Ababa, Ethiopia

Healthinfo
P.O. Box 9051
Addis Ababa, Ethiopia

Web Sites

CIA World Fact Book, Ethiopia: www.odci.gov/cia/publications/factbook /geos/et.htm
www.icomp.org.my/ and type "Ethiopia" in box
For Ethiopian recipes: www.sas.upenn.edu/African_Studies/Cookbook /Ethiopia.html

Chapter 5

GHANA

Kwabena O. Akurang-Parry
and Dorothy A. Akurang-Parry

INTRODUCTION

Ghana is situated on the west coast of Africa. It shares borders with Togo in the east, Burkina Faso in the north, and the Ivory Coast in the west, while the Atlantic Ocean borders the south. Ghana was formerly known as the Gold Coast due to its abundant gold deposits. The Gold Coast remained under British colonial rule from 1874 to 1957 and was the first colony south of the Sahara to experience decolonization. Ghana has maintained peaceful relations with its neighbors and has contributed to the relative stability that exists in West Africa.

Since independence, Ghana has experienced two types of governments. One is similar to the American system of constitutional democracy. Four democratically elected governments have ruled Ghana: in 1957–60, 1969–72, 1978–79, and from 1992 to the present. Ghana's constitutional democracy involves three levels of government: the executive level or the president and his or her team, the legislature or the law-making body, and a parliament where elected representatives debate issues of national interest. Ghana's constitutional democratic system of government is far younger than that of the United States, but while endemic problems of ballot counting occurred during the 2000 election in the United States, the Ghanaian election held in the same period was not burdened by any major problem. This shows that, contrary to popular opinion, Ghana and other African countries are becoming mature democracies.

Dictatorship, Ghana's other form of government, may be divided into two forms. The first is a one-party state and this occurs when a party that has been democratically elected uses its power to stifle all opposition. Ghana experienced this from 1961 to 1966. The second type is a military dictatorship in which soldiers use arms to coerce citizens to accept their rule. This type of government occurred in Ghana in 1966–69, 1972–79, and 1981–92.

Ghana's export economy is based on agriculture and mining. The main export cash crops include cocoa, palm oil, pineapples, and oranges. Since the beginning of the last century, cocoa has been Ghana's leading export crop. During the 1950s and 1960s, Ghana was the leading exporter of cocoa to the world. In fact, more than 60 percent of Ghana's arable land is used for the cultivation of cocoa. Thus, less than 30 percent or so of Ghana's arable land area is used in the cultivation of staple crops for local consumption. This agricultural system, known as a monocrop economy, is one of the negative effects of the European colonial rule in Africa. Also, the prices of cash crops produced by Ghana and other African countries are determined by the consumers or buyers in the "developed world," including the United States. Overall, substantial human resources and capital are put into the production of raw materials for Western consumers. This explains some of the economic problems that face not only Ghana, but also other African countries.

Farming involves the use of simple tools, mainly hoes, cutlasses, and machetes. There are also large-scale farming methods that involve the use of tractors and animal-driven plows. Gender division of labor is the norm; for example, males perform specific tasks such as clearing and preparing the land for cultivation. Female roles include harvesting and carrying the yield from the farm to the home. Age also determines farming tasks; for instance, teenagers carry the harvest from the farm to the home and help to store the yield in barns.

Other export commodities are forest products or timber and animals such as monkeys and parrots. Additionally, Ghana produces staple food for both local and regional consumption in West Africa. This includes yams, cocoyams, plantains, rice, bananas, cassava, vegetables, and spices. Ghana is well endowed with minerals, including gold, diamonds, bauxite, and manganese. These are mined by companies and sold on the international market for the much-needed foreign exchange. One of the important gold mining companies is the Ashanti Goldfields Corporation.

Contrary to popular opinion in the West, African states have manufacturing industries and Ghana is no exception. Like the United States, Ghana produces canned foods, household wares, pharmaceuticals, and clothes and textiles. Some Ghanaian industries engage in assembling vehicles and machines imported from overseas. Hydroelectric power forms the basis of the industries and is generated by the Akosombo Dam, built in 1961. A considerable part of the energy from the dam is supplied to the industrial port city of Tema, where most of the advanced industries are located.

Fishing and hunting are important sources of fish and meat. Most of the communities along the coast have fishing industries based on fish caught in the Atlantic Ocean. Some of the fish are sold fresh to consumers. Others are dried in the sun, smoked on locally built ovens, or refrigerated in large quantities. Although the fishing industry is dominated by independent traders, the State Fishing Corporation (SFC) plays a crucial role. The SFC is not only involved in fishing, but also buys surplus fish and stores it for future use. Above all, it protects fish stocks in Ghana's waters from foreign fishing predators. Traders, mostly women, transport and sell dried and salted fish in the interior markets, and a substantial quantity is sold in the landlocked country of Burkina Faso. Ghana has several rivers and lakes, and most of them are endowed with different species of fish, including mudfish or *adwene*, which is a staple Ghanaian fish. The Volta, Pra, Densu, Ankobra, and Birim are some of the most important rivers, while the lakes include Bosumtwe and Volta.

Ghana's forests abound with game, including antelope, grass-cutter, rabbits, and deer. These are hunted for their meat, leather, and sometimes wool. Special seasons for hunting exist for the preservation of animal species and these are enforced by law. Since time immemorial, inhabitants of different regions in Ghana have practiced animal preservation, enforced by social and religious sanctions that prevent hunting during animal gestation seasons. Additionally, there are forest and game reserves protected by law that nurture endangered animal species. Similar to those in the United States, Ghana's forest and game reserves attract a flood of visitors, both local and foreign. The most important ones are Kakomdo National Game Reserve in the Central Region and the Bole National Park in the Northern Region.

Fortunately, unlike African countries such as Somali and Rwanda, Ghana has not experienced any major civil war, only sporadic ethnic conflicts in its Northern Region. Overall, Ghana is one of the most peaceful countries in the world. It is common knowledge that Ghanaians offer excellent hospitality to foreign visitors. The peace and stability that exist in Ghana and other African countries dispute the popular notion that the whole of Africa is a violent place.

TYPICAL DAY

Like teenagers worldwide, there is no one special pattern of daily life for Ghanaian teenagers. The daily activities of Ghanaians depend on where they live, their family backgrounds, the day itself, and so on. In the rural areas, Saturday is set aside for farming and teenagers accompany their parents to the farm. Rural teenagers also take farm animals to graze. Those who live in urban centers and cities may engage in wage labor, visit friends, or watch soccer. Daily activities are gendered; for example, girls clean the house while boys fetch water.

The weekday rituals of Ghanaian teenagers also involve going to school or preparing for school by doing homework. Unlike most American schoolchildren, who are bused to school, most Ghanaians walk to school. This may differ slightly in the urban areas due to considerable distances from home to school. As a result, some parents drive their children to school or the children take public transportation. Schools normally break for the day around 4:00. Students engage in extracurricular activities, including soccer, or "hang out" before returning home.

Daily activities on boarding campuses include rising in the morning and preparing for a morning assembly where prayers are said and daily routines are spelled out by the school authorities. Breakfast and classes then follow until lunchtime. The afternoons and evenings are set aside for private studies either in the classroom or library. Extracurricular activities of sports and club meetings also take place in the evenings. Most of these activities are compulsory and students are expected to participate in all of them. Student leaders assist the school administration in maintaining law and order on campuses. Overall, Ghanaians put a premium on education because it is one of the major means of social advancement or social mobility. For this reason, parents, peer groups, and school authorities pressure students to do well in school. Sports and other physical activities are encouraged. However, unlike in the United States, sporting activities do not serve as tickets to scholarships and avenues for lucrative future careers. In fact, some parents vigorously discourage their children from engaging in any form of sports.

There are three holidays per school year: Christmas, Easter, and the long vacation. During the holidays, a few students work, but most assist their parents at home. School holidays enable students to visit friends and relatives. In recent times, rich teenagers have traveled overseas, especially to England and the United States, to visit family and friends.

FAMILY LIFE

The ideal Ghanaian family consists of a father, a mother, several children, and their extended families, including grandparents, uncles, aunts, cousins, nephews, and nieces. The Ghanaian family structure is defined by a network of clans and lineages. Members of the extended family (for instance, the wife's niece or nephew) may live with the nuclear family. Thus, a typical Ghanaian household includes several members of both the nuclear and extended families.

The husband dominates in the Ghanaian family structure. Patriarchy is the norm, but wives exercise authority and make their own decisions, especially among families that are urban-based and highly educated. Families in Ghana spend a lot of time together except during working hours, when the parents go to work and children go to school or work. Weekends are normally spent together at home.

In a typical Ghanaian family, both parents have jobs. Work is gendered and men's jobs are usually considered more prestigious than women's. Increasingly, women are being hired to do prestigious jobs. Unlike in the United States, there are no salary differentials between men and women. Many Ghanaian women are housewives and at the same time workers. This means that while their daily tasks involve chores at home, they also work (for example, in offices) or have small-scale businesses such as selling wares at the local market.

Part-time jobs are uncommon in Ghana. Therefore, if a woman has a baby she either has to return to work or stay at home. Due to the fact that part-time jobs are virtually nonexistent, full-time working parents usually use the services of live-in nannies, who are sometimes relatives. Apart from caring for the children, the live-in nanny performs other chores, such as cooking and cleaning. Live-in nannies are paid cash or receive free board and lodging and other forms of remuneration. Although servants are mainly preteen girls, sometimes boys serve as servants, and their roles mostly involve weeding, laundry, and cleaning.

Like office work, household chores are gendered, and just as in the United States, women perform most of the tasks. Male tasks include ironing and the fetching of firewood, while females are in charge of cooking and other household chores. Overall, the factors of urbanization, social change, globalization, and the global women's movement are reshaping some of the gendered roles, especially among the urban-based educated elite.

Until quite recently, children did not work in the formal sector of the economy; their main preoccupation was education. But due to economic problems, a great number of children work, especially in the urban centers. Most of them peddle items, ranging from orange juice, newsprints, and apples to dog chains. This has a negative effect on the educational achievement of children. Hence, it has become an issue of great concern to the Ghanaian government and social workers. Most of the child ped-

Girl in Ghana preparing food. Courtesy of A. Olusegun
Fayemi.

dlers are from the interior backwater of the country. Their work barely
yields enough money for survival in the harsh urban environment. As a
result, some of them live on the streets and are forced to resort to desper-
ate means, such as prostitution.

Teenagers from affluent families may use their parents' cars, but do not
necessarily own them. The price of a car is not within the economic reach
of the average Ghanaian. The legal driving age in Ghana is 18. There are
no laws that dictate at what age a person can drink; however, strong
parental and communal bonds prevent teenagers from wanton drinking.

Overall, in recent years significant social and structural changes have occurred in family life. Parental control of children, which bordered on authoritarianism, has been minimized. Also, the typical large family size has been considerably reduced. Parents now pay attention to the education of both male and female children. While extended family bonds are still a powerful force and a source of familial strength, individuals pay more attention to the nuclear family. These and other changes are the result of social change and the diffusion of global ideas.

TRADITIONAL AND NONTRADITIONAL FOOD DISHES

Eating habits vary and have been affected by social change and other variables. Specific age groups eat together; for instance, a father and his brothers or cousins may eat together, and teenage boys do the same. The same applies to females, but in addition, they eat with children. While eating from the same bowl and drinking from the same cup have been the norm, this is changing. Educated and affluent parents sit at a table and each family member eats from his or her own plate and drinks from a separate cup. Also, instead of using their fingers in the traditional way, they use silverware, and may have dessert.

Ghanaians eat breakfast, lunch, and supper. Most Ghanaian dishes are spicy and include several condiments. Families pay particular attention to supper because it is eaten at a time when all family members are at home. In spite of the variations based on region, ethnicity, and class, breakfast may include porridge, tea, bread or kenkey, fried fish, and hot pepper. Boiled rice and beef stew, for example, are served either as lunch or supper. The only difference is that what is served for supper tends to be heavier than lunch.

There are different types of "restaurants" in Ghana. The most popular one is known as a chop bar. These chop bars serve local staple food, particularly *fufu* (pounded yam or plantain with soup), yam and stew, rice and stew, and fried plantain and bean stew. The chop bars cater mostly to workers in the urban setting. One may eat at the restaurants or take the food out. Unlike in the United States, in Ghana, patrons who want to take out food bring their own containers or plates. The bars do not use disposable plates and cups but metalware and earthenware plates and cups that are washed and reused. In comparative terms, unlike restaurants and bars in the United States, the Ghanaian ones are environmentally friendly.

There are restaurants that resemble those in the United States. These are more expensive and are patronized by the affluent and mostly by foreign tourists. The restaurants serve both local and international menus. Sometimes music, both Ghanaian and international, is played in the background. Some of the restaurants also function as hotels and serve as discos. Patrons may eat at the restaurants or order takeout just as in the United States.

SCHOOLING

Ghanaians are committed to education because it is a major means of social advancement. Parents and communities alike encourage children to go to school. Like the United States, Ghana has all the formal educational structures. These are nursery school, primary school, secondary or high school, polytechnic or community college, teacher-training college, and university. School days are similar to those in the United States. Classes begin on Monday and end on Friday. Extracurricular activities, such as sports or symposia, can take place on any day. School sessions begin in the morning with variations in specific hours depending on the level of education. Schools break for lunch at noon, close around 4:00 P.M., and then students return to either their homes or student apartments. Night classes are usually held for polytechnic and university students.

Ghana teens line up for school. Courtesy of A. Olusegun Fayemi.

Unlike in the United States, until quite recently a greater number of high schools were not day schools, but boarding schools. Students spend about eight to nine months on campuses and return home during public or school holidays. High-school students tend to go to schools that are far away from home. There are boarding schools for both boys and girls. Overall, the boarding schools are considered more prestigious than the day schools because their academic and social training are better than those of the day schools.

From Ghana's independence in 1957, when mass education was adopted, to about the end of the 1970s, the distinction between rich and poor kids' schools was negligible. This was because the Ghanaian government adequately funded all schools. Certainly, in terms of preparation for high school and college, rich kids tended to have an advantage over poor kids. But such advantages were not as pronounced as they are in the United States. To a large extent, the Ghanaian educational system provided opportunities for anyone who was prepared to study.

However, this seemingly equitable system of education changed due to the government's failure to provide substantial financial assistance to the schools. At the college level, students receive loans, but harsh economic realities make the loans virtually insufficient. Today, rich kids go to the best schools and enter into the most prestigious professions of law, medicine, accounting, and engineering. Overall, poor parents are unable to pay for the education of their kids beyond the primary school level. As a result, the dropout rate has increased considerably. Although it is higher in rural areas and among the urban poor, the dropout rate is still lower than that of the United States. Parents and communities place a premium on education; consequently, students have very little choice in making the decision to drop out of school.

Admission into any school beyond primary school is based on examination scores. The examinations are organized nationally and sometimes regionally among the former British colonies in West Africa, namely Nigeria, Sierra Leone, and the Gambia. The competitiveness of nationally and/or regionally organized examinations has a direct impact on academic achievement. Hence, schools, students, teachers, and parents go to great lengths to make sure that students are well prepared for entrance examinations. Rich parents pay for extra classes for their children's preparation toward the exams. Each school organizes its own examinations for each class at the end of every term. Cumulative test scores determine whether a student will be promoted to the next level. This process is repeated until the student reaches the equivalent of grade 10; then he or she takes another competitive national examination to move to grades 11 and 12.

To enroll in any of the universities or polytechnics, the student has to take a nationally organized competitive examination. Unlike in the United States, a student's test scores determines not only the courses he or she will be allowed to pursue, but also which university will admit him or her. While student applicants select the course they would like to pursue, it is the university that eventually makes the final decision, except in cases where a student excels beyond doubt. For example, a student may choose to pursue law, but based on his or her grades, the university will make it mandatory for him or her to study political science. The fact is that there are more applicants than the universities can accept. Hence, if an applicant is offered political science instead of law, there is no other option but to accept it.

The teacher-training colleges are distinct from university colleges: the graduates of the former teach in primary and high schools, while the graduates of the latter teach in high schools. The technical schools are similar to trade schools in the United States. They prepare students in the fields of masonry, carpentry, mechanics, and engineering, in addition to the humanities, the arts, and the social sciences. Graduates of the technical schools go on to become professionals, such as carpenters, masons, electricians, and mechanics, or continue on to the polytechnics and the universities for advanced degrees.

The school programs or curricula are similar to what exists in the United States. Schools in the United States, however, have technological advantages over their Ghanaian counterparts—for example, computers. There are general programs in the sciences, arts, humanities, and social sciences, and special curricula for the hearing-impaired and the blind. Curricula tend to be national, devised by the Ministry of Education. Teachers are allowed to use a wide range of textbooks and material to meet the goals of the ministry. The study of the English language is compulsory because it is Ghana's official language. However, the study of local languages is strongly encouraged, and the French language tends to be a popular subject in the elite schools. Islamic-based schools, mostly in the northern part of the country due to its large Muslim population, also study all of these in addition to Arabic and Koranic studies. Teaching methods often take the form of lecturing, but increasingly other methods, including group work, student presentation, and films, are being used. Homework is common and it takes the form of book work.

Schools have socials as American schools do. These include dances, parties, debating, and symposia held on campus or off campus. Students in the urban centers and rich kids tend to have socials that are splendid and

Teens in Ghana play the drums at school. Courtesy of A. Olusegun Fayemi.

more similar to socials in urban America. Parties may entail the consumption of alcohol and food, but music and dancing form the most significant part. The music played at such parties is distinctively American and current, but local music can also be heard. The dance forms are universal, mirroring what is globally current but also enriched by indigenous Ghanaian dance forms.

Symposia, debating, and other extracurricular events are usually organized by various clubs and associations. Topics for such occasions are current and address social and political issues that affect not only teenagers but society as a whole. The discussions also deal with international issues, such as the role of the United Nations in global affairs, the position of women in society, and human rights.

Each school has other functions, including speech day, parent-teacher association day, founder's day, and alumni day. During speech day, a prominent member of the community, such as a minister or secretary of state, is invited to give a talk on a topical issue. The head teacher then gives an overview of the year's achievements and activities, followed by the awarding of prizes to deserving students and teachers. Speech day is attended by the community, parents and guardians, students, and teachers. Alumni day is similar to founder's day, but the former's activities are more informal than the latter's. Alumni day involves sports activities between students and alumni or between various alumni groups. Founder's day is the annual celebration of the date when the school was established. Alumni and influential members of the community are invited to campus to take stock of the achievements of the school, reminisce about the past, and plan for the future.

SOCIAL LIFE

Teen life in Ghana is not markedly different from that in the United States, although there are certain defining cultural differences. For example, Ghanaian teens do not have the freedom from parental control that American teenagers have. In fact, the Ghanaian social structure allows parents to influence the choices and actions of their children, irrespective of gender and age. While Ghanaian teenagers have social choices, parental influences and constraints limit their options.

Meeting and dating among Ghanaian teenagers occur in several ways. The place can be a school setting; a community setting; a social gathering, such as a party or sports function; or an accidental meeting in a public place, such as the market. The meeting can be initiated by parents, friends, or siblings. Overall, occasions for developing friendships are similar to those that exist in the United States.

In the past, the role of the nuclear and the extended families in dating and mate selection was pronounced. This was due to several factors, including the prevalence of closely knit communities. But today, due to rapid urbanization and social change, teenagers are free to choose their own dates. Marriage is considered a solemn social undertaking, and all involved, including the couple, the in-laws, and the larger extended family, take it seriously.

Overall, acceptable forms of behavior are not different from those that exist in the United States. Ghanaians value respect and obedience to authority, individual responsibility that leads to the common good, and so on. But unlike Americans, Ghanaians put special emphasis on age, and hence, show deference to older persons and pay special reverence to senior citizens. The Ghanaian respect for old age is based on a religious worldview that underscores reverence for ancestors and a belief that old age comes with unquestioned wisdom. Thus, teenagers are expected to be circumspect before their elders. Also, Ghanaians consider sociability as an individual asset and hospitality as a prime communal asset. Gracefulness to visitors, foreigners, and strangers is encouraged. It is now axiomatic that Ghanaians are very hospitable. Foreign visitors to Ghana use the proverbial Ghanaian hospitality as a scale by which to assess the level of hospitality in other African countries.

Parents exercise minimal control over what is an acceptable code of dressing when it comes to casual wear for everyday occasions. Ghanaians pay special attention to dressing for special occasions such as funerals, weddings, and church services. On such occasions, unlike with everyday casual dress, parents make sure that their teenagers' appearances are dignified and communally acceptable. The style of dress and its color should suit the occasion. For example, if the occasion is a funeral, one's dress should not reveal sensitive body parts, and the acceptable color is dark. In comparative terms, teenage boys may have the parental license to dress as they please, but overall, teenage girls are required to be circumspect about the type of dress they wear. For example, a short, revealing dress on a teenage girl is not considered proper.

The Ghanaian traditional dress is known as *ntama* or literary cloth. Men wear it by throwing one end of the piece of cloth over the shoulder, allowing the rest to loosely cover the body. Women wear it in three or more pieces: a top, a long loose skirt, and a piece that either is used for headgear, or covers the top and the long skirt, or is tied around the waist. Parents teach and encourage their children to wear the local dress, and teenagers wear it especially on important occasions such as funerals and festivals. Ghanaian teenagers like jeans, T-shirts, baseball caps, and sneakers as much as Americans do. Both rural and urban teenagers wear Western dress, but urban rich kids tend to exhibit a sense of fashion and style similar to pop culture fashion in the United States.

Ghanaian teenagers, like their American counterparts, engage in premarital sex. Social observers have noted that premarital sex is a recent phenomenon. In the past, strong social control networks and normative social sanctions did not allow teenagers to experiment with sex. In fact, pregnancy outside wedlock was considered an imprint of disgrace not only on the teenagers involved, but on their families as well. Today, however, social change, urbanization, tourism, and globalism have weakened the bonds of social control, hence premarital sex is as common in Ghana as it is in America. However, the growing scourge of HIV/AIDS has energized parents, community leaders, youth groups, churches, and nongovernmental organizations to mount campaigns that seek to eradicate or minimize premarital sex.

RECREATION AND ENTERTAINMENT

Recreation is determined by several factors. Teenagers in rural regions do not have the same recreational facilities as those in urban areas. Hence, rural-based recreation often uses improvisations of urban-based facilities. For instance, instead of a large dance hall in an urban area, the rural area may have a small corner drinking bar. In the rural setting, recreation includes indigenous games like draught or an improvised game of *ludo*. Both boys and girls take part in these games, but others like *ampe* and *olu*, are the exclusive preserve of girls. In rural communities, boys engage in group hunting and fishing as a form of recreation.

Every community, rural areas included, has at least one field where soccer, the most popular sport in Ghana, is played. Teenagers form on-the-spot soccer teams or permanent ones with names. The rules of the game are observed, administered by linesmen and referees. Like their counterparts in the rural areas, teenagers in Ghanaian urban settings play soccer. In addition, the Ghana Football Association organizes soccer games involving professional teams that are based in urban areas. Each team has its loyal supporters. Teenagers in urban areas get to watch their teams play during the weekends. International matches that involve Ghanaian and foreign teams from Africa play at urban stadia and attract a sizeable number of teenage fans.

Ghanaians have both local and international sports heroes. Local sports heroes tend to be prolific soccer players in the national soccer leagues and Ghanaian internationals playing in the European leagues. But other sports heroes have been athletes and boxers. The retired international featherweight boxing champions, David "Poison" Kotei and Azumah "Zoom Zoom" Nelson, were very popular with Ghanaian teenagers. Overall, international sports personalities, including Americans Carl Lewis, Michael Jordan, Mike Tyson and countless others, are very popular in Ghana.

Urban residents have access to other forms of recreation that for the most part are unavailable in rural areas. These include video bars, cinema halls, playgrounds or parks, the beach, discos, and dance halls. A few video bars, where video games are played, exist in the major urban centers of Accra, Kumasi, and Tema. The video bars are patronized by rich teenagers, mainly boys. Those who have computers at home and can log on to the Internet to access video games. Cinema halls abound in most Ghanaian urban centers and are a significant form of entertainment. Three types of films are available at these film theaters: Hollywood films; Asian films, mainly Chinese Kung Fu films; and Indian ones. While the last two genres have existed longer, Hollywood films are the most popular. Consequently, the average Ghanaian urban-based teenager knows the names of some of the popular film stars and can provide overviews of some of the latest films from Hollywood. There is no doubt that the lifestyles, story outlines, and fashions in such films influence Ghanaian teenagers' pop culture.

Another set of films is made in Ghana by independent film companies and the Ghana Film Board. More recently, the Ghanaian-made films have become popular with mass viewing due to the fact that they address themes that the average Ghanaian can identify with. Some of the film companies have latched onto the soap opera genre, which allows them to address variations of the same themes. The thematic relevance of such soap opera films are a subject of popular conversation among Ghanaian teenagers, just as American teens discuss soap opera shows. Films from other African countries, such as Nigeria, are highly patronized by Ghanaians.

Television is increasingly becoming a source of entertainment and information for Ghanaians. Apart from popular local TV shows, Ghanaians watch CNN, *The Oprah Winfrey Show, The Jeffersons*, and American soap operas including *All My Children*. European and other African TV programs are also available. Television is significant in several ways. It allows Ghanaians to learn about what is going on in the rest of the world. The average Ghanaian teenager is very much schooled in global developments. Television also serves as an agency of diffusion of innovations in fashion and lifestyles. Lastly, ideas, ideologies, and social mores can be assimilated from watching TV, and Ghanaian teenagers do benefit in that regard.

Swimming is another important form of entertainment, particularly for those who live in the coast towns bordering the Atlantic Ocean. There are several swimming spots and attendance is very high during weekends and national holidays. In the urban centers, jogging is a common form of exercise among teenagers. There are a number of "keep-fit" clubs in urban centers where teenagers exercise.

Ghanaian teenagers listen to several types of music genres that may be divided into local, continental, and international. The local music includes hi-life, spirituals, and innovative versions of rap and reggae. The continental musical genres from other African countries include Congolese and South African genres. The international music is mostly American and includes rock, soul, R&B, and rap as well as Caribbean-based music such as reggae and calypso. Apart from local music idols, the most popular musicians among Ghanaian teenagers are Americans. Most radio stations play American songs. For this reason, American pop culture dominates the Ghanaian teenage social scene.

RELIGIOUS PRACTICES AND CULTURAL CEREMONIES

Three major religions exist in Ghana and they help shape the religious practices and lifestyles of teenagers. They are indigenous African religions, Christianity, and Islam. There are Ghanaians whose religious worldview and practices cut across all three religions. Overall, Ghanaians have succeeded in grafting either Christianity or Islam onto indigenous African religions, which are an important part of socialization and rites of passage, notably the rituals of birth, marriage, and death.

Indigenous African religions vary in different parts of Africa and sometimes in the same country. They deal with how Africans perceive the interconnectedness between the secular and the sacred world and the place of humans in it. Contrary to popular notions, the indigenous African religious worldview shares some tenets with Christianity and Islam. These consist of a belief in a supreme being or god, the use of intermediaries, and the existence of bad or evil spirits. Other commonalities are the liturgical practices of prayers, incantations, and song.

Indigenous African religious practices form an important part of the rites of passage and affect Ghanaians in several ways. Ghanaian ethnic groups have ritual practices that are enacted to usher the prepubescent teenager into adulthood. Although such rituals are increasingly being abandoned due to social change and urbanization, some ethnic groups still practice them. For example, among the Krobo of southern Ghana, a special ceremony known as *dipo* is performed for prepubescent girls. The ritual prepares them for adulthood, marriage, and motherhood. During such ceremonies the initiates are taught the ways of the world by older women. In the past, *dipo* was compulsory before marriage, but today it is no longer obligatory but still a respectable thing to do.

An aspect of indigenous African religion that affects teenagers is the celebration of festivals. Each ethnic group in Ghana has its own religious festivals that are celebrated annually. Such festivals are like Oktoberfest in the United States. They are celebrated to commemorate harvesting seasons, thanking the gods for ample food and health. Some of the festivals are *Aboakyere, Odwira, Ohum, Homowo,* and *Kundum.* These and others have attained both national and international popularity. Teenagers form a substantial number of those who attend the festivities, which entail food, music, dance, and opportunities for making new friends.

The way that Christianity affects Ghanaians is similar to the way Christianity affects Americans. Christians in Ghana go to church regularly, are baptized and confirmed. They form a network of Christian groups and engage in specific lifestyles defined by church doctrine. Just as in the United States, the celebration of Christmas involves both Christians and non-Christians. Christmas is celebrated by families and communities. It is a time of festivities, including dance, music, food, lively communal interactions, and sharing. People who have left their home districts to work in other regions return home to celebrate Christmas with their extended families. Gift-giving, Christmas cards, and Father Christmas or Santa Claus form a part of the Christmas celebration in Ghana. Overall, the activities of teenagers, including parties and organized dances, dominate Christmas.

The Muslim presence is stronger in the northern part of the country, but large concentrations of Muslims can be found in any urban and commercial center. Muslim teenagers, like their adult counterparts, perform all the Islamic rituals—for example, ablutions and praying five times per day. Muslim teenagers tend to dress differently from non-Muslim teenagers. The former tend to wear loose white gowns and caps in the tradition of Muslims, while the latter wear Western-style clothes. The Muslim festival of Ramadan is popular with non-Muslims and during Ramadan, Muslims share festive food with non-Muslim members of the community.

CONCLUSION

Several factors have continued to shape Ghanaian society, culture, and history. These include the defining influences of the indigenous society, vestiges of colonialism, and the global winds of change. While the factors of social change, both from within and without, continue to shape the Ghanaian social landscape, cultural features that are unique to Ghana have persisted. Ghanaian teenagers share certain commonalities with American teenagers. These include music, sports, pop culture, movies, dress, and religious worldview. But there are also subtle differences, including the Ghanaian teenagers' deference to the aged, parents, and authority. Also, in comparative terms, Ghanaian teenagers are shielded from the violence that plagues American society.

RESOURCE GUIDE

Books and Articles

Aidoo, Ama Atta. *Dilemma of Ghost and Anowa*. New York: Longman, 1995.
Akurang-Parry, Kwabena. "Otherizing Space and Cultures of Africa: The American Media's Coverage of President Bill Clinton's Visit to Ghana." *Journal of Cultural Studies* 3, 1 (2001): 74–89.
———. "The Internet and the Debasement of Women in Ghana." *Refuge* 17 (1998): 13–17.
Barnett, Jeanie M. *Ghana*. Philadelphia: Chelsea House Publishers, 1999.
Buah, F. K. *A History of Ghana*. London: Macmillan, 1998.
Darko, Ama. *Beyond the Horizon*. Portsmouth, N.H.: Heinemann, 1995.

Douglas, Rimmer. *Staying Poor: Ghana's Political Economy, 1950–1990*. Oxford: Pergamon Press, 1992.

Geography Department of Lerner Publications. *Ghana in Pictures*. Minneapolis: Lerner Publications, 1989.

Ghana, A Country Study. Washington: Federal Research Division, 1995.

Lake, Obiagele. *A Taste of Life: Diaspora, African Repatriation to Ghana*. Ann Arbor: University Microfilms International, 1990.

Levy, Patricia. *Ghana*. New York: Marshall Cavendish Corp., 1999.

Owusu-Ansah, David. *Historical Dictionary of Ghana*. Metuchen, N.J.: Scarecrow Press, 1995.

Saum, Steven J., and Toyin Falola. *Culture and Customs of Ghana*. Westport, Conn.: Greenwood Press, 2002.

Sweet, Nancy Horton. *Oh Africa, My Africa: A Personal Encounter with the Ghanaian People and Culture*. Malvern, Pa.: Marcus Horton, 1994.

Web Site

Ghana home page: http://www.ghanaweb.com

Chapter 6

KENYA

Christian Jennings

INTRODUCTION

Kenya is an extraordinarily diverse country in East Africa, nestled between Lake Victoria and the Indian Ocean. Kenya occupies an area of nearly a quarter-million square miles, roughly the same size as Texas. Kenya's spectacular diversity is apparent just about anywhere one looks, from its people, cultures, and languages to its geography, ecology, and wildlife. The 30 million people who live in Kenya usually think of themselves as belonging to one of more than 40 ethnic groups. The Gikuyu are the most populous, comprising about 20 percent of Kenya's population. Other major groups include the Luhya, Luo, Kalenjin, and Kamba, each of which make up more than 10 percent of the population. In addition to the 35 smaller African ethnic groups, small minorities of Asians, Europeans, and Arabs also live in Kenya. Kenya is also home to the famous Masai pastoralists, whose pictures adorn countless postcards and coffee-table books. While the official languages of Kenya are English and Kiswahili, each ethnic group also speaks its own language, meaning that many Kenyans are fluent in at least three languages. About 70 percent of Kenyans are rural farmers or cattle-keepers, but there is also a large and rapidly growing urban population in Nairobi, which has a population of 1.5 million, as well as in other major cities such as Mombasa, Nakuru, and Kisumu. Kenya's landscape is a marvel of contrasts, from snow-capped Mount Kenya to the fertile soils of the Kenya highlands, from the broad savannas of the Great Rift Valley to the lush tropical beaches of the coastline. The wildlife of the country is world-famous, including elephants, rhinos, and great herds of wildebeest, zebra, and antelopes, which are stalked by lions, leopards, cheetahs, and hyenas.

Kenya's history is as ancient as humanity. Some of the earliest known human remains have been found in the Great Rift Valley. Agriculture and animal domestication developed here many thousands of years ago. During the past thousand years, waves of migration have swept into East Africa, displacing or intermingling with the region's original inhabitants. These waves of migration consisted of Bantu-speakers from the west, Cushitic-speakers from the north, and most recently, Nilotic-speakers, also from the north. Today, most of Kenya's languages fall into one of these three major language groups. Along the coast, a chain of loosely connected city-states developed, and the people who inhabited them came to be known as the Swahili. The Swahili were linked to a vast Indian Ocean trading network, sending goods from the interior to places as far away as China. The Swahili also incorporated elements of Islamic culture from the Arab settlers who intermarried with them. Kiswahili, the language of the coastal people, became the language of commerce and travel throughout East Africa. During the era of European expansion, several Western nations attempted to colonize East Africa. First came the Portuguese, who conquered areas of the coast and constructed fortresses to guard their lucrative trading outposts. The Swahili and Arabs eventually reclaimed these areas through their own efforts. During the nineteenth century, however, Britain, Germany, France, and even the United States launched more successful commercial ventures in East Africa. At the end of the nineteenth century, Britain formally colonized the area known today as Kenya. British rule lasted until the years following World War II, when an unsuccessful yet tenacious guerrilla campaign, known as "Mau Mau," signaled that Kenyans would no longer tolerate colonial domination.

In 1963, Kenya attained its independence peacefully, and nationalist leader Jomo Kenyatta became the country's first president. In the era of Cold War politics, newly independent nations such as Kenya were strongly pressured to declare their sympathies for either the capitalist United States or the socialist Soviet Union. Kenya chose the capitalist route, and forged close commercial ties with the United States. Although elections were theoretically democratic, Kenya was in practice dominated by a single party, the Kenya African National Union (KANU). During the 1960s and 1970s, Kenya was widely praised as a commercial success, but freewheeling capitalism eventually took its toll in the form of rapid urbanization, high unemployment, environmental problems, and rampant corruption in government. When Kenyatta died in 1978, power was transferred peacefully to his handpicked successor, Daniel arap Moi, a remarkably smooth transition in a region plagued by coups and military dictatorships. But Moi's regime grew increasingly authoritarian, especially following a failed coup attempt led by factions of the Kenyan Air Force in 1982. In 1991 Moi finally conceded to international and domestic pressure, and agreed to allow multiparty elections in Kenya. KANU held on to power through questionable elections in 1992 and 1997, but Moi is constitutionally required to step down in 2003, leaving Kenya's future uncertain.

Today, Kenya is a vibrant and dynamic country, but one that faces stark challenges to its environment, economy, and social structure. Kenya's wildlife and scenery are among the most spectacular in the world, but the country's environment is threatened by industrial pollution, deforestation, dangerous pesticides, and a sprawling human population. The tourist industry, which forms the bedrock of Kenya's cash economy, feels the effects of these problems, and in addition must cope with a new world in which many would-be tourists are no longer comfortable traveling abroad. Perhaps even more alarming is the rise of ethnic conflict in recent years. Although Jomo Kenyatta was from the Gikuyu ethnic group, Moi's KANU is dominated by the Kalenjin. During the past few years, government-sponsored violence against Gikuyu, Luo, and Luhya people has displaced more than 300,000 people, the vast majority of them children, from the countryside to the cities. In the cities, Kenya again proves itself to be a land of contrasts. Wealthy families, part of the small urban elite, live in luxurious suburban villas, drive expensive new cars, and work in downtown high-rise buildings. Just around the corner, though, is Nairobi's Mathare slum, with a population of 700,000 desperately poor people—one of the largest on the African continent, and growing at a rate of 10 percent per year. Mathare's people live in a crowded urban landscape with no electricity, no running water, and no sanitation services.

With this diversity in mind, we can begin to appreciate the difficulty of describing teen life in a country where half the population is under 20 years of age. Teens from wealthy families have a great deal in common with teens in the United States—they go to school in a cosmopolitan setting, wear up-to-date fashions, listen to the latest popular music, and watch the same blockbuster movies that American teens watch. At the same time, poverty is a fact of life for many teenagers in Kenya. There are 60,000 homeless children in Nairobi alone, plus many more who sleep with their families at night but roam the streets during the day for lack of anything better to do. Then again, life is entirely different for teens living in a rural setting. Their lives often revolve around traditional ideas of farm, family, and culture. While most rural Kenyan families view education as a cherished opportunity, some find it too costly to send their children to school, as we will learn below. Life can be strikingly different for young Kenyans based on gender, as well. Men are generally expected to take the lead in education, business, and politics, but women are responsible for 80 percent of all agricultural labor in Kenya, and also bear considerable family burdens. There has been a strong movement for women's rights in Kenya, but gendered social and cultural expectations still exert a strong influence on the choices that young men and women are forced to make. So, at the outset, it is important to remember that Kenyan teens find themselves in a wide variety of situations, and there is little "typical" about Kenyan life as a whole, much less about its youth. In the following pages, we will try to find common elements that cut across social, economic, ethnic, and gender lines, but we will also take time to describe the many different experiences that make up teen life in Kenya.

TYPICAL DAY

In describing a "typical day" for Kenyan teens, the key word is diversity. A typical day can vary greatly for different teens in different parts of the country, depending on their location, gender, and economic status. For an urban teen who attends school, the daily routine is almost the same as that of an American teen. He or she might wake up in the morning, put on a school uniform, eat breakfast with the family, and walk or ride to school. After school, an urban teen might change into jeans and a comfortable shirt, eat dinner with the family, and then spend the evening studying, watching TV, or hanging out with friends. For this student's rural counterpart, the day would be similar, except that community social life still predominates where televisions are scarce, and some days might be spent working in the fields or pastures rather than attending school.

For Kenyan teens who do not attend school on a regular basis, daily life can be quite different. For example, a young Masai *moran* (warrior) might wake up after spending the night underneath the stars, guarding the family's herd of cattle. He wears a *kanga* (cloth wrap) and blankets, and carries a spear, club, and knife. After leading the cattle out to the pastures to graze, the *moran* might spend the day with his peers, learning about range management, combat, or the various medicinal uses of plants. At the end of the day, he will bring the cattle back to their fenced enclosure for the night. While this Masai teen's typical day might seem adventurous to an American teen, for this *moran* it can be an adventure to hitch a ride to school or town. Many rural teens do attend boarding schools far away from their rural communities, but they are usually expected to maintain close ties to their roots and to return home to take part in the family's social and economic life whenever possible.

For a rural girl who does not attend school, the typical day usually starts very early, as she wakes along with her mother to prepare a small breakfast. After the men have eaten and left for the day, she will probably help her mother clean the compound. In rural areas of Kenya, cleanliness is considered very important, and women are responsible for keeping the huts, clothes, dishes, and latrine clean and sanitary. But the physical labor doesn't end there for this young woman. During the course of a typical day, she might carry water from a well or river, chop and collect firewood from a nearby forest or grove, or harvest crops from the fields. If there is any spare time, she might practice making jewelry with beads, a skill she

Kenyan teen. Courtesy of A. Olusegun Fayemi.

has learned from her mother. In the afternoon, she helps her mother prepare dinner, eats with her family, and goes to bed early.

Finally, at the opposite end of the spectrum, we should consider a typical day for urban teens who do not attend school, a common situation for
the thousands of young people who live in the sprawling slums, such as
Mathare in Nairobi. These teens spend most of their days trying to make
a little money. Boys collect scrap metal and paper to turn in to recycling
centers in exchange for a bit of cash, or they work as "parking boys" downtown, finding spots for drivers to park their cars. These teens sometimes
find a lunch of bread and water at a shelter, where they can also work with
tutors on remedial learning skills. If a "street teen" has a stable family, he
will usually spend the night with his parents. If not, he will probably sleep
in a *chuom*, an alleyway he has claimed with a group of other boys. Half of
Nairobi's 60,000 street children are girls, whose daily activities are mostly
confined to begging or working as "twilight girls" (prostitutes). These
young women face a harrowing day-to-day life and must cope with the
constant threat of sexual abuse, physical violence, and AIDS.

The daily routine of teens from well-to-do Muslim families in the
Swahili towns along the coast revolves not only around school and work,
but also the five daily prayers (*salaat*). The morning begins with the sound
of the *muezzin* (a Muslim official) calling the faithful to prayer. Men slip
away to the mosques, while women remain in the houses. After prayer,
the women make tea and wake the children to get them dressed for
school. The men go to work, the children and teens who attend school
leave as well, and the remaining women and teenage girls stay at home to
do household work. Late in the morning, the women retreat to the private
rooms of the house to pray, while the men stop again at the mosque on
their way home from work. The entire family gathers at home for a lunch
of rice, fish, and curried vegetables, the men seated at the table to eat
while the women and children sit around a large mat on the floor. After
lunch, the men return to work, the students return to school, and the
women relax inside, away from the pounding afternoon sun. Late in the
afternoon, it is time again for prayer, then baths and tea. The cool evening
hours are time for socializing and visiting friends across town, perhaps taking in a movie or visiting a café.

FAMILY LIFE

In most parts of Kenya, family ties are of paramount importance, taking
precedence over individual concerns or desires. Families in Kenya, especially in the countryside, include extended ties to uncles, aunts, and

cousins, who interact with each other much more frequently than typically occurs in American family life. Elders are highly respected family members, while children are very important as well. Kenyan parents tend to have between four and six children, who usually take on responsibilities at an early age, such as household chores or caring for younger siblings. Polygamous marriage is practiced in many parts of Kenya, allowing men to take two or more wives. However, the demanding social and material investments required of men in traditional marriage arrangements is a strong factor limiting polygamy. Wealthy men can sometimes take quite a few wives during the course of a lifetime, but the reality for most Kenyan men is that they cannot afford to marry multiple women. At the same time, urban Kenyans and those who are influenced by Christianity usually choose to remain in monogamous marriages.

In the country, families live in homesteads or compounds, with several houses of extended family members linked together. Houses or huts are made of earthen walls and thatched roofs. Some newer houses have cement floors, and it is becoming more common to see houses built with corrugated metal or bricks. Rural compounds have outdoor latrines, use oil lamps for lighting, and have open hearths for cooking. Electric service is available in some rural areas, but can be intermittent. In farming communities, the compound also typically includes a garden adjacent to the houses, while in pastoralist communities the houses often encircle a central, fenced cattle ground. Within the compounds, parents, their daughters, and younger children live together in a house. Older boys typically have their own huts, as do grandparents. In polygamous families, each wife has her own house. Women usually build and own the houses in their compounds, while husbands divide their time, staying in the houses of their wives or extended family members. Women are also responsible for cooking, cleaning, collecting firewood, fetching water, caring for children, and farming. Men tend to congregate at workplaces, bars, churches, and the houses of local chiefs or politicians. Many men from rural areas migrate to the cities to find work, where they must go long stretches without seeing their families, and live in crowded apartments or shanty towns.

Urban families in Kenya, especially those of the middle class and the wealthy elite, tend to focus much more on the nuclear unit of parents and their children. Family life in these economic groups is relatively similar to that in American households. Middle-class families live in apartments, with one or both parents working full-time, while the children attend school. These families usually maintain ties to their rural roots, visiting relatives on a regular basis. Many stable urban dwellers also own farms in their rural ethnic communities. Upper-class Kenyans, meanwhile, live in expensive villas in Nairobi's posh suburbs. The parents might be successful business owners or political figures, and employ a household staff to take care of domestic matters. Their children usually attend elite private schools, and rarely, if ever, visit their parents' ancestral communities in the countryside.

The Swahili towns along the coast are famous for their classic architecture. Houses are traditionally built from coral stone and mangrove timber. Most buildings have two floors, with an open courtyard facing north towards Mecca, which also allows for the cooling monsoon breeze to filter through the house. Customarily, these houses have no windows, but recently families have begun adding them as they strive for "modernity." The Swahili Muslim family home typically revolves around two areas: the reception room, which is used by men to entertain visitors, and nowadays is also an area for women to share; and the master bedroom, which is the most private and secluded spot in the house. Physical cleanliness is a sign of moral purity and social rank, so families try to install the most modern toilet and kitchen facilities they are able to afford.

TRADITIONAL AND NONTRADITIONAL FOOD DISHES

Most Kenyan families eat one full meal per day—dinner (or in some places lunch), which most commonly consists of bread and a kind of vegetable stew. The bread comes in two main forms. Families in the countryside usually make *ugali*, a thick porridge made of maize meal, while coastal and urban families prefer to make *chapati*, a fried flatbread made of flour. The *ugali* or *chapati* is then used to dip and pick up the stew, *sukuma wiki*, which is usually made by boiling a leafy green vegetable (such as collard greens) with tomatoes and onions. Other typical dinner foods include potatoes, rice, beans, carrots, and other vegetables. In urban areas, a dish called *githeri*, made with beans, maize, and vegetables, is popular. Coastal families often make a delicious meal of fish, spiced rice, and *chapati*. After-dinner desserts usually consist of fresh fruits such as banana, papaya, mango, or passion fruit. Of course, like teens everywhere, Kenyan youth prefer to eat junk food whenever possible. Urban teens in Kenya eat burgers, fries, and sodas, along with other fast foods such as sausage, *samosas* (deep-fried pastry shells usually filled with ground meat, onions, and spices), and hot dogs.

The type of food one eats in Kenya is limited by economic factors. Middle-class and wealthier families enjoy more sophisticated foods and go to restaurants, many of which are strongly influenced by Indian cuisine, but the average Kenyan family cannot afford to eat this way. Breakfast, for example, is sometimes not eaten at all, or is kept very simple. A hot cereal called *uji* is a typical morning dish, while a special breakfast treat might be a donut-like pastry called *mandazi*. Along the same lines, meat is eaten sparingly in Kenya, because it is expensive. Typically, meat is reserved for a special occasion such as a visit from a friend or relative. For such a meal, a family might slaughter a chicken, goat, or even a cow. A popular meat dish is goat barbecue served like a shish kebab, in bite-sized pieces, accompanied by *ugali* or a curried stew.

Chai (tea) is by far Kenya's most popular beverage, and also one of its primary exports. The cultural preference for drinking tea was brought to Kenya by the British colonialists, but the particular style of tea that all Kenyans prefer can be traced to the Indian traders who began to settle in East Africa during the 1800s, after centuries of contact via the Indian Ocean trading network. In Kenya, chai is made by boiling tea together with milk and sugar in a large pot. Whenever possible, spices such as cinnamon, cardamom, and ginger are added as well, creating a delicious and highly satisfying brew. Chai is served at breakfast, during the morning work break, after lunch, at afternoon tea, and after dinner. It is standard practice to drink several cups at each sitting.

SCHOOLING

Education is considered one of the highest priorities in Kenyan society. A Swahili proverb says *Ilmu tafute China kama ikulazimu*, "Seek knowledge, even if you have to go to China." Schools in Kenya are modeled after the British school system. After independence in 1963, schools were arranged in a "7-4-2-4" system, meaning seven years of primary school, four years of secondary school, two years of advanced secondary, and four years of university. To move on to the next level of education, each student had to pass a rigorous examination. In 1984 Kenyan schools were streamlined into an "8-4-4" system much like the one used in the United States, with eight years of primary school, four years of secondary school, and four years of university. At the end of primary school, a national examination determines which students go on to high school, after which another exam, called the Kenya Certificate of Secondary Education, determines which students will be admitted to college. Classes in Kenyan schools are taught in English, and school uniforms are mandatory. Despite this strong emphasis on the value of learning, Kenya's education system is beset by tremendous problems.

Theoretically, primary education is free for all students in Kenya. However, schools in the country face a crippling lack of resources, and in practice, families are required to pay for uniforms, books, registration fees, examination fees, supplies, transportation, and building maintenance. These expenses can easily add up to more than U.S. $100 per year, an astronomical amount for most Kenyan families. Because education is not compulsory in Kenya, families must decide whether to send their children to school, and many parents simply cannot afford it. An estimated 4 million Kenyan children do not attend school for this reason alone. Many families send one child to school while another works at home. In addition, the dropout rate in Kenyan schools is high. In urban areas, children as young as nine are removed from school if they are not performing well, leaving them to become "parking boys" or "twilight girls" on the streets. Only two-thirds of standard-one (first-grade) students complete standard eight. Kenyan girls are especially disadvantaged in the Kenyan educational system. The dropout rate for girls increases dramatically for each successive grade level. Less than half of Kenyan girls finish primary school, and only one-fourth go on to university. Young women in Kenya face tremendous social pressure to marry early, and many have to drop out of school because of pregnancy. These pressures have begun to ease in recent years, as the average age of marriage has risen, and hopefully more young women will be able to pursue higher education in the coming years.

In rural areas, education is looked upon as a beacon of hope for the future, and the challenge of paying school expenses is often the primary focus of family efforts. Parents and older siblings take extra jobs to help pay for younger family members to attend school. A rural community will often pool its resources to create a school by holding a building party called a *harambee* ("let's pull together," a slogan employed by the Kenyan government to garner support for public self-help efforts). Once a school is in place, students are usually expected to clean and maintain the grounds. In addition, many students work on adjacent farms, ranches, or sawmills to help raise money for their schools. Still, rural schools have to make do with few supplies. Books are usually shared, and some classes are taught outside for lack of building space. In a pinch, walls can simply be painted black and used as chalkboards.

Not surprisingly, parents who can afford it almost always prefer to send their children to boarding school. These schools typically require high grades for admission, and are very expensive, but offer a much higher quality of education and better facilities than day schools. Teens who attend boarding schools consider themselves fortunate, because this is their first chance to live on their own, away from family. For many, this is also their first experience of living side-by-side with young people from different ethnic groups or social backgrounds. Although life at a boarding school is still disciplined, with constant supervision from the teachers, students at these schools experience a certain sense of freedom from the confines of their communities, where individual activity can be severely curtailed by social convention.

SOCIAL LIFE

The recent trend for young people in Kenya to delay marriage until they are in their twenties, along with the increasing influence of Western popular culture, has allowed the development of a teenage social milieu fairly similar to that found in other cosmopolitan nations. The kinds of social activities and opportunities Kenyan teens enjoy depend mainly on whether they live in the city or the country. In rural areas, choices are fairly limited for teens, and social life still tends to revolve around the village community as a whole. Many teens also take jobs when they are not in school, limiting their free time. But teen-focused social activities are available, including sports clubs, youth groups, and especially church-sponsored activities such as plays, dances, and field trips.

In the city, teens have many more possibilities at hand, although even here, many teens do clerical work or manual labor during weekends and holidays. Young Kenyans enjoy going out in the evening. The main mode of public transportation is the *matatu*, a privately operated shuttle van that is usually packed with passengers, more often than not bearing a pile of cargo on top and at least one young person clinging precariously to the back. *Matatus* are painted in bright colors, and often feature a catchphrase or slogan on the back, such as "Wing and a Prayer." But public transportation doesn't run late at night, so whenever possible, teens pile into a friend's car to drive to clubs and parties. The driving age in Kenya is theoretically 18, but children from wealthier families usually start driving much earlier. There are several upscale dance clubs in cities like Nairobi and Mombasa, where DJs spin soul, R&B, and hip-hop records that would be instantly recognizable to American teens. Many clubs have ladies' night on Wednesdays, and Friday is the busiest night, when many young people stay out club-hopping until Saturday morning. If a group of teens isn't in the mood for dancing, they might go to one of the dozen or so multiplex theaters in Nairobi, where they can watch first-run American and Indian blockbusters.

Fashion is very important to Kenyan teens, especially those in the city, and styles change as frequently as they do in Western countries. Currently, the "in" look for boys includes baggy designer jeans with plenty of pockets, while girls wear low-hipped jeans that reveal their stomachs.

Fancy button-down shirts are popular, especially if they display a designer logo. In general, the desire among city teens is to distance themselves from the "country" look—plain shirts, shorts, and trousers. While Western fashions come and go, there is still a strong affection among all social and economic classes for the Swahili *kanga,* a brightly colored cloth wrap. *Kangas* come in a multitude of symbolic patterns, usually including Swahili proverbs woven into the design. Women generally wear two *kangas* at a time, one wrapped around the torso and one tied around the head. Hairstyles are also very important to Kenyan teens, especially for girls, and a great deal of time and money can be spent in capturing the right look.

When it comes to dating, most Kenyan teens prefer to mind their own business. Gossip is frowned upon, although close friends might talk confidentially to each other. Dating tends to be a group activity, and parents don't feel the need to chaperone their teens. Group dates for middle-class city teens usually involve going out to dance at a club, to a café, or to a movie. Most of the time is spent talking, eating, or playing games, and not much physical contact occurs. Romantic relationships are discussed among close friends, but are generally not discussed with older people. Despite this conservative attitude toward dating, however, sexually transmitted disease is a major problem among Kenyan teenagers. Over 2 million Kenyans have HIV, and many are teenagers who contracted the virus through unprotected sex. The proper response to this crisis is a hotly debated topic among adult Kenyans, many of who blame young people for their irresponsible decisions. But the fact is that most teens in Kenya, especially those from working and farming communities, simply lack the basic medical information necessary to make informed choices regarding their health.

RECREATION

Opportunities for recreation for young people in Kenya range from organized sports to the latest video games. Teens in Kenya are very athletic and love to play sports. The country produces many world-class athletes, especially in track and field. The most popular sport in Kenya, though, is also the world's most popular sport—soccer. Kenyan teens avidly follow their national team, the Harambee Stars. School kids compete in organized soccer and track, as well as rugby, field hockey, cricket, basketball, and other sports. There is still some cultural bias toward males participating in sports that involve physical contact, while low-contact sports such as badminton are sometimes seen as "proper" for girls. Schools also sponsor competitions in drama, dance, and music. Away from school, teens enjoy bowling, swimming, billiards, and board games such as chess. Well-to-do Kenyans are increasingly taking up golf. Urban teens—at least, those who can afford it—also love to play video games and use the Internet. In rural areas, though, many teens have never even seen a computer.

For teens who live in poorer urban areas, opportunities for recreation are depressingly scarce. Soccer is one of the few sports that any group of people can play, under almost any circumstances, and this fact has contributed to the sport's enduring position as the world's most beloved pastime. With this fact in mind, the Mathare Youth Sports Association (MYSA) was founded in 1987 to promote athletics and to help community cleanup efforts in Nairobi's sprawling Mathare slum. MYSA's soccer club, Mathare United, has grown to become the largest youth football club on the African continent, with squads for both young men and women. In addition to fielding competitive teams, MYSA promotes social responsibility and leadership among young people, both on and off the field. All of the members of Mathare United's 18-to-20-year-old senior squad are trained as AIDS peer educators. These athletes work on an informal basis with other teens to communicate medically accurate information. This program is highly effective because the soccer team members are seen as heroes by their peers.

ENTERTAINMENT

Urban Kenyan teens enjoy most of the same entertainment outlets as their American counterparts. In particular, Kenyan teens feel a strong affinity for black popular culture from the United States. The latest R&B and hip-hop songs dominate radio airwaves and boom from stereo speakers in the cities, but some young people still keep an ear tuned to their favorite African styles. Street vendors in Nairobi hawk cassettes featuring pop music sung in regional languages such as Luo, Luhya, Kamba, and Gikuyu, but Kenyan music that reaches a nationwide audience is almost always sung in Kiswahili. Kenyan pop is diverse and vibrant, influenced by Congolese *lingala* (an African language) music as well as Tanzanian *rumba*. The most successful homegrown music is the *benga* sound of energetic guitar-based versions of traditional Luo and Kikuyu songs popularized by Luo musicians. Whatever the style, though, Kenyan popular music is always very dance-oriented and features strong melodic guitar lines that interweave with the vocals. Most teens consider these local styles to be old-fashioned. Lately, though, there has been a resurgence of *tarabu*, a popular music from the coast somewhat analogous to blues music, with lyrics that focus on the perils of love and romance.

Kenyan teens love to go to the movies. Theaters in the major cities show up-to-date hits from the United States and India. Theaters showing American stars like Denzel Washington and Tom Cruise always do brisk business. But theaters are practically nonexistent in rural areas, so teens from these areas might not even recognize the names of Hollywood movie stars. Mobile movie theaters sometimes bring films to rural areas, though, and these presentations always attract a large crowd. Televisions are fairly common household items in the cities, and VHS movies are a popular diversion for many young people. Teens from wealthier families spend a lot of time watching satellite feeds of networks from the United States, the UK, and South Africa, including the most recent hit comedies and soap operas. TVs are rare, and often impractical, in rural homes, but virtually every family in these areas keeps a portable radio tuned in to music, news, and sports broadcasts.

RELIGIOUS PRACTICES AND CULTURAL CEREMONIES

As with so many areas of life in Kenya, religious practices are strikingly diverse, with indigenous beliefs, Christianity, and Islam flourishing side by side. Kenya is predominantly Christian: nearly 40 percent of the population is Protestant, while Roman Catholics, the single largest denomination, make up nearly 30 percent. In urban areas, many teens view church as a peripheral activity, if they attend church at all. But in the countryside, church activities are often the focus of social life for teenagers, providing one of the primary forums in which they can interact and have fun with other teens. Many rural teens are active members of church youth groups, which sponsor sporting events, seminars, and other social gatherings. Churches frequently organize week-long youth gatherings, bringing together teens from all over the country. Such gatherings, usually held in cities such as Nairobi, Mombasa, or Nakuru, allow rural teens to broaden their perspectives and mingle with young people from different backgrounds. Rural teens who participate in church youth groups are often viewed with pride and respect by their families and local communities.

Islam is practiced by less than 10 percent of Kenyans, but it is far and away the predominant faith in the Swahili towns and cities along the coast, and in the northeast where the population is mainly Somali in origin. In these parts of Kenya, many children attend *madari*, Islamic schools, where they receive training in the arts and sciences as well as religious instruction. Young people are encouraged to take an active role in Muslim communities, and there are several organizations for them to get involved with, such as the Young Muslim Association (YMA), which was founded in Kenya in 1964. The YMA operates an orphanage and sponsors many other social welfare projects. In addition, women in recent years have begun to take a more active role in defining their place in Islamic society, in many cases forming associations of their own. Islam's historical presence along the East African coast, dating back several centuries, instills a sense of pride and perseverance for Muslims, who must cope with a predominantly Christian government that is usually less than accommodating to their interests and needs.

About a quarter of Kenyan people subscribe to indigenous African religious traditions, not counting the great number of Kenyans who combine indigenous beliefs with their understanding of Christianity. In the rural setting, there is a very thin line between sacred and secular aspects of life. Traditionally, children grow up learning the rituals, practices, and spiritual precepts of their cultures, as reflected in songs, dances, and visual arts. Most indigenous belief systems in Kenya hold that there is a creator or supreme being (called *Ngai* by the Masai), who inhabits, or is closely connected to, natural phenomena such as rivers, rain, trees, and mountains, but who is rather aloof and disconnected from human concerns. Many traditions in Kenya also include spirits, often believed to be ancestors, who are much more involved in the daily affairs of the living, and must be appeased by those whose lives they affect. Diviners, or prophets, are prominent figures in Kenyan spiritual systems. Diviners can bring rain, treat sickness with herbal remedies, and often serve as advisors for their followers. Drums are often used for divining, and music in general is a crucial component of African spirituality.

Rites of passage are a crucial part of life for most Kenyan teens, applying to both young women and men. These cultural practices vary between different ethnic groups, but in general, they are used to mark pivotal transitions in the life cycle, such as birth, adulthood, and marriage. For teenagers, the most relevant rite is initiation into adulthood, which most ethnic groups mark by performing circumcision. Modern initiations are often scheduled during the school breaks in August or December, and a few teens even choose to have their circumcisions performed in a hospital instead of their home communities, but some ethnic groups, such as the Masai and Samburu, insist on maintaining their own traditional schedules and locations for initiation. Initiation commonly takes place between 12 and 18 years of age, and involves ceremonial activities that can take up to two months to complete. Initiates are often separated from the rest of society for a certain amount of time. In most ethnic groups, initiation not only involves circumcision, but the imparting of cultural knowledge and lessons which are considered necessary for the initiate to become a full-fledged adult member of society.

Circumcision itself is performed differently among the various ethnic groups, but there are several common features. For boys, circumcision symbolizes the transition from the protection of their mothers to young adulthood and bachelorhood, so a high premium is placed upon the demonstration of bravery. In most cases, boys are strictly forbidden from showing pain—even a slight flinch or batted eyelash can be interpreted as failure. Girls' circumcision is symbolically equivalent to that for males, but the procedure itself is physically much more severe, and can have negative long-term health effects. Although controversial, female circumcision is an ancient practice, often controlled by women themselves, and today it affects more than one hundred million women worldwide. Female circumcision is officially illegal in Kenya, but many ethnic groups still practice it. Defenders, including many women, argue that the practice is a fundamental symbol of traditional cultural unity, loyalty, and womanhood. Many Kenyans especially resent the perceived arrogance of Westerners who would simply sweep away indigenous cultural practices as they see fit. In recent years, however, one-on-one dialogue at the local level, accompanied by accurate, unbiased medical information, seems slowly to be changing the attitudes of mothers and daughters who are in a position to make their own choices about circumcision.

CONCLUSION

Diversity can make the experiences of one Kenyan teenager seem a world apart from those of another living not too far away. This diversity stems in part from Kenya's long history of interaction with the world at large, which has brought influences from as far away as India, the Middle East, Britain, and the United States. At the same time, Kenya boasts a wealth of vibrant and persistent indigenous African cultures, which today are still in the process of learning to flourish together within the context of a modern nation-state. We have seen how family life, educational opportunities, religious activity, recreation, and entertainment can vary greatly depending on each teenager's ethnic, social, and economic background. These contrasts combine to make life very interesting for Kenyan teenagers, who will bear the challenge of continuing the legacy of diversity that has made Kenya the unique country it is today.

ACKNOWLEDGMENT

The author wishes to thank Peter Kamara Mburu for his help in supplying information for this chapter.

RESOURCE GUIDE

Books and Dissertation

Fuglesang, Minou. "Veils and Videos: Female Youth Culture on the Kenyan Coast." *Stockholm Studies in Social Anthropology* 32 (1994). This fascinating dissertation focuses on the lives of modern teenagers in Lamu, an ancient town on Kenya's northern coast.

Ngugi wa Thiong'o. *Petals of Blood*. New York: Penguin Books, 1991. Ngugi is Kenya's greatest novelist, and this book, first published in 1977, is perhaps his greatest work.

Sabania, Neal. *Culture and Customs of Kenya*. Westport, Conn.: Greenwood Press, 2003.

Watson, Mary Ann, ed. *Modern Kenya: Social Issues and Perspectives*. Lenham, Md.: University Press of America, 2000. An up-to-date collection of papers on many aspects of life in modern Kenya, including education and poverty as they affect young people.

Fiction

Dinesen, Isak. *Out of Africa*. New York: Modern Library, 1992.

Gallmann, Kuki. *I Dreamed of Africa*. New York: Penguin Putnam, 1991.

LeCarré, John. *The Constant Gardner*. New York: Pocket Books, 2001.

Mwangi, Meja. *The Last Plague*. Nairobi, Kampala, Dar es Salaam: East African Education Publishers, 2000.

Web Sites

Daily Nation newspaper: http://www.nationaudio.com

The Kenyan Embassy in Washington, D.C.: http://www.kenyaembassy.com

Mathare Youth Sports Association homepage: http://www.mysakenya.org

Pen Pal/Chat

http://www.pen-pals.net

Chapter 7

LIBYA

Edmund Abaka

INTRODUCTION

Located on the Mediterranean coast of North Africa, Libya—together with Morocco, Algeria, and Tunisia—constitute the *Maghrib*, or area of North Africa west of Egypt. Water-poor, oil-rich Libya has one of the highest per-capita incomes in Africa. Most Libyans live on the Mediterranean coast in the largest cities of Tripoli and Benghazi.

Beginning in antiquity, the people of Libya had been subject to varying degrees of foreign control until independence in 1951. Phoenicians, Carthaginians, Greeks, Romans, Vandals, and Byzantines controlled parts of Libya at one time or another.[1] In the seventh century, the Arabs conquered Libya, and the policy of Arabization and Islamization which they pursued led to the adoption of Islam as the official religion, and Arabic as the language of the people.[2] The invasions absorbed communities of Berbers and Jews. In the sixteenth century, Ottoman Turks, in turn, conquered Libya and maintained a hold—sometimes strong, at other times tenuous—over the territory until the Italian invasion of 1911 incorporated Libya as a colony.[3] The invasion and occupation were fiercely resisted because the Italians were Christians, whereas Libya was a Muslim state.

Literary, monumental, and ceramic evidence show that Libya and the rest of North Africa constituted the world's greatest granaries and produced large quantities of agricultural produce in medieval times. In spite of scanty rainfall, the fertile enclaves of Cyrenaica and Tripolitania enabled Libyan farmers to grow grapes, wheat, barley, dates, olive oil, and citrus fruit.[4] Livestock production was also an important occupation. Cattle, sheep, goats, and poultry were raised on the plains of Cyrenaica and Tripoli to provide meat, milk, butter, and cheese. During the Ottoman period, transportation was mainly by camel and donkey caravan, but from the end of the nineteenth century, the caravan trade declined and alternative forms of transportation emerged. Tripoli and Benghazi did brisk business in cattle, sheep, wool, camel hair, dates, barley, and wheat, which were exported to Italy, England, Malta, Egypt, Tunisia, France, Austria, and Germany in return for cotton and silk textiles, glass, firearms, rice, tea, sugar, and coffee.[5] Small-scale industries weaving cotton silk tents and carpets, and private factories making bracelets, rings, and earrings existed side by side with government-owned industries processing salt and tobacco. But Turkey was too preoccupied with its own problems to improve roads and ports to assist these economic activities.[6]

Italy embarked on colonization in the early twentieth century. Initially, it pursued "economic imperialism," establishing the *Banco di Roma* for financial business in Tripoli in 1907, and later, for business ventures in industry, agriculture, transportation, sheep farming, shipping, and land purchase. Italy also started shipping services between Libya and the neighboring countries, and Italian survey teams began prospecting for minerals. These activities aroused suspicion about Italy's role in Libya, and Turkish authorities frustrated the *Banco di Roma*'s activities. Using this as a pretext, Italy invaded Libya in 1911.[7]

After the fascist coup of 1922, Italy aggressively promoted "demographic colonization" in Libya. The plains of Tajura, the hills of Khums, the Tarhuna Mountains, the central Jaffara plains, and (after the Italo-Sanusi war) the Sanusi estates, were all acquired for Italian settlement. Large numbers of Bedouins, a nomadic people, were incarcerated, and in 1930 the Cyrenaican resistance leader Umar al-Mukhtar was captured and hanged.[8] The Italian government granted large estates to wealthy Italians for agriculture; the government leased 58,087 hectares (116,174 acres) of land by 1929. It also provided £62 million (about $104 million) in subsidies and £158 million (about $265 million) in loans to promote Italian settlements in Libya. After 1932, however, the Italian government entrusted the effort to semipublic institutions such as the *ENTE per la colonizzione delle Libia, Instituto Nazionalle della Providenza Social*, and *Azienda Tabacci Italiani*. These institutions cleared land, provided water supplies, erected farm buildings, and provided stock to settlers who were, in turn, to sell their farm produce to these institutions.[9]

The Italian government also invested in infrastructural projects, most of them at the expense of the Libyan people. The colonial Italian administration pushed the local population onto marginal land in the interior, resettled Italians in their place, and reduced the sheep and camel population through slaughter and confiscation.[10] Under the fascist program of "demographic colonization" (approved by Mussolini in 1938), 20,000, and later 12,000, selected Italian peasants left for Libya in 1938 and 1939, respectively. By 1939, about 120,000 Italians were settled in Libya.

During World War II, British forces pursued Axis forces across North Africa (October 1942 to February 1943) and ended Italian rule in Libya.[11] After failing to agree on a trusteeship system for Libya, the great powers called in the United Nations, which resolved in November 1949 that Libya should be independent in two years. The Sanusi leader Sayyid Muhammad Idris was accepted by Tripolitanians, and later Cyrenaicans, as their leader, and in December 1951 Libya became an independent constitutional monarchy under King Idris I.[12]

King Idris provided an effective focus of national unity, but he left most of the affairs of the state in the hands of wealthy elite families who progressively lost touch with the people and used their positions to enrich themselves. The discovery of oil in 1959 and subsequent petroleum sales transformed Libya from one of the world's poorest nations into a very wealthy state. In 1969, a young army officers' coup led by Colonel Muammar al-Qadhafi abolished the monarchy and proclaimed a new Libyan Arab Republic. The new Revolutionary Command Council, led by Qadhafi, pledged to take an "active role in Palestinian Arab causes; promote Arab unity; encourage domestic policies based on social justice, nonexploitation, and equitable distribution of wealth."[13] It vigorously attacked manifestations of European influence and demanded the withdrawal of American and British troops from bases at El Adem and Wheelus Field in Libya.[14] The new regime then established diplomatic relations with the United Arab Republic and Sudan.

Boosted by oil revenues, the government embarked on infrastructural development: roads, ports, airports, and communications facilities. Good roads along the coast connected Tripoli with Tunis (Tunisia) through Benghazi and Tobruk, and with Alexandria (Egypt). Another road network connected Sabha in the interior with the coastal roadway. The government also embarked on an ambitious program to provide isolated villages with schools, health and welfare facilities, and extended loans for the development of low-cost, government-controlled housing, small businesses, and industry.[15]

On March 3, 1977, Qadhafi convened the General People's Congress to proclaim the establishment of people's power, and changed the name of the country from the Libyan Arab Republic to the Socialist People's

Libyan Arab Jamahiriya. Borrowing from Islamic and pan-Arab ideas, Qadhafi created a political system that rejects Western democracy and political parties and establishes a "third way" in addition to capitalism and communism. The governing principles are predominantly derived from Qadhafi's *Green Book.* This system of government implies that Libya is ruled by the citizenry through a series of popular congresses, as laid out in the Constitutional Proclamation of 1969 and the Declaration on the Establishment of the Authority of the People of 1977. In practice, however, Qadhafi and his inner circle, aided by Revolutionary Committees and a Comrades Organization, exercise control.[16] The aim of Jamahiriyan society, Qadhafi asserted in 1982, is to lead change in the Arab world and the rest of the world, as much as to create a new life worth living. The new government gave scholarships for young people from high school to study abroad; 80 students ended up in the University of Missouri.[17]

The discovery of oil transformed Libya from a poor desert country into a rich one. The government began to exploit its oil deposits and to use the money for the benefit of its citizens. Schools, roads, airports, communications facilities, and hospitals were built, and loans were appropriated to develop low-cost, government-controlled housing. Loans were also provided to small Libyan businesses and firms. Some Libyans, moreover, were sent abroad to study and acquire the skills necessary for the development of the new economy.[18] In addition, the need for people with technical and managerial skills, and teaching and nursing skills and qualifications also led to the importation of workers from around the world, particularly the Muslim countries of Egypt, Tunisia, Morocco, Sudan, Turkey, Pakistan, and from South Korea and Thailand. The investment in infrastructure, oil, and foreign workers changed Libya from a desert country to a modern country with beautiful high-rise office buildings in the major cities. Good roads link all parts of the country and facilitate travel by bus or car.

In terms of dress, Libya blends, to some extent, the modern and the traditional. Most Libyan men wear the traditional Arab dress, the *djellaba*, a long-sleeved cotton tunic, together with sandals and cotton turbans or caps. Teenage boys wear the *djellaba*, but they replace the traditional turban with baseball caps like some Western teens. Libyan women usually wear a long black cloak, the *abayah*, and cover their hair with a black scarf, usually in public. The older, more traditional women are likely to wear a *burqa*, a "mask" designed to cover the upper part of the face. Underneath their *abayahs*, however, Libyan girls, especially university students, may very well be wearing Western clothes, especially Italian and some American or French fashions. Foreigners generally dress either in Western clothes or in their national dress, and some combine Western dress with Islamic standards of modesty. It is not uncommon to see girls in Italian designer jeans and Islamic headscarves, societal injunctions notwithstanding.

On the whole, life in Libya seems easy for teenagers, especially since the discovery of petroleum and Qadhafi's establishment of a welfare state. Crude oil exports peaked at 3.7 million barrels a day in 1970, and global reliance on oil has made Libya a wealthy country. Libyans are generally well off. Teenagers from other countries are fairly well off too, because their parents make decent wages that enable them to resettle their families in Libya and cater to them. Teenagers from Europe and the United States growing up in Libya belong to the middle class, usually as the children of technical and skilled personnel working in the oil industry or on international projects in Libya. Teenagers from many African and Asian countries, however, tend to be poor because their parents are laborers and servants, earning just enough to take care of their families. Such families do get by, although without much savings.

Libya has a very low rate of violent street crime due to the strict implementation of Koranic laws on crime (such as amputation of limbs), so teenagers do not fear being mugged or assaulted. All the same, some Libyan teens find access to illegal drugs. A worrisome trend unheard of in the 1980s, drug consumption among youth has emerged in Libyan society. According to a report from government departments in charge of the "fight against atheism, drugs, and hallucinogens," Libyan police seized 781 kilograms of hashish, 8.66 kilograms of heroin, and 136.5 kilograms of cocaine between 1997 and 1998. Hospitals have created specialized units for the care of drug addicts, the majority of whom are rich kids.[19]

The harsh Libyan weather has an impact on life in the country. Annual rainfall averages less than 50 centimeters (20 inches) on the coast and less than 20 centimeters (8 inches) in the interior. Occasionally, the rains fail to fall altogether. Another special feature of the Libyan climate is the *ghibli*, a hot, dry, dust-laden southern wind lasting one to four days. It occurs usually in spring and fall and can cause temperatures to rise within hours to over 110 degrees Fahrenheit. The Great Manmade River project, expected to cost about $25 billion, was begun in 1984 to transport water from wells in southern Libya to irrigate about 74,870 hectares (about 185,000 acres) of land and provide Libya's water needs.[20]

Summer outdoor activities are almost impossible. Many homes and offices have air-conditioners to make life comfortable in the extreme heat. Nighttime temperatures are sometimes a bit chilly, as Libya experiences the extremes of a desert climate.

TYPICAL DAY

The typical day for a teenager in Libya varies somewhat according to nationality and in which part of the country he or she resides. All teens in Libya go to school because of free and compulsory education. These schools generally start around 9:00 in the morning. In the Mediterranean cities of Benghazi, Tripoli, Tobruk and others, teenagers on the way to school by bus or in the family car have to contend with rush-hour traffic. Further inland, as well as in the rural areas, roads are less congested, and some schools are close enough for some students to walk, especially when the weather is cool.

In the hot summer months, with temperatures over 100 degrees during the day, schools close early and students go home to eat lunch with their families and possibly take a nap. Stores often close around 2:00 and open again at 4:00 or 5:00. Teenagers spend the late afternoon and early evening on homework, listening to the radio, relaxing with friends and family, and watching television and videos. Libyans were estimated in the early 1990s to own about 1.1 million radios and 467,000 television sets.[21] One of the favorite hangouts of teens is fast-food restaurants in the cities. They also congregate to play soccer. The evening meal is usually fairly late, sometime between 8:00 and 10:00. Families often stay up quite late, as cooler temperatures after sundown make it pleasant to be outdoors.

Libyan teenagers hardly work outside the home, especially when there is no financial need to do so. North Africans generally consider the menial or unskilled work that teenagers do to be demeaning. Teenagers who work are more likely to be Asian or children from other African countries. Libyan teens generally rely on parents or other relatives for money. Hence, there is no incentive to work. They see no reason why teenage children of some foreigners should do menial work.

Libyan families, like African families, are generally large, consisting of a man, his wife, his single and married sons with their wives and children, unmarried daughters, and other relatives, such as a widowed or divorced mother or sister. In traditional North African society, family patriarchs rule over extended families. Despite changes in urban and rural society (especially in the aftermath of the 1969 revolution), the family as an institution in Libya has survived somewhat more tenaciously than elsewhere in North Africa.

Most Libyan families have servants. Foreign servants and housemaids are paid low wages, and even families who live on government subsidies can afford at least one. Wealthier families might employ several housemaids, cooks, drivers, and maids to work in and around the house and pick up children from school. Teens go to parties, or just go on errands. The servants or domestic workers usually live in separate quarters within the family compound. They usually work on a contract basis for two years or even longer. Some families have nannies to care for young children.

Having servants at home eases the household responsibilities for some of the teenagers. While the wealthier families can afford many servants who might do all the work, teenage girls in less affluent households help their mothers with cooking and directing the housework. Boys are usually not expected to help out around the house.[22] Both boys and girls usually spend some time, however, with younger brothers and sisters, and in that respect, help out the family.

In the case of non-nationals, most girls are expected to help their mothers, more especially when they cannot afford servants. Following general cultural trends in many African states, and in other places, girls are much more likely than boys to be expected to help with housework.[23] Non-Libyan boys and girls both are likely to feel the pressure from their parents to take their schooling seriously and work hard to graduate and possibly find a job. Non-Libyans are not guaranteed jobs when they graduate from high school, and can be asked to leave the country, as has happened to Ghanaian and Nigerian citizens in Libya several times in the last decade. Non-national boys must find jobs when they finish high school, or college, if they wish to continue living in Libya. Foreign teenagers, both boys and girls, often continue to live with their parents after school in order to save money and assist with family chores.

FAMILY LIFE

The family life of Libyans, like that of other North Africans, is markedly different from that of non-nationals from Europe or North America. Libyans often live in extended families. They often live in large houses, or in walled compounds containing several houses. Generations of the same family—grandparents, parents, brothers, sisters, aunts, uncles, and cousins—sometimes live together. Families that live in different parts of the city or in different places often visit one another. As a result of this, Libyan teens get to know their aunts and uncles and socialize with their cousins while growing up.

Non-nationals often live in nuclear families. Usually, the extended African or Asian family resides in the home country and only a father, mother, and a child or children reside in Libya. Some non-Muslims leave their families in their home countries to go to Libya to work for a brief spell, make money, and return to their countries. Be that as it may, members of the extended family, those in Libya and those outside the country, communicate with one another, and remittances from those working in Libya are often sent back home.[24] These remittances are very important to the families in the home country. Non-nationals with family members in different parts of Libya are more likely to visit each other, usually on weekends. By the same token, if a non-Libyan teenager's relatives, such as grandparents, aunts, and uncles, live in another country, the family usually will visit them every year, especially during leave times and vacation. They may take two or more trips home if they are very well off.

Family levels of education sometimes differ between Libyans and non-Libyans. Mass public schooling in Libya began right after independence and increased with vigor during the revolution. Generally, Libyan parents born in the 1940s and 1950s are more likely to have very little education because there were very few schools during the colonial period, especially with the struggle for independence. The exceptions are wealthy families who sent their children abroad for education after independence. Because of the shortage of teachers in the period after independence, it took some time for the level of literacy to rise. It was only during the revolutionary period that schools were located throughout Libya, in both urban and rural areas. Today, there are schools in every neighborhood and many public universities, so the generation of Libyans currently in high school has far greater educational opportunities than their grandparents and parents. In fact, many teens say that although some parents are themselves not well educated, their families value education and want them to take advantage of the free university education that the government provides. Those teens whose parents come from other countries are in a different position. Many of these parents are college graduates or have had some professional training beyond high school. This translates into strong support for school or college and teenagers can get help with their homework and guidance for college education.

The discovery of oil and the attendant infrastructure and social development has also led to a generational split. Before the "oil revolution," the grandparents of present-day teens lived in a poor desert country with few roads, old houses, and few places of entertainment. Libyan teens today are growing up in an oil-rich country with material goods, appliances, clothing, cars, and video games and other entertainment forms that did not exist before.

Certainly, the new wealth and social changes have given girls greater opportunities than their mothers and grandmothers. Currently, some Libyan women hold important positions in the society. While many

Libyan women have large families that keep them busy at home, those women who work outside the home tend to do so for the sense of independence and professional accomplishment that come with being a qualified professional. Young Libyan women are now attending universities and seek work after they graduate.

The social setting of the family significantly affects the circumstances of a wife. Until the discovery of petroleum and the 1969 Revolution, conservative attitudes and values toward women dominated Libyan society. The Qadhafi government enacted several statutes that improved the position of females in Libyan society. It raised the marriage age to 16 for girls and 18 for boys and forbade marriage by proxy. The government also placed great emphasis on education and stressed the need for the education of women. Female enrollment in both primary and secondary schools increased. By the 1980s, the education of women had resulted in modifications in the traditional relationship between the genders in Libya. The most important changes were in the traditional role of women.

Men, however, are not constrained by societal norms to stay at home. In the post-revolution period, they usually belong to societies based on school, workplace, athletic clubs, or circles of friends and meet in cafés and other places. Like all Arabs, Libyans value men more highly than women. Girls are socialized to accept being the weaker sex and that they must cater to boys. The honor of families is damaged by the bad conduct of girls and women. Wives, sisters, and daughters are expected to be circumspect, modest, and decorous, with their virtue above reproach. Female virginity before marriage, and sexual fidelity thereafter, are essential to maintaining a family's honor. Consequently, women who break these societal norms are usually punished by their families for tainting the family name. Impropriety is, therefore, swiftly avenged.[25]

Girls are often married at an early age, probably to forestall the loss of their virginity. After marriage, the young bride goes to the home of her bridegroom's family. In traditional society, girls were married in their early teens to men considerably their seniors. Marital security in traditional society was predicated on having boys, and mothers appeared to favor sons throughout life. Very little has changed.

Libyan parents, like parents in other Arab countries, generally have more control over their children's lives. In Libya, and throughout many traditional societies, an individual is a representative of his or her family, and the family member's behavior reflects on the reputation of the family as a whole. For example, girls with lax morals bring shame upon the entire family. Teenage girls are therefore more closely supervised than boys, so they tend to spend more of their time with other girls than with boys.[26]

TRADITIONAL AND NONTRADITIONAL FOOD DISHES

Libyan cuisine is a mixture of Arabic and Mediterranean, with a strong Italian influence. The popularity of pasta, especially macaroni, in Libyan dishes shows the legacy of Italian colonization. Couscous, a very popular local dish, is made of boiled cereal used as a base for meat and potatoes. Traditionally, millet was used for couscous but nowadays wheat is often used and the meat is often mutton or chicken. *Bazin*, a local specialty which is a hard paste made from barley, salt, and water, is also popular,[27] as is a spiced Libyan soup, *sherba*. Libyans eat a lot of fruits and vegetables, especially dates, oranges, apricots, figs, and olives. Much of the fresh produce is grown in Libya, thanks to a year-round growing season in the oases, but some of the produce is imported from around the world. Produce is sold in supermarkets and vegetable markets. The latter are very popular because the traditional method of shopping is for buyers and sellers to meet, talk, and haggle over prices. Libyans prepare dishes like other Arabs. Breakfast consists of Arabic bread and cheese. *Hummus* (an exotic blend of pureed chickpeas, lemon, sesame, tahini, oil, and spices; usually used as a dip with pita bread), tabouli (parsley and bulgur salad), *mootabol* (a kind of dip made from *hummus* and eggplant), vegetables stuffed with rice, and grilled meat or fish are served for lunch, together with Libyan tea, a thick beverage served in a small glass, often accompanied by mint or peanuts. Dinner is served later in the evening and when the weather is cool, might be cooked and served outdoors.

Libyans have large families, and tend to buy in bulk. They also entertain guests and need to have food supplies ready at home. Bread, especially Arabic bread and pastries, is often bought from a bakery in the neighborhood, while other types are prepared at home.

The menu differs, according to nationality. Non-nationals still try to prepare their own traditional dishes; for example, Ghanaian and Nigerian families in Libya are apt to prepare West African dishes if they can secure the ingredients.

Libyans generally eat at home, but on Fridays, some people enjoy beachside picnics or cookouts. Some Libyans and many foreigners eat at restaurants and cafés. Larger hotels generally serve international cuisine, but they also serve local offerings consisting mainly of meat and vegetables with couscous or macaroni. In addition, they also serve Libyan tea and American or British coffee. Nescafé instant coffee is very popular. Alcoholic drinks are banned in accordance with Muslim custom, but local "brews" are available.[28]

The cuisine of the small Jewish population is different from the local cuisine. Some of their dishes are borrowed from Tunisian and Moroccan cooking, but also reflect Spanish and sometimes Italian influences.[29]

Libyans traditionally sit on the floor to eat, with the food placed on a low, portable table. They wash their hands and often eat with their hands, using the flat Arabic bread to pick up morsels of food from central platters. Others sit at a table to eat and use silverware. This is also the case when the family receives visitors.

Fast food is becoming popular. Libyan youths drink Coca-Cola and eat hamburgers and pizza, or enjoy a form of Arabic pizza called *zaatar*: pizza crust sprinkled with olive oil, sesame seeds, and thyme. In many cities, there are stands selling *shuwarma*, an Arabic sandwich made with thin bread.

SCHOOLING

The Libyan constitution at independence made education compulsory for children of both sexes. In his throne speech upon opening the first session of the new Libyan parliament, King Idris noted that:

> My government fully realizes that education is the only factor apt to make a nation an effective force keeping abreast with the procession of dignified and modern civilization; it is the beacon which guides the people and enables them to realize their ideals and grasp the effective means of progress towards perfection. The first step worthy of great care is to unify the curriculum of education in the United Kingdom of Libya on the basis of the Egyptian programmes, and to make its purpose clear and definite, that purpose being to create a good fruitful generation, straightforward in its morality, organized in its thinking, believing in God and loyal to the fatherland.[30]

Thus, right from independence, Libya has emphasized education as an important element of development. It developed an extensive public school system to provide free education to Libyans. Under the monarchy, all Libyans were guaranteed the right to education. Primary education in Libya is divided into two stages: the first four years for reading, writing, counting, and verbal expression, and the next two years (years five and six), during which the curriculum is expanded to include history, geography, science, and even a foreign language. The half-day shift system was started in the postindependence period because of the inadequacy of the infrastructure for education. In the secondary realm, three types of educational establishments were set up: secondary schools, teacher-training centers, and technical or vocational schools.[31] Koranic schools, which had been closed during the struggle for independence, were reopened and new ones established. Total enrollment rose from 34,000 on the eve of independence in 1951 to about 150,000 in 1969. By 1986, 1.24 million students (670,000 or 54 percent males and 575,000 or 46 percent females) were enrolled in schools.

Apart from the official schools, there were also community schools in Libya at independence. Benghazi was home to four community schools: a Jewish school, a Greek school, a school maintained by Italian brothers (with 90 pupils), and a school run by Italian nuns.[32] These schools catered to specific communities, usually foreigners, who wanted to preserve their educational system and culture. Many of these schools were dismantled, however, after the 1969 military takeover.

From the beginning of its administration, the revolutionary government placed great emphasis on education. It continued and expanded programs begun under the monarchy. In 1987, the school program consisted of six years of primary school, three years of preparatory school (junior high), and three years of secondary school (high school). A five-year primary teaching program could be elected upon completion of primary school. A technical high-school program (including industrial subjects or commerce and agriculture) and two- and four-year programs for training primary school teachers were among the offerings at the secondary level. Education was free at all levels up to university. Attendance was, however, compulsory between the ages of 6 and 15 until the preparatory cycle of secondary school was completed.

By mid-1950, nearly half of all schools were in the cities of Tripoli and Benghazi, but by the late 1970s and early 1980s, schools were distributed throughout the country. Expansion in teacher-training programs in the 1970s was designed to increase the number of qualified Libyan, rather than foreign, teachers. In 1987, school attendance was compulsory between ages 6 and 15 years or until completion of the preparatory cycle of secondary school. During the 1980s, primary and secondary schools offered a variety of courses. English was introduced from the fifth primary grade onward. Islamic studies and Arabic were offered at all levels of the curriculum, and several hours were devoted to Qadhafi's Green Book.[33] In 1981, weapons training was made part of the curriculum in secondary schools and universities as part of a general mobilization process.

Due to Islamization, Arabic is the native language of a majority of Libyans. Under the colonial regime, Italian was the language of instruction in schools but as very few people attended school, the language did

Schoolgirls walking home from school in Libya. © J. Sweeney/Trip Archives.

not take root. During the 1970s, English was taught from primary school onward and even in many scientific, technical, and medical programs. This widespread practice was curtailed, however, in the late 1980s.

The literacy rate has dramatically increased since Qadhafi came to power. Unlike some Arab leaders, Qadhafi has stressed the importance of education for women. While boys still outnumber girls in schools, the percentage has narrowed over the last 10 years. Education is free in Libya from first grade through university. Scholarships are available for university study outside Libya, though this practice has been drastically curtailed over the last 10 or so years.

Most Libyans go to the government schools, as do Arabs of other nationalities, for whom education is also free. However, because of the language of instruction (Arabic) and the fact that religious study, which includes memorization of the Koran, is part of the curriculum, non-Muslims seldom attend these schools. Many non-Libyans who can afford it send their children to private schools. The government schools are quite strict and all follow the same rules. The Ministry of Education determines the curriculum, the same in all government schools throughout the country. In addition to religious instruction, the curriculum includes Arabic, science, math, and social studies. Extracurricular activities at the government schools are few. Some Libyan parents hire tutors to help their children with their homework, so that the schoolwork does not stop when the students come home.

SOCIAL LIFE

Libya has a large Arab (and Arab-Berber) population, as well as a fairly large number of guest workers. In 1979, there were some sixty-five thousand workers from Western and Eastern Europe, the United States, Turkey, Pakistan, and China, and about fifteen thousand Italian short-term contract workers.[34] In the 1980s, a lot of guest workers from West Africa (especially from Ghana and Nigeria) also came to Libya to work. The society is, therefore, made up of a number of nationalities and cultural groups. Most teens socialize with others from their own nationality, or at least within their culture and language. Teens from Arab countries tend to mix with one another more than with other groups. Thus, Tunisian, Moroccan, Egyptian, and Syrian teens are more likely to be friends, as opposed to teens from Ghana or Nigeria. However, teens meet at school, at the restaurants and other places and by so doing, some of the cultural barriers are sometimes broken.

Schools are usually same-sex and contact between boys and girls is limited. However, at community events, in cafés, and in restaurants, teens sometimes meet brothers, sisters, and cousins of their classmates. Most Libyan teenagers are not allowed to date because of religious and social traditions. However, non-Libyan teenagers in Libya can date as they would in their own countries, but are likely to be very circumspect when it comes to petting and kissing, and often do so without their parents' knowledge.

Teenage experiences in Libya vary. Teens from Europe or North America as well as some non-Westerners generally go about life in the same way as they would in their countries, with the exception of religious and cultural prohibitions imposed by an Islamic society. More commonly, teenage boys have much more social freedom than girls in Libya. Boys can go out with friends or relatives to play soccer, meet in cafés or fast-food restaurants, hang out with older friends, or go driving with relatives or friends. In spite of prohibitions, it is easier for teenage boys to date if they find a girl in whom they are interested. But societal restrictions and the burden of family honor (the issue of bad reputation) make it difficult for many girls to date.

Teenage girls are often allowed to go out with other girls or with relatives their own age or slightly older. They can attend parties at the homes of friends or relatives, go to the shopping mall, or to the movies, but they will almost always be chaperoned by an older relative, family member, or close family friend. In this way, parents know (or at least think they know) where their daughters are and who they are with. Some parents object to their daughters associating with teenage girls of questionable reputation for fear that such girls might corrupt their daughters by arranging for them to meet boys. In spite of this strict "policing," teenagers sometimes outwit parents about their whereabouts, relying on friends as decoys and alibis. However, such activities carry heavy penalties when scandal erupts and a girl is found to have misled her parents about her activities and whereabouts. The restrictions on girls are common throughout North Africa, and are predicated on the fact that both Islam and Libyan custom forbid premarital sex. But more importantly, a girl is supposed to be a virgin at marriage and it is a disgrace to the family if she is not. Additionally, a girl with a bad reputation may find it difficult to find a husband to marry. Many Libyan families arrange marriages for their children and the question of reputation counts. Since many Libyan women are educated and professionals, they make their own choices when it comes to marriage, albeit not without societal angst.

RECREATION

On Thursday evenings at the beginning of the Muslim weekend, cars can be seen everywhere in some of the major cities of Libya. In southwest Tripoli, young rich boys gather on Gargaresh Avenue wearing flashy Italian shirts and try to impress the girls. In northern Tripoli, on the waterfront, there is a funfair (amusement park) where the youth gather to listen to the latest Rai, or Algerian pop music, hits. At the Al Fatah campus, a university that caters to 70,000 of Libya's 240,000 university students, young flashy men come and go as they please, driving their Maximas, Nubiras, and Galants. Mostly these cars belong to their fathers, who are given them by the government. The cars are important symbols of power and pleasure.[35] While not necessarily typical of youth in general in Libya, "Libya's lost generation," a phrase used by Qadhafi himself at a meeting of the popular congresses at the end of 1996 in Libya, opens a window into teen recreational and social life in Libya. They appear to be "going where their parents and grandparents never went," and doing what their parents did not do in their time.

Libyan teens love sports, especially soccer, which is a national sport with a huge following.[36] Foreign teens play the sports of their own countries as well. Libyan boys and girls follow soccer but only boys play the game. On weekends and on special occasions, families visit other family members. Libyan teenagers also spend a lot of leisure time in cafés, restaurants, malls, and clubs.

ENTERTAINMENT

Soon after taking office, the Qadhafi government closed bars and nightclubs, banned entertainment deemed provocative and immodest, and mandated the use of the Muslim calendar.

Social life starts in the late afternoon and extends late into the night. Teenagers love to hang out in shopping centers, either just walking around or sitting in a café or fast-food restaurant. These provide a good meeting ground. Going to movies in the malls is another favorite pastime.

Many Libyan teens enjoy music, as do teens everywhere else in the world, and in Libya they have a wide range of music from which to choose. Many teens enjoy Algerian Rai pop, Libyan Arab music, and some Western music. Many teens can play the folk music and dance to the music of the country. Although clubs are restricted, some teens find ways to get in and dance. Moviegoing is also very popular among the youth. Others watch TV or movies on video, play video games, listen to music, or surf the Net.

RELIGIOUS PRACTICES AND CULTURAL CEREMONIES

Islam (Sunni) provides both a spiritual guide for individuals and a keystone for government policy in Libya. Islam stresses unity of religion and state, not separation or distinction between the two. Sunnis, or orthodox Muslims, emphasize that what the Muslim community as a whole agrees on over time is the guarantee of what is right (religious experts assist the community in preserving Islamic truths). Since the 1969 coup, the Qadhafi regime has explicitly endeavored to reaffirm Islamic values, enhance appreciation of Islamic culture, elevate the status of Koranic law, and to a considerable degree emphasize Koranic practice in everyday Libyan life.

The five pillars of Islam—*shahadah* (oneness of God), *salat* (daily prayer), *zakat* (almsgiving), *sawm* (fasting), and *hajj* (pilgrimage)—are promoted and enforced by the government of Libya. Men are obliged to observe the Friday congregational prayer at a mosque under the direction of an *imam*. Even though it is permissible for women to attend public worship at the mosque, they are segregated from men and their attendance is not encouraged. More often than not, women pray at home. Most teenagers regularly attend Friday prayers in the mosque, and many boys and girls pray the five required prayers every day.[37]

As citizens of a strict Muslim nation, Libyans observe all Muslim holidays and festivals. During Ramadan, Muslims abstain from food, drink, smoking, and sexual activity from sunrise to sunset. Fasting during Ramadan is designed to remind Muslims of the suffering of the poor, emphasize the importance of charity, and stress the duty of Muslims to lead pious lives. Teenagers are expected to fast just as adults do. Many businesses and restaurants close during the afternoon to allow Muslims a chance to rest and open again after dark and stay open late into the night. Restaurants offer special Ramadan meals (*iftar*) at sunset, and many families invite friends and relatives to their homes to share the *iftar*.

Government offices and schools remain closed during Muslim holidays such as the Eid Ul-Adha, which celebrates God's providing a ram to Ibrahim for sacrifice in place of his son Ismail. Most workers in both the public and private sectors are given time off. Members of extended families usually gather together to share meals during the celebration that follows the holidays.

In Libya, among the strictest of Muslim countries, cafés must remain closed for the holidays during the day. But they open their doors after dark, and feasting occurs during the night. Although consumption of alcohol is irregularly enforced in most Muslim countries, the Libyan revolutionary government has been strict in ensuring that its prohibition is effective, even in the households of foreign diplomats.

CONCLUSION

Libya is a strict Islamic country, and teenagers are required to obey the laws of Islam because they constitute an integral part of their life and culture. They are raised as Muslims. At the same time, Libyan teenagers are like teenagers everywhere. They spend their evenings playing soccer or hanging around the new fast-food restaurants. Libya has one of the highest ratio of cars per capita in Africa and since it costs only six dinars ($8.44) to fill a tank, driving has become a major recreational activity among the young. They watch movies and TV shows, drink Coca-Cola, eat hamburgers and pizza, wear Benetton clothes, and listen to Algerian Rai pop.

NOTES

1. Vassilios Christides, *Byzantine Libya and the March of the Arabs towards the West of North Africa* (Oxford: J. and E. Hedges, 2000): 6–8.

2. For details of the Arab conquest, see Christides, *Byzantine Libya*, especially Chapter 2, "Muslims in the March towards the West," 37–57, and Chapter 3,

"Epilogue: Warfare and Consolidation of the Arab Conquest of the Maghrib," 59–69; and Jamil M. Abun-Nasr, *A History of the Maghrib in the Islamic Period* (Cambridge: Cambridge University Press, 1987), especially Chapter 2.

3. Robin Hallett, *Africa since 1875* (Ann Arbor: University of Michigan Press, 1974): 195.

4. Christides, *Byzantine Libya,* 2–3.

5. A. A. Abdussalam and F. S. Abusedra, "The Colonial Economy: North Africa. Part II: Libya, Egypt and the Sudan," in *UNESCO General History of Africa. VII. Africa under Colonial Domination 1880–1935,* Adu Boahen ed. (Paris: UNESCO, 1985): 440–41.

6. Abdussalam and Abusedra, "Libya, Egypt and the Sudan," 443.

7. Ibid., 443–44.

8. Hallett, *Africa since 1875,* 236–37; Abun-Nasr, *History of the Maghrib,* 401–2.

9. Abdussalam and Abusedra, "Libya, Egypt and the Sudan," 444–45.

10. Ibid., 446.

11. Hallett, *Africa since 1875,* 236–37.

12. Ibid., 238.

13. U.S. Department of State, Bureau of Public Affairs, *Background Notes, Libya* (August 1985): 3.

14. Ibid., 3.

15. Ibid., 4.

16. U.S. Department of State, Bureau of Democracy, Human Rights, and Labor, *Libyan Report on Human Rights Practices for 1997* (January 30, 1998).

17. Noemi Ramirez, "The Trials and Triumphs of Discovering a New Home-land." Cited November 20, 2001. http://digmo.org/winter98/religion/benghazi.html

18. U.S. Department of State, *Libyan Report on Human Rights,* 4.

19. Raymond Mansour, "Libya's Lost Generation," *Daily Mail and Guardian* (Johannesburg, South Africa, September 17, 1999).

20. Ronald Bruce St. John, *Historical Dictionary of Libya,* 2nd ed. (Metuchen, N. J.: The Scarecrow Press, 1991): 46–47.

21. "Libya. General Information," http://www.iief.de/medisat/D1/libya.html. Cited December 31, 2001 (5 pp.).

22. Vincent B. Khapoya, *The African Experience, An Introduction,* 2nd ed. (Upper Saddle River, N. J.: Prentice Hall, 1998): 51–52.

23. Ibid., 51.

24. Such remittances constitute an importance foreign exchange pool in many African countries.

25. Library of Congress, "Libya—A Country Study," http://lcweb2.loc.gov/cgi-bin/query/r?frd/cstdy:@field(DOCID+ly 0060). Cited December 15, 2001. See section on the Family, the Individual and the Sexes.

26. Ibid.

27. ArabNet, "Libya, Culture, Food & Drink," http://www.arab.net/libya/culture/la_food.html

28. ArabNet, "Libya: Culture, Food & Drink," http://www.arabnet/libya/culture.la_food.html. Cited December 15, 2001 (2 pp.).

29. "The Last Jews of Libya," http://sunsite.berkeley.edu/Jews ofLibya/libyanJews/museum/food5.html. Cited December 15, 2001 (2 pp.). For Libyan Jews, see Harvey E. Goldberg, *Jewish Life in Muslim Libya* (Chicago: University of Chicago Press, 1990).

30. United Nations Technical Assistance Program, *The Economic and Social Development of Libya* (New York: United Nations, 1953): 114.

31. Ibid., 115–16.

32. Ibid., 125.

33. See St. John, *Historical Dictionary of Libya*, 33–34.

34. John L. Wright, *Libya: A Modern History* (Baltimore: Johns Hopkins University Press, 1982): 261.

35. Mansour, "Libya's Lost Generation."

36. Soccer is the most popular sport in Africa, and children and teens do not need expensive equipment to play the game.

37. For Islamic beliefs and practices, see, for example, Emory C. Bogle, *Islam Origin and Belief* (Austin: University of Texas Press, 1998): 26–46.

RESOURCE GUIDE

Books and Article

Harris, Lilian Craig. *Libya: Qadhafi's Revolution and the Modern State*. Boulder, Colo.: Westview Press, 1986.

Joffe, George. "Libya." *Africa Contemporary Record* 23 (1990–1992): B468–483. This article has information on the Socialist People's Libyan Arab Jamahiriya.

Metz, Helen Chapin, ed. *Libya: A Country Study*. Washington, D.C.: Department of the Army, 1989.

Simon, Rachel. *Change within Tradition among Jewish Women in Libya*. Seattle, Wash.: University of Washington Press, 1992. This is a useful introduction to teenage Jewish women in Libya. Family life, work, and education for women are covered in a couple of chapters.

Web Sites

Encyclopaedia of the Orient: http://i-cias.com/cgi-bin/eo-direct-frame.pl?http://-cias.com/e.o.Libya_5.htm

For information on Qadhafi, the Green Book, and other topics, see www.geocities.com/Athens/8744/mylinks/htm

For information on the Italian occupation, see http://ourworld.compuserve.com/homepages/dr_ibrahim_ighneiwa/resist.htm

See Faisal Kutty, "Middle East Youth Crisis: A Source of Global Instability?", Middle East News Online: www.middleeastwire.com/newswire/stories/20010817_1_meno.shtml

Organization

Mission of Libya to the United Nations
309 E. 48th Street
New York, NY 10017
U.S.A.
Tel: (212) 752-5775
E-mail: lbyun@undp.org
Home page: http://www.undp.org/missions/libya

Chapter 8

MOZAMBIQUE

Kirsten Walles

INTRODUCTION

Mozambique is located on the southeastern tip of the African continent. It is bordered by Tanzania to the north, Malawi and Zambia to the northwest, Zimbabwe to the west, and South Africa and Swaziland to the southwest. With a landmass of 801,590 square miles, Mozambique is roughly twice the size of California. Seven out of its 10 counties are located along 2,400 kilometers of beautiful, sandy coastline. Miles of unpolluted coral reefs stretch along the coastline and the waves are perfect for surfing. Turtles, whales, sharks, and dolphins can all be found within these waters.[1]

The interior of Mozambique varies from dense tropical forests, about 22 percent of the landscape, to wooded plains. Zebra, lions, giraffes, and the endangered black rhinoceros can be seen in wild game preserves throughout the interior region. Two of southern Africa's longest rivers, the Zambezi and the Lompopo, flow through the country.

Sugar and cashew nuts are the main agricultural exports of this country, although coal, salt, diamonds, and bauxite are mined and exported as well. Most of the country's wealth is made from agricultural production and the export of lobster and shrimp.

Since the ninth century, Mozambique has been a key stopping point for traders from Europe, Arabia, India, and China. First came Arab traders, who traveled from the Middle East across the Indian Ocean. Many of these visitors decided to settle in Mozambique. These Arab immigrants intermarried with the indigenous population, forming a new mixed community of Arab-Africans. This new community adopted Islam and the

Arab way of dress and diet.² Gold, ivory, and slaves were the main trade items between Africans and Arabs.

The settlement of Arab/Islamic traders occurred through agreements between the Arabs and the head African chiefs of the region. The benefits were mutual in that both parties obtained luxury items from each other. The African communities gained access to such items as chinaware, cloth (silk), and beads. The Arabs in return had access to axes, daggers fashioned from ivory, palm oil, and slaves.³

Beginning in the fifteenth century, the Portuguese began to expand trade interests with Mozambique, encroaching upon the established Arab trade relations. One of the most important historical events in Mozambique's history is the visit of the famous Portuguese explorer Vasco de Gama in 1498. De Gama was definitely surprised at finding such a "sophisticated trading society" and ports filled with large ships as well as "navigational charts and instruments more refined than those of the Portuguese."⁴

Unfortunately for the Mozambican inhabitants, this discovery by de Gama meant the Portuguese became resolved to winning control of the Indian Ocean trade by establishing ports along the Persian Gulf and Red Sea and seizing "control of the seaborne trade from the Arabs."⁵ The Portuguese dominated Mozambique for about five hundred years, until a revolution in 1974 transferred power from the Portuguese to the Front for the Liberation of Mozambique (Frelimo). Mozambique declared independence from Portugal on June 25, 1975.

The first Mozambican president was Samora Machel, who attempted to implement a communist system of government. He was killed on October 19, 1986, in a plane crash. A new constitution was written on November 30, 1990. A peace agreement was reached between the acting government and the rebel forces known as the Mozambique National Resistance (MNR). This accord allowed mass elections to take place in October 1994. This meant that refugees that had fled Portuguese rule and the rebel fighting that followed were free to return to Mozambique.⁶

Although Mozambique gained independence from Portugal in 1975, conditions for social and economic development have not been favorable for the newly independent Mozambicans. In the 1980s, severe drought and civil war between the Frelimo and the MNR (Renamo) caused famine and heavy loss of life. The organization Renamo (Resistencia Nacional Mocambicana) was established by Rhodesian security forces in the mid-1970s to hit back at the newly independent Frelimo government for their stance against Rhodesia's Unilateral Declaration of Independence and for harboring guerrillas during the liberation war in Rhodesia.⁷

When Rhodesia became Zimbabwe in 1980, control of Renamo was moved lock, stock, and barrel to Phalaborwa in South Africa's Transvaal, and Renamo activities stepped up.[8] The Frelimo government was hostile to both the Zimbabwean National Guerrillas in Rhodesia (ZANLA) in Zimbabwe and the African National Congress (ANC) in South Africa because of the support they lent the Renamo movement.[9] This support forced the Frelimo government to battle Renamo forces both within and outside the Mozambican borders.

As in most of the civil war-torn former colonies in Africa, thousands of live land mines were scattered and left in the ground all over the countryside. Most of these weapons had been placed quickly and no one has a map of where they are located. The great majority of the land mines remain hidden in the ground. Removal requires the slow process of searching and destroying mines one at a time. The loss of limbs and innocent lives is too great to count. The mines were placed in fields where Africans grew their crops, so many farmers gave up their homes and farmlands because of the danger to themselves and their families and the constant fear of tripping a mine.

Mozambique has three main cities: Maputo, Beira, and Nampula. The rich can be found in these cities, because only they can afford the luxury houses, Mercedes cars, and high-class restaurants. However, most people live in rural areas, following a traditional and poorer way of life. Four out of five Mozambicans depend on the land for a living.[10]

In 1999–2000, Mozambique experienced the worst flooding in four decades. One of the climatic realities in Mozambique is the rainy season, usually occurring each year from October to March. Some flooding is generally expected and residents are updated on the status of the expected rainfall throughout the year. The flooding is worse in the southern and central provinces rather than the northern ones, due to the Limpopo and the Xia Xia Rivers.[11]

For a while, efforts to rebuild the economy and the infrastructure after the civil war put advances in flood awareness and prevention temporarily on hold. However, the catastrophic floods of 1996 and 1998 emphasized to the government the necessity of flood awareness in the country. Although more than 40,000 Mozambicans lost their homes in the floods of 2000, only 700 lives were lost. This is credited to the flood awareness programs established by the government.[12]

Farms, factories, schools, and entire villages were completely flooded and some were still saturated with water by the time the rainy season began again in October 2000. Almost 200,000 people were left homeless. Agencies from all over the world offered assistance to the residents of

Mozambique, most notably OXFAM, the Mozambique Red Cross, and the Save the Children foundation. In 2000, as the country was still trying to overcome this disaster, the diseases of AIDS and malaria, largely unchecked by medicines or government warnings, and fostered by dangerous social habits, reached epidemic proportions.[13]

Today the current president of Mozambique, Joaquim Chissano, is working to restore the self-esteem of his country. He and his ministers, with the aid of other African nations and the United Nations, have set goals to boost the country's economy by rebuilding and revitalizing factories and plantations and reinvigorating its agriculture. In addition to increased activity by mine-detonating squads, new steel-protected trucks detonate land mines so farmers can feel safe on their land and grow crops again.

Other improvements include a new toll highway completed in 2001 to connect the capital city of Maputo with Johannesburg, South Africa. The main port of Maputo is being rehabilitated with the hope that tourism and exports will once again be revived and improve the economy of Mozambique.[14] Mozambican authorities are trying to boost tourism in the northern provinces of Cabo Delgado, Nampula, and Zambezia. These regions are famous for their white sandy beaches and unblemished coral reefs.

The new government is investing heavily in education for its youth. In an address to UNESCO, President Chissano stated, "Today's youth represents the future of humanity. If they are to develop, they must be cared for and be respected through the creation of a climate of co-existence, free of war, of racial discrimination, hunger, poverty, and illiteracy."[15] President Chissano is fully aware that Mozambique will not become a modern country without educated people to help run it.

Mozambique is rebuilding again, and young people are the key to this growth. Young people under the age of 18 make up 3.8 million of the total population of Mozambique of 19.5 million.[16] This is a relatively small percentage of young people, around 20 percent, on a continent where the average life expectancy for adults is 45 years of age. This is a very small percentage of youth compared with other countries. The percentage of young people in the United States averages around 26 percent; however, the life expectancy is 76.7 years of age.[17]

As the capital and only modern city of Mozambique, Maputo has become the place where most Mozambican and outside companies make investments in this region. Therefore, the suburban centers are appealing areas for work and education.

Although many youths gravitate to the capital city of Maputo, most young people still reside in the rural areas of Mozambique. Outside of the

major cities, lack of improvements in transportation and economics prohibit many young people in rural areas from having the opportunity of experiencing life in the city.

Agriculture remains the basis of Mozambique culture. Cashew nuts,
sugar plantations, and fruit orchards cover much of the rural agricultural
land. These plantations are being rebuilt and improved to rev up the export economy of Mozambique. Child laborers ranging in age from eight
years to early teens are hired to work in the fields and scare birds from eating the crops. The government protects the rights of Mozambicans to own
and harvest land. Because most of the residents of the country survive on
subsistence farming, this is a guaranteed way for most youth to survive and
maintain a reliable source of food.[18]

Another view is offered in the book *Kalashnikovs and Zombie Cucumbers: Travels in Mozambique* by Nick Middleton. He notes that many residents of rural regions, specifically the northern coastal provinces, remain
in those areas because they hope that the new independence of Mozambique, established by the Frelimo government, will encourage the same
prosperity in their regions as during the Portuguese colonial period.

This new generation of Mozambicans comprises an interesting mix of
ethnicities and cultures that portrays the modern image the country is
striving for. Although influenced by Arabia and Portugal, most regions
within Mozambique still depend upon tribal relationships and culture.
That means that even with the push to modernize as a cohesive country,
the system of relying upon family and the community rather than the government or the economy remains the backbone of Mozambican culture.

The group history of working collectively within the community has
been the main reason each province has survived up to today. Despite
hundreds of years of Arab and Portuguese influence and rule, almost 90
percent of the residents are of African descent (the Makua of the northern provinces, the Makonde, the Sena, and the Shanagaan to name a
few), with a few of Arab, Asian, and mixed descents as well.

Although the formal language of Mozambique is Portuguese, most
youth do not speak this fluently. Rather, they speak the tribal languages
prevalent in their regions. Most young people do not need to speak much
Portuguese because they will not travel to major urban centers where it is
spoken. Likewise, not many foreigners travel to the remote areas outside
the major cities of Mozambique, so passable Portuguese is all that is required for an effective business visit.

During 20 years of war and 10 years of natural disasters, most teenagers
were unable to attend or receive the formal education they needed to become part of the new economy. Due to the chaos of civil war, lasting from

1975 to 1992, most families in the rural provinces could do no more than concentrate on daily survival. If Renamo soldiers were not destroying their homes and villages, their crops were being damaged by the continual placement and detonation of mines. In cities like Maputo, funds were used to fight the civil war and were not available to maintain roads or infrastructure, to build the workplace, or to improve education.

Travel between towns and out to the country became very dangerous. Most roads were destroyed and it was not uncommon to be fired upon by rebels when driving down a road. Trade between the various regions within the country became minimal. Most families ended up relying upon their communities and family members to survive. However, the war did not completely isolate Mozambicans from each other.

Travel for face-to-face trading kept families and groups informed even though they were not able to travel or work without danger. Therefore, many families relied upon the oral tradition of storytellers from other communities for education about the world, subsistence farming for food, and other basic survival skills to avoid the warfare.

The modern rebuilding of Mozambique offers teenagers an opportunity they have not had before in their lives. Though this effort is only now beginning to take hold, young people are offered skills and experiences that will allow them to find their place in a different Mozambique. The hopes for a new Mozambique rest in their hands and will develop with their minds.

TYPICAL DAY

The effects of civil war, drought, and flooding have restricted the opportunities for teens to have a consistent lifestyle. Life for teenagers in Mozambique is significantly different from that for teens in the West. If the family lives in a rural area, or is poor, as is common for most city families (52 percent), teens will not be in school long. Rather, they will be expected to work to help feed the family. The United Nations Children's Fund reported in July 2001 that the majority of children under the age of 15 were found to be working in 7 out of 10 provinces. Work for these youth means prostitution, farm labor, and hawking.[19]

Prostitution by teens is seen in every province. These girls either live in different regions than their parents or their parents are no longer alive. Recent UN reports indicate that prostitution is still a major employment option for young girls who need to earn money for food and shelter. Most girls spend the entire day preparing to look presentable at night. Then they hang out at bars or dancing areas in the hope of meeting someone for the evening.[20] With few options for employment and little education or trade skills, these young women are forced into this unfortunate but common practice throughout Africa.

Most teens living on farms with their families or in rural areas are expected to help work on the family plots. Others are hired at bigger farms and the money is used to help feed the family. Other youths hawk packs of cigarettes or roasted cashew nuts to supplement the family income. Those young people who are able to attend school have very busy schedules, schedules that most teens in the Western world could not imagine having every day.

One young woman from Maputo, Caterina, 15, is determined to get an education. Every morning she rushes to complete her chores before school. Caterina is up and dressed at 5:30 A.M. to fetch water from the piped tap about one kilometer away from her home. She has to make five trips with a 20-liter water carrier on her head. Then she helps her younger sisters and brothers wash and dress, and gets herself ready to walk to school, which is an hour's walk away. She has to be there at 7:15 A.M. Lessons are not easy for Caterina, partly because there are more than 60 children in her class. Sometimes the teacher sends Caterina home, because she is not dressed in the school uniform. Her mother cannot afford to buy it.[21]

When Caterina returns home, she must cook and clean before she can study. Then she studies before it gets dark, because there is no electricity in her home.[22] These daily routines are very similar to those that young people have in the rural provinces. To receive an education, chores on the farm must be done in the morning before attending school, and afterwards before the sun sets.

FAMILY LIFE

Most Mozambican families still feel the effects of the previous 25 years of war and chaos. Many young people lost their parents in the fighting or were temporarily separated from them. These youths gravitated to the major cities, like Maputo, in the hope of finding food and family. With the scarcity of jobs and the lack of skills among young people, most of the youth in the cities became street children. These teenagers make a living selling cigarettes and other items to pedestrians. Unfortunately, many resort to prostitution in order to make enough money to eat because they have nothing other than their bodies to offer. A few have been lucky enough to find relatives that escaped the civil war, and they are being reunited with family. Divisions of the United Nations, nongovernmental organizations, and missionary groups have been working tirelessly to assist Mozambique's youth in reuniting with their families.

A small minority of families in Mozambique is wealthy. They invariably are easy to spot by the Mercedes cars they drive and the large houses they own. In cities like Maputo, these families are given exclusive service in restaurants and stores, and their children are guaranteed an education, usually up through the university level. However, 70 percent of the families in Mozambique exist at the poverty level.

In most regions outside the major cities, the families are struggling to put food on the table and provide for their children. Ernesto Cossa and his wife, Amelia Ndava, live in one of the southern provinces known as Ilha Josina Machel. Here, he and his wife grow maize, beans, and potatoes to feed themselves. Amelia works at the local sugar factory and Ernesto trains others to work on a cooperative farm. Their son Antonio left home at 17, to look for work in Maputo. He is still unemployed.[23]

Although Ernesto and Amelia's situation may not change much in future years, Antonio still has opportunities. New programs implemented through the government are specifically designed to train young men and women in basic job skills. Such programs include basic administration training, auto mechanics, and agricultural awareness.

In the northern provinces of Mozambique, most families are still recovering from the civil war as well as from the drought and floods of recent years. However, because they are not near major urban centers and better jobs, the families tend to remain in close proximity to each other for mutual support. They live in poverty, inhabiting reed huts, and try to harvest food from the meager farms. A few acquire some of the scarce jobs available in factories.

Most communities in Mozambique observe a patrilineal society, which means that when a woman marries she leaves her home and moves in with her husband's family. There are a few cases of matrilineal communities in the northern provinces, but most regions now observe the patrilineal pattern.

Upon the decision of marriage, a "bride wealth" (*lobolo*) is paid by the groom to the bride's family. This process is called "gratification gifts." Arranged marriages (in which parents decided which boy and girl would be married) used to be the norm, but more young people are taking a modern approach and choosing mates for themselves. Men like Jose Sitoye agree with the modern way. He remarked, "Now we don't have to buy our wives and this is very important. I fell in love with my girlfriend and I asked her to marry me. I didn't ask her father for permission."[24]

In towns like Ribaue in the northern regions, young women sometimes become pregnant in their teen years.[25] Most teenage women in Mozambique today can expect to be pregnant by the age of 17, although most do not marry. Single teenage mothers or teenagers with multiple partners are not unusual. Promiscuity is expected of the male population.

However, because education about safe sex is difficult to discuss due to local taboos, and AIDS and sexually transmitted diseases are still very new topics in most regions of Mozambique, the majority of male and female youths have not been educated on the use of condoms. Therefore, the pregnancy rate for teens is high, as is the percentage that contracts the AIDS virus. AIDS/HIV activists perform theater productions during the bar socializing hours in the hope of educating the populace in a relaxed atmosphere.

These problems of unprotected and promiscuous sex exist in the major cities as well. In the cities, teens battle sexually transmitted diseases and HIV/AIDS just like their rural counterparts. However, in the cities today AIDS and HIV awareness is becoming easier to discuss. The government is promoting mass education about these diseases and urban teens have better access to medical and counseling resources. There is even a house established for AIDS victims.

The fate of teens is not completely dismal. For example, in the regions surrounding Maputo, there are many middle-class families. Like many parents around the world, the father and mother work to send their children to school. Some households are very large and include multiple wives and many children. In Fernando Chavango's house, there are three wives and 12 children. Five of his children are under the age of eight, one daughter is away attending middle school, another daughter is attending high school, and one son is studying agriculture in Namaacha. His other children are either married or helping out at home.[26] Chavango works hard to make sure his children receive an education because he understands that to succeed in a new modern country, his children must be educated.

Polygyny (a man married to multiple women) was a common practice among indigenous Mozambicans and practicing Muslims. One of the common explanations given for the marriage of a man to more than one wife was "because women's labor is so relentless, it was in a household's best interest to have more than one wife to share the work, ensure the household's survival, and give it the chance to accumulate wealth."[27] Young teenage girls are usually the choice as second wives in polygynous marriages. This arrangement is done for several reasons: either to provide the husband with an heir, to provide the girl's family with some political ties, or for monetary reasons.

Today young and old women are campaigning against polygynous marriages. Many young men have expressed their desire to only wed one wife. Divorce is becoming a more accepted option for those who do not wish to remain married, so polygyny is not such an appealing solution to marital problems.

TRADITIONAL AND NONTRADITIONAL FOOD DISHES

Teens in Mozambique do not have a wide variety of options to choose from at mealtime. Because families grow most of what they eat, their diets consist mainly of vegetables with meat included occasionally. Rice is the staple part of their meal; spicy vegetables add some flavor to the dish. The northern provinces will eat goat with their rice. Most all of the provinces add fish and prawns to their meals because they are easily accessible from the sea. Mangoes grow in abundance around the country and are an excellent addition to most meals.

Portuguese cuisine is interspersed with rice and vegetables. Urban centers, such as Maputo and Zambezia, offer some variation to the staples. Portuguese cuisine, seafood, vegetable dishes (matapa and mucapte), and chicken grilled in palm oil are well-known specialties of this region. In Maputo, a couple of restaurants even offer some Chinese dishes, and recently two restaurants opened which offer Italian-style pizza.

SCHOOLING

During colonization by the Portuguese, most of the indigenous youth population was not given the privilege of attending school. Only the children of wealthy parents were sent to private schools established by the Portuguese. This opportunity was available, provided the youth understood that they would be loyal to and trained for work with the Portuguese government. Assimilados, Mozambicans who were "both black and mestizos (mixed race), whom the colonial state considered to have met Portuguese language and cultural standards," were the other fortunate group allowed to receive an education.[28]

Becoming assimilado was very beneficial to a Mozambican family, not only because they would not have to take part in the "forced labor system" (military service) but because, as one Mozambican stated, "In those days obtaining the status of assimilado was a way of seeking a less-degrading life for our children. It was a way of ensuring that they have access to an education."[29]

After independence in 1975 and during the civil war, education became difficult to provide. Initially the new Frelimo government pushed to provide education throughout the country. However, the civil war made this goal temporarily unattainable. During this time, entire villages and lines of communication were routinely destroyed. Many Mozambicans fled the country, and a child's focus was more on survival than improving his or her education.

The United Nations released a youth profile of Mozambique in the year 2000. According to the figures gathered in 1995, the total percentage of illiterate teens (aged 7–13) was more than 59 percent. There are more illiterate teens in rural areas than in urban centers and the percentage of illiterate girls is higher than the percentage of illiterate boys by 30 percent.[30] Illiterate adults have little chance of finding employment in the modern job arena.

Missionaries provide education for teens in the rural northern provinces, such as Niassa. Parents can send their children to live and be educated at schools established by various missionary groups. If the children do well, they can continue their education at high schools and colleges in the capital city of Maputo. Teens have greater access to education within the towns and cities where private and public schools are provided.

After the civil war, the education of youth became a top priority of the government. Almost 18 percent of the governmental budget of 1995 was set aside for education.[31] This is actually a very big percentage of the government's budget. In the same year, the United States allotted only 7 percent of its budget to education for American youth.

When independence was declared in 1975, the minister of education stated that the goal of the new government was to establish universal education in Mozambique. In the decade from 1975 to 1985, student enrollment in primary and secondary schools rose 40 percent for all school-age children. Today, although progress is being made within the more populated areas such as Maputo, the rural regions still lag behind.

According to the United Nations Youth Profile, one of the projected goals of the new education policy was to provide literacy training to more than 2,000 young women and adolescent girls.[32] Other agencies focus directly on those who participated in the civil war. One agency, titled The Peace Education Project, focused on assisting groups of disadvantaged youth, including former child soldiers.[33] This still means that only 30 percent of the youth population is literate.

One of the top universities of Mozambique, Eduardo Mondlane University, announced in March 2001 that it was attempting to provide equal opportunities for teens from each province in Mozambique to get an education at the school. Until this announcement, most young people could receive postsecondary education only from Catholic and Muslim schools operating in the northern and central region of the country.[34] Despite the increased emphasis on education and its importance in the new economy, most teenagers do not aspire to go on to a secondary education. Their goal is to complete primary education and become trained in the workforce.

SOCIAL LIFE

During Portuguese colonization and the civil war, many youth were kidnapped for military use and opportunities for the remaining young people to socialize were limited. Teenagers who were not separated from their towns and families were discouraged from traveling and spent most of their time working in factories or on farms. Some youth had opportunities to play soccer on the weekends or meet friends at night. However, the stress of colonization and civil war prevented the formation of youth organizations. In the past decade, the government of Mozambique and organizations from the United Nations have focused their attention on providing the young people of the country with opportunities to meet other teens. The goals are to establish social outlets for the youth of Mozambique, where they can begin to heal the wounds of war and experience the positive aspects of youth unity.

According to the Mozambican youth and sports minister, "more than ever the youth are today called upon to give their contribution for the solution of their problems, which are the nation's problems."[35] The government is trying to help young people attain this goal by communicating with and through various youth organizations. There have been two assemblies in Maputo of the National Youth Council (CNJ) focusing on the role of young people in Mozambique. No one disputed the fact that the youth are the "guarantors of peace, stability, and national unity."[36] One of the priorities established by this assembly is to bring awareness of AIDS to the whole community.

Several other organizations have been established to provide avenues for youth to share ideas with each other. One such organization, the Organisation of Mozambican Youth (OJM), was established in 1977. The OJM is a nongovernmental organization designed to educate the young people. After the civil war, many branches were placed throughout the

Three boys posing in Metangula, Mozambique. Courtesy of Painet.

country in the hope of educating the young people about the peace process and providing moral, civic, cultural, and professional education.[37] OJM, according to the United Nations, has a membership of 1 million young people and provides an opportunity for Mozambicans to meet through conferences, seminars, voluntary service projects for national development, study groups, and exchanges.[38]

Both the CNJ and the OJM are examples of how the government is attempting to establish supportive organizations among the young people of Mozambique. It is apparent that the government believes these newly independent youth are the backbone of the country.[39] Organizations such as these will assist young people in focusing on the country as a whole and will educate the youth on the obstacles they have yet to overcome.

Other groups interested in the social welfare of Mozambican youth include divisions of the United Nations, such as the United Nations Development Program (UNDP). They have provided programs for the social welfare of the youth population. One of the projects established by the UN is geared towards encouraging young women in entrepreneurial endeavors, like starting small, home-based businesses. This organization has set aside up to $380,000 U.S. dollars to assist these young women in their pursuits.[40]

RECREATION

Although the country is rebuilding from war and natural devastation, the youth of Mozambique still have fun. Many teens play soccer during their free time, not only in the city but in the rural regions as well. Soccer is the national sport, though most games are played not on regulation fields but on any open terrain where kids can gather. The national soccer team competes in the African Cup of Nations.

A few sports activities do deserve notice. Both male and female basketball teams compete throughout the continent. The women's basketball team from Academica Maputo of Mozambique is known throughout the continent for their championships. Most notably, this team has brought home medals from the pan-African competitions.

One of the woman athletes, dubbed the "African Queen" by the press, is an inspiration to the adolescents of her country. Maria Mutola is the first Mozambican to win Olympic gold for her country. She has put Mozambique on the map in most 800-meter races around the globe.

ENTERTAINMENT

Most villages in the seven provinces bordering the ocean have easy access to the beach. On the weekend, it is not unusual to see most of the community spending their day along the sandy beach. It is in this atmosphere that most teens have an opportunity to relax, talk, fish, and play without having to worry about chores or responsibilities. In the evenings, young people gather to dance at outside cantinas/cafés that provide music from either local bands or the jukebox.

As in America, music is an integral part of Mozambican youth culture. On the weekends, bars and clubs throughout the country are filled with youth dancing to a blend of traditional and modern musical styles. Music is used in traditional ceremonies as a reminder of Mozambicans' cultural heritage, a motivator for dancing and meeting new people, and a way to express feelings.

Opportunities to dance and meet new people are available in the numerous clubs and cafés in each town. Young people regularly gather in the evenings and weekends at the cafés and drinking establishments for a chance to meet new people and listen to music. The music in these establishments is heard from jukeboxes, radios, or local bands. Young men and women dance and talk while music from all parts of the world plays in the background. Peaceful independence and new international relationships have allowed for new musical types ranging from traditional African beats to Caribbean to hip-hop to be heard throughout the country.

Traditional music is widely played in Mozambique. The strong African beat accentuated with drums can be heard in most bars throughout the country. Variations of African music are mixed with pop sounds or jazz. Groups from Angola and South Africa are especially popular in Mozambique. Recently, local bands have been experimenting by mixing hip-hop with the local African sound. In the urban areas of Mozambique, the big thing is the *marrabenta* style. The Orchestra Marrabenta Star de Mocambique is the most recognizable group that utilizes this style. They use local imitations of the original instruments to produce a sound and rhythm that is similar to salsa and calypso. However, the lyrics are not tied to one standard. They range from social criticism to love songs to praise songs.[41]

Marrabenta is perhaps the most typical Mozambican music, with a light style inspired by traditional rural *majika* rhythms.[42] Even the modern artists of today incorporate the traditional *Marrabenta* style. One of the current CDs brings together the "grand old men" of the *Marrabenta* style with the young stars of the Mozambican hip-hop movement.[43]

Some provinces capitalize on their own unique styles of music. The Makonde in the north are noted for their wind instruments, known as *lupembe*. In the south, the Chope musicians play the *timbila,* a form of xylophone that uses keys called *munje*. These are made of a special wood only found in Inhambae. The sound box is made from hollow calabashes. At a *timbila* dance, it is not uncommon to have an orchestra including 18 to 23 of these marimba chopes playing together.[44]

Venancio Mbande is perhaps the most famous of the *timbila* musicians. He was in exile in South Africa for most of the last days of colonization in Mozambique and during the civil war. However, the *timbila* festivals have begun again and Mbande has returned to perform. The *timbila* festival is held annually in August in Chopiland, located in southern Mozambique. There is a yearly pan-African hip-hop festival held each year, usually in July in one of the participating countries within Africa (Benin in 1999). A group from Mozambique attends almost every year. One popular group, The Baseball Track (Yuss), evolved from four members in 1989 to 16 members currently. They even have a Web site where listeners can locate them.[45]

Music can be heard all over Mozambique, from live bands in clubs, jukeboxes, and on the variety of radio stations filling the airwaves of the country. There are over 730,000 radios in use in Mozambique. This is the main form of communication in the country, especially since there is only one television station and most households are unable to afford a television. Recently, Internet service has become available in the urban areas of the country. Currently, there are 6,250 Internet users and two cybercafés just opened in Maputo.[46] However, only a small percentage of the population has access.

When not at the beach or meeting friends at the cafés, Mozambican teens go to the cinema. Before independence, the opportunity to see movies was extremely limited due to lack of movie theaters and films. After independence and the civil war, an effort has been made to restore many of the cinemas in the cities and to build new ones. Today young people have opportunities to see all types of films from America, Spain, Africa, and England.

RELIGIOUS PRACTICES AND CULTURAL CEREMONIES

The diversity of religion in Mozambique is comparable to the diversity of its people. After the loosening of Portuguese control, Mozambicans returned to honoring religious practices established long ago. The independence constitution "guarantees the freedom of citizens to practice or not to practice religion."[47] The ruling Frelimo government does not claim any religious affiliation and is not supportive of the Roman Catholic Church in Mozambique, because it considers the Catholics to be a "bulwark of the Portuguese colonial regime."[48] Currently, the religious population includes Muslims (20 percent), Christians (30 percent), and those with indigenous beliefs (50 percent).[49]

As in the other countries of southern Africa, animist religions have existed in Mozambique for thousands of years, and many people retain these traditional beliefs, sometimes alongside their practice of an organized religion. Animism is the belief that all living things—trees, water, and animals—have a soul.

The young people generally follow the belief of their parents. The *Annual Report on International Religious Freedom*, released by the U.S. Department of State, reported most of the population professing not to belong to any religious organization. However, it does note that traditional beliefs are prevalent in most Mozambican societies. Traditional beliefs were even incorporated into the religions of Christianity and Islam. Some examples include church members regularly visiting their ancestors' graves to pray for rain. Other visits to graves are to inaugurate a special occasion, like getting a new job, by saying prayers and pouring libations over the grave.[50] Traditional practices occur across the country, while Protestants are predominately in the south, Catholics in central Mozambique, and Muslims in the northern and coastal regions.[51]

Arab traders introduced Islam to the coastal regions beginning in the eighth century. Through a process of intermarriage and assimilation, the

Islamic faith was adapted into the indigenous culture. In 1500, after the introduction of the Portuguese community, Catholicism was introduced to the populace as well. Today the Muslim population exists mainly in the northern provinces and coastal areas. The Catholic population and the animist/indigenous-beliefs populations are interspersed throughout the country.

One note of interest: Because the toleration of religion is paramount to the independence of the country, conflicts between religious bodies are not very common.

Events such as birth, puberty, and death are extremely important within the community, and traditional ceremonies mark these occasions. One such traditional practice that continues today is the male initiation ritual in Capo Delgado and the initiation dances in Tete.

The male initiation rituals of Capo Delgado usually occur when a male reaches the age of transition from boyhood to manhood. A dance is performed using *mapio* masks. Traditional tattooing and teeth sharpening are still additional practices of the transition. The Makonde wear masks during ceremonies that symbolize initiation into adulthood or marriage.

CONCLUSION

The youth of Mozambique have had to survive many harsh realities in life: rebuilding after civil war, overcoming the ravages of drought and flood, the new epidemics of AIDS and sexually transmitted diseases, and the painful reality of trying to catch up to a modern world.

However difficult the challenges they face, Mozambican youth display a hope for the future. Education is becoming available, and families are rebuilding even while valued traditions have endured. One young man, Delmo Absalao Mahandjane, has survived all of these problems and faces the future with realistic hope. His father was killed in the civil war and he was relocated to Maputo with the rest of his family.

Expressing hope for Mozambique, Delmo has this to say to his fellow youth: "We young people in Mozambique are not in an enviable situation. Every time we try to take an initiative, it normally ends in failure because of lack of support from all sides. With all the poverty and the hurt and history of our country, there is little to encourage us. A lot of things have lost their meaning. What's the point in going to school if there are no jobs? What's the point of going home if there's nothing to eat? Most of us just survive, end up with low-paying jobs in the construction industry or selling things in the streets. Some fall into drugs. There is violence, petty theft, and delinquency. It is rarely a choice; it's just to be able to eat. You need to have courage to carry on. Real courage. My message to other young people is: Let us not get lost in images and superficial things, but let us be ambitious for the world. Here in Mozambique, so many young people have grown old before their time. They have lost their identity because they have lost their hope. We have to reconquer our youth culture and initiative. We need to learn to value ourselves."[52]

In a country with few developed resources, the greatest resources—young people—are finally feeling the growing efforts for positive change. Education has become critical. The government, their parents, and industry all understand that investments must be made to improve the opportunities for young people, not only for their individual health but for the growth and health of the nation.

In Mozambique, adults, youth, and children are rebuilding life from scarcity and poverty to self-sufficiency and opportunity. At the moment, there is hope throughout the land. The people see the way ahead. Bolstered by friends around the world, Mozambique is creating a better world for teens.

NOTES

1. Central Intelligence Agency. "Mozambique" in the *World Factbook* (Washington, D.C.: Brasseys, 2003). Or this information can be found at: http://www.odci.gov/cia/publications/factbook/geos/mz.html

2. Irving Kaplan et al., *Area Handbook for Mozambique*, 2nd ed. (Washington: , 1977), 20.

3. Ibid.

4. Ibid., 22.

5. Ibid.

6. "Nations of the World: Mozambique," *The World Almanac and Book of Facts 2000*.

7. Nick Middleton, *Kalashnikovs and Zombie Cucumbers* (: Sinclair-Stevenson, 1994), 4.

8. Ibid.

9. Cascon Case Mozambique: http://web.mit.edu/cascon/cases/case_moz.html

10. Oxfam: http://www.oxfam.org.uk/coolplanet/kidsweb/world/Mozamb/mozpeop.htm

11. CIA *World Factbook*, "Mozambique."

12. Frances Christie and Joseph Hanlon, *African Issues: Mozambique & the Great Flood of 2000* (Great Britain: James Currey, 2001), 2.

13. "Nations of the World: Mozambique," *The World Almanac and Book of Facts 2000*.

14. James Hall, "Economy—Mozambique: Rehabilitated Port Promises to Lift Tourism," Inter Press Service English News Wire, November 23, 2001.

15. See President Chissano's address to UNESCO, http://www.unesco.org/opi /29gencon/97–191e.htm

16. United Nations Youth Information Network, Mozambique Youth 2000 Profile: http://www.visionoffice.com/unyin/countrya.asp?countrycode=mz.

17. Statistics located through fastats: http://www.cdc.gov/nchs/fastats/life expec.htm

18. John Hanlon, "Mozambique: Will Growing Economic Divisions Provoke Violence in Mozambique?," article found at Swiss Peace Foundation Institution for Conflict Resolution and SDC—Federal Department of Foreign Affairs: http://www.isn.ethz.ch/pub/ihouse/fast/crp/hanlon_00.htm

19. IOL, "UN Warns on Aids Danger for Child Labour," Independent Online, http://www.iol.co.za/general/newsprint.php3?art_id=qw995902262230B252. Cited July 23, 2001.

20. Descriptions of this situation can be found in multiple UN reports regarding youth, AIDS/HIV, and child pornography/prostitutes dating back to 1990. The most recent report is the United Nations World Youth Report, April 2003.

21. Information obtained through the UNICEF Web site on AIDS: www .unicef.org/aids/aids_mozambique.htm

22. Ibid.

23. Merle L. Bowen, *The State against the Peasantry: Rural Struggles in Colonial and Postcolonial Mozambique* (Charlottesville: University of Virginia Press, 2000), 173–75.

24. Stephanie Urdang, *And Still They Danced: Women, War, and the Struggle for Change in Mozambique* (New York: Monthly Review Press, 1989), 210.

25. Charles Mangwiro, "Spreading the Word on AIDS in Mozambique," Reuters, November 18, 2001.

26. Bowen, 164–65.

27. Urdang, 202–3.

28. Raul Honwana, *The Life History of Raul Honwana: An Inside View of Mozambique from Colonialism to Independence, 1905–1975*, Allen F. Isaacman, ed. (Boulder: Lynne Rienner, 1988), 10.

29. Ibid., 15.

30. United Nations Youth Information Network, Mozambique Youth 2000 Profile, http://www.visionoffice.com/unyin/countrya.asp?countrycode=mz.

31. Ibid.

32. Ibid.

33. Ibid.

34. "Sparks Fly over Moz Varsity Quotas," South Africa Press Association [Web article], http://www.news24.co.za. Cited March 8, 2001.

35. "Minister Praises Role of Youth Play in Society," Pan African News Agency [Web article], http://allafrica.com. Cited May 19, 2001.

36. Ibid.

37. IISD Youth Source Book, http://iisd1.iisd.ca/youth/ysbk136.htm

38. United Nations Youth Information Network, Mozambique Youth 2000 Profile, http://www.visionoffice.com/unyin/countrya.asp?countrycode=mz.

39. "Minister Praises Role of Youth Play in Society," Pan African News Agency, 19 May 2001, [Web article], http://allafrica.com

40. United Nations Youth Information Network, Mozambique Youth 2000 Profile, http://www.visionoffice.com/unyin/countrya.asp?countrycode=mz.

41. http://www.ethnobass.org/afr_south.html

42. Lonely Planet World Guide Destination Mozambique, http://www.lonely planet.com.

43. "Marrabenta Mozambique," Africa Online Correspondent, http://www.africaonline.com. Cited March 28, 2001.

44. Official Mozambique home page, established by Eduardo Mondlane University Informtics Centre, http://www.mozambique.mz/eindex.htm

45. http://www.africanhiphop.com/crew/crew.htm

46. CIA *World Factbook*, "Mozambique."

47. Kaplan, xi.

48. Ibid.

49. Lonely Planet World Guide Destination Mozambique.

50. U.S. Department of State International Report on Religious Freedom for 1999: Mozambique, Bureau for Democracy, Human Rights and Labor, Washington, http://www.state.gov/www/global/human_rights/irf/irf_rpt/1999/irf_mozambiq99.html. Cited September 9, 1999.

51. Ibid.

52. Delmo Absalao Mahandjane, "Learning to Survive," article written for News of the Education to Fight Exclusion Project by UNESCO, http://www2.unesco.org/ece/actus/uk_mozambique.htm

RESOURCE GUIDE

Books

Honwana, Raul. *The Life History of Raul Honwana: An Inside View of Mozambique from Colonialism to Independence, 1905–1975*. Boulder, Colo.: Lynne Rienner, 1998.

Middleton, Nick. *Kalashnikovs and Zombie Cucumbers*. London: Sinclair-Stevenson, 1994.

Poetry and Fiction

Couto, Mia. *Under the Frangipani*. David Brookshaw, trans. United Kingdom: Serpents Tail Publishing, 2001.

———. *Voices Made Night*. David Brookshaw, trans. United Kingdom: Reed Educational & Professional Publishing, 1990.

Mankell, Henning. *Secrets in the Fire*. Anne Connie Stuksrud, trans. Toronto, Ont.: Annick Press, 2003.

Web Sites

Africa Online, for a compact resource to news, music, and chat rooms: http://www.africaonline.com

Mozambique home page: http://www.mozambique.mz/eindex.htm

Oxfam Cool Planet, the Amazing World Category: http://www.oxfam.org.uk/coolplanet/index.html

Youth-Related Organizations

Cruz Vermmelha de Marocambique
C.P. 2986
Maputo, Mozambique

Jos Mateu Muaria Kathupa, Minister
Ministry of Culture and Youth
Avda Patrice Lumumba 1217
C.P. 1742
Maputo, Mozambique

Mozambican Youth Organization (OJM)
C.P. 2998 Rua Pereirado Lago 147
3 Andar, Maputo, Mozambique

Youth for Development Association (JODESE)
Ms. Celmira Silva, Coordinator
Av. 25 De Setembro
No. 917 7 Andar
C.P. 1742
Maputo, Mozambique
Tel: +258 428167
Fax: +258 428650

Pen Pal/Chat

Penpal International. http://www.ppisearchy.net

Chapter 9

NIGERIA

Ikechukwu Enwemnwa

INTRODUCTION

Centuries before Europeans came to the coasts of Nigeria and before Islam came through the Sahara Desert to the north, the indigenous people who make up contemporary Nigeria had been living as independent societies and maintaining forms of inter-relationships among one another as the need for survival and the ability to communicate allowed. As the president of Nigeria, Olusegun Obasanjo, puts it:

> Our people, the ancestors of Nigerians of today, have been living to-
> gether as neighbors, visiting, trading among ourselves...blended our
> cultures, fought wars and made peace, and formed the great empires
> that once existed in Benin, Oyo, Songhai, Sokoto, and Borno.[1]

Among these indigenous societies and peoples were the Hausa, Fulani, Kanuri, Tiv, Nupe, Birom, and many smaller societies in the northern and central regions of the country. To the southwest were the Yoruba, Edo, Urhobo, Igbo, Itsekiri, and Ijo, while to the southeast were the Igbo, Efik, Ibibio, Ijo, Kalabari, Ogoni, and many other smaller groups. Between the ninth and sixteenth centuries, these people had established empires, kingdoms, clans, and villages—political entities with different levels of autonomy and inter-relations, different languages and religious beliefs, as well as different levels of sociocultural development.

Despite their political, cultural, and ethno-linguistic differences, these indigenes of precolonial Nigeria shared some similar cultural value systems, including elements such as respect for elders, honesty and accountability, industry and hard work, the pervasive connection between religion and all aspects of social life, the extended family system and the primacy of kinship, social responsibility, and the ethic that each individual is his or her brother's keeper. Resources and capital, including land and labor, were communally owned; these were not commodities to be sold and bought in the market for capital and profit.[2]

It was in amalgamating these people and territories—emirates, kingdoms, fiefdoms, clans, and villages—into the Northern and Southern Protectorates and the Colony of Lagos, that the British Government constituted the Federal Republic of Nigeria in 1914. The British ruled these villages, clans, districts, emirates, divisions, and provinces using the system of Indirect Rule until October 1, 1960, when independence was won and the country became the Federal Republic of Nigeria.

During this long period of Indirect Rule, the British created and gave the impression that each group was ruled through its own traditional authorities. Effectively, however, the system enabled the British to superimpose a north-south dichotomy of identities, interests, and values on Nigeria's more than 250 ethno-linguistic groupings and integrated them around three core ethnic groups and hundreds of other smaller ethnic groups. This foundation only consolidated a three-region political structure in which the core ethnic groups Hausa-Fulani, Igbo, and Yoruba dominated the smaller ethnic groups around them as they jostled for the control of the federal government.[3] It is this structure of regional political inequality that explains the political instability, the religious violence, the involvement of Nigeria's military in government and the creation of 36 states that have characterized Nigerian political history since independence.

With a population estimated at 120 million, the Federal Republic of Nigeria is Africa's most populous country. This makes one in every five black persons in Diasporas a Nigerian. The country is in West Africa and is situated north of the Gulf of Benin in the Atlantic Ocean, with the Republic of Benin to the west, Cameroon to the east, and Niger and Chad to the north as neighbors. It occupies a total area of 923,773 square kilometers, making it slightly more than twice the size of California. The climate is equatorial in the south, tropical in the center, and becomes semi-savanna to arid toward the north. The River Niger is the largest river in the country. It flows from its source in Fouta Jalon Mountains in the Guinea Republic, entering Nigeria through the northwest, to its confluence at the center of the country with the River Benue, from where it flows south to empty into the Gulf of Benin through many creeks.

Since its independence some 41 years ago, Nigeria has been ruled al-most continuously for 33 years by military administrations. Elected gov-ernments ruled only from October 1, 1960, to January 15, 1965, and from October 1, 1979, to December 31, 1983. During this long period of mili-tary rule, 33 new states were created, raising the number of states consti-tuting the federation from three in 1960 to 36 today. In addition, the nation's capital was moved from Lagos in the south to Abuja in the north in 1991. The Federal Republic of Nigeria was returned to a civilian ad-ministration with the democratic elections that produced Olusegun Obasanjo as president on May 29, 1999.

Nigeria is richly endowed with both human and natural resources. Its natural resources include natural gas, tin, coal, columbite, iron ore, lime-stone, lignite, lead, zinc, cocoa, rubber, timber, and palm produce. Nigeria is the world's sixth-largest producer of crude oil. The United States buys 54 percent of Nigeria's oil, which is about 20 percent of its oil consumption.

Even with all the natural resources, the economy of Nigeria is mono-cultural in the sense that petroleum has become its primary product, con-tributing about 85 percent of the annual budget and accounting for about 95 percent of the nation's total exports, with agriculture contributing a mere 3.7 percent. Today, the Gross National Product (GNP) per capita is estimated at $350, with the inflation rate at 53 percent.[4]

Thirty-eight percent of Nigeria's population is urban. Nigeria's urban growth rate of 5–7 percent makes it one of the most rapidly urbanizing countries in the world. Some of Nigeria's urban towns and cities devel-oped around provincial and divisional administrative capitals. Industrial and commercial centers hold populations of 50,000 to 200,000. Others, including Kaduna, Benin City, Enugu, Port Harcourt, and Abuja (the na-tion's new capital since December 1991) have grown into huge urban areas with populations of 1.5–3 million. Lagos, the former national capi-tal, has grown into a sprawling megalopolis with an estimated population of more than 8 million. Each of Nigeria's traditional cities of Ibadan and Kano have a population estimated at between 8 and 10 million.

Nigeria's annual population growth rate of about 2.8 percent over the past decade outpaces the average annual GDP growth rate by about 1.6 percent. The unemployment rate is estimated at about 45 percent, espe-cially among primary- and secondary-school graduates. Unemployment of university graduates and professionals such as bankers and engineers is also on the rise.

Children aged 14 and under constitute 43 percent of Nigeria's total population of 120 million. This age bracket is distributed almost equally between males and females, with a sex ratio of 1 male to 1.01 females. The proportion of the population aged 15 to 19 years is 9.4 percent, with a sex ratio of 1 male to 1.11 females; those in the age bracket of 20 to 64 years constitute 45.5 percent, with 1 male to 1.03 females; and those over 65 years are 2.1 percent, with a sex ratio of 1 male to 1.02 females.[5]

The poor economic condition of the country reflects the structural inequities in the inherited political order, mismanagement of the economy, and corruption and looting of the public treasury, as well as a lack of accountability by Nigeria's former military-political leaders. These developments have created political strife and conflicts with serious negative effects on the lives of Nigerian teenagers.

TYPICAL DAY

A typical day in the life of a Nigerian teenager may not vary as significantly on the basis of religion or ethnicity as much as on the basis of sex/gender, parents' occupations, household income, and rural or urban residence.

Across the cultural spectrum, children 10 to 12 years old are seen as being in the "Age of Responsibility," while those aged 13 to 20 are described as in the "Age of Consolidation of Adulthood."[6]

When the child enters the "Age of Responsibility," he or she will be expected to assume certain responsibilities, including contributing to the well-being of and providing some services to the household. Specific role expectations will vary depending on the size of his or her family, birth order, gender, the occupation(s) of parent(s), and whether they live in an urban or rural area. Nigeria is largely a rural country with about 62 percent of the population living in towns, villages, and hamlets with as few as 1,000 and as many as 20,000 people.[7] In larger families, typical of rural areas, each older sibling is more quickly weaned to maturity.

Small towns in Nigeria are usually truly rural, isolated and without industry. Rural people engage, for the most part, in peasant agriculture. Nigeria's rural farms are the "breadbasket of the nation." The peasant farmers are completely dependent on nature, barely exposed to modern technology, and lacking storage and preservation facilities for their perishable products. They produce more than 75 percent of the people's staple foods. As Nigeria's *Vision 2010 Report* shows, "agriculture now offers employment to over 65 percent of the working population, accounts for over 70 percent of non-oil exports, and contributes about 30 percent of the Gross National Product."[8] Teenagers living in Nigeria's rural areas, therefore, live in poverty. About 50 percent of Nigerians are categorized

Nigerian teen carrying grain sheafs. Courtesy of A. Olusegun Fayemi.

as living below the poverty line. In Nigeria, being poor means earning an
annual income of about 15,000 Naira (equivalent to $150), far below the
47,040 Naira ($470.40) required by an individual Nigerian for minimum
sustenance.[9]

Rural poverty in Nigeria is due mainly to the absence of business and
employment opportunities because of inadequate infrastructure—including lack of electricity and potable water; an inadequate and undeveloped
network of roads, transportation systems, and communications; lack of social amenities such as health care; and insufficient and dilapidated educational facilities. Though these conditions are improving measurably in
many areas, they affect to a large extent the quality of the lives of
teenagers who live in such rural areas.

Not all rural dwellers are poor, though. Many rural farmers earn incomes far above the poverty line and spend far less because they live mostly on produce from their farms. Peasant farmwork is a full-time job for families and tasks are gender-specific. The father, oftentimes accompanied by the mother, will leave home early in the morning and return at sunset; sometimes this routine is maintained at least six days a week. When both parents go to the farm, it becomes the responsibility of the oldest teenage child to watch over his or her younger siblings, take care of their basic needs during the day, and be accountable for the affairs of the family. He or she will be expected to get out of bed by 6:00 A.M., clean up the house, get himself or herself and the younger siblings ready for school, and walk them to the neighborhood school at 8:00 A.M. and back about 2:00 P.M. Such routines change, of course, if the child has school, church, or club activities in the afternoon hours. In other words, the teenager is not only a responsible role model, but also serves as an active mentor to younger siblings.

Gender differentiation of functions comes into play, too. Traditionally, all of Nigeria's cultures differentiate men's and women's functions in the house and on the farm. While teenage boys do assist with housework, such jobs are the designated responsibilities of the teenage girl in the family. In addition to the daily routines, a teenage girl is expected to help the mother out in the kitchen as she prepares the family meals, relieve her of some house chores, sweep and tidy up the home, wash dishes, and do her own laundry as well as that of her younger siblings.

She is also expected to accompany her mother to the marketplace when necessary and to be able to negotiate her way through buying some essential foods and ingredients if asked by her mother. Similarly, in some rural areas, especially during the peak season of farmwork, teenage boys are expected, as soon as they come back from school, to eat their lunch and run off to the farm to join their fathers at work. At sunset, teenage boys are expected to take some firewood home to their mothers for cooking the family meal.

Generally, after the family dinner, usually after 8:00 P.M., children are expected to work on any school homework they may have, or just get themselves ready for the next day's schoolwork. They may also play games in the village square with siblings and cousins under the moonlight before going to bed.

Expected daily responsibilities of a teenager 10 to 14 years old will vary if his or her family lives in an urban area, are educated and working for the government or business, or if either parent is a self-employed private business owner. In urban situations, higher qualities of life and conveniences can be reasonably assumed.

Nigerian girls with earthenware. Courtesy of A. Olusegun Fayemi.

Though city services may function erratically and even break down, sometimes for many days, the fact that they are available makes life easier and more fulfilling for urban teenagers. Unlike their rural counterparts, urban teenagers are not saddled with trips to fetch drinking water and firewood for their households. Instead, urban teenagers are expected to wake up much earlier, some before 5:00 A.M. and others at 6:00 A.M., depending on the distance and available means of transportation to school. Because of rapid urban growth, lack of proper priorities, forward planning, and inadequate government funding, most Nigerian urban roads and streets are clogged by traffic buildup, creating long hours of travel time for urban school teenagers. Unlike in the United States, there are no school buses for either urban or rural students in Nigeria.

The socioeconomic status of a family also makes a difference here. In Nigeria, unlike in the United States, middle- and high-school students don't own cars or drive themselves to school. Instead, middle-class parents drop their children off at school. Families that can afford a chauffeur have him do the rounds. There are no school lunches for Nigerian students. After children have returned from school and have had lunch, they are expected to spend their afternoons at lessons—privately organized prep schools that give children additional preparations, usually in English language, mathematics, and the sciences. For some teens, parents may engage the services of home tutors. After their lessons, children of affluent or middle-class families may go home to watch televisions or video movies, listen to music on CDs, or play video games.

Many professional, affluent, two-income families engage the services of housemaids or servants for housekeeping and cooking their meals while the mother of the house is at work. Few professional and middle-class families are able to get home for family dinner with their children. In such cases, the servant or an older family relative living in the household will cater to the needs of the children.

Children of low-income urban families, on the other hand, may go to their schools in commercial transportation like buses, otherwise known as *Bolekaja*, *Tuke-tuke*, or *Molue*; taxis, or even on "drop-off" motorbikes called *Okada*. Still, urban low-income children, especially girls, usually rush after school to the marketplace to help their mothers with the sale of their wares or to take home food items and make the dinner.

Teens between 15 and 19 years are culturally seen as in their "Age of Consolidation of Adulthood." At this stage it is as if teenagers are on their own. Parents expect them to show who they are and what kind of adult they want to be. But unlike in the United States, where middle- and high-school students work and contribute towards the cost of their education, there is no full-time employment for Nigerian secondary-school or college students. As a result, it behooves parents to support their older teenage children until they graduate with allowances for transport, the cost of books, and out-of-pocket expenses.

Tuition fees are completely free or minimal for students in all public schools. Parents pay for boarding and lodging when their children move into school boarding houses. Rural teenage boys in day schools are expected to help out with housework during weekdays and with farmwork only at weekends. In most families, teenage girls come home to relieve their mothers of the majority of house chores. Student boarders are expected to come home and contribute to the family's well-being only during the end-of-term holidays. Because parents finance their schooling, the children do not expect wages when they work for the family, though some may be given some cash emoluments.

School, club, and league sports like soccer and table tennis are highly encouraged for teenagers in Nigeria. Many teenage students spend much of their afternoon at soccer arenas, clubs or school fields for supervised practices. In general, teens aged 15 to 19 are required to serve as good role models and effective advisors to their younger siblings. Even as Nigerian teenagers at this stage are, to a greater extent, still economically dependent on their parents, some parents experience an authority crisis with their children when they begin to develop tastes and needs beyond what their parents can provide, and when they begin to interpret their presumed adulthood and freedom literally. Such problems tend to be greater among rural and semi-urban residents and with teenage girls.

FAMILY LIFE

Belief in the institution of the extended family and its values provides the foundation of family life in Nigeria. Most ethno-linguistic groupings are organized on the basis of a patrilineal system of inheritance and patrilocal system of residence. In the rural areas, where traditions and customs survive longer, an ideal extended family unit consists of at least three generations of paternal relatives living together in a family compound, or what Americans would call a homestead. It includes the head of the extended family, the oldest male, his younger brothers and their wives; their unmarried, widowed, or divorced sisters; their sons and grandsons and their wives; and their unmarried, widowed, or divorced daughters, and all their children. An extended family therefore consists of many nuclear families, each consisting of a man, his wife, and their sons, daughters and grandchildren. Oftentimes, teenage grandchildren and great-grandchildren in an extended family will include second and third cousins.

Land ownership, especially of land for residence, is communally held in the extended family. The head of the extended family controls the allocation and utilization of the family land in trust for other members. He has the responsibility to ensure that, to the extent possible, the land is allocated to family members according to their ages, need, and ability to develop a homestead. The head of each nuclear family will be allocated a piece of land within the extended family compound to build his own house for himself and his family. For as long as there is space within the family compound, the houses of all nuclear units of an extended family tend to be contiguously located. Each nuclear family lives together under one roof, but in close proximity to the other members of the extended family. Given this system of land use, it becomes natural where relationships are cordial for children to mix freely, enjoying relationships with their uncles and cousins, and in some cases eating from whichever mother has food ready. Teenage children in an extended family may even sleep over at the homes of their uncles and cousins around the corner.

The head of the extended family is an important authority in the marriage or wedding of any member of the lineage. Tradition sees the marriage of a member of the family as a process of admitting an "outsider" into the lineage. It is in this sense that marriages in much of Africa become "unions of two families." Bonds of marriage between families are truly perpetual because they are not broken by the death, divorce, or separation of the partners. Only a marriage in which there is no biological offspring can be permanently dissolved. Hence, a woman is married to the extended family of her husband and can, in the event of the untimely death of her first husband, under the custom of widow-marriage, remarry any of her late husband's brothers or cousins. It is therefore the responsibility of the head of the extended family to establish the ancestry of a man wanting to marry one of the family's daughters or that of a girl that one of the sons wants to marry. This does not mean, however, that the head of the extended family arranges marriages or chooses whom the young ones in the family will marry.

These traditions, however, are changing rapidly as members are forced by lack of additional space to move out of the extended family land. Even in the rural areas, available spaces in family compounds are decreasing as more permanent houses are built, as better health and better living standards increase the life expectancy of people, and hence as the population of family members increases.

In the towns and cities, the nuclear family of a man, his wife, and their children is becoming the norm. If, however, the husband and his wife are both holding jobs and the wife is still having babies, the couple may bring from the rural home into their household either of their mothers-in-law, a sister, or an aunt to help nurse or take care of their baby. Many families find this a more convenient solution to the lack of established day care centers or nurseries or the high cost of existing ones. In many cases the maturation of a teenager may be under the guidance of relatives other than the child's parents.

These conditions affect family life and the teenager in it. In both rural and urban areas, responsibilities, roles, and functions are differentiated according to gender. In the rural farms, there are crops that wives must cultivate, tend, harvest and sell to make money for themselves. At home, there are female chores: for example, home management and housekeeping, cooking the family meals, and taking care of the children are responsibilities of the wife. It is also the basic responsibility of mothers to socialize their daughters into the cultural expectations of women and the intricacies of womanhood. On the other hand, it is the responsibility of the husband to provide the staple foods and an accommodation for the family. The pattern is more or less the same for urban families, except that the independent income of a professional career woman enables her to make more effective contributions to her family.

There are no traditional women's jobs in the workplace. In fact, there is a long history of women professionals who have had successful careers as chief executives, directors, and heads of many big corporations and government agencies, and as medical doctors, lawyers, engineers, professors, school principals, and teachers. Some have even been elected to legislatures or appointed to ministerial positions.

Most of these developments have been among Christians, however. Muslim women were prohibited under Islamic injunction from holding public offices. But even this is changing somewhat as a few Western-educated Muslim women have started taking positions in government and in the business sector.

As indicated above, middle- and high-school teenage students do not work, mainly because there are no employment opportunities for them. Even at the university level, students are in school full-time and may only seek or take up vacation jobs during the three-month annual school holidays.

Whether in rural or urban areas, even after children have turned 21, they are expected to continue to live with their parents until they have graduated from college or university, obtained some employment, or gotten married.

There are many differences in the lifestyles of the poor and the rich and between rural and urban residents. In the rural areas almost every family owns and lives in its home. Only a few strangers, students, traders, small businessmen, teachers, and local government workers rent flats and rooms.

In the urban areas, most families do not own the houses, flats, or apartments they live in. They rent their accommodations.

Teenage family life for members of the well-to-do class is similar to the life of American teenagers in the same socioeconomic circumstances, with a few exceptions. The few differences relate to children owning cars, driving cars, and time schedules. In Nigeria, although 18 is the official age for obtaining a driver's license, teenagers do not generally own cars, even when their parents can afford to buy one for the children. This is in part because cars, whether used or new, are too expensive. Since teenagers do not work, they need substantial help from their parents not only to buy cars but also to keep cars on the road. Another reason is the high incidence of teen-driver accidents on Nigeria's roads. Some affluent parents have indulged their teenage children, allowing them to drive family cars around. Many such experiments have ended in fatal accidents, partly because of the conditions of the roads and partly because of the undisciplined driving habits of many a Nigerian driver. Consequently, parents prefer to hire family drivers to chauffeur their children to school and on their outings or trips.

It is only among Nigeria's *nouveau riche*—well-to-do persons without much education or a profession who have made money as government contractors or political agents of people in office—that you find parents indulging their teenage children with cars, sometimes as a way of keeping the children in school. The fatal accidents experienced by quite a few of such spoiled kids have helped to reduce this indulgence.

Religion, too, has a big impact on family life and makes a lot of difference in types of families and how children are raised. Religion determines the system of marriage a family adopts. Thus, Christians implant the Western concept of monogamous marriage into the traditional extended family system. The result is that many family members become genuinely and honestly involved in the normal lives of married family members. Thus, when marital problems develop, the intervention of such relatives helps to pull couples away from the precipice of separation and divorce. Though the records of divorce courts are not often correctly kept, available evidence suggests the divorce rate of Nigerian Christians is less than 2 percent. It is even lower for non-Christian believers in traditional religions who practice polygamous marriages and live in the extended family compounds in the rural areas. In addition to enhancing family stability, many uncles and aunts in the extended family are involved in raising the children in the family. These extended family relationships protect Nigerian teenagers from some of the destabilizing effects that high rates of divorce, separation, and single-parent families have on American teenagers.

The situation is different for Muslims. A Muslim man is allowed under Sharia, the Islamic law, to marry and keep up to four wives at the same time, if he shows that he is in a position to satisfactorily and adequately maintain each woman and her children without making her work to fend for herself. In those Hausa-Fulani northern states where a rigid interpretation of Sharia is imposed and practiced, and in parts of the Yoruba Muslim states, the requirement that a man must be able to satisfactorily take care of his wives is stringently applied. Thus, once married into the family of a practicing Muslim, a wife never goes out for paid employment, unless she was an educated professional and had developed a career before her marriage. The stay-at-home wives hardly ever go out of their harem—the compound or homestead of their husband—without escorts and without covering up from head to toe in traditional attire, called *bakha*. The system means that all the wives of the same man stay at home essentially to raise their children, do their housework, and take turns in attending to their husband. Mothers are expected to teach their daughters from an early age the cultural definition of the role of a woman in a family. In many cases, Muslim daughters are not allowed to be educated in the Western values of Nigerian schools. As they grow up, most Muslim teenage daughters are encouraged by their parents with huge dowries to marry early, usually before they turn 13 or 15 years old. Because of their protected lives and upbringing, daughters easily become acquainted with the circle of approved men from which to choose their spouse. A girl may then get betrothed between ages 10 and 12. These arrangements are intended to reduce the incidence of premarital sex or the loss of virginity by daughters of a family. In the Muslim tradition, a daughter brings social dishonor and shame to her family if she is known to have lost her virginity before marriage. Loss of virginity by a Muslim bride provides sufficient grounds for sending the girl back to her parents. It further provides a sufficient reason for the mother of the dishonorable daughter to be divorced by her father. The father of such "a girl of shame" is merely required to chant or pronounce some words of "dishonor and divorce" from the Koran to his wife, the child's mother, and her divorce is final. This tradition accounts for higher divorce and remarriage rates for Muslims than for Christians.

But these customs too are slowly giving way to the globalizing influence of a Western-value-oriented democracy, education, technology, and trade. In the past, it was thought sufficient for Muslim sons, before they are eight years old, to be put through Koranic schools and Arabic classes under Islamic teachers, or *Mallams*. Today, however, many Muslim boys and girls in Nigeria are sent to single-gender boarding schools where they are taught many of the same subjects that American teenagers study. The only difference is that the Nigerian Muslim teenager is protected from receiving religious instruction in Christianity. The 1999 Nigerian Constitution at Section 38 (2) "forbids a Nigerian child attending any place of education from receiving religious instruction other than the one that relates to a religion of his parent or guardian."[10]

TRADITIONAL AND NONTRADITIONAL FOOD DISHES

The integration of Nigeria's multicultural society has led to the emergence of Nigeria's "national dishes," which are truly cherished by most Nigerians. In the past, culture and geographical factors such as climate and vegetation determined the system of agriculture, the food products, and the menus of each of geo-ethnic cultural group.

Today, however, with interethnic migrations and marriages, increased urbanization, industrialization, and commerce, as well as improvements in transportation and communication networks across the country, foods previously characteristic of particular cultures have become staple items in the diets and menus of other ethnic groups. Thus, tuberous products like yams and cassava, indigenous mainly to the rain-forest vegetation of the south, have become staple foods to people from all over the country. Plantains, the mainstay of the riverine peoples of the Niger Delta and eastern Yoruba lands, have become part of cherished meals in faraway Sokoto, Kano, and Borno in the north. Similarly, rice and beans, traditionally produced in the semi-savanna; and beef, beef *Suya* (roasted or barbecued on an open fire), and pasteurized milk or *fura donono*, central to the dietary habits and culture of the Hausa-Fulani of northern Nigeria, have all become part of everyday meals all over the country.

While men sometimes help, it is a generally accepted tradition that women, either as mothers or daughters, prepare family meals in Nigeria. It is a measure of the upbringing of a Nigerian girl that she is comfortable with preparing many traditional dishes. And Nigerian women are very deft and savvy at doing so.

While these previously ethnic foods have become staple foods to all groups and classes in Nigerian society, how each dish is prepared, what people eat with it, and how frequently it is eaten differ by class or ethnic culture. Nigerian women often process the same staple foods differently and combine them with different types of soups to produce different dishes for family breakfast, lunch, and dinner. Thus, yam and plantains may be boiled or fried as chips and eaten with tomato, fish, or beef stew. Both also may be boiled and pounded into a paste and eaten with different types of soups with cultural flavors. Yams, plantains, rice, beans, and corn are often milled, sifted, and dried to produce flour for different types of pastes, puddings, or cakes. Similarly, cassava may be fermented for four or five days to produce *akpu*, traditional to the Igbo people but now popular across the country. *Akpu* is now known among urban construction and blue-collar workers, called "six-to-six," the euphemism for the energy to keep one going from 6:00 A.M. to 6:00 P.M. The same cassava may be milled or grated, pressed dry, and fried to produce *garri*, a preferred meal of the Yoruba people but now a staple food of all Nigerians.

In general, Nigerians use very few refrigerated or frozen foods or foods with preservatives added. Across rural Nigeria, women generally cultivate in farms or around their houses different types of vegetables for family meals. These are used in the preparation of different soups that go with staple dinners. Most Nigerian cultures believe that organically cultivated and grown foods without biochemical additives and preservatives have some herbal effects on health when cooked and eaten fresh. One should not attribute this preference entirely to a lack of the technology of food preservation in the culture. Indeed, where people find it necessary to preserve any food items, as is sometimes done with okra, maize, nuts of the date palm, or other fruits, they will cure the produce under the heat of the sun.

Nigerians also prefer their meals well cooked in boiling water or deep-fried in peanut or palm oil. Even leftover foods must be reheated for breakfast, snacks, or lunch. Sometimes the same items of food may be served as breakfast or lunch. Usually, however, they are prepared as different dishes. Most families eat a heavy breakfast, a light lunch, and a full meal for dinner at night. Thus, for Nigerians of all classes, breakfast for children rushing to school or for parents rushing off to work may consist of *akamu,* a cereal meal made from milled corn or millet flour mixed in boiled water and eaten with *akara* or *moi-moi,* made from beans or black-eyed peas and fried in cooking oil or boiled in water. At other times, the same corn or millet flour may be turned into *ogi* when it is mixed in cold water, stirred to a paste in boiling water, wrapped in some leaves, and eaten with *akara* or *moi-moi* or fried plantains, called *dodo.*

While meat pies, hot dogs, shortcakes, sandwiches, and other such snacks are sold in some supermarkets, many Nigerians have not acquired the appetite for McDonald's-type "fast foods" or the European-type fish 'n chips. Nigerians have yet to accept the "eating on the go" habit common in American culture. Also, most Nigerian families hardly dine out. People eat out essentially to mark a special event, business occasions, or parties. And even on such occasions, only a few middle- or upper-class executives who have acquired the taste ask for European dishes of steak, ham, or roasted chicken. Most ordinary Nigerians will still stick to African dishes, what they eat at home.

Most families eat their full meal of dinner at night. Mothers (or wives) put in their utmost to ensure good dinners for their families. Dinnertime, especially in the rural areas, is when mothers bring their families to roost and fathers get an account of everybody's affairs during the day. For teenagers who might be beginning to cut their independent paths, family dinners may be seen as encroachment on one's schedule.

To make dinner the event it is supposed to be, women are expected to bring the staples and the supply of vegetables from the farm while the other ingredients may be bought from the market. The men are expected to provide meat or fish for family meals. In the past, most rural farmers were also hunters or fishermen on the side. Much of the meat or fish a family needed used to come from the hunting or fishing successes of the father or older boys in the family. This is, however, changing rapidly as only a few men now go hunting in the wild.

In the urban areas, nearly all families now rely on the marketplace for the supply of beef, chicken, fish, vegetables, and other foods they need. Nigerians buy their foods at open or stall markets. In such urban market-places, it is a very common sight to find many heavy and light trucks off-loading bulk produce and food products transported from distant rural towns and villages. The supermarket chains and malls characteristic of the United States do not exist in Nigeria, even in the huge metropolitan cities. The so-called supermarkets that dot many neighborhoods provide only small items (canned foods, juices, sugar, and the like) that people tend to run out of between weekly shopping trips. Only a few educated, rich urban families actually depend on such shops for most of their needs. Most urban people still buy all of the same items and goods from city markets at much lower prices than in the supermarkets.

Nigerians eat much the same foods on all occasions. On special days of celebrations and festivities like Sundays, Christmas, New Year's Day, or traditional festivals, the quantities of fish or meat (goats, rams, chicken, and so forth) are increased to reflect the number of persons expected to participate in the feast. In the past, when rice and chicken were not in sufficient supply, these items were reserved or set aside as meals for children and women. Now that these foods are in good supply, the food preferences between children, teenagers, and adults are not so clear.

SCHOOLING

Nigeria's National Policy on Education is structured to follow what is called the "6-3-3-4 System." Thus, a child who goes to school at age five will spend six years in primary (elementary/grade) school, three years in junior secondary (middle) school, another three years in senior secondary classes (high school), and finally may go to a college or university for another four years.

Despite state, gender, and religious differences in education, it is increasingly being accepted that schooling provides for the Nigerian teenager the transition from a tradition- and custom-dominated life to a life of new values, new norms, and new standards. Primary, secondary, college, and university education have continued to enable the Nigerian child and youth to participate and share in the formative pan-ethnic experiences of Nigeria's governmental, political, economic, and legal institutions and its rapidly growing global Western influences.

Nationally, secondary-school enrollment grew in the 1980s from 1.99 million in 1980 to 3.1 million in 1990. Secondary-school enrollment increased from 3.60 million in 1992 to 4.8 million in only five years. At the university level, the student population increased at an even higher rate, by an annual average of 18.9 percent during 1981 and 1992.[11]

To further increase the enrollment rates of Nigerian youth in the school system, the federal government introduced various educational policies. Among these are the Universal Basic Education (UBE) Program, the creation of the National Primary Education Commission (NPEC), and the National Board on Technical Education (NBTE). At the secondary-school level, during 1989 and 1991 the federal government embarked on a policy aimed at boosting female education by establishing 11 additional federal government girls' colleges and by making 36 formerly all-boys federal government colleges co-educational. These policies are already having the effect of closing the national gender gap in secondary-school enrollments. The distribution was 56.3 percent male and 43.7 percent female in 1990, while in 1996 it became 51.2 percent male to 48.8 percent female.

About 95 percent of all educational institutions in Nigeria are owned and controlled by both the federal and state governments. This means that tuition fees are free in all public schools. Some state governments have gone further to supply free textbooks also. In general, therefore, who goes to school in Nigeria does not depend on the parents' ability to pay. Instead, who goes to school and how far on the educational ladder one goes depend more on the child's ability, family values, and the religious affiliation of the parents.

However, the socioeconomic status of the parents, meaning the parents' income and educational backgrounds, combine to determine the type of school a child attends, the quality of schooling he or she receives, and how long he or she stays in school. During the many years of military rule, national investments in education unfortunately plummeted to the point that the government's allocation for education averaged a mere 6 percent of the annual budgets. This inadequate allocation of funds resulted in the fact that most primary and many secondary schools all over the country have suffered from years of neglect and a lack of basic infrastructure, instructional materials, and supplies. In addition, it created a poor pupil-teacher ratio of 76:1 and a lack of motivation among teachers that resulted from low salaries and poor conditions. The growing increase in numbers and population of private schools throughout the country, especially in the cities, reflects the reaction of parents to the deplorable situation of the public schools. As in the United States, private or parish schools in Nigeria are being established by churches and private entrepreneurs. Many parents, especially from educated middle- and upper-class families who can afford the higher fees and other charges the private schools impose, prefer to take their children out of the ill-equipped public schools to enroll them in private schools for a better education.

With the exception of entrance examinations conducted by individual university demonstration and staff schools, admissions into public secondary schools are based on two sets of examinations. There are the highly competitive National Common Entrance Examinations conducted annually by the national examining body, the West African Examinations Council. There is also the set of common entrance examinations conducted by the ministries of education of the respective states. For admission into one of the prestigious federal government colleges, a child is expected not only to be successful in the National Common Entrance Examinations but to reach the merit level. In general, a child's score on the National Common Entrance Examinations is as important for admission into the federal government colleges as the SATs are for the admission of American teenagers into colleges and universities in the United States. Usually, the results of candidates are compiled on national, state, or educationally less developed states' merit lists. Drawing successful candidates from these lists enables the federal Ministry of Education to comply with the federal character principles requiring that students be selected with a view to promoting equality of opportunity and national integration through these federal government colleges.

Since the entrance examinations are highly competitive and selective, admission into the federal government colleges confers enormous prestige on entrants. Consequently, many ordinary Nigerian families who place high value on education and educationally conscious middle- and upper-class parents spare no time or expense in preparing their 9- and 10-year-olds for these examinations. Many parents send their children to years or months of after-school tutorials in prep schools to improve their children's chances of making the admission marks. Admission into state public secondary schools is not as competitive, in part because there are more schools to choose from, but also because only those children who failed to get into the prestigious federal government colleges end up in the state secondary schools.

Secondary school education in Nigeria builds on the foundation laid at the primary level by expanding students' knowledge in the English language, mathematics, the sciences, the arts, history, geography, and other social sciences. Most secondary schools are nonboarding schools. This means that students are expected to get to school at 8:00 A.M. and remain in school until 3:00 P.M., allowing for about 30 minutes of break or recess for snacks. Nigerian schools do not provide school lunches for students.

In the boarding schools, students begin the day with dormitory jobs, with breakfast between 6:00 and 8:00 A.M. Formal classes begin at 8:00 A.M. and run until 2:00 P.M. After lunch, student boarders are allowed a one-hour break time or siesta, followed by sports and athletic activities from 4:00 to 6:00 P.M. Students are required to return to classrooms for prep from 8:00 to 10:00 P.M., after which they are expected to retire to their hostels for the night.

Unlike in American middle and high schools, Nigerian students are not often exposed to many vocational studies like typing, computer literacy, and dancing. Also, there are no special programs that select or track and target particular students for some special attention intended to facilitate their admission into a university, polytechnic, or technical college. Instead, all students in senior secondary class one are encouraged and guided on the basis of their performance on the Junior Secondary Certificate Examinations to select subjects for their major/specialization from either the science group or art group of subjects. In effect, they will take their Senior Secondary School Certificate or General Certificate Examinations in the group of subjects of choice. These blocks or groups of subjects correspond to the requirements of universities and the Joint Admission and Matriculation Board for admission into the faculties of medicine, the sciences, humanities, social sciences, arts, and law.

During a typical day at school, students receive lectures from teachers who are professionals in the individual subject areas they teach. Teachers assign lots of readings and exercises as homework as a means of inducing students to study privately beyond class lecture notes. During any one session, a student must successfully fulfill the requirements of all courses or subjects in which he or she was enrolled in order to move to the next higher class.

Computer technology and access to the Internet are not widely available in many Nigerian schools and universities. Consequently, teachers deliver their lessons in lecture formats without as much reliance on instructional materials and visual presentations as is the case in American schools. But this varies from one faculty or department to the other as lots of teaching aids are required and used in the medical, science, arts, and teaching fields.

While the rate of students repeating classes for failing courses is low, the school completion rate is about 80 percent in secondary schools. Higher school dropout rates are observed in the predominantly Muslim states of the north, where as many as 20 percent of the children attend Islamiya or

Koranic schools. Also, in the more Islamic states, higher dropout rates result from parents withdrawing their sons to apprenticeships and street trading while daughters are withdrawn to early marriage, household labor, and childcare.

SOCIAL LIFE

In most parts of Nigeria, including the Islamic states in the north and among the Yoruba Muslims in southwestern Nigeria, teenage boys and girls do mix freely, select their own dates, and go dancing together. As was pointed out earlier, public day schools are coeducational institutions. Even in public, parish, or private boarding schools, authorities set up visiting-day rosters when boys and girls receive visitors of the opposite sex under the supervision of boarding house or hall officials. They therefore provide teenage students with opportunities to meet, interact, and develop relationships, much as middle- and high-school teenagers do in America. But Nigerian schools do not organize proms for students. Also, while students may organize social clubs, there are no student fraternities. Thus, only a few Nigerian boys in their teenage years may have had any sort of alcoholic drinks other than beer. The strongest alcoholic drink commonly available to Nigerian teenagers is beer. Teenage binge-drinking parties are unheard of in Nigeria. Less than 2 percent of teenage boys are on record to smoke a cigarette a week. It is estimated that less than 1 percent of Nigerian teenage girls have had an alcoholic drink, beer, or cigarette. Incidents of hard drug use among teenage students, boy or girl, are rare and far apart.

Across ethnic groups in southern Nigeria, among both Christians and practitioners of indigenous African belief systems, boys and girls belong to the same youth organizations, church choirs, and social clubs and participate in social activities together. In rural areas, teenagers of both sexes enjoy folk tales and telling stories outside their homes at night under the glare of the moon. Such traditional events and activities often become some of children's most enduring and memorable common experiences of growing up in villages. The extended family system ensures that most of the young ones who play together are siblings, or first, second, or third cousins. Usually children are socialized before becoming teenagers to believe that tradition and custom prohibit any romantic, sexual, or amorous relationships between children who are biologically related in an extended family. Such behaviors amount to incest, and parents and children revere taboos associated with such misdeeds. Understanding and accepting these customs and traditions enable teenagers to build honest and lasting relationships in those moonlight sessions.

Marriages are no longer prearranged. Today's teenagers in southern Nigeria hear stories of prearranged marriages between families in the past just as Americans hear it of Africans. Some three or four generations ago, prearranged marriages among chiefs and notable families were one way families stabilized their aristocratic status and prestige in communities. In the circumstances of contemporary living, such customs no longer serve any useful or relevant function, even in the rural areas. Consequently, families no longer impose such obligations on their young ones.

In the cities, teenagers are even freer to decide whom they date, whom to socialize with, and whom to marry. Today, teenage daughters and sons choose when they take their suitors and girlfriends home for presentation to their families. In many cities, it is a common sight to see teenage boys and girls holding hands and strolling along the streets. But it is rare to see Nigerian teenagers kissing on the street. This lack of public demonstration of affection by teenagers is often mistaken by non-Nigerians to mean that, "for their part, most Nigerians don't kiss at all."[12]

Among the educated middle- and upper-class families in the cities, schools and colleges provide young ones with the freedom to choose their friends and dates. From such school contacts, they organize social activities, parties, and go to popular Sunday afternoon dances known as "Sunday jumps."

In general, urban teenagers are encouraged to invite friends home. Because parents do not often allow children younger than 15 to go out on dates, teenagers tend to sneak out to meet their dates in the company of friends of the same sex. In the past, premarital sex by a daughter was regarded as bringing shame and disgrace to her mother, who thus would not be presented with the traditional gifts that signify that her daughter's husband found his bride a virgin upon consummating their marriage. Society now seems to accept that with long years of schooling, and with girls marrying as late as 25 to 30, sex before marriage is an understandable result of social changes, lengthy schooling, and late marriages.

The dress styles of Nigerian male and female teenagers are quite similar to what Americans in the same age bracket wear. All Nigerian schools insist and ensure that students come to school wearing the approved school uniforms. At home, on the streets, and for social occasions, Nigerian teenagers wear the same brand-name blue jeans, dress pants, shirts, sweatshirts, sunglasses, sneakers, and heavy boots that teenagers buy in any shopping mall in America. Nigerian girls are equally fond of the spaghetti-strap or sleeveless blouses and body-hugging shirts that many American girls wear. Nigerian girls, however, wear blouses and skirts, formal dresses, and shoes to school and social occasions more than their

American counterparts do. In fact, a Nigerian girl would look odd wearing a pair of sneakers and pants outside a sports arena. While boys in southern Nigeria rarely wear traditional dresses of *sokoto*, *khaftan*, and *agbada* to school and nonformal occasions, the fashion for Nigerian girls is Nigerian designer styles in skirts, blouses, and *long booboo* made out of Nigerian cotton prints and *adire*, tie-dyed cotton materials.

The situation is completely different in the Muslim north. There, especially among devout Islamic families, stringent regulations and rules limiting movements and freedoms are imposed on girls. While daughters are especially adored and loved by their fathers, a daughter is expected to grow up within her mother's accommodation and under her tutelage in the harem, the women's section of a Muslim family compound.

Many daughters are usually betrothed to suitors between age 10 and 12 and are given out in marriages with a lot of household wares and wealth as dowry. This is because in the Hausa-Fulani tradition, marriages between the offspring of long-time friends and notables are the most honorable way of cementing relationships. Sometimes, the girl may in fact be given away to her father's best friend with no concern for age difference.

Just as her mother would not be allowed to leave the family compound without a male escort, so a daughter may not go out without a chaperon. If her father is rich enough, she will be driven to wherever she wants to go or visit. But as more boys now go through college, many rich Muslim parents are finding it necessary to allow their daughters to obtain a secondary education with a view to making them suitable wives to the emerging Western-educated Muslim young men.

Dress codes are enforced for both Muslim boys and girls. Hausa-Fulani women are required to cover up from head to toe with a robe, the *bakha*. However, single teenage girls are expected to cover from head to toe but with their faces exposed. Muslim boys normally wear *sokoto* and *khaftans*, a pair of pants worn under a long robe that hangs down to the knees. For a more formal outing, a Muslim boy is expected to wear a complete *babanringa*, a three-piece flowing gown with an inner long-sleeved *khaftan* and a pair of *sokoto*. All Muslim males must wear a cap to go out of their homes.

RECREATION

It is a popular belief in Nigeria that the teen years are a developmental period when children become most physically active. Thus, in-school and out-of-school teenagers, both boys and girls, are encouraged to participate in organized sports, athletics, and recreational activities. The popular sports are soccer, basketball, table tennis or Ping-Pong, tennis, boxing, swimming, and wrestling. Girls particularly like handball, netball, and tennis. Both the federal and state governments fund national and state sports councils to organize these sports in schools for state and national league competitions.

Soccer, called football in Europe and Nigeria, has become a national pastime for both sexes, though female soccer is a recent development. Soccer is believed to be so important in the national psyche that many of the former military dictators buoyed up their stay in power by encouraging the development of soccer. Almost everyone in Nigeria enthusiastically watches soccer, although only teenagers and young adults play it.

Children begin to be involved in street, village, and town soccer teams and clubs even before they get to school. Soccer is to all levels of Nigerian schools what football is to American colleges. Schools organize their student populations into junior, medium, and senior soccer teams for seasonal competitions among schools in different zones and leagues within each state. While every student is encouraged to participate at one level or another, selection into the school team is competitive and based on superior performance. Schools and leagues that emerge as zonal or state champions go on to the national championship competitions. Victories in these competitions bring trophies and honors to school teams that popularize colleges. Also, aspirants to the states' major leagues and Nigeria's national professional teams are often recruited at these school competitions and at the National Challenge Cup competitions.

Nigeria's male professional soccer teams are organized into the Under 18, Junior Eaglets, the Under 21 Eagles, and the National Super Eagles. For female soccer, the two national teams are the Female Eaglets and the Female Under 21. That the national soccer teams are named after the eagle, the official emblem of Nigeria, clearly points to the high esteem Nigerians accord the sport of soccer. This national pride in Nigerian soccer is increased by the fact that nearly every generation of teens in the last three decades has produced teams of Under 18 or Junior Eaglets or National Super Eagles that have competed or won trophies at the finals of the Olympics, the World Cup Series, and the African Cup of Nations Competitions.

Soccer has also given to Nigerian teenagers their soccer legends and national heroes. The most famous heroes in the recent past include Tasilimi Balogun, Chuks Okala, and Sunday Onyeali. Today's national heroes include Kanu Nwankwo, who became world-famous at the Atlanta Olympics in 1996, Sunday Olisa, Austin Okocha (popularly known by teenagers as "Jay Jay"), Stephen Keshi, Omeokachie, Odegbami, and

Babayaro, to name but a few. These Nigerian soccer stars and others not so well known are currently living in Europe where they play professional soccer for different European major-league clubs. The fact that these stars make money playing soccer in Europe and come home when called upon to play for Nigeria at international events inspires the spirit of soccer among Nigerian teenagers.

Though many other sports are similarly organized, only swimming, table tennis, boxing, and field athletics are nearly as popular as soccer. Boxing has produced its heroes too, including an Olympic champion, Stephen Konyegwachie, and a professional world champion, Hogan Bassey. Table tennis or ping-pong has become so popular that teenagers in rural and urban areas can be seen at street corners playing it. In the coastal towns and villages in the delta of the River Niger, swimming is a way of life of the people. Children are taught to swim at infancy. Many such children have grown up to represent their states in swimming competitions as teenagers. Officials of state sports commissions provide systematic and technical training in ping-pong, tennis, swimming, and athletics in many public stadiums across the nation.

Sporting and athletic activities provide boys and girls recreational opportunities that enable them to mix, make friends, and compete, not only among students of the same school but also with students from other schools in different zones or states. In many cities, youth clubs encourage jogging, running, wrestling, and bodybuilding exercises. Participation in other sports such as rugby, polo, hockey, and horse riding are limited to students of a few elite schools founded by the British colonial administration.

ENTERTAINMENT

Entertainment is one of those areas where Nigerian teenagers have successfully broken from the past their parents knew. Traditionally, entertainment for teenagers included only community- or village-wide dance groups of boys and girls, age-group activities and festivities, or storytelling and musical shows presented by itinerant artists. In the 1970s and 1980s, groups of teenagers from the same neighborhood sought entertainment by going to theaters to watch movies or by going to Sunday jump dancing. Going to movie theaters is no longer in vogue for today's teens, nor is dancing to popular *highlife* and *Juju* music or learning formal dance steps like the waltz and fox-trot.

Instead, today's teens enjoy watching video movies on the VCR, listening to music on CDs, and going disco dancing in pubs and clubhouses serviced by popular DJs. There are no Blockbusters renting movies and videocassettes. Hence, in many towns and cities, video clubs and movie rental shops, set up as small businesses by teenagers, are springing up in increasing numbers.

Many Nigerian teenagers are current with developments in rap, metal, rock, and pop music. Many also follow the movements of American or international artists and their recordings/songs on rating chart boards as closely as many American teenagers do. Among Nigerian teenagers, Michael Jackson, Britney Spears, Celine Dion, Janet Jackson, Mariah Carey, and pop groups like Destiny's Child, U2, 'NSync, TLC, and the Backstreet Boys are household names. When teens organize dance festivals in school halls, clubs, or village centers, CDs of international artists top their lists.

The older teens, 18- and 20-year-olds, however, do still have some fascination for the music of Nigerian artists, including the late Fela Anikulapo-Kuti, Osayimore Joseph, and King Sunny Ade. This attraction may probably be a result of the captivation of this cohort with the flavor and anti-military lyrics of the local artists. These older teens also patronize club-houses and pubs, where they drink beer and dance. Nigerian girls do not ordinarily go to clubhouses by themselves, even as all-girl groups. This means also that boys do not go to clubhouses hoping to meet girls they didn't know before.

While Nigeria's adult rate of alcoholism is very low compared to rates for adults in American and European societies, the comparative rates between teenagers is even lower. A few Nigerian teenage boys may try beer or some locally brewed alcoholic drinks before they turn 20. Still fewer of them, however, go out of their way to buy and drink beer on a regular basis. With the average temperature during much of the year at 80 degrees Fahrenheit, few Nigerians indulge in alcoholic beverages. Also, binge drinking or boozing in college fraternities and dorms are unheard of in Nigeria. It is estimated that less than 2 percent of Nigerian teenage girls have tasted any alcohol before they turned 18 and even less than 1 percent has smoked more than one cigarette in any one day.[13]

This much lower rate of beer and alcoholic consumption among teenagers may be explained in part by the low living standard of most teens and by the high costs of beer and alcohol in the country. The standard Nigerian 1.5-liter bottle of beer sells for 50 to 60 Naira, equivalent to about 55 U.S. cents. A Nigerian teenager who is in school, who does not work, but depends on his or her parents for all out-of-pocket expenses would rather spend his or her money on renting videocassettes and movies than buy a beer. In the same way, with temperatures between 70 and 100 degrees Fahrenheit, very few Nigerian teenagers are tempted to smoke cigarettes, much less do cocaine, crack, or hashish.

Until 1996 in Nigeria, the use of hard drugs was punishable with the death penalty. Much as Nigeria is now notoriously presented in the Western media as a transit center for drugs from southeast Asia and Latin America bound for the North American and European markets, hard drugs are unavailable to all but possibly a very small number of Nigerian teenagers. The exception to this is marijuana, which is traditionally grown and smoked or used in herbal medicines for treating some ailments in the southern riverine areas. Consequently, the low rate of arrests for the use of hard drugs has been recorded among children of the *nouveau riche*, some of whom spent their earlier years in middle or high schools in Europe or America.

More recently, the explosion of Internet shops in towns and cities has provided teenagers with a new form of entertainment. Few Nigerian families can afford to have telephones and PCs in their homes. Therefore, Internet shops are springing up in many cities and towns to provide Internet access at exorbitant prices for middle- and upper-class children who can afford to pay. Many kids use such facilities to surf for educational materials, for entertainment, and to send e-mail messages to relatives, friends, and pen pals outside the country.

RELIGIOUS PRACTICES AND CULTURAL CEREMONIES

This is another area where indigenous Nigerian cultures have diminished importance among teenagers. Nearly all teenagers have abandoned the traditional ancestral worship and indigenous belief systems of their cultures. Most teenagers, while in school, especially in the Christian south, become converts to the numerous denominations of Christianity that exist in Nigeria today. Since many parents themselves are treating the idol-worshipping associated with traditional belief systems as a relic of the past, children are embracing the break with that aspect of culture without any sense of loss. Thus, joining Christian churches has become the in thing for all non-Muslim teenagers. In the last decade or so, many evangelical churches and prayer houses have sprung up and have become more appealing to teenagers, especially to girls. Many orthodox Christian denominations, such as the Roman Catholic, Anglican, and Methodist churches are losing youths among their congregations to the new evangelical churches because the latter accommodate more congregational participation, singing, and dancing, and feature little liturgy.

In the Muslim north, children naturally follow the Islamic religious faith of their fathers. However, teenagers are not required to become active members of or participants at the mosques, or even attend the *jumat* on Fridays. While a father may insist on taking his son along, daughters are not encouraged to appear in the mosque until they are married or have become old women.

In line with British tradition, the Nigerian government recognizes such Christian festivities as Christmas, Easter, and New Year's Day as public holidays. Similarly, the Muslim festivals of *Eid Fitr* and Ramadan are observed as public holidays. The government has also set aside May 29 of every year for the celebration of the Day of the Youths. On this day, no class activities are carried out in schools. Instead, students from different schools in a town or city will assemble in the city stadium, or town or village field, to listen to an address on some civic lessons from the President of Nigeria. After the address, the salute of Nigeria's national flag, and some cultural performances, the children will be feasted by state authorities.

Every ethnic group has its own annual traditional and cultural festivities. In many cases, these festivities are related more to seasonal agricultural activities and customary rites of passage for boys and girls, or to homecoming by migrants, than to religious practices. The forms that such festivities take and the roles of youth or teenagers in them vary from one culture to the other. In many cases, however, such festivities often entail physical exercises, reenactments of traditions, masquerades, and dances that most teenagers enjoy participating in. Indeed, teenagers, especially those living in cities with their parents, appreciate such opportunities of going back to their home villages to participate in such annual festivities.

CONCLUSION

With its 250 indigenous nations and ethno-cultural societies, Nigeria became a multiculturally diverse nation following the British amalgamation of those societies into the Federal Republic of Nigeria in 1914. To different degrees, many African countries, and indeed many countries the world over, have been founded and developed as multiculturally diverse nations.

The indigenous nationalities and societies who became the Federal Republic of Nigeria had lived at different levels of interrelationships, cooperating in trade, politics, and cultural exchanges, and had occasionally fought wars and made peace with one another before the white man came to the shores of Nigeria. It was in the British colonial amalgamation of these people into a political structure of ethnic majorities and minorities characterizing today's Federal Republic of Nigeria that the multi-ethnic diversity of the country became translated into an instrument of cultural and political power manipulations. The Nigerian political leaders, in their struggle to take over power at independence in 1960, and the military dictators who monopolized political power for 35 years, have merely exploited and exacerbated these religious, linguistic, and ethnic group memberships and educational differences for the purpose of gaining control of the political power of the Nigerian state. But at no time, either in the precolonial era or in the recent past, has Nigeria been like those countries where ethnic warlords control the civil society. This state and civil society distinction provides the framework for a clearer understanding of the Nigerian society and political state structure that provide the social context of teenage life in Nigeria.

Below the state level, in the civil society where Nigerian teenagers live and grow up, multi-ethnic diversities in language and religion are recognized and accommodated in inter-ethnic migrations, inter-ethnic marriages, trades, lifestyles, sports and athletics, and emerging national foods or dishes. Nigerian teenagers are located and identified in civil society through the extended families of which they are members. Civil society protects the Nigerian teenager from the destabilizing social unrests characteristic of Nigerian politics and the state.

Thus, the main determinants of a teenager's life experiences in Nigeria are the extended family system, Western education and lifestyles, Christian or Muslim religion, rural or urban residence, the level of education of parents, and the socioeconomic circumstances of family and gender. Ethnic group of origin becomes relevant only in conjunction with state of origin, as this relates to the north-south dichotomy when the child seeks admission into one of the prestigious federal government colleges.

Across most of Nigeria's ethnic groups, the extended family provides the Nigerian teenager with a stable family heritage in land, with uncles and aunts who accept their responsibility to be there for the teenager, and with the support of cousins beyond that which their nuclear families can provide. The extended family stabilizes the marriages of parents so that, even in the event of a separation or divorce of parents, the extended families protect the teenager against the psychological and economic effects and moral consequences of unstable families. The extended family further socializes the Nigerian teenager to an early sense of responsibility to self, family, and community. The Nigerian teenager, especially if he or she resides in a rural area, is therefore more likely to mature into adulthood earlier than children the same age in the cities or in the Western world.

Western education or schooling provides the Nigerian teenager with a transition from a life dominated by custom and tradition to a life of participation in the Nigerian political economy. At school, he or she is exposed to new peers, new knowledge and values, and new skills or ways of life in the community and in the outside world. Schooling expands the horizon of Nigerian teenagers, exposing them not only to formal education and knowledge but also to the global influences of Western values and culture. Much of Nigerian teenagers' exposure to Western tastes in fashion, music, and entertainment is acquired either directly in school or through peers met in school. It is at school that the teenager becomes exposed to competitive sports and norms of living and participating in the Nigerian polity. For many Nigerian teenagers, school life provides them with lifelong social experiences and enduring friendships.

The extent of a teenager's exposure to the outside world is determined by the factors of residence, the religious affiliation of the parents, and the gender of the child. Rural teenagers are more likely to be tied to tradition and cultural life than city residents. Teenagers with strong Muslim family backgrounds are more limited in their educational and social exposures and orientation. Muslim restrictions are stronger for the teenage girl than for a boy. On the other hand, the values of equality, success, and competition in the socialization of Nigerian children from urban, educated, middle-class Christian families is comparable to the experiences of American children in equivalent age and socioeconomic brackets.

NOTES

1. Federal Ministry of Information, "National Broadcast by His Excellency, President Olusegun Obasanjo on the Occasion of the 40th Anniversary of Nigerian Independence, October 1, 2000." (Abuja, Nigeria: Government Printer, 2000).

2. Nnoli Okwudiba, *Ethnic Politics in Nigeria* (Enugu, Nigeria: Fourth Dimension Publishers, 1977).

3. Ikechukwu Enwemnwa, "Ethnicity and Political Development in Nigeria" (Unpublished thesis, University of Wisconsin, Madison, 1974).

4. Federal Ministry of Information, *Nigeria: Vision 2010 Report* (Lagos: Government Printer, 1999).

5. T. M. Yesufu, *The Nigerian Economy: Growth without Development*, The Benin Social Science Series for Africa (Benin: University of Benin, 1996).

6. Philip E. Leis, *Enculturation and Socialization in Ijo Village* (New York: Holt, Rinehart & Winston, 1972).

7. *Nigeria: Vision 2010 Report.*

8. CIA, *World Factbook*, Nigeria, 2000. In addition see these Web sites: http://www.nigeriaembassyusa.org/f_index.html;   http://www.nidoamericas.org; http://nopa.net; and http://www.nopa.net/Other_Government_Sites/frame.html

9. CIA, *World Factbook*, Nigeria, 1999. In addition see these Web sites: http://www.nigeriaembassyusa.org/f_index.html;   http://www.nidoamericas.org; http://nopa.net; and http://www.nopa.net/Other_Government_Sites/frame.html

10. Omowale Kuye, "What the Constitution Should Look Like," VAN-GUARD: Politics This Week, May 2001: http://www.vanguarngr.com

11. *Nigeria: Vision 2010 Report,* 5.

12. J. J. Macionis, *Sociology* (Upper Saddle River, N.J.: Prentice Hall, 2001): 39.

13. Enwemnwa.

RESOURCE GUIDE

Book

Falola, Toyin. *Culture and Customs of Nigeria.* Westport, Conn.: Greenwood
    Press, 2001.

Web Sites

http://www.nigeriaworld.com
http://www.afbis.com

Chapter 10

SENEGAL

Jacqueline Woodfork

INTRODUCTION

Senegal is a fascinating country in West Africa and teenagers there play a vital role in the life of their nation. Senegalese teenagers go to school, participate in family activities, and are central players in religious, political, and civil life. For many years, Senegal has been a meeting place of many cultures, but the new and growing influence of American culture and its impact on teenagers is worrisome to many. In this chapter, we will look at the nation of Senegal and the teenagers who live there, and we will see how their lives are different from and the same as teenagers in the United States. On the surface, their lives may seem very different; however, they share the same hopes and aspirations as teens everywhere.

The country's official name is the Republic of Senegal. It is the part of West Africa that projects the farthest into the Atlantic Ocean. The nation is a little smaller than the state of South Dakota. Senegal's geographic location has resulted in a fascinating combination of religions and cultures that makes Senegal a unique country in Africa. It includes both the Sahel (the dry area south of the Sahara desert), and the coastal area along the Atlantic. Countries on its borders are Mauritania, Mali, Guinea, and Guinea Bissau. Also, Senegal surrounds the country of The Gambia, except where the two touch the Atlantic Ocean. Senegal's climate is hot and tropical during the rainy season, which lasts from May to November. The other season is typically dry; it is chilly along the coast in the months of December and January.

Senegal is important to West Africa for a number of reasons. Its economy has been relatively stable. Senegal has been a leading force in the

Economic Community of West African States, which links Senegal with other countries. There are a little more than 10 million people who live in Senegal, and approximately 3 million of them live in Dakar. The capital city of Dakar is a trade center, a transportation hub, and a center for education. In 1987, 55 percent of the population of Senegal was under the age of 20.[1]

Senegal is truly a crossroads for Europe, sub-Saharan Africa, and North Africa. Some of the first people in West Africa to embrace Islam were the Senegalese. The country's place along the Atlantic meant that it had some of the first contacts with Europeans. Senegal's residents include people from other African countries and other foreigners such as the French and the Lebanese.[2]

There are many ethnic groups in the country, such as the Wolof, the Serer, the Diola, the Tukulor, and the Lebu. In the precolonial era, Senegal had many powerful kingdoms. These kingdoms interacted with each other and with non-Africans, such as the European sailors who came to the shores of West Africa in search of trade. Eventually the trade in goods changed to a more sinister trafficking, that in human beings. Gorée Island, off the coast of Dakar, was a major slave trading center.

One of the most important changes that took place before the colonial era was the arrival of Islam. Many Senegalese readily accepted this new religion, and they did so for a number of reasons. Certainly, there was true religious sentiment, but conversion also facilitated trade for some; for others, it helped them fit into their communities. No matter what the reason, the religion spread and was well-established in the country when the French arrived and began to colonize the area.

Europeans initially looked for trading opportunities on the west coast of Africa; later they established colonial rule in Senegal and other parts of the continent. Senegal was the center of France's empire in West Africa and that has greatly affected the past and present of the country. The Senegalese reacted to the French in a variety of ways. Some violently opposed the presence of Europeans; leaders such as Lat Dior (who died in 1884) and El-Hadj 'Umar Tall (who died in 1864) led their followers in armed conflict against the French. Eventually France was able to control Senegal. After World War II, the Senegalese demanded political liberation. Senegal and the Sudanese Republic (present-day Mali) were briefly united in the Mali Federation, from April 1959 to August 1960. During this time, France transferred power to its colonies in West Africa. Senegal withdrew from the Mali Federation in August 1960 to become an independent nation state.

GOVERNMENT

Senegal is a multiparty democracy, and it operates under a constitution that was adopted in 1963 and revised in 1991. The president is elected to a seven-year term and can stand for reelection for one additional term. The governing bodies of the country are the *Assemblé Nationale*, akin to the House of Representatives, and the Senate. Senegal has seen two successful and peaceful transitions of presidential power. The first was when the first president of the independent state, Léopold Sédar Senghor, left office and his successor, Abdou Diouf, took power in 1981. The second was when Abdoulaye Wade won the presidential election in March 2001 and Diouf left office.

Muslim leaders play an important role in the government of Senegal. In the colonial era, the government did favors for religious leaders who helped the French administration. Thus, the system was in place at the time of independence. Politicians court the heads of Muslim brotherhoods and hope to have these leaders endorse them and their policies, thereby getting their followers to vote for them. Muslims in Senegal see no difficulty in mixing religion and politics.

Students and teachers play an important, if unofficial, role in government because their lives are greatly affected by government decisions about education. The university in Dakar, the Université Chiekh Anta Diop, named after a famous Senegalese historian, has been the site of many political demonstrations by students. In the late 1990s, students and their instructors often went on strike to protest a number of issues, including the increasing costs of university education and teacher shortages. Because of budget problems, the government has had difficulty in meeting all of the university's needs.

ECONOMY

Senegal is a developing country whose government has to make difficult choices about how to spend its limited money. Senegal is primarily an agricultural economy, but industry in the cities, especially Dakar, is increasing. These industries include the processing of agricultural products and petroleum refining. The main crops that people grow for food are sorghum, millet, rice, cassava, and corn. People also raise cattle, goats, and sheep. Peanuts are the most important agricultural product in Senegal's export economy. For the foreign export market, the Senegalese coastal fishing industry sends much of its catch to Europe.

Compared to the drier, Sahelian regions of Senegal, the economy of the coastal area is strong. People who live in the coastal area have more economic opportunities than the people in the interior of the country. Because of the relative lack of poverty along the coast, it is easier to find medical care, hospitals, public schools, and maternity clinics. Maritime Senegal has good ports and fishing. There is also the attraction of its beaches. Tourism is an important part of the economy of Senegal, and its often mild weather, especially during the winter months, draws many Africans and Europeans to the country for vacation.

In the interior where the population density is high, young people who would like to farm for a living are concerned that they will not have enough land to feed their families, never mind growing surplus crops to pay for other things that they need or want. Because of these uncertainties, many young people choose to migrate to urban areas in search of employment. In rural areas, village elders and the government are trying to find ways to stem the tide of urban migration. One solution has been forming training programs in rural areas.

Both Senegalese teens and adults think a lot about finding work. Unemployment rates in Senegal have increased because of drought condi-

Teen in Senegal carving wood. Courtesy of A. Olusegun Fayemi.

tions, and farming has also suffered. The drought has led many to move to cities in search of employment. Many of those who migrate to urban areas end up working in the informal sector. That means they sell goods in marketplaces or become street vendors. Unemployment has hit teens the hardest of any working age group; almost one half are looking for jobs.

Now many young people are migrating to cities in search of work. It is easier to find jobs with wages in urban areas. This urbanization has left more of the very old and the very young in villages. Many who have spent some time in cities do not wish to return to village life because they find it dull or they do not think that farming is how they want to make their living. There is a gap in each family that has a member leave and live elsewhere.

Finding employment for the youth of Senegal has been an enormous challenge for the country. Each year, nearly 100,000 people enter the job market, and almost all of them are under the age of 25. At the end of the 1980s, 25,000 high school and college graduates competed for 4,000 to 5,000 job openings in the formal sector. Because of the poor outlook for jobs, many Senegalese university students stay in school for as long as they can. With an ever-larger number of people seeking university degrees, the problem will continue to grow.[3] Some university graduates look for work overseas, particularly in France and the United States. While this solution can be a great advantage because they can earn high salaries and send money home to their families, it is also a problem because it creates a "brain drain" from the country. Adjusting to life in a foreign country can be very difficult for young people who have moved overseas alone.

CHALLENGES FOR TEENS IN SENEGAL

There really is no such thing as a stranger in Senegal, only a guest, and the Senegalese are very proud of their hospitality, *teranga*. In a country where there is so much emphasis on being kind to each other, on reciprocal obligations, and maintaining good relationships, social tensions are particularly difficult to accept. Some problems stem from economic difficulties, some from politics, and some of the most significant are about cultural change.

Many teenagers in Senegal are seeing rapid changes in their country and they are worried about their futures. Equally, older Senegalese people are worried about these changes, and they tend to see youth as less moral and serious than themselves when they were the same age. Older people often claim that alcohol and drugs are ruining the country's youth. An equally serious potential problem is disease.

One of the areas in which Senegal has made a lot of progress is in the prevention of HIV/AIDS. The country's remarkable progress in preventing the spread of the disease comes in part from rap musicians. These rappers have spread the word, through their music, about the disease and how to prevent it. The government deserves a lot of the credit for helping to contain the disease. The government of Senegal quickly became involved in the fight to prevent HIV/AIDS, and its program easily could be a role model for other countries. Today Senegal has one of the lowest rates of infection on the continent, under 2 percent.[4]

Senegal has been fortunate to have fewer problems with HIV/AIDS and armed conflict than some of its neighbors, but problems do exist. Young people experience tremendous hardships during civil strife. School, farming, marketing activities, and other regular aspects of life are all interrupted. There is also bodily injury and loss of life. In the Casamance region, an armed separatist movement started in 1982. The Diola people of the Casamance were very involved in the struggle for independence from the Senegalese nation. The people of the Casamance resented the lack of resources allocated to them by the national government and the influence of emigrants and government workers in the area. People believed that Senegalese from other parts of the country were threatening their traditional way of life, their religion, and the natural resources of the area. There have been occasional outbreaks of fighting while people search for peaceful solutions.

Another incident of unrest was in 1989, when the killing of Moorish shopkeepers in Dakar led to the departure of the rest of the Moorish population. Moors are people from Mauritania who often have lighter skin than the Senegalese. Although the Senegalese and the Mauritanians in Senegal often held negative opinions about each other, relations between the two were usually cordial. One cause of the problem was the expansion of agriculture on both sides of the Senegal River, which separates Senegal from Mauritania. In Mauritania, Moors discriminated against the black African population—the Wolof, Soninke, Peuhl, and Tukulor farmers whose land they wanted to take. In April 1989, Mauritanian soldiers killed two Senegalese who were in a village in Mauritania. Villages on both sides of the river responded with reprisals against "foreign" villagers. Rioters in Nouakchott, the capital of Mauritania, retaliated by assaulting and killing numerous Senegalese and dark-skinned Mauritanians. In Senegal, the response to this action was the looting of Mauritanian shops and the revenge killings of Mauritanians. The violence continued until the two countries exchanged populations across the border. Since then, tensions have decreased and people are going about their everyday lives.

TYPICAL DAY

The typical day for teens varies considerably, depending on where they live and whether or not they go to school. Nevertheless, most teens rise early in the morning. Those who attend school have to do their chores and get ready for school. Those who work in the home must begin the many activities it takes to keep a household running. Teens who work in agriculture or fishing need to start the journey that will take them to the fields or to the sea.

Many teens head to school after their morning chores. In urban areas, students go to school on public transportation, sometimes city buses or privately run vans (*car rapides*) that act as public transportation. There are not many privately owned vehicles in Senegal, so students do not have the luxury of driving themselves to school. Students are in school from approximately 8:00 in the morning until 3:00 in the afternoon. For the midday meal, a few students go to restaurants close to school, while the majority bring food from home. Then they return to classes until 3:00. This is a recent development. Students used to start school at 8:00 and go to classes until noon, at which time they would go home and eat lunch with their families. Students had the opportunity to do some schoolwork, chores, or simply relax with family and friends before returning to school at 3:00 in the afternoon for two more hours of classes. This change, which has the school day looking more like it does in the United States, is more evidence to some of how Senegalese society is becoming Westernized. Those who support the change claim that this schedule is better, especially because students have fewer transportation costs and spend less time traveling.

When the school day is over, Senegalese teenagers still have a lot of work to do. There are usually chores to do at home. Teens generally have at least two hours of homework to do at night, and often a lot more. Senegalese high-school students like to study in groups; they will often drink tea, eat snacks, and do a bit of socializing while they get their homework done.

Teens who do not go to school are very active as well. There is a gendered division of labor in Senegal, and teens' tasks are divided into men's and women's work. Girls help with the household chores, which can be very time-consuming in rural areas of Senegal. In places without running

Girls in Senegal haul sticks for firewood. Courtesy of A. Olusegun Fayemi.

water, girls and women often have to walk long distances to fill containers and bring them back to the house. They carry heavy basins on their
heads, and some also carry pails in their hands. Balance is very important—if there is a pail in one hand, there should be one in the other and
they should weigh the same. This helps to even out the load. It is a real
misfortune if a water pail or basin spills. Not only is it a waste of a precious
resource, but it is a waste of labor because the person must go back to the
water source for more. Women are in charge of farming and domestic activities, including food preparation, clothes washing, home repair, the
collection of firewood for cooking, and anything related to the house.
Women and girls also participate in marketing activities, both as buyers
and sellers.

Young men have different responsibilities. Some young men are often
responsible for the families' herds. Some travel long distances to find grazing land, while others make day trips to places where the herds can find
food. Males are also responsible for growing cash crops, in this way bringing money into the household economy.

Some teens, particularly girls, work outside the home or the home economy. Girls will often work in the home of another person, a family member or a person who does not have a blood relationship with the girl. These girls work as domestics, performing the types of chores that they would do at home: cooking, washing clothes, doing the marketing, taking care of children, and cleaning the house. In households where there are servants, mothers still make sure that their daughters know how to do all the activities needed to keep the house running, in part because the daughter may need to do these things for herself some day, but also because it is good training for supervising those who will work in her household in the future.

FAMILY LIFE

The most important unit of Senegalese society is the family and the Senegalese typically live in extended family systems. Unlike in the United States, where a family usually consists of parents and their children, the Senegalese family has the same units as Americans plus aunts, uncles, grandparents, nieces, and nephews. These extended families, especially in rural areas, live in the same compound, which encompasses a number of houses. Extended family members are so close that those whom Americans would call "aunt" or "uncle" are "mother" and "father" to the Senegalese, while a cousin is referred to as a brother or sister. The core of the polygynous family (or family with more than one wife) is the mother and her children. The bonds between the mother and her children and the children to each other are incredibly strong. There is competition between siblings, as there is in all societies, but the group presents a united front to people from outside their immediate family.

One important way of reinforcing the family bond is eating together, and meals are very important to family unity. Those who can come home during the day for the midday meal do so. Everyone looks forward to the evening meal. The Senegalese eat late, perhaps to ensure that every family member can be home for the evening meal. Dinner is usually eaten between 9:00 and 10:00 at night. After that, there is tea, relaxing, and conversation. Most Senegalese are Muslims, and they do not drink alcohol.

Families of different socioeconomic levels live different lives. The more affluent families may have running water, electricity, automobiles, and larger homes. In the extended family system, there is a way to spread wealth around the family. If there is a family member who makes a good living in a city, relatives from the village may send their children to live with that person. The children go to school and help out around the house.

People who live in cities often visit their relatives in rural areas, bringing with them things from the city such as electric fans, luxury goods, or simply money, which goes to the family. When they return, they carry with them food items they would otherwise have to buy in the city. This system shares the wealth and allows people to display their generosity by helping family members.

Family life has changed somewhat in the last few years because of changing economic situations. One change has been in the number of polygynous marriages and the number of wives in these marriages. Both Islam and traditional religions allow a man to have more than one wife. The first wife or wives should approve of the new addition to the family. Another consideration is that the husband must have enough money to marry another wife. The understanding is that the husband must be able to take care of all wives as well as the first one—that no wife or child should suffer or receive less support by adding another wife to the family.

Teens in Senegal meet each other as friends and potential mates in many ways. Senegalese parents generally do not keep tight reins on their teens, who have the freedom to meet people at school, dances, and other events. Many teens meet the people they spend time with in their homes or the homes of relatives or family friends.

One way in which youth and their elders diverge is in what they look for in marriage partners. Teens are now meeting and selecting their mates on their own, whereas previous generations had more family involvement in the selection process. This was because marriage was not seen just as the union of two people, but the union of two families. Therefore, it is a major decision with many issues to consider. Adolescents in Senegal, especially in urban areas, are less concerned about the castes and ethnic groups of prospective partners than previous generations. Although times have changed, family approval is still important. Both males and females very much want to get married and have children.

In Senegal's family code, a girl cannot marry if she is younger than 16 years old, and there must be agreement about whether the marriage will be monogamous or not. Yet many girls in rural areas get married before the legal age, and the agreement about the form of marriage rarely happens.[5] The average age at which women marry depends mostly on where they live and how much education they have. Girls who go to school marry later, as do those who live in urban areas. Some girls move to cities to get jobs and accumulate goods to bring to their new households before they get married.[6]

Some young women see marriage as a way to change their circumstances; for example, in rural areas, they may look for marriages that will take them to an urban area. Some girls see marriage as a way to move out of the constraints of living with their families, or to improve their financial conditions.

Although virginity is highly prized in Senegalese society, the Senegalese usually do not pass judgment on the children produced from sexual relations out of wedlock.[7] Yet not being a virgin can have an impact on a girl's marriageability, as nonvirgins cannot legally have a Muslim wedding.

The overwhelming urge to marry comes from social norms; people are expected to get married and have children. For a woman, bearing children secures her place as a member of her husband's family and acceptance from her in-laws, especially her mother- and father-in-law. For a man, children are tangible proof of his virility as well as a source of wealth. For parents who live in rural areas, children are important sources of labor on family farms. But children are also a sort of wealth because of the prestige attached to being a parent. Having a large family is the same as having a large resource network that can provide love and support.

TRADITIONAL AND NONTRADITIONAL FOOD DISHES

Food and the sharing of meals are very important parts of Senegalese culture. The food in Senegal is very tasty and interesting, in part because North African and sub-Saharan African cuisines meet in Senegal, producing fantastic combinations of spices, tastes, and dishes. More recently, the French influence has made an impact on the food that the Senegalese eat (the Senegalese are as enthusiastic about baguettes as the French), but the Senegalese continue to enjoy traditional foods. In urban areas, there are fast-food restaurants that serve burgers, pizza, and Lebanese dishes like *shawarma,* which is roasted lamb marinated in lemon juice, garlic, and other spices, served with sauce and fries wrapped in pita bread. (Yes, the fries are wrapped in the bread with the meat!)

Bread, butter, jam, and coffee or tea are commonly eaten by city dwellers for breakfast. The Senegalese national dish is *ceebujen* (which means rice and fish in Wolof, one of Senegal's indigenous languages), a delicious dish consisting of rice made with a tomato base, surrounded by vegetables and topped with a fish stuffed with spices. It is so popular that many Senegalese eat *ceebujen* for lunch and dinner. Chicken yassa is another popular dish; pieces of chicken are marinated in lime juice and grilled and then served over rice. *Mafé,* a peanut-based sauce made with chicken, beef, or lamb and served over rice, is a favorite of many. Most Westerners really like Senegalese foods, although two dishes that often take getting used to are *lakh* and *thiakry*. *Lakh* is a dish prepared from roughly kneaded millet flour that is then cooked in water and eaten with curds. *Thiakry*, similar to *lakh*, is prepared by mixing sweetened curds with well-kneaded millet flour and steaming it.

Food in Senegal comes from a number of different places. Much of the produce in Senegal comes from the Casamance region. People in rural areas are accustomed to eating locally produced grains, like millet, while people in urban areas are very much dependent on rice imported from Vietnam, once a French colony. Imported luxury foods come from Europe and the United States. Senegal's coastline provides much of the fish that the people consume. People also eat lamb, chicken, and some beef. There are almost no pigs in Senegal because Muslims do not eat pork.

Some people in urban areas eat in the Western style, at a table with flatware and individual plates. More often people eat from a large, circular, communal platter. People sit on the floor at the edges of the platter and eat with their hands. Hand washing before and after the meal is imperative.

There is etiquette to eating from the communal bowl. People must eat with the right hand only; the Senegalese believe that the left hand is unclean. Also, a meal is not a free-for-all: if you see a large chunk of fish resting in front of a fellow diner, you cannot reach and take that food. The highest-ranking woman in the household serves as director of the meal, keeping an eye on all those who are eating and pushing choice tidbits toward guests.

After meals comes tea, or *ataaya*. One person is in charge of preparing the tea, Chinese green tea prepared with fresh mint and sugar. A small kettle is placed on a portable coalpot stove to boil. The person who prepares the tea pours it from a great height so that there is a frothy head on each glass. Three rounds of tea are served in short glasses. Each round is sweeter than the one that preceded it, but since the leaves are not changed, the tea gets weaker. The first glass is very strong and bitter, the last is weaker, but *very* sweet. Because it takes a long time to prepare the tea, people sometimes call it a ceremony; it is a time when people relax after the meal and talk. It is proper to consume all three glasses; leaving after only two may offend the host. This tea is a good example of Senegal's mixed legacy because it is a custom they adopted from the people of northern Africa. Like people in other parts of the world, after the noon meal, the Senegalese have a siesta, or a rest period, before they return to their jobs.

SCHOOLING

As is the case in the rest of the world, Senegalese parents want their children to go to school. Both parents and teens realize that education can open many doors of opportunity, but it is not always easy for Senegalese teens to go to school. Who gets to go to school often depends upon whose families have the means to excuse children from participating in activities that help the household. When there are many children of school age in a family, some difficult decisions must be made.

There are a variety of schools that teens can attend in Senegal. Many start their Western educations after attending Koranic (Islamic) school. Because many parents believe that it is best to learn the Koran (Islam's holy book) before going to secular school, boys and girls start Koranic school when they are 2 to 3 years old and stay for four years. Some people attend Western and Koranic schools simultaneously. People believe that it is as important for girls to learn the Koran as it is for boys.

There are also technical courses and schools which prepare young people for a variety of careers, from working in the airline industry to agriculture to computer programming. Many students choose academic training for high school. They take the same kinds of courses that American students take, but most have more foreign-language classes to choose from, including Arabic and Russian. After school, students have many extracurricular activities, such as drama and organized athletics.

Secondary schools in Senegal have a curriculum inherited from the French during colonization. Schools are elitist and not very well adapted to the needs of the Senegalese students. Secondary school lasts for seven years and is divided into a four-year lower-level program and a three-year upper-level program. The end of the three-year cycle is the baccalaureate examination. This exam is quite difficult and competitive, and passing it offers access to higher education.

SOCIAL LIFE

Senegalese society is highly stratified and people know what their social niche is. Nonetheless, the interaction of people of different social classes takes place on a daily basis, although these interactions may not be profound. Within the household, residents and domestic servants interact daily. Teens participate in this dynamic in their households, and to some extent at school, mostly in public settings like football games and markets.

The Senegalese believe that people should dress appropriately for all occasions and that one's dress should reflect one's status in society. While a mixture of African and Western styles can be seen in the streets, religious celebrations such as funerals, baptisms, and other momentous events usually find their participants in traditionally styled clothes. The style of dress that teenagers adopt depends upon their families' means, their religion, and their level of Westernization. The styles that are available and acceptable in Dakar may raise eyebrows in more rural areas.

Women who are traditional usually wear skirts and dresses that cover their knees and usually fall close to the ankle. The *boubou* is a favorite of girls and women in Senegal. *Boubous* are made from many meters of cloth that cover the body from the shoulders to the ankles and from the wrist of the right hand to the wrist of the left; although there is a great deal of cloth, tailoring makes the garments fashionable and flattering. Often there is intricate embroidery around the shoulders, wrists, and hemline. The cloth is produced either locally or overseas. Plain cotton is the most popular material, and damask is also highly sought-after. Women and girls do not usually wear pants. Shorts are not acceptable for adults of either sex, no matter how hot it is. Traditional and Western dress both are worn in Dakar, but the majority of women who favor Western styles are young or working professionals. Students who attend Western-style primary and secondary schools wear uniforms that are very much like the uniforms that some American children wear to school. Men also have the option of traditional versus Western clothes. Traditional clothing for men is a different version of the *boubou*, a long robe worn with a shirt and pants underneath. Often those who wear Western-style clothing to work change into African clothes when they go home in the evening.

The fashion industry in Senegal combines Western and Senegalese elements to create unique clothes. Very often designers do this by combining Western styles, such as shorter skirts, with traditional African prints and cloth. The results are outstanding. These items are usually out of the price range for teens.

Hair is very important as well. Girls have many more options for hairstyles than boys. Girls create elaborate hairstyles from braids. Beads are often added for ornamentation. These elaborate hairstyles take a long time to create, and female family members and friends do the braiding, allowing women a chance to gather and socialize. Although women may have complicated hairstyles, some opt to cover their heads. These women wrap their heads with cloth, elaborately tied, that matches the outfits they are wearing. This is particularly the case for women who wear traditional clothing. Leather sandals are popular footwear. Jewelry is the last item to

Girls in Senegal braiding hair. Courtesy of A. Olusegun Fayemi.

add to the outfit, but not the least important. The Senegalese value gold very highly, although silver, copper, and iron are also used. The country's highly skilled jewelers create pieces that perfectly compliment many kinds of outfits.

RECREATION

Senegalese teens enjoy recreational activities just as much as American teens do. Many of their activities are the same, though one difference is in telephone use. Not all teens have phones in their homes, and those who do know that telephones are luxury items and fairly expensive. Phone users are charged by the minute, so parents limit the amount of time teens can spend on the phone. In Senegal, there are *télécentres* instead of public telephone booths. Some Senegalese teens have cell phones.

Sports are a major form of recreation in Senegal. The sports scene in the country reflects the various cultural influences. Senegalese of all ages enjoy sporting events. Those who cannot see games or matches in person often listen to them on the radio.

The French introduced soccer to Senegal and it is popular in both rural and urban areas, in part because it is an inexpensive and easily accessible sport. Villages have youth teams that compete against each other in the hopes of going to the country's national championship match. Senegal's performance in the 2002 World Cup, in which it won the match against France, raised hopes for the future of teens playing the sport.

More recently, basketball has been growing in popularity in Senegal, and not just as a spectator sport. Many people play basketball, especially young adults. Some young Senegalese men dream about making their way to the United States to be professional basketball players, following the example of DeSaganna Ngagne Diop. Diop's mother is an accountant and his father is a high school principal. They moved to the United States so that Diop could have an opportunity to play in the National Basketball

Senegal teens playing basketball. Courtesy of A. Olusegun Fayemi.

Association. He was successful in his quest and joined the Cleveland Cavaliers when he was selected in the first round of the 2001 draft.

Canoe racing is well liked and draws crowds to the shores to watch the competition. Some canoes are small and have few rowers, while others are large and have many. Often, one village rows against another. These canoes are specially designed and brightly painted. The oarsmen seek the blessings of a patron, usually a local saint or hero, by naming the canoe after that person.

Wrestling, known as *beré*, is an ancient art in Senegal; it combines athletic skill with spectacle. People often refer to this sport in French as *la lutte*. Each wrestler has an entourage of people who follow him to the matches. These followers include praise singers who sing about his courage, strength, and past feats in an effort to psychologically intimidate the other opponent, much the way American boxers do in prematch publicity. One of the most well known wrestlers is Mohammed Ndao, who adopted the name of the American boxer Mike Tyson.

Mike Tyson is known throughout the country for fighting while wearing an American flag. His entourage also makes clothes from the American flag. These young men refer to themselves as *boulfalé*, which means "boys who don't care" about their traditions and who prefer to take their inspiration from American culture.[8]

Punching used to be forbidden in these matches, but because it pleases modern audiences, punches have made their way into the sport. Even in sports, there is a battle about traditions and new ways. Traditionalists, mostly older people, dislike the money and hype that surround today's wrestling matches and long for wrestlers to compete for the pride of the family, village, or ethnic group. In either case, traditional or modern, wrestling is a great form of entertainment for the Senegalese.

ENTERTAINMENT

Many teens in urban areas of Senegal use the Internet. There are Internet cafés along many streets and access is quite easy, although not everyone can easily afford to buy an hour of time online. Senegalese teens learn a lot about the world outside their country via the Internet. In this way, they are able to keep up with news and events that are not shown on the Senegalese information networks. Senegalese teens know a lot about teenagers in the United States, but they also keep up with political and cultural events in America. Senegalese teens believe that Americans do not know as much about the Senegalese people and their lives as the Senegalese know about the United States and Americans.

Many Senegalese listen to the radio for news and music. Televisions are less common than in the United States. People may visit friends and relatives who have television sets if there is a program that they want to watch. In more rural places, people may gather at a public place to watch TV. There are programs from Senegal, France, Mexico, and the United States. People who have satellite access can receive stations from Morocco, Saudi Arabia, the United States, France, and other European countries.

Music is a very important aspect of Senegalese cultural life. Adolescents and other Senegalese people learn about their culture and heritage from *griots*, oral historians and musicians who teach people through their performances. The Senegalese listen to many types of music, and Cuban

Senegalese teen playing an instrument. Courtesy of A. Olusegun Fayemi.

music is very popular. Youssou Ndour is one of Senegal's biggest pop music stars and his audience enjoys his mixing of traditional *mbalaax* music with Western soul, pop, and rock. Baaba Maal, another popular Senegalese musician, has traveled throughout the country to talk with people about HIV/AIDS. The music industry in Senegal has grown very quickly in the last few years and Senegalese singers such as Ndour and Maal have gained respect and listeners across the world. Compacts disks are available, but most people purchase cassettes, which are easy to find in markets and from street vendors. Also popular are live performances using traditional instruments such as the *kora* (a type of lute), the xylophone, and the many varieties of Senegalese drums.

Senegalese youth use music as a way of expressing displeasure, like young people throughout the world. One way that they do this is with rap music. Rap has become increasingly popular and it is an influence that older people point to as an example that the youth of Senegal are being seduced by American culture. Rappers in Senegal insist that a major difference between their music and that of American rappers is that their lyrics are trying to reach a teenage audience and encourage young adults to be upstanding people. One such group is Positive Black Soul, a duo of young men from Dakar. The former college students tour frequently in West Africa and have also gone to South Africa and Europe. They explain that rap may seem to be an odd choice as a musical form for Africans, but it is actually well suited to their musical needs. Because *mbalaax* music is often used to sing the praises of wealthy patrons, it is limited in its ability to criticize social or political institutions, unlike rap. Like other young Senegalese people, Positive Black Soul is concerned with issues like pan-Africanism, materialism, and the negative images of Africa that persist in the world today.[9] The group sings in Wolof, French, and English, reflecting the linguistic trend among the youth of the country.

The Senegalese enjoy maintaining aspects of their traditional culture, and dance is one of the ways that they do this. Dancing is a favorite form of recreation in both rural and urban areas. Sometimes there are organized performances by the national ballet company, or another dance troupe. The Senegalese use any chance they can to have a dance party. People in rural areas will often gather in a wide, sandy opening to dance.

In urban areas, there are dance clubs for those teens whose parents allow them to go. Some have live music, while others offer recorded Western music or African, especially Senegalese, music. Going to these clubs can pose an economic hardship because they often have entrance fees. Thus, the ability to go out to these places depends not only on parental permission but on having the money to get in the door and perhaps to purchase soft drinks.

In rural areas, conversation and storytelling have endured as a major form of entertainment that has not changed in many, many years. Story-telling is not just the recounting of an event; in Senegal it is an art. Some storytellers are *griots,* men and women who have been trained from a young age to tell the histories of families and ethnic groups and play music to accompany their tales. These *griots* memorize stories accompanied by music, often the *kora.* The audience is not passive during the perfor-mance, they participate in it. The audience responds to the *griot's* story and the *griot* reacts to the audience as much as the audience to the *griot.* However, not all storytelling comes from the *griot.* People will recount tales whenever they can, entertaining each other through words.

RELIGIOUS PRACTICES AND CULTURAL CEREMONIES

The two main religions in Senegal are Islam and Christianity, and the overwhelming majority of the population is Muslim. Though there are some tensions between the two groups, there is still a general spirit of re-ligious tolerance, and Muslim and Christian people in Senegal generally get along very well. There are some who practice "traditional" religions or religions that existed before the arrival of Islam and Christianity, but they are few and many have converted to one of the two major world religions.

Most Christians in the country are Catholic, and they comprise only about 5 percent of the population. Catholic Senegalese tend to live in urban areas such as Dakar, Thiès, Mbour, and the lower Casamance in southern Senegal. Many Senegalese believe that Catholicism and colo-nialism are very closely tied, because Europeans, especially French colo-nizers, brought the religion to the land. Those Senegalese who converted to Christianity often had more educational opportunities and were more likely to get jobs working for the French. Thus, Senegalese Christians continue to be seen as favoring colonialism or the West. Those who op-posed the French presence often chose a religion that was in opposition to the French presence: Islam.

Senegal is one of the first places to which Islam went in West Africa and it is one of the most Muslim countries in West Africa. Many who fought colonialism, such as Cheikh Amadou Bamba and El-Hadj 'Umar Tall, were Muslims. It is important to note that no Christians are believed to have been early resistors to the French presence. In more recent history, however, Catholics such as the first president of independent Senegal, Léopold Sédar Senghor, were instrumental in the country's inde-pendence from France in 1960.

Senegalese Muslims practice the same rites as Muslims in other parts of the world. Many of the religious holidays involve families interacting with other people, so in a sense religious holidays are social events. One special event is *Korité* (Eid-al-Fatr), the last day of Ramadan, the month of fasting observed by every Muslim once a year. During Ramadan, people abstain from food, water, smoking, and sexual relationships during daylight hours. Ramadan is a time for spiritual reflection and cleansing. For *Korité*, the men in the family go to the mosque to pray and eat *laax* when they return. A big feast takes place in the middle of the day. After that people go to visit their friends and neighbors. They greet the people they meet by saying "Dewenati" or "May God grant us life for the next year." Because it is an important holiday and time of social interaction, people save their money to buy a special outfit for the day.

Tabaski (Eid-al-Adha) is the Feast of the Sacrifice. The feast takes place two months and 10 days after *Korité*. It is celebrated in honor of the sacrifice that Abraham was willing to make to fulfill the will of God. The day starts with prayers in the mosque followed by the ritual slaughtering of a ram. The meat is shared with neighbors and some is saved to be cooked for the family's feast. Each family tries very hard to save money to buy a ram and new clothes for *Tabaski*.

Islam has seen a phenomenal growth in Senegal since the country gained independence in 1960. While the political and intellectual elite remain committed to a secular state, some Muslims want the state to become an Islamic one. One interesting phenomenon is that Muslim teenage girls are choosing to wear veils. Veils are appearing in secondary schools and universities. These young women are choosing to display that they are good Muslims and will be good Muslim wives, even though they have chosen the path of Western education that might lead to a well-paying job. While many adults complain that teenagers are turning to the West for role models and that their morals are eroding because of it, the wearing of the veil is a clear example of a conservative choice that adolescent girls have made.

Some Muslim teens are choosing to follow the teachings of the Mouride sect. The sect was founded at the beginning of the twentieth century, and its center is in the city of Touba where there is a fantastic mosque. The Mourides' philosophy is to include everyone, to accept anyone into the sect. Mourides believe that it is important to submit to a religious guide who accepts the followers' devotion and agrees to intercede on their behalf. The Mourides give offerings to their guide and work for him. They often work on collective farms and are responsible for much of the peanut production in the country.

One part of the Muslim brotherhood are the Baay Fall. They forsake the five pillars of Islam in favor of dedicating themselves to their spiritual leader. The Baay Fall believe that they will find salvation by doing everything that their leaders ask of them. They are easy to recognize—they wear multi-colored robes and stocking caps over their dredlocks. Many Senegalese disapprove of the Baay Fall because of their aggressive requests for money and playing music in the streets, while others applaud them for their religious devotion.

A yearly pilgrimage of Mourides, the *Magal* (to celebrate the return of Chiekh Amadou Bamba, the founder, from exile), to the city of Touba, takes place 48 days after the Islamic New Year. Touba is a sacred city in the interior of the country, in the heart of the peanut-growing region. This day commemorates the return of a Senegalese hero, Cheikh Amadou Bamba, to his homeland from exile by the French colonial government. The route that the pilgrims take is the same that Bamba walked when he went home. Bamba always opposed French colonial rule, and he proposed that Islam was a way to achieve his goal of ousting the Europeans. The number of Mourides in Senegal continues to grow and teens are a large part of that group. Although older generations voice their concerns about teens today, it is clear that there are many devoutly Muslim adolescents in Senegal.

Teens in Senegal deplore the events of September 11, 2001. They disagree with the methods used, but believe that the United States needs to be more aware of how its policies have affected Muslims in the Middle East.

CONCLUSION

No matter what their religion or whether or not they go to school, teenagers in Senegal share many traits and interests with other teens across the globe. They wish to live in a just and fair society, want interesting jobs, and want to get married and have families. Senegalese teens face challenges that do not exist in other areas of the world, but they also enjoy advantages that people do not find elsewhere. The economic situation of the country often prevents teens from doing all the things they want to do. Teens will have to find a way of balancing the traditional Senegalese culture they admire and enjoy with aspects of Western culture that now coexist in the country. In general, young people are more accepting of the influence of the West than the older generations. That influence once came from France, but now the United States is very important. English words are slipping into the vocabulary of Senegalese teens. They discuss Michael Jordan and American rappers as much as they talk about Senegalese sports heroes and musicians. While teens enjoy some aspects of Western culture, they have a deep respect and love for Senegalese culture.

In the past, Senegal has had a very successful meeting of cultures, and there is no reason to expect that this group of young people will not be as successful as previous generations. In the words of teenager Boubacar Sanga: "Yes, I may wear my baseball cap backwards, but I know my culture tells me to be faithful, respect your mother and father, say prayers, don't drink alcohol, don't just eat anything, don't dance anyhow, respect others and respect yourself. That's what my culture tells me."[10]

NOTES

1. Amy Wright, *The Girls of Jeunesse Action: A Sociological Study of Street Youth in Dakar* (Dakar: ENDA, 1987): 1.

2. When the French were in power in Senegal, they invited the Lebanese to come and work as merchants in the country. They remain to this day, although many Senegalese people resent the economic power that the Lebanese have.

3. Sheldon Gellar, *Senegal: An African Nation between Islam and the West* (Boulder: Westport Press, 1995): 124.

4. "Senegal Contains the Spread of HIV," http://www.who.int/inf-new/aids3.htm

5. Barbara Callaway and Lucy Creevy, *The Heritage of Islam: Women, Religion, and Politics in West Africa* (Boulder: Lynne Rienner Publishers, 1994): 37.

6. Giles Pison et al., *Population Dynamics of Senegal* (Washington: National Academy Press, 1995): 83–85.

7. Wright, 24.

8. Rosalind D. Muhammad, "Culture Clash—How American Culture Is Seducing African Youth," from *Final Call*, June 8, 1999, http://www.ncmonline.com/in-depth/1999–06–11/clash.html

9. "Positive Black Soul Biog," http://www.urbanimage.tv/backgrounds/Positive-Black-Soul-Biog.htm

10. "Pop Stars and Youth Break Taboos to Spread AIDS Message," http://www.reggaeontheriver.com/year2000artist/PositiveBlackSoul.htm

RESOURCE GUIDE

Articles

The Associated Press. "Senegal Celebrates WCup Advance." June 11, 2002.

Creevey, Lucy E. "The Impact of Islam on Women in Senegal." *The Journal of Developing Areas* 23 (April 1991): 347–68.

Klein, Chrescht. "Dakar's Kermel Market: The Rediscovered Soul of a Witness to History." *Courier: Africa, Caribbean, Pacific European Union* 163 (May–June 1997): 68–70.

McLaughlin, Fiona. "Islam and Popular Music in Senegal: The Emergence of a New Tradition." *Africa* 67, 4 (1997): 560–81.

Moszynski, Peter. "The Making of Baaba Maal." *West Africa* 3921 (November, 1992): 9–15.

N'Dour, Youssou, Sophie Boukhari, and Seydou Amadou Oumarou. "Youssou N'Dour: Africa's World Musician." *UNESCO Courrier* (July–August 1998): 78–82.

Novick, Adam. "Sabar drums, sabar culture." *Traditions* 6 (May 1997): 10–13.

Parker, Ron. "The Senegal-Mauritania Conflict of 1989: A Fragile Equilibrium." *Journal of Modern African Studies* 29, 1 (March 1991): 155–71.

Pop Stars and Youth Break Taboos to Spread AIDS Message, http://www .reggaeontheriver.com/year2000artist/PositiveBlackSoul.htm

"Senegal Contains the Spread of HIV," http://www.who.int/inf-new/aids3.htm

Urbanimage.com. "Positive Black Soul Biog.," http://www.urbanimage.tv /backgrounds/Positive-Black-Soul-Biog.htm

Books

Berg, Elizabeth. *Senegal.* New York: Marshall Cavendish, 1999.

Brownlie, Alison. *Senegal.* Crystal Lake, Ill.: Rigby Interactive Library, 1997.

Callaway, Barbara, and Lucy Creevy. *The Heritage of Islam: Women, Religion, and Politics in West Africa.* Boulder, Colo.: Lynne Rienner Publishers, 1994.

Else, David. *Lonely Planet: The Gambia and Senegal.* Oakland, Calif.: Lonely Planet, 1999.

Gellar, Sheldon. *Senegal: An African Nation between Islam and the West.* Boulder: Westview Press, 1995.

Gordon, Eugene. *Senegal in Pictures.* Minneapolis: Lerner, 1988.

Koslow, Philip. *Senegambia: Land of the Lion.* Philadelphia: Chelsea House, 1997.

Lutz, William. *Senegal.* New York: Chelsea House, 1988.

Pison, Gilles et al. *Population Dynamics of Senegal.* Washington: National Academy Press, 1995.

Vanderwiele, M. *Les Aspirations de l'Adolescent Senegalais.* Dakar: Centre de Recherche et de Documentation Pedagogique de l'Ecole Normale Superièure de Dakar, 1980.

Wills, Dorothy Davis. *Culture's Cradle: Social, Structural, and Interactional Aspects of Senegalese Socialization.* Ph.D. diss., The University of Texas at Austin, 1977. Ann Arbor, Mich.: Xerox University Microfilms.

Wright, Amy. *The Girls of Jeunesse Action: A Sociological Study of Street Youth in Dakar.* Dakar: ENDA, 1987.

Fiction

Bâ, Mariama. *So Long a Letter.* Portsmouth, N.H.: Heinemann, 1991.

Lowerre, Susan. *Under the Neem Tree.* Seattle: University of Washington Press, 1993.

Sembene, Ousmane. *God's Bits of Wood.* Portsmouth, N.H.: Heinemann, 1995.

Web Sites

http://www.senegal-online.com/senega55E.htm
http://www.africanet.com/africanet/country/senegal/home.htm
http://www.sas.upenn.edu/African_Studies/Country_Specific/Senegal.html
http://www.africanet.com/africanet/country/senegal/home.htm
http://www.au-senegal.com/decouvrir_en/
http://www.peacecorps.gov/countries/senegal/index.cfm
http://www.au-senegal.com/
http://www.africa-ata.org/afmap.htm
http://www.senegalpost.com/
http://www.newafrica.com/news/country.asp?CountryID=42
http://www.afrol.com/Countries/Senegal/senegal_news.htm
http://www.sas.upenn.edu/African_Studies/Cookbook/Senegal.html
http://www.foodtv.com/cuisine/senegalrecipes/0,5140,,00.html
http://www.countrywatch.com/cw%5Fcountry.asp?vCOUNTRY=151
http://www.catholicrelief.org/where%5Fwe%5Fwork/africa/senegal
http://www.nationbynation.com/Senegal/index.html
http://www.cia.gov/cia/publications/factbook/geos/sg.html
http://www.senegal-online.com/senega00E.htm
http://www.worldrover.com/history/senegal%5Fhistory.html
http://www.wtgonline.com/data/sen/sen.asp

Organization

The Embassy of the Republic of Senegal
The Honorable Mamadou Mansour Seck, Ambassador
2112 Wyoming Avenue, NW
Washington, DC 20008
(202) 234-0540

Pen Pal/Chat

http://www.pen-pals.net/

Chapter 11

SOMALIA

Mohamed Diriye Abdullahi

INTRODUCTION

Somalia is a popular name for the Somali Republic, which was formed out of two newly independent states in 1960: Somalia (the South), previously an Italian colony, and Somaliland (the North), previously a British protectorate. The Somali Republic is situated on the easternmost region of Africa, which projects out to the sea, forming a peninsula, with one side being the Gulf of Aden and the other, the Indian Ocean. It has borders with the tiny Republic of Djibouti and with Ethiopia, on its northern and western sides, and with Kenya, on the southern side. Since 1991, the year that the Barre dictatorship fell, the Somali Republic has been practically nonfunctional as a state due to a continuing civil war in the South. However, on May 18, 1991, the North declared that it had reverted back to its former name and identity as Somaliland and has since been stable and functional as a state despite lack of international recognition. The largest city in the South is Mogadishu, an ancient coastal city, which shows a blend of Italian and local architecture. In the North, Hargeisa is the largest city but not the oldest. Hargeisa is situated inland on mountainous terrain.

The majority of the people are Somalis. However, the Somali people are not confined to the Somali Republic (the North and the South). They also inhabit parts of the Republic of Djibouti, the Somali region of Ethiopia (eastern Ethiopia) and the Somali region of Kenya (northeastern Kenya). The Somali people have a predominantly pastoralist culture, even if their ancient cities have a history spanning several millennia. Somalis speak one language, Somali.

This chapter is concerned with the life of teenage Somalis irrespective of the region and state where they might reside, be it Somalia, Somaliland, the Somali region of Ethiopia, northeastern Kenya, or Djibouti. The lives of Somali teenagers, as well as of teenagers from minority groups among Somalis, are basically the same, at least as far as cultural upbringing and parental expectations are concerned.

TYPICAL DAY

The teenage period is one of many experiences, and the daily life of a Somali teenager depends on whether he or she resides in a town or in the countryside. Thus, depending on the activities of the family, the teenager's life might involve mostly work with livestock, agricultural work, going to school in a town, or assisting a parent who is a trader or who practices one of the many trades such as carpentry, masonry, and so forth.

In the countryside itself, there are two modes of life: agriculture and livestock breeding. The latter is led by pastoralist families or nomads. Most country Somalis are pastoralists who wander far and wide with their flocks of sheep, goats, camels, and cattle. There are also some families who might be called agro–pastoralists, meaning they practice agriculture as well as livestock breeding.

Preteens in pastoralist families are already expected to fully participate in the activities of their families; this starts, naturally, when they are small children. In fact, as small children, they are trained to go out with the herds by first tending young baby animals (*maqal* in Somali) kept in and around the family's camp. Thus, by the time they are preteens, they are able to go out with the larger flocks to pastures farther away from the family's camp.

At a tender age, there is a division of chores between boys and girls. For example, little girls may go out with the flocks of sheep and goats but usually never with cattle (cows, oxen) or camels. This is strictly the domain of young boys and men, since these animals are usually led out to greater distances from the home camp.

By the age of 14 or so, the life of a country teenager is centered around preparing him or her for the responsibilities of adulthood. Already, if the family has a herd of camels, a country teenage boy might be a *geeljire* (camelboy), while a country teenage girl is on her way to becoming a *gashanti* (a marriageable girl)—this same word refers to any young girl of marriage age in both town and country.

The *gashanti* usually stays at home in a pastoralist family, as younger siblings relieve her of her chores outside the perimeter of the settlement such as going out with the sheep and goats, although she might still occasionally do so. She usually does other duties around the settlement home, such as the incessant milking of the sheep and goats. She might also be preparing objects that might eventually become part of her trousseau. This includes the weaving of such items as mats and various other items that go into the traditional Somali nomad home. Such objects will become part of her bridal home. At this age, she also becomes more conscious of and more involved in her personal grooming and dressing, and may receive gifts of beautiful clothing and jewelry from her parents.

As for the young *geeljire*, he is out in camel country, situated usually far away from the family camp or settlement. Camelboys typically range in age from 8 years to as old as 24; in fact, many young men will stay out with the camels until such a time as they marry and become household fathers. The life of a camelboy revolves around taking care of the camels, taking them to pastures and watering holes, staying on the lookout for camel rustlers and raiders, and occasionally defending the camels against rustlers, as well as from the attacks of wild beasts, such as hyenas or marauding lions in the old days. The life of a camelboy is certainly harsh but it is also full of adventure and hardihood, which is thought to be good for young men.

The daily life of a teenager in an agriculturist family is similar in many ways to that of the pastoralists, since most agriculturalist families also keep flocks of livestock such as goats, sheep, cattle, and camels. The only difference is usually the additional work in the fields.

Although there are a few large cities, most towns are small and life tends to be provincial. In a town, many teenagers go to school, are abreast of what goes on in the outside world, and even know a tune or two of the latest American or British pop music. However, many others do not go to school and might instead work in stores or in workshops, such as a carpentry workshop, with their parents and other relatives. At the same time, many teenagers combine both work and school by either working with their parents or working for an employer.

In towns, the focus of daily life is therefore either school or work. Both school and work start early in the morning; however, while schools close at around at about 2:00 P.M., working teenagers may work very long hours.

FAMILY LIFE

Somalis are brought up to respect their parents and to seek advice and blessings (*du'o*) from them. Lack of deference to parents brings forth a parental curse (*habaar*). Teenagers take part in caring for older relatives staying with the family, such as grandparents. Grandparents not living on their own usually stay with their older children, since there are no seniors' homes.

Teenagers also help to take care of younger brothers and sisters. Girls, especially, may spend a lot of time taking care of younger siblings as well as doing other household chores. Sometimes, if the mother is away, a teenage girl might do all the work that the mother does for the family, including cooking, shopping, and other household duties.

The sense of family or belonging to the family is much wider or more extended among Somalis. Thus, less immediate relatives are part of the extended family, and teenagers learn to respect them. Also, all relatives will help the teenagers if the parents are unable to do that; for example, a teenager may stay with an aunt or uncle to go to school in town if his own parents reside in the countryside.

CLOTHING

The kind of clothing worn by teenagers can be traditional or modern, which usually means Western-style clothing. Truly traditional clothing is today worn only during cultural festivals or on special occasions. Traditional clothing for a teenage girl would be a *saddehqayd* and its more modern adaptation known as a *guntiino*. This is a dress that consists of several yards of cotton, which is worn by a knotting technique that needs to be mastered for any efficient wearing of the cloth. It is usually knotted atop the right or left shoulder, and is then passed around the chest and waist, finally falling to the feet while leaving a fold in the back of the torso to be used as a hood when the wind blows sand or when it gets cold. A band of clothing with several colored strips is then worn around the waist as a complement; this latter piece may have a beautiful tassel, known as a *boqor*, which hangs down to the feet. Girls who have come of age exclusively wear the *boqor* piece.

In cities, a variation on the theme of traditional clothing consists of three pieces of cloth for women: one worn as a long skirt, another as a blouse or chemise, and another piece as a shawl. Nowadays, however, most women wear a loose dress known as a *diric*; some teenage girls also wear the veil, which is not part of Somali traditional dress but whose use has spread since the wars that wrecked the land starting in the 1980s.

Traditional dress for teenage boys consists of a cotton sheet worn around the waist and another sheet, also of cotton, which is used for the torso or is sometimes just carried on the shoulder if it gets too hot; this can also be used as a hood against the sand or as a blanket when it gets cold.

This is known as a *go*. Tassels of gold and red may adorn the more expensive sheets of clothing. Sometimes a sleeveless shirt is used with the lower piece of clothing. Nowadays, in both town and countryside, many young men and teenage boys wear the sarong, a sheet of clothing worn around the waist and reaching to the ankles. The sarong has been borrowed from Muslim Asian countries such as Malaysia and Indonesia.

Modern dress for teenagers consists of trousers, with jeans being a favorite, and a shirt, completed by sneakers. In towns, teenagers, as in most other countries, particularly prize jeans and sneakers from major international brands.

TRADITIONAL AND NONTRADITIONAL FOOD DISHES

The kind of food eaten by Somali teenagers is largely dependent on family table food, since as a general rule most young people eat only at home. However, in larger towns, cafés and restaurants might be found where boys can eat snacks. Girls do not frequent public restaurants or cafés; if they go to eat in a restaurant, it is usually in the company of their family.

The types of home and restaurant foods are varied and cannot be fully covered here. Snack foods include a variety of cakes and pastries that are sold either in snack restaurants or in street stalls. Among them are a large number of puffy and spicy pastries in yellow colors as well as sesame balls and milk-based caramels. These are sold usually by street vendors from wheelbarrows, and young people particularly like them and buy them as snack foods. Pastry shops in large towns sell a variety of pastries (*ma'-ma'aan*) and sweets, including the sweet known as *halwad* and snack foods. Fast-food outlets serving pizza or hamburgers are unknown, although snack restaurants usually serve sandwiches.

At home, cooking is usually done by the mother, and it is common that all family members eat from the same platter, with all the males eating from one platter and the females from another one. Teenage girls help with the cooking as well as with all the other household chores. Boys usually are not taught to cook but they might run errands to the corner store or fetch water from a water source.

A typical home breakfast that a teenager would eat consists of *injera*, which looks like thin large pancakes. Butter or honey is used as a spread on *injera*. A typical lunch, which is the main family meal, usually consists of a cereal like rice served with a meat sauce, known as *suugo* or *sanuunad*, accompanied by a salad, and fruit for dessert. A typical home dinner is a usually a light meal of *injera* served with a sauce or spread.

Teenagers do not drink many bottled soft drinks; these are usually not very cheap and are sometimes not available except in very large cities. However, teenagers, especially boys, might drink a lot of tea, as do older males. The tea is traditional Somali tea, which is a sweet and fragrant drink. Its ingredients are tea, cardamom, cloves, fresh ginger, and lemon.

SCHOOLING

Most teenagers living in a town, if they are in school, will be in public school, although a few might be in private schools. Public school means a government school, as the government through the Ministry of Education runs all schools. Rural teens do not usually go to school, except perhaps Koranic school.

Being in school for a teenager is in many ways similar to being in school anywhere in the world. Classes start in the morning and end in the afternoon, and students graduate after having passed through 12 grades. At the end of the school cycle, some students will then find employment while

Adolescent Somalis sing a Muslim song before starting school in Hargeisa, Somalia. © AP Wide World Photos.

others, if lucky enough, will go to a university. However, Somali schools differ in several ways from what exists in developed countries. First, because of the limited number of schools and educational opportunities, teenagers have to work hard not to lose their school position. And secondly, while corporal punishment in schools does not exist anymore, breaking the school rules warrants strong disciplinary actions from the teachers, including temporary or permanent suspension.

School life means going to school every day at 7:00 A.M. for six days instead of five. However, school hours last only up to 1:00 or 2:00 P.M., unless the school is an "afternoon school," in which classes are held in the afternoon because of a lack of rooms in the morning. Schools do not provide cafeterias or food services unless they are boarding schools. Otherwise, students usually sit in class, engaged in their work unless they have some activity outside the classroom. A typical class period lasts for an hour or so.

Schools teach only the core curriculum, which means subjects such as biology, physics, chemistry, math, history, geography, languages, and religious or civic instruction. Recreation and the arts are limited or nonexistent in most schools. However, a few schools might have playgrounds for playing soccer or basketball. While school life is spartan, being devoid of recreational activities and the arts (such as music), the core education is excellent, and Somali students in overseas universities have been known to do exceptionally well.

Since the adoption of a Latin script for Somali in 1972, the language of instruction has been mostly Somali. Languages such as English and Arabic are taught in schools and are popular with teenagers. Somali literature and its large repertoire of poetry are also popular with teenagers; this is so because Somalis have a tradition of oral poetry, poetic contests, and poetic series in which several poets engage each other over a long period of time.

As a matter of fact, Somalis have been described as a "nation of poets" and teenagers are no less ardent in memorizing poetry and trying their hand, or rather tongue, at composing some verses. Teenagers try to learn to compose poetry by listening to recitals either by reciters or by older poets, or more recently, by listening to the radio or a recorded tape, or by reading poems at school or at home. Many young poets, before they fall into a style of their own, mimic the style of a particular poet. If the source model for their poem is evident, they are said to have composed a *gabay-dheeg* (derivative poetry). Generally, the best young poets are those from the countryside who have learned from the recitals of nomadic poets true to the tradition of oral poetry.

SOCIAL LIFE

Family and social life in many ways are closely intertwined, since in rural areas relatives at all times surround teenagers. In general, teaching the mores of a society, or socialization, is a long process that turns young children into the men and women of the society. Teenagers learn what is expected or acceptable from either parents, relatives, or their friends. Older people are always ready to dispense lessons to them if the occasion arises. Teenagers are expected to show good behavior and it is entirely normal for an adult stranger to disapprove of teenagers engaging in behavior not conforming to what is expected of their age. This is more true of rural and small communities than of large towns, in which people are more preoccupied with their own problems than with the care of young people.

Passing from childhood into the teenage years is not ritually celebrated among Somalis, as Somalis do not have an age-set system that formally marks the passing from one stage to another. However, the passage is more visible in girls than in boys. Teenage girls, for example, no longer have their hair shaven as was the custom in the old days; instead, they wear it braided or loose. However, because of Muslim customs, hair has to be covered at all times with bright scarves or shawls. Teenage girls are also supposed to adopt the particular gait or style of dignified walking associated with well-bred ladies—they should not, for example, scamper like little girls when outside; instead, they should walk in a slow and dignified way.

Teenage life is considered a period of transition to adulthood, and it is common, especially for teenage girls, to get married. Thus, teenage life is a time when both boys and girls are likely to become more interested in getting to know each other. In the countryside, young people have sufficient time to get to know each other. However, opportunities for conversation are not limitless and the young have to make ingenious use of all occasions to have a conversation. One of the favorite occasions, and one which marks the coming of age of young women among pastoralist Somalis, is the leading of the water-camel to the wells. For this occasion, the young woman dresses in her best clothes and jewelry, takes the halter of the camel, and leads it to the wells where gallant young men hang out for the chance of filling her water jars. In towns, there are far more occasions for teenagers to meet and converse. Perhaps the greatest occasion for the young to socialize is during community events such as marriages. When there is a wedding, dances are held at the home of the newlyweds for seven nights, and the young and unmarried are allowed to dance. Such dances additionally allow the young aspiring poets of both genders to sing their pieces and to expose their intelligence and verbal artistry to their peers.

In towns as well as in villages, teenage boys may sit in a tea shop to socialize or listen to Somali music played from a cassette tape player. Girls do not frequent tea shops but socialize through home visits. No alcoholic beverages are sold in public places, so drinking alcohol is not a problem for Somali teenagers. Street drugs such as marijuana or heroin are unknown in rural areas, although some marijuana use has been episodically reported in large towns; thus, it is safe to say that street drugs are generally unknown to teenagers as well as to adults.

However, there is a local drug, known as khat (sometimes written as "qat"), to which many teenagers become initiated. Khat (*Catha edulis*) is an evergreen shrub native to northeastern Africa and southern Arabia, especially Yemen. Its fresh leaves, when chewed for a long period of time and in sufficient quantities, give an amphetamine-like high, which is to say that it has a stimulating effect like coffee and keeps one alert and euphoric for a while. However, fatigue, drowsiness, and loss of appetite set in the next day. Once hooked, teenagers become regular khat-chewers who must daily find their bundle of leaves. However, stopping the use of khat is not as traumatic as quitting hard-core drugs such as heroin and it is possible for some teenagers to quit it after having tried it for a period of time.

MARRIAGE

For most boys, marriage usually does not happen until past the teenage years—that is, after the age of 18 or 19. However, marriage may well happen for teenage girls starting at about 16 years of age. But when it does happen at such a tender age, the family has a lot to do with it—older women have more latitude about whom they should marry. In general, marriage is considered as entailing or bringing forth a new relationship between two families, clans, or villages. Thus, the involvement of the family.

In the Somali language, the word *guur* has two meanings: to marry and to move away. Marriage in Somali society is therefore viewed as both a break and a new beginning. It is a break because one is leaving the household of one's parents—one is flying out of the familial nest, but it is also a renewal because a new household is being founded. Thus, to marry is a rite of passage that changes the social status of both man and woman. In the countryside especially, the act of marrying signifies for the young man that he is now a member of the informal club of household fathers and can participate in meetings (*shir*). Whereas before he was merely "the son of X," people will now readily refer to him by his own name. Similarly, the young woman, who was until then a mere "daughter of X," will become the "lady of the house" and participate in the councils of household mothers. To mark this change in status, especially in the old days, the young woman would change her headgear and start wearing a gray or black scarf. Marriage might be therefore an empowering stage for young men and women in the sense that they will have more control over their daily lives.

Family involvement in marriage does not necessarily mean that the family decides whom one marries (although that may happen in some cases), but that they are heavily involved in the ceremonies and rites of marriages from start to finish, especially in the case of teenage marriages. The first ceremony consists of the older men from both families meeting to formally approve of the marriage between the two families; this is usually the occasion for the man's family to present gifts to the family of the young woman, in the form of either monies or livestock. Such gifts, called *yarad*, are not a price paid for the young woman's hand but rather part of the ceremonial and reciprocal gifts. The family of the young woman provides many items and accessories to furnish the home of the newlyweds; at the same time, they return on the spot some of the gifts provided by the suitor's family as a way of balancing the costs of each side. The obligations of the young woman's family regarding her well-being, however, do not end there. Over the years, if the new couple is not successful or have a financial problem, their daughter will turn to her parents and siblings for help. The parents will also welcome her back in the event the marriage ceases to exist for some reason.

However, not all marriages are contracted according to tradition and through the elders of the two families facing each other. Sometimes, because of either the destitution of the young man and his family or some other interdiction making it impossible for the young man to approach the young woman's family, elopement seems to be a way out of a predicament.

RECREATION AND ENTERTAINMENT

Somali teenagers in towns band together sometimes for the sake of recreation or to pass the time. At such times, they usually either play soccer or just hang out somewhere, usually places where they might be allowed to linger, such as on the fringes of the town market. The Somali mall is called a *suuq* and consists of a series of small shops connected by covered or open alleys, and loitering teenagers are not tolerated.

Of all sports, soccer is the most popular among boys, and groups of boys playing on empty grounds are a regular sight. Schools sometimes organize soccer tournaments between different schools. In general, sports does not figure among school subjects, and playing soccer is usually learned from other players. The same is true of most sports. However, in large towns, one may find places where certain kinds of sports are practiced.

Teenagers may watch imported films and videos. Some teenagers may also watch television, either at home, at the neighbors', or at some public place such as a café in towns where there are TV stations. However, there are no dancing clubs at all. The theater, where Somali plays are shown, has a wider appeal for the whole population and teenagers usually never miss seeing the latest play in town and listening to the new tunes in the play—Somali plays are part song shows, part comedy shows, and part drama.

Young people usually listen a lot to Somali music on the radio, as well as to other radio programs—the radio reaches everyone and thus is important in the diffusion of music and other programs. Somali music is perfect for quiet listening and for savoring the poetry and the wisdom of the song, but anyone who wants to dance in the energetic and swiveling style of Western pop dances would find it inadequate; therefore, teenagers who like to dance à la Western usually do so in the privacy of a home by playing Western pop tunes from cassettes. However, such dancing is considered quite inappropriate by parents and older people and has to be kept a secret. This is because Somali culture, deeply rooted in pastoralist and Islamic values, is quite ascetic when it comes to hedonistic pleasures and having fun.

However, a quite acceptable form of entertainment for teenagers is folk dancing during weddings and holidays. In the countryside, there is much more folk dancing and sometimes, especially after a particularly good season when both water and pastures are plentiful, young people organize impromptu dances with the acquiescence of their parents, who are never far away from the grounds of the dance.

RELIGIOUS PRACTICES AND CULTURAL CEREMONIES

Somalis are Muslims and their religion is Islam. Islam means submission to God and Muslim means one who has submitted to the supremacy of Allah. Mohammed is the messenger of Allah (*rasuul*) and the prophet of Islam ('*Nabi*). Very few among the Somalis belong to other religions.

Somali children are taught at an early age the five tenets of Islam: belief in the oneness of Allah (monotheism), belief in Mohammed as the *rasuul* (messenger), saying a prayer five times a day, fasting in the month of Ramadan, the offering of *zakat* (alms), and the *hajj* or pilgrimage to Mecca when possible.

By the age of 14, everyone is expected to fast and pray. However, in practice, while most teenagers observe fasting during Ramadan, not very many young people in either country or town practice five prayers a day. Older people, however, tend to be more assiduous of religious observances. This does not mean that young people are flippant about religion, but that they tend to be less observant of daily religious practices and that society does not enforce religious practices in a formal way. In general, young people have a very great respect for religion and for the *wadaad*, a man of religion or local priest.

There are some young men who aspire to become learned in the religious sciences and who may spend many years learning at the foot of a scholar erudite in Islam. These are known as *her*. Groups of these young students of religion sometimes travel around the country, with or without their teacher, and expect and get hospitality from all the people they meet along the way.

CONCLUSION

While the aspects of teenage life given here are true and typical, sometimes especially during war and turbulence, teenagers as well as children may find themselves in roles that do not belong physically or morally in the domain of the young. Unfortunately, among today's Somalis two generations of teenagers have seen war and violence, first under the Barre dictatorship from 1980 to 1990, then under the era of civil war and instability. As a result, thousands of teenagers may have seen fighting or may have been directly involved in fighting as teenage militia and hired gunmen. Thus, in general, the lives of Somali teenagers have been difficult for the last two decades; war and life in refugee camps have taken their toll among them. That does not mean that there are no bright spots; in places, where the guns of war have fallen silent, teenagers are back in school or learning a trade and looking to brighter futures.

RESOURCE GUIDE

Books

Abdullahi, Mohamed Diriye. *Cultures and Customs of Somalia.* Westport, Conn.: Greenwood Press, 2001.

Andrzejewski, B. W., and Sheila Andrzejewski. *An Anthology of Somali Poetry.* Bloomington: Indiana University Press, 1993.

Laurence, Margaret. *A Tree for Poverty: Somali Poetry and Prose.* Canada: McMaster University Library Press and ECW Press, 1993.

Loughran, John, Katheryne Loughran, John Johnson, and Said S. Samatar, eds. *Somalia in Word and Image.* Washington: Foundation for Cross-Cultural Understanding, 1986.

Samatar, Said S., and David Laitin. *Somalia: A Nation in Search of a State.* Boulder, Colo.: Westview Press, 1987.

Web Sites

Somalia proper (South):
http://www.midnimo.com
http://www.banadir.com
http://www.hiiran.com
http://www.somalinet.com

Somaliland:
http://www.somalilandforum.com
http://www.somalilandnet.com
http://www.somalilandnews.com
http://www.somalilandgov.com (Government of Somaliland)

Chapter 12

SOUTH AFRICA

Edmund Abaka

INTRODUCTION

South Africa, at the southern tip of the African continent, has emerged from one of the most brutal and racist regimes in history into a multiracial democracy and a power broker on the continent. The Afrikaners' (white descendants of Dutch settlers) desire to be independent and dominant shaped the history of South Africa for decades until 1994. The award of a Nobel Peace Prize to African National Congress leader (and later president) Nelson Mandela and President F. W. de Klerk signified the acceptance by the world community of a country that had attained pariah status for its apartheid system of racial separation and discrimination.

Before 1960, South African historiography attributed the political and economic domination of whites to the fact that the region was almost empty at the time of white settlement in the 1650s. The argument contended that black Bantu-speaking farmers only moved into the region between 1500 and 1600.[1] Archeological research, oral literature, rock paintings, and other sources have now been used to dismiss these claims. South Africa, like the African continent itself, is a country of diverse people and cultures. Archeological evidence, rock paintings, and even records of early European travelers, traders, and missionaries indicate that the earliest inhabitants of the region were the San. They inhabited South Africa thousands of years ago and lived in relative abundance, given the good climate and vegetation.[2] The San eventually came into contact with the pastoralist Khoikhoi who, it is believed, originated from the dry grasslands of the northern Kalahari desert or could have been a branch of San hunter-gatherers who adopted a pastoral way of life.[3] Linguistic and archeological evidence have also shown that between A.D. 1000 and 1800, Bantu-speaking migrants entered southern Africa, having moved from parts of West Africa. They traversed central Africa and occupied the arable farmlands of southeastern Africa. This group lived in semipermanent villages and established strong political systems.

In 1497, the Portuguese explorer Vasco da Gama, looking for a sea route to India, sailed around the Cape of Good Hope. The first permanent European settlement in South Africa began in 1652, however, when the Dutch East Indian Company sent a party of 90 men under the command of Jan van Riebeeck to establish a refreshment station at Table Bay to supply fresh water, fruit, and vegetables to ships en route to the Far East, especially to the Dutch colonies of Java, Sumatra, and Borneo.[4] By the end of the second decade after initial settlement, further migration from England and France had buttressed the size of the settler population. The settlers gradually moved further inland, displacing the Khoikhoi, San, and others, forcing them to move inland or become farm laborers. The importation of slave labor from Benin, Mozambique, Angola, Madagascar, and Malaysia fueled expansion of the Dutch commercial enterprise, especially cattle ranching and wheat growing.[5] By 1800, a tiered society based on racism and discrimination had already emerged in South Africa, putting Afrikaners (Dutch) and British settlers at the top, coloreds[6] in the second tier, and Africans at the bottom.

Britain took control of South Africa in 1785, relinquished it, and took control again after the Napoleonic wars. From 1815 onward, Britain pushed for the abolition of slavery in South Africa. Additionally, the English educational and judicial systems were introduced in the Cape Colony, and British missionaries promoted Anglicanism, the state religion of Britain. Afrikaner resentment of British control eventually culminated in the Great Trek of the 1830s, in which as many as 1,500 Afrikaners moved inland to rid themselves of British authority and control.[7] The march inland brought the *voortrekkers* into conflict with the Zulu, Nguni, Sotho, and other African groups in the region. The trekkers' push inland brought them into new areas where they staked out claims to far more land than they actually occupied. Eventually, they established the Transvaal and the Orange Free State. During the high point of European imperialism in the period after 1850, British concern for the safety of the sea route to India resulted in increased British intervention in South African affairs.[8]

By 1860, settler expansion had displaced many of the indigenous people. The discovery of diamonds at Kimberly in 1867 changed the history of South Africa forever as an influx of Europeans into the region gradually changed the established racial order. The British government sanctioned the annexation of an area from Griqualand west to the Cape to consolidate British control over the diamond mines. The new racial order made it difficult for South Africans to own or trade in diamonds and would presage the later apartheid policy of racial segregation.[9]

The discovery of gold at the Witwatersrand in 1887 similarly meant an influx of people from Europe, the United States, Australia, and New Zealand. This immigration, together with a lot of European capital, set the stage, wittingly or unwittingly, for tighter white control of economic resources and economic activities in South Africa.[10] The influx of British mining capital intensified Anglo-Dutch rivalry in the region, since Britain was determined to consolidate its control of the Cape all the way to the Transvaal and the Orange Free State to ensure the safety of the sea routes to its possessions in India. Control over South African gold meant domination of worldwide money markets. This rivalry culminated in the Anglo-Boer Wars of 1899–1902.[11] The Boers lost the war but won the peace, and the white population solidified its rule through a pervasive and virulent system of racial discrimination.[12] The Transvaal and the Orange Free State eventually received a new constitution which provided for self-government in 1906 and 1910. In May 1910, a unitary government under British control was created, with the former colonies transferring sovereignty to a central authority. The constitution also provided for a legislature in which only Europeans were enfranchised. The exception was the Cape Province. Suddenly, this union excluded 80 percent of South Africa's population from the legislature.[13] The National Party, which came to symbolize Afrikaner domination, systematically eliminated all vestiges of black participation in politics.

After World War II, the National Party regularized and systematized racial discrimination through the policy of apartheid (apartness). It passed a series of laws designed to ensure a separate and unequal state in which an African "nation" was to develop separately under white tutelage in the "homelands." These laws were concretized in 1948 and South Africa became a nation of two societies. Cognizance is taken of the fact that the laws of 1948 formalized a situation that had existed since the arrival of the Dutch settlers in 1652. The Dutch had pushed the Khoikhoi out of their "territory." Then, political and legal inequality was established before the British reintroduced the pass laws, created "native reserves," levied hut taxes, and controlled land and labor. After union in 1910, the government wasted no time in adding legislation that intensified what was not too different from the later apartheid system.[14]

From World War II onward, the virulent system of separation of the races known as apartheid was instituted, with migration and urban slums becoming endemic features of its presence.[15] Fourteen-year-old Sandile Dube summed up his experiences as a teen living in apartheid South Africa in a poem titled *Echoes That Shiver the Sky*.[16]

Under the apartheid system, the gap between poor Africans and wealthy whites widened further. Informal opposition to racism and discrimination coalesced in the formation of the first African political opposition group in 1912: the African National Congress (ANC). The formation in 1944 of the youth wing of the ANC, headed by Nelson Mandela, Walter Sisulu, and Oliver Tambo marked a watershed in the development of African political consciousness and activism. The National Party government countered ANC-organized protests, boycotts, and armed struggle with the arrest of ANC leaders Mandela, Sisulu, and others. After the long Rivona trials of 1964, the ANC leaders were sent to prison.[17] Even with the leaders in prison, the ANC organized an international campaign against the pass laws, nurtured a culture of black protest against apartheid, and worked with other black and white organizations, including South African churches, to dismantle apartheid.

One of the insidious consequences of apartheid was the destruction and desolation that resulted from the breakdown, or decay, of moral, social, and religious institutions that were the backbone of a people, a community, and the country as a whole together. Young men left the rural areas to seek employment in the urban centers and mining towns and, as they did so, left behind their wives and children.[18]

Poverty or scarcity of resources was endemic in the black society of South Africa. Whites owned most of the best land, leaving poor land to blacks. Consequently, African farmers' crop production was poor. The migration to the cities resulted in the emergence of shanty towns on the outskirts of cities, as fortunate Africans found work, and those who did not were all crowded into small living spaces in these shanty towns.[19]

The apartheid system restricted the movement of Africans and required passes indicating where they lived and for whom they worked. For young people at this time, the restriction of parents' activities and the limitations placed on where and for whom they could work placed a tremendous strain on families. When parents were unemployed and could not renew passes, they could not send their children to school. Life was very difficult and children often had to go to bed hungry. This situation, fueled by a lack of opportunities, resulted in part in the emergence of gangs and turf wars, many of which were "wars of survival." The lawlessness in the ghettoes that arose near the big cities often led to police raids, and children watched in horror while the police (peri-urban) dragged their parents off to jail.[20] Life for those who migrated to the city seeking work was no bed of roses either. Work was nonexistent, and many women became prostitutes and sold liquor illegally to survive.

The restrictions imposed on Africans can be summed up thus: the Prohibition of Mixed Marriages Act of 1949 (prohibited interracial marriages), the Population Registration Act of 1950 (ensured that every South African was classified into a specific group), the Pass Laws of 1952 (controlled the movement of Africans), the Bantu Education Act of 1953 (segregated education from nursery to university), and the Group Areas Act of 1955 and 1956 (imposed different residential areas in cities for blacks and whites).[21]

The stark reality of life for youth in apartheid-era South Africa, especially in the ghetto outside Johannesburg, was harsh. Many children eked out an existence in shacks of the ghettoes where midnight police raids (peri-urban) and gang warfare were facts of life. It was a state of helplessness and daily humiliations of parents by police. Many teens lived in abject poverty and inhumane conditions. One teen told of his experience:

> I was born of illiterate parents who could not afford to pay my way through school, let alone pay the rent for our shack and put enough food on the table; when black people in Alexandria lived under constant police terror and threat of deportation to impoverished tribal reserves; when at 10 I contemplated suicide because I found the burden of living in a ghetto, poverty-stricken and without hope, too heavy to shoulder...[22]

The pressure from the combined opposition of the ANC, other men's and women's organizations, the South African masses, the South African churches and students, the countries of southern Africa (the Frontline States), and the international community finally paid off, as the ruling Labor party agreed to multiparty nonracial elections.[23] In 1990, President De Klerk lifted the ban on the ANC and other political organizations. Mandela was released from prison after spending 27 years in jail, and in April 1994, South Africans voted for the first nonracial government. The ANC won the elections, and on May 10, 1994, Mandela assumed the presidency of South Africa.

High hopes attended Mandela's term in office, which began in 1994. Teens who were chafing under the Bantu education system and other indignities saw the collapse of apartheid as an end to all of South Africa's problems. Since President Mandela's term, many gains have been made. The racial restrictions on access to education, finance, and housing have all been abolished. It is not easy, however, to undo in four mere years the work of centuries. Many teenagers are frustrated by the lack of opportunities, but at the same time are very hopeful about life in the new South Africa. Many young people have reached across the racial divide to establish friendships[24] and acquaintances in the new South Africa, which has desegregated schools, shops, and public places like beaches, parks, and restaurants.

Soon after assuming office in 1994, the ANC government began to exploit the resources of the country, this time for the benefit of its citizens. The first challenge was bridging the disparity between blacks and whites. The government desegregated schools and all institutions. It also started to lend money to blacks to start or improve their businesses. Many black Africans had neither the education nor skills to work in the new economy and schools were built in black areas that had long been abandoned by the apartheid government. The ANC government preached tolerance and racial equality. It encouraged investment and the diversification of the economy.

Today, South Africa represents a "tale of two cities." It is a very modern country with a good infrastructural base. The cities are filled with beautiful high-rise office buildings, luxurious homes, good roads, shopping malls, and other conveniences, but the areas of major black residence, like Soweto and other townships, are still trying to realize their dreams of a good life. The level of prosperity, while high, is skewed in favor of the white South Africans. Nonetheless, it allows people to buy computers, cell phones, satellite dishes—indeed all the latest technology. Many of the major South African cities resemble U.S. cities.

This impression changes as soon as you move to black townships and rural areas. Palpable neglect dating back to the days of apartheid has resulted in a lack of infrastructure, rundown buildings, bad roads, and a lack of medical facilities.

In terms of dress, most South Africans wear both African and Western clothes. South African girls may very well be wearing the latest French, Italian, American, or African fashions. As for the rest of nationalities, dress is up to the individual. Some wear Western clothes, some wear their national dress, particularly the Indian *salwar kamees* (long, embroidered dresses), since South Africa has a large Indian population.

The South African government has aggressively pursued the education of youth, especially black and colored youth. The practice of providing different subsidies for education for black and colored youth has long been discontinued.

The South African economy has undergone changes under the ANC government. Yet, as Zwelinzima Vavi, the Trade Union secretary general, noted at a national meeting in 2001:

> What we have in South Africa is a very successful political transformation. But at the economic level, what we cannot miss is that the economy remains in white hands and the black majority remains trapped in unemployment, deep inequality and poverty.[25]

The paradox of postapartheid South Africa is summed up by Neil van Heerden, a diplomat during the era of apartheid (and under Mandela) and now a businessman who runs the South African Foundation, an association of more than 40 of South Africa's biggest companies. Commenting on the changes in the new South Africa, he notes, "There is no question that there was a sense of loss, of confusion, of fear of the future. Suddenly, I'm being ruled by my enemy."[26] On Afrikaner reaction, van Heerden notes, "But I believe since 1994, the Afrikaner has taken stock.... He has looked at the quality of the people who are now his rulers, and he's beginning to say, 'Although we have black empowerment and affirmative action, I can find standing room in this country.' "[27]

In June 2000, the Afrikaner youth league, the Afrikanerbond (the postapartheid incarnation of the Broederbond, the powerful secret society that advanced Afrikaner interests), and the youth league of the ANC held a joint conference to focus on building trust and unity among the next generation of South African leaders.[28]

TYPICAL DAY

The typical day for a South African teenager, especially from a poor family, starts with early morning chores before going to school. This may involve fetching water, washing pots and pans, or sweeping the compound. Most teens in South Africa attend school now, either public or private, and these schools generally open at around 8:30 A.M. Every weekday morning, urban teens have to fight rush-hour traffic on the congested roads of the cities to reach school in many places throughout the country. In the rural areas of South Africa, schools tend to be in residential areas and teens commute on foot to and from school all year long.

After school, teens go home to be with family members. While fairly well-off teenagers visit friends, play together, watch television and videos, or chat with friends on the phone, their counterparts from poor families help parents at home, play in the neighborhood with other teens, or go to work for a few hours to make some money to supplement family income. In rich neighborhoods, teens are likely to spend time in shopping malls, restaurants, and similar places where they hang out. Africans generally eat a big evening meal and South Africans are no exception. Supper is eaten anywhere from 6:00 P.M. to 9:30 P.M. Teenagers, and even small children, often stay up quite late swapping stories or playing at home.

Children in communal societies make contributions to the family welfare earlier than their counterparts elsewhere. In areas where jobs are available, many black South African teenagers work. In many instances, there is a real financial need to do so—to supplement the meager wages of parents, or to enable teens to purchase items like clothes and shoes they crave but their parents cannot afford. Such teens do not generally rely on parents for spending money since they earn income themselves. But generally, teens rely on parents, or other relatives, for spending money, which is also called "pocket money."

Many white families have servants, often black South African or Indian. Wealthy families with mansions and large plots of land might employ several housemaids, cooks, drivers, and nannies to tend smaller children. These domestic workers often travel from their own homes in poor black neighborhoods, or in the cities, to go to work in affluent homes. After the day's work they return to their own homes. In a few instances, domestic workers have separate quarters outside the main building, usually referred to as "boys' quarters," where they may live alone or in some cases with their families. Many young white South Africans have been cared for by black South African women since colonial times.

African families, both rich and poor, are generally large and highly valued. An ideal family size of four to six children can be found across the continent.[29] And since only wealthy households have servants, the majority of South African households are without servants. Therefore, teens have household responsibilities: sweeping or mopping rooms, washing pots and pans, and even fetching water. In Africa, a gender division of labor exists and in many households girls assist their mothers with cooking and housework. In rural areas, boys are usually expected to help with fetching water if there is no standing water at home or even fetching firewood on the weekends or occasionally when the situation warrants it.

Some non-nationals have a servant or two to help at home. At the same time, girls might be expected to help mothers with housework. These non-nationals are also more likely to live in apartments rather than the poor rundown neighborhoods in rural South Africa. In addition, they are likely to insist that girls spend more time on schoolwork than on housework, although this varies from one family to another.

Teens doing homework, Soweto, South Africa. Courtesy of A. Olusegun Fayemi.

FAMILY LIFE

Most South Africans, like other Africans, live in extended families. Whether rich or poor, compounds contain several houses in which several generations of the same family live: grandparents, parents, brothers and sisters, aunts, uncles, and cousins. Where families live apart, there is a sense of obligation to visit members as often as possible, on weekends, or during holidays like Christmas and Easter. South African children always know their aunts, uncles, and cousins extremely well and socialize with them

People from other African countries are much more likely to live in nuclear families in South Africa but stay in contact with the extended family in their own countries and often send remittances home. Teenagers of such families likely visit their grandparents, aunts, and uncles living in another country once in a while, usually at the end of the year. Alternatively, family members from their country may visit them in South Africa.

Expatriate teens often have parents with college or university degrees from their own countries or some professional training beyond high school. This background enables them to help their children with their homework and tell them what to expect in school.

Many grandparents and parents grew up under apartheid, with its notorious segregation and restrictions. Many black South Africans still live in urban slums and poor rural areas. But South African teens of today are growing up rich, with access to the Internet and other technological appliances that were not possible in their parents' time. They have access to material things, including trips to other countries.

The new dispensation and attendant social changes have undoubtedly given girls greater opportunities in public and private employment than their mothers and grandmothers. Some educated South African women hold important, albeit limited, positions but the opportunities can only grow in the future. Due to the extended family system, women can leave their children with relatives and go to school and to work. Thus, a new generation of South African women are working outside the home in order to get independence and professional accomplishment.

Parents make financial decisions at home. Many teens live with their parents or their mothers. Others live with uncles, aunts, grandparents, and other relatives. About 34 percent of teens depend on their parents for all their needs. The mean age of first birth for women is in the teens, but it is slightly higher for men. Fifty-two percent of women in their teens have children. Some have children when they are still in school.[30]

On the whole, life for many black South African teenagers whose families have lived in poverty for a long time is very difficult, even after the collapse of apartheid. On the other hand, their white counterparts are generally fairly well off. Teenagers from other African and Western nations are certainly not poor, because their parents are sometimes categorized as expatriates and paid higher salaries. Many of these expatriates—from Africa, Europe, and the United States—were recruited after the collapse of apartheid to help build the new multiracial democracy. Expatriate teenagers often live in middle-class neighborhoods. There is also a sizable Asian population, descendants of Indians who have been in South Africa since the 1800s. South Africa has a very high rate of violent street crime, so young people worry about being mugged or assaulted. The worst problem South African teens face, however, is the HIV/AIDS pandemic that has gripped the nation.[31]

There is one important difference between family life in South Africa and in America. As in other African countries, South African parents have more control over their children's lives than their American counterparts. The individual lives not only for himself or herself but also for the family. The individual's behavior, therefore, reflects on the family. If the individual is a criminal, or has a bad reputation, this behavior reflects on the reputation of the family as a whole. Families put pressure on children to avoid behavior that would soil the family name. This often means fairly close supervision.

South African teens cannot get a driver's license until they are 18 years old. Teenagers normally use public transportation, which is widely available in many parts of South Africa.

TRADITIONAL AND NONTRADITIONAL FOOD DISHES

Due to its location and diverse population, South Africa has a complex mix of British, Dutch, Indonesian, and African cuisine. The cuisine represents a unique intermingling of vastly different cultures and native cuisines. The traditional foods of the San, the hunter-gatherers who occupied South Africa before the Dutch arrival, consisted primarily of game and food derived from local crops such as corn and millet. The pastoralist Khoikhoi raised sheep and cattle and had a meat-based diet. To these were added Dutch, English, French, and Indian cuisines.

The Dutch demand for labor led to the importation of slaves from Java, Borneo, and Sumatra.[32] Furthermore, the demand for labor in the post-emancipation period attracted many workers from the Indian subcontinent. With these people arrived cuisine: curries, chutneys, sambals, and atjars. These were imported specialties of India, China, and Indonesia and increasingly became an integral part of South African cuisine. Indian-style spices are available in bulk both in the supermarkets and open markets. The Dutch settlers, mostly farmers and herders, introduced baked goods and other specialties from Holland. The temperate climate, the fertile land, and the *el dorado* of South Africa attracted many European migrants—French settlers (Huguenots) escaping religious persecution as well as Germans in the decades after the initial settlement in 1652. The French brought with them grape vines, the art of wine-making, and French dishes. The Germans introduced pastries, and the British, who increasingly sought to control South Africa and safeguard their commercial empire in the Far East, introduced meat pies and other British delicacies. Consequently, the native African cuisine was broadened to accommodate the dishes of all the migrants to the region.[33]

The main meals in South Africa, like other African countries, are starch- and stew-based. A popular meat, *biltong*, which is spiced, wind-dried meat, is usually used as a snack. In addition, game and lamb are also favorite dishes. Due to proximity to the Atlantic and Indian oceans, lobster (especially rock lobster), fish (including pickled fish), lentil soups,

and salt cod are all important dishes. Curries from the Indian subcontinent are also important in South African cuisine. Finally, vegetables like
tomatoes, peas, green beans, and cabbage and various kinds of fruit form
the core of South African cuisine. *Boerewors* or farmer's sausage, a traditional barbecue sausage, is also important. Typical dishes also include
sosaties (a type of kabob), *bobotie* (a curried mince dish), *bredies* (meat,
tomato, and vegetable casseroles), and crayfish (or rock lobster). There is
also wine and local home-brewed sorghum beer, *umqombothi*.

Today, South African dishes reflect the food and cooking techniques
brought from the East and the West. New foods have merged with native
coconuts, chile peppers, pumpkins, tangerines, and tamarind to create a
complex and unique set of dishes that are global in scope and have the
best of both worlds. A lot of fresh produce is imported from around the
world, and people buy this produce in supermarkets or in open-air markets.

The migration of Mozambican, Zambian, and Tanzanian mine workers
has added elements of cooking from these countries. But these tend to be
more limited to the mining areas. American fast-food chains like Mc-
Donald's and Kentucky Fried Chicken are everywhere in the major
Southern African cities.

SCHOOLING

Levels of education also differ between white and black South Africans.
Mass public schooling with equal access and similar facilities for blacks
and whites started only in the postapartheid period of the mid-1990s. Unless a black South African family has been wealthy for a long time, the
parents and children are likely to have very little formal schooling.
Schools were restricted for black South Africans, and where they were operated, resources were so inadequate that children boycotted the schools.

Under the apartheid system, depriving blacks of education was a deliberate goal. To this end, a system known as Bantu education was instituted
to provide inferior education to blacks. South African Prime Minister
Hendrik Verwoerd captured the essence of this ideology in 1960 when he
stated in Parliament that, "The natives will be taught from childhood to
realize that equality with Europeans is not for them."[34] But the revolt of
schoolchildren in 1976 and the attendant massacre of innocent schoolchildren initiated a full-scale attack, local and international, against the
final strongholds of apartheid.

Until 1950, the government had left African education to missionaries.
In 1953, the government assumed control of African education in a

highly segregated system. Though South Africa had as many as five times more black African children than white, the government spent 10 times more per person on white than on black children, and universities were forbidden to accept black students. During the apartheid era, schools became centers of resistance and mass student strikes became part of the protest culture. Today, schools are integrated and funded equally, but the all-black township and rural schools have seen very little change. Schools are everywhere, so the generation of black South Africans currently in high school has far greater educational opportunities than any previous generation. Even when the parents have very little education or none at all, they want their children to take advantage of the opportunity to go to school up to the university level.

After 1994, the ANC government moved to change the education system and ensure equal access for everyone regardless of race or creed. The South African Constitution of 1996 made education a basic right: no child is to be denied admission to a school on account of race, gender, creed, color, inability to pay school fees, language, or age. The constitution also established the South African Schools Act (1996) and the Na-

Student government office in Soweto, South Africa, high school. Courtesy of A. Olusegun Fayemi.

tional Education Policy Act (1996) to streamline education. Schools were subsequently recognized as either public (state) or private (independent). The government restructured the 19 apartheid-era education departments into one national and nine provincial education departments.[35] The government spends 23 percent of its national budget and 7 percent of its gross domestic product on education. The result is that South Africa has achieved near-universal education for children aged 7 to 16 years, but inequalities have not been eliminated.[36]

South African teens go to school until they are 17 or 18 years old. Then they may go to a technical school (similar to the American community college) or to a university. Since they are in the southern hemisphere, the school year ends early in December and they start a month-long summer break. Most South African schools, unlike American schools, require students to wear uniforms. Some students like the practice of wearing uniforms and others do not.

There is a different education attainment for blacks and whites in South Africa, which has implications for economic prospects. There is a strong belief that education is the key to employment and a better future. A member of a focus group composed of 16- to 24-year-old men intoned:

Soweto, South Africa, classroom. Courtesy of A. Olusegun Fayemi.

I would say that our future and opportunities are bright in that the standard of education is high. Our parents were denied a brighter future because of the low level of education, which was prevalent then. They used to use sticks and stones to count; education is now advanced because of the advent of technology. This provides various opportunities for the youth in South Africa.[37]

Similarly, a woman in the 16- to 24-year-old group maintained that:

Yes, there will be job opportunities but the only thing that will be lacking will be money. So if we have money we can go to school and be educated and have a wide variety of job opportunities. But if you don't have money you won't be able to go to school and you won't have job opportunities.[38]

The youth also believe that companies should give high school graduates a chance to work and gain valuable experience, an important key to employment.

South African teens usually live with their parents and are usually dependent on them. Given the current economic conditions, teens, especially black teens, are looking for jobs. A Community Agency for Social Enquiry study of youth in South Africa showed that even though youth who have matriculation certificates are more likely to be employed than those who do not, African youth with matriculation certificates do not appear to have a better chance of getting jobs; the unemployment rate for black youth stands at 70 percent. White and colored youth stand a better chance of employment.[39] Additionally, women are most affected by the high unemployment rate in South Africa. At the same time, the general unemployment rate is even higher in the rural areas, at 75 percent. About 21 percent of South African youth (out of a sample of 2,500) believe that employers and the government should be encouraged to hire more young people. In all, they see education, or better-quality training, as the ticket to "better employment."[40]

Like the inner cities of the United States, the climate of unrest in the black townships has disrupted schooling. Some black schools are "no-go" areas. School attendance is poor and teaching is not very effective. Consequently, some parents, especially those who can afford it, have sent their children to other schools. Gang wars in the Cape Flats, for example, have resulted in the migration of some students to Cape Town, and from township schools to suburban schools in Johannesburg and other cities.[41]

In the dying days of apartheid, the pressure to desegregate schools and open half-empty white schools to black students forced the government to create three models of schooling: Model A would be private or independent schools receiving no state subsidy; Model B would maintain the status quo and receive 70 percent of the current level of funding; Model C schools would receive state funding for staff and would be allowed to determine their own admission policies. While the overwhelming majority of white schools chose Model C, and most voted to admit black students, very few—mainly poor Afrikaans-speaking schools—opted for Model B. Only a few schools opted to become independent or private.[42]

New independent schools which required parents to purchase a R40,000 (US$5,817.47) debenture in addition to annual school fees were established at the top end of the market, and so were fly-by-night colleges which were set up to provide education to a starved public.[43] Today, some ex-Model C English-medium schools are predominantly black, especially those in town or city centers or in the suburbs close to city centers. Similarly, many previously Indian and "colored" schools have now changed in composition since the days of integration.[44]

There are higher levels of integration (especially at the lower grades) in English-medium schools because English is the language of business and politics. Additionally, the fear of racism in Afrikaans-medium schools, coupled with the images from apartheid, have kept many blacks from Afrikaans-medium schools, including children of mine workers who can speak only Afrikaans.[45] Currently, some erosion of confidence in public schools has led to an increase in the growth of independent or private schools as the black and white middle class have moved their children from public to private or independent schools. That trend is evident in the working class as well. Independent schools have grown from 518 in 1994 to 1,302 in 1998 and 1,557 in 1999.[46]

In addition to these, expatriates working on contracts for multinational companies or for the South African government have built their own schools: American, German, and French. Added to these, there are about 445 Catholic schools (300 of which have been taken over by the government due to financial difficulties) that serve poor communities, as well as extraterritorial schools in neighboring countries. These extraterritorial schools, which are organized under the rubric of the Independent Schools Association of Southern Africa, are based in Johannesburg.[47]

In terms of computer literacy, only a quarter of South African youth have access to computers. An equal number know how to use a computer, even if they do not have access to one. There is an urban-rural disparity in both access to and knowledge of computers. In the 16–19 age bracket, for instance, about 15 percent of youth in the urban areas are significantly more likely to have access to, and know how to use, computers than their rural counterparts. The disparity widens when figures are compared for boys and girls.[48]

SOCIAL LIFE

The restrictions of the apartheid period meant that white teenagers generally associated with their white counterparts and blacks with their black counterparts, since there was limited contact between the two groups. Segregation meant that there was no interaction between black and white teenagers at schools, playgrounds, malls, or on soccer or cricket fields. By implication, there was virtually no dating between whites and blacks. With the demise of apartheid and the integration of schools, sports, and all areas of national life, inter-racial dating between white and black South African youth, while not the norm, has gradually become a reflection of the changing landscape of South Africa. Schools are coeducational and inter-racial, and so whether at school, in restaurants, or at the mall, South African teenagers can date, albeit under the watchful eye of parents or older siblings.

In the southern part of South Africa, HIV/AIDS is presumed to be higher among the youth than among adults. The political agenda of South Africa over the past year has been dominated by HIV/AIDS. There seem to be gaps among awareness, beliefs about HIV, action to prevent HIV, and negative attitudes toward the disease. President Thabo Mbeki's ANC government has been accused of dragging its feet in the fight against the scourge in South Africa, but the media campaign against it appears to be having a positive impact on teens. Sexually active teens, especially those in urban areas and those who are in school, have gradually come to accept the importance of condoms in HIV/AIDS and sexually transmitted disease prevention. At the same time, the proportion of teenagers that have never used condoms seems relatively high. Additionally, less than a quarter of the youth have been tested for HIV. Again, the distribution varies between urban and nonurban areas.[49]

RECREATION

One of the most popular pastimes in South Africa is sports. Teens love to both watch and participate in sports. The three big sports in South Africa are soccer, rugby, and cricket. Teens also enjoy swimming, skiing, running, basketball, golf, and many other sports. Every year, many teens participate in the Cape Times Big Walk. As with teens in the United

Boys at a pool in Soweto, South Africa. Courtesy of A. Olusegun Fayemi.

States, scouting is popular with South African teenagers. Boy Scouts and Girl Guides go camping and participate in other group activities.

South African teens, like teens everywhere, are also faced with the problems of teen pregnancy, drug abuse, crime, and the spread of HIV. Many teens tend to be active in their communities and volunteer to help fix these social evils. They are also interested in world events.

During apartheid, marginalized and disaffected youth found solace in street gangs, which fulfilled their need for a rite of passage from childhood to adolescence and adulthood in the apartheid period. They were made to feel important in these organizations and strove for social acceptance.[50] South African townships were beset by very limited economic activity and poverty, high rates of illiteracy, unemployment, and an educational system that did not provide them with a sense of belonging or identification, but rather, imposed a foreign Afrikaner culture on them. Teenagers, in the immediate aftermath of the collapse of apartheid, spent a lot of time in the streets. However, economic improvement, a sense of power, and acceptance of purpose, coupled with the ANC government's efforts to empower black youth by investing in their ideas and their participation in local and national activities, have changed the tide, in spite of the slow pace of the recovery efforts by the government.

ENTERTAINMENT

South African teens love music. There is a wide distribution in the taste of music. Africans prefer gospel, *kwaito*,[51] rhythm and blues, and ballads, in that order. Colored teens have a somewhat similar taste in music: rhythm and blues, gospel, jazz, ballads, rap, and *kwaito*. White teens prefer rave, rock, pop, 90s music, and contemporary music.

South African teens generally enjoy the music of Ladysmith Black Mambazo. The group's music chronicles the life and toil of black workers in the mines far away from their home and families. Their music has become somewhat popular in the United States. Paul Simon's *Graceland* album showcased the music of the group. There is also the ubiquitous Miriam Makeba, whose music was produced outside South Africa during the apartheid period. Claire Johnstone and the Mango Groove have also made South African music popular.

Music radio stations and television programs are very popular with South African teens. Whereas a majority of black and colored teens watch South African Broadcasting Corporation channels, white teens prefer M-net (which broadcasts in English and Afrikaans) and satellite.

One by-product of the love for music in South Africa is the popularity of raves. Raves are one of the hottest crazes for teens in South African cities. Raves are all-night happenings with loud music by rave bands. Everybody dances the whole night then goes home and sleeps the next day. Only nonalcoholic energy drinks, packed with vitamins and natural ingredients, are served at raves, but they provide the energy boost that teens need to keep going.

South African teens also like to read fantasy and horror fiction and go to the movies (mostly American movies). Many teens (and schools) are getting computers and spending lots of time surfing the Internet.

RELIGIOUS PRACTICES AND CULTURAL CEREMONIES

Religion in South Africa is as diverse as the population itself. While almost 80 percent of South Africa is Christian, Hindus, Jews, and Muslims also constitute sizable religious communities. With the exception of the major indigenous African churches, many Afrikaans, Pentecostal, and charismatic churches are members of the South African Council of

Churches (SACC). African independent churches have also grown considerably since the collapse of apartheid. Originally, members of the mission churches—independent churches, about 4,000 in all—commanded a membership of more than 10 million from both rural and urban South Africa. The Dutch Reformed Churches are also home to about 3.5 million people, with a few English- and Portuguese-language congregations.[52]

South African practitioners of traditional religions recognize a supreme being. More importantly, ancestors or departed members of the community are believed to be intimately connected with the lives of the living. As a result, the ancestors are venerated.

Additionally, about two-thirds of South African Indians are Hindus. Of the remainder, 20 percent are Muslim, and 20 percent are Christian. Islam, while small, is increasingly growing. Added to the mix are 100,000 mostly Orthodox Jews and adherents to the Baha'i faith.[53]

CONCLUSION

In postapartheid South Africa, teens, like everyone else, are trying to make the most out of a very difficult transition to a new reality. Black teens have identified education as the panacea to many of their problems: access to better jobs and administrative and political positions, and acceptance in the international community. While high crime and HIV/AIDS continue to bedevil South Africa, most teens help their parents at home, seek employment to supplement household income, avidly consume education programs, and enjoy the international reputation that the country has gained over the past six years. They love the national sports (soccer, rugby, and cricket) and South African and international music. They continue to make strides in healing the race wounds in the country. Many teens are also actively involved in international programs to other countries.

Table 12.1 Educational Attainment by Race

	African	Colored	Indian	White	All
None/Primary	19%	13%	2%	2%	16%
Secondary	55%	62%	40%	38%	53%
Matric	21%	18%	47%	29%	22%
Post-matric	6%	7%	11%	32%	9%

Source: Youth 2000 Report. A Study of Youth in South Africa.

NOTES

1. Bantu was a language family that covered the area from Cameroon in West Africa down to South Africa. The Xhosa, Zulu, Sothu, and others are all Bantu speakers. However, at the height of the apartheid regime, "Bantu" became a pejorative term for all Africans.

2. John A. Williams, *From the South African Past: Narratives, Documents, and Debates* (New York: Houghton Mifflin, 1997): 1; Kevin Shillington, *History of Southern Africa* (Harlow, Essex: Longman, 1995): 1–5.

3. Williams, 6–9; Shillington, 5–6.

4. Williams, 1–2, 6; Shillington, 21–24.

5. Williams, 34–48; Shillington, 24.

6. "Colored" was a racial category used in twentieth-century South Africa to refer to descendants of Europeans, Khoikkoi, and slaves. They became a rural and urban proletariat.

7. Norman Etherington, *The Great Treks: The Transformation of Southern Africa, 1815–1854* (Harlow, Essex: Longman, 2001); A. E. Afigbo, E. A. Ayandele, R. J. Gavin, J. D. Omer-Cooper, and R. Palmer, *The Making of Modern Africa. Vol. I: The Nineteenth Century* (Harlow, Essex: Longman, 1986): 239–50.

8. Ronald Robinson and John Gallagher, with Alice Denny, *Africa and the Victorians* (New York: St. Martin's Press, 1961), especially Chapters III and XIV.

9. Williams, 141–83.

10. Afigbo et al., Chapter 11.

11. Robert July, *A History of the African People* (Prospect Heights, Ill.: Waveland Press, 1998): 352–56.

12. For the Anglo-Boer Wars, see Robinson and Gallagher, 410–61.

13. July, 356.

14. Williams, 221–38.

15. Ibid., 239–56; Vincent Khapoya, *The African Experience: An Introduction* (Englewood Cliffs, N.J.: Prentice Hall, 1998): 232–40. Alan Paton, *Cry, the Beloved Country* (New York: Macmillan, 1987).

16. Sandile Dube, "Echoes That Shiver the Sky." In *Nelson Mandelamandla*, eds. Amelia Blossom House and Cosmo Pieterse (Washington: Three Continents Press, 1989): 8–9.

17. Williams, 257–321; Khapoya, 245. For the struggles of various groups, see Martin Murray, *South Africa: Time of Agony, Time of Destiny. The Upsurge of Popular Protest* (London: Verso, 1987).

18. Paton. See also Mark Mathabane, *Kaffir Boy: The Story of a Black Youth's Coming of Age in Apartheid South Africa* (New York: Macmillan, 1986).

19. Paton.

20. Mathabane.

21. Williams, 246–56; Khapoya, 235–40.

22. Mathabane, ix.

23. For details of the struggle against apartheid, see Nelson Mandela, *No Easy Walk to Freedom* (Oxford: Heinemann, 1990); Murray, 195–493.

24. See for example, Rachel L. Swarns, "Only Joking. But Healing South Africa Too," *New York Times* (14 January 2001).

25. Rachel L. Swarns, "South Africa Sees Turmoil Dividing Ruling Party," *New York Times* (20 November 2001).

26. Rachel L. Swarns, "For South African Whites, Money Has No Color," *The New York Times on the Web:* www.nytimes.com/library/world/africa/042000 asfrica-afrikaner. Cited April 20, 2000. (5 pp.).

27. Ibid., 5.

28. Ibid., 4.

29. Khapoya, 50–52.

30. Ibid.

31. Ibid.

32. Williams, 34–48.

33. Global Destinations, South Africa, www.globalgourmet.com/destinations/southafrica.html. Cited January 10, 2002. (2 pp.).

34. Peter Tygesen, "The ABCs of Apartheid," *Africa Report* (May–June 1991): 14.

35. Jane Hofmeyr, "The Emerging School Landscape in Post-Apartheid South Africa," March 30, 2000. In www.sun.ac.za/hofmeyr.htm. Cited January 10, 2002. (19 pp.).

36. Ibid., 2.

37. Youth Report—Chapters 1–3," in Youth 2000: A National Study of Youth in South Africa, December 2000: http://www.case.org.za/html/yo1-3. Cited November 27, 2001. The Community Agency for Social Enquiry (CASE) Youth Study was commissioned by the Royal Netherlands Embassy in South Africa.

38. Ibid.

39. Ibid.

40. Ibid.

41. Hofmeyr, http://www.sun.ac.za/hofmeyr.htm

42. Ibid., 5.

43. Ibid., 5.

44. Ibid., 6.

45. Ibid., 7.

46. Ibid., 9–10.

47. Ibid., 11–12.

48. Ibid.

49. Rachel L. Swarns, "Newest Statistics Show AIDS Still Spreading in South Africa", *New York Times* (21 March 2001).

50. See Amamda Dissel, "Youth, Street Gangs and Violence in South Africa," in *Youth, Street Culture and Urban Violence in Africa,* proceedings of the International Seminar held, Abidjan, Ivory Coast, May 5–7, 1997.

51. *Kwaito* is South African pop music—a mixture of South African disco, hip-hop, R & B, reggae, and American and British music with a strong local flavor.

52. South Africa YearBook 2000/01. "The Land and the People." http://www.gov.za/yearbook/rainbow.htm, 1/10/2002, 4–5 (28 pp.).

53. Ibid., 5–6.

RESOURCE GUIDE

Books

Abrahams, Peter. *Mine Boy.* London: Heinemann Educational, 1963.
Afoloyan, Funso. *Culture and Customs of South Africa.* Westport, Conn.: Green-wood Press, 2003.
Mathabane, Mark. *Kaffir Boy: The Story of a Black Youth's Coming of Age in Apartheid South Africa.* New York: Macmillan, 1986.
Paton, Alan. *Cry, the Beloved Country.* New York: Macmillan, 1987.
Thompson, Leonard. *A History of South Africa,* rev. ed. New Haven, Conn.: Yale University Press, 1995.

Web Sites

Bernard Makhosezwe Magubane, "Reflections on the Challenges Confronting Post-Apartheid South Africa." Discussion Paper Series, No. 7. Presented at Conference on Struggles against Poverty, Unemployment and Social Exclusion: Public Policies, Popular Action and Social Development, organized by UNESCO in Bologna, Italy, in collaboration with the University of Bologna and the city of Bologna, December 2–3, 1994. http://www.unesco.org/most/magu.html
Global Destinations, South Africa, Menu Guide. Deals with cuisine in South Africa. http://www.globalgourmet.com/destinations/southafrica/safrwhat.html. Cited June 1, 2000. (4 pp.).
Lou Seibert Pappas, "South Africa." http://www.sallys-place.com/food/ethnic_cuisine/south_africa.html. Cited June 1, 2002. (9 pp.).
South Africa YearBook 2000/1. The Land and Its People. http://www.gov.za/yearbook/rainbow.html. Cited January 10, 2001. (28 pp.).
"Youth Report." Youth 2000: A National Study of Youth in South Africa, December 2000. http://www.case.org.za/htm/yo9.htm. Cited November 27, 2001.

Organization

Embassy of the Republic of South Africa
4301 Connecticut Ave., NW Suite 220
Washington, DC 20008
(202) 939-9261

Chapter 13

UGANDA

George O. Ndege

INTRODUCTION

Uganda is in eastern Africa. Together with Kenya and Tanzania, the three countries make up the East African Community. Uganda, like many other countries in Africa, is both multi-ethnic and multilingual. There are 13 African ethnic groups, of which Baganda is the largest, comprising about 20 percent of the entire population. Each of the 13 groups has its own language, although some are closely related. Besides the African groups, Uganda also has members of European and Asian communities.

Britain colonized Uganda in the late nineteenth century. At the time, most of the Ugandan communities were fairly independent. Some had centralized political systems headed by chiefs or kings, while other communities were decentralized and governed by councils of elders. Notwithstanding the various political systems and their autonomous status, the populations interacted through trade, migration, and intermarriage. The British declaration of protectorate over Uganda in 1894 had the important effect of bringing together the disparate African communities under the umbrella of the colonial Ugandan state. Colonialism necessitated cultural encounters between the indigenous societies and the newly introduced British colonial order. British colonization was also manifested in the large numbers of Christian missionaries that flocked into the country, the establishment of schools and health care facilities, and the establishment of colonial administration.

British colonial control was exercised indirectly through chiefs, kingdoms, and the resident British administrators. However, the British colonization did not supplant the preexisting African customs or Islamic values. Although Western schooling became entrenched as the dominant system, the traditional, informal educational system continued to play an important role in the lives of most Africans. Thus, colonial Uganda became a melting pot of the three traditions: African, Islamic, and European.

Uganda attained independence from Britain in 1962. Although the transition was fairly peaceful, Uganda's postcolonial history has been tumultuous, with only a few interludes of peace. General Idi Amin, the army commander, toppled the first civilian government of Uganda, headed by Milton Obote, in 1971. The military government of Amin remains the most brutal and repressive regime in Uganda's history. It was infamous for political assassinations, violation of human rights, and economic ruin.

Ugandan rebels removed Amin from power in early 1979 with the active support of the Tanzanian defense forces. However, the removal of Amin failed to restore peace in the war-torn country. Protracted civil war plagued the country throughout the 1980s. Yoweri Museveni led successful guerrilla warfare and assumed power in early 1986. He moved fast to restore order, cracking down on militants and bandits. He mobilized people and established National Resistance Councils (NRC) at the local level in order to ensure public participation in his government. President Museveni also focused on revamping the economy by attracting foreign investors. His reign marked the first serious attempt to restore order and stability since 1971. Nevertheless, factional fighting among various warring groups persisted well into the mid-1990s.

The civil war led to the emergence of child soldiers. Thousands of children died in the war, and many more were orphaned as the war coincided with the spread of AIDS.

The situation, however, has changed significantly since the mid-1990s. Under Museveni's leadership, the country has been fairly stable. Although the country has a no-party political system, Museveni encourages political participation from all citizens of Uganda, regardless of their political, ethnic, and religious convictions. The spread of AIDS infection has slowed down drastically due to aggressive, open, and bold steps taken by the Museveni government with the support of international donors.

Peace is still elusive in northern Uganda. As a result, teenagers from such areas still experience tremendous responsibilities and hardships as soldiers and orphans. The instability in Uganda is a function of many factors, including ethnic and regional conflicts and the attendant competing nationalism. Nearly seven decades of colonial governance, as well as fragile institutions, also have been contributory factors to the incessant civil wars in Uganda.

Uganda has a vibrant, liberal economy. Investor confidence is high. The country's gross domestic product (GDP) growth rate has stabilized at 5 percent, which is a remarkable achievement considering the poor performance of the economy throughout the 1970s and 1980s. However, Uganda is still plagued by high unemployment and nearly 55 percent of the population still lives below the poverty line. The country has a weak industrial base. Agriculture remains the backbone of the economy, employing nearly 80 percent of the entire country's workforce. Uganda's population of nearly 21 million is disproportionately rural, with 86 percent of the people living in rural areas. Out of the 14 percent that is the urban population, 40 percent live in the capital city of Kampala.

English is the official language: the language of commerce, law, and government. Luganda and Swahili are the two most widely spoken indigenous languages. The electronic and print media in the country have been instrumental in maintaining the preeminence of English and these two indigenous languages. Uganda Television (UTV), which is state-controlled, broadcasts in Swahili, English, and Luganda. Radio Uganda, patronized by the government, broadcasts mainly in Swahili, English, and Luganda, with some airtime dedicated to other Ugandan vernaculars. Meanwhile, the two newspapers with the largest circulation in the country, *New Vision* and the *Monitor,* are printed in English, while the third-largest newspaper, *Taifa Uganda Empya,* is printed in Luganda.

The preeminence of Luganda is also due to the fact that the most populous community, Baganda, speaks it. During the nearly seven decades of colonial governance, the Baganda were given special status within the protectorate. As a result, Baganda agents were utilized in spreading British influence. Luganda was imposed on communities where the Baganda worked as imperial agents. Meanwhile, Swahili is the most widely spoken indigenous language in eastern Africa. With Kenya, Uganda, and Tanzania forging greater political, economic, and educational ties, the role of Swahili is likely to increase.

TYPICAL DAY

A teen's typical day is influenced by a number of factors: level of education, urban or rural residence, and gender. The day begins quite early for those in day schools. They have to wake up early, eat breakfast, and walk to school because the government does not provide public transport, and failure to reach school on time (which is usually 7:30 A.M.) can result in the student being reprimanded or punished. On reaching school, students engage in a number of cleaning activities, including sweeping their classrooms and trimming grass. Classes run from around 8:00 A.M. in the morning to 3:00 P.M., with one hour for a lunch break. Those whose homes are close to the school usually return home for lunch, while those who live far often carry their lunches when they go to school in the morning. Those in the lower grades do not return to school after lunch.

In the evening, students help their parents with domestic chores. Girls help by fetching water and cooking. Boys help with milking cows and splitting firewood. School assignments are done after dinner, which is usually eaten between 6:00 and 7:00 P.M. Teens preparing to take national standardized examinations are often required by teachers to stay in school late, or report very early in the morning to ensure that they complete their assignments. Schools do this because of the awareness that it is much harder for the students to complete their homework because of the many chores they have to perform at home. Teens in day schools also spend the weekends helping their parents.

In order to overcome some of the foregoing problems, parents who are financially able may prefer to send their children to boarding schools. Boarding schools provide the students with the facilities and time to focus on their studies without being distracted by too much work. Thus, students do not have to worry about what and when they are going to eat.

Meanwhile, teenagers from wealthy families have a more relaxed schedule than those from poor families. Their families usually employ housemaids who help with cooking and cleaning the house. They wake up to a ready breakfast, after which they are driven to school. For those in private schools, the management organizes transportation and the students are picked up at home every morning. On return from school in the evening, they eat dinner and then either complete their assignments or watch television.

There are teenagers who for one reason or another do not attend school. Their typical day begins early, as in the case of those who go to school, but their routine is primarily focused on eking out a living. If they are not working on their parents' farms or tending cattle, they are offering their services in return for payment. There are those who engage in petty trading, selling wares and other related commodities. Their daily routine is challenging and long. They have to be aggressive and effective in enticing customers to buy their products to be able to make a living. Often they frequent bus stations where they try to sell to commuters, or the open-air markets.

Teenagers who are employed by wealthy families as domestic workers in return for payment are the first to wake up. They go and buy milk and

Ugandan teens. Courtesy of Catherine Agnes Nantongo.

bread from the kiosk if that was not done the previous evening. They have to fix breakfast for the family. If there are children who carry a packed lunch to school, the maid must make sure that the meal is ready when the child leaves for school. After the children and their parents have gone to school and work, respectively, the maid washes dishes, mops the floor, and washes clothes. The schedule becomes quite hectic if there is an infant who must be taken care of in addition to the aforementioned chores. The maid must also prepare lunch if the family returns home for lunch. The irony, however, is that these maids, who are mostly teenagers, are poorly paid despite being the force behind chores performed in the household.

FAMILY LIFE

As in most African communities, the family is the most important unit in Uganda. It is at the family level that the teen is introduced to complex social and kinship relations. The immediate and extended family members have enormous influence on teens' lives. The family in Uganda is not only a biological unit; it is also a social institution. However, the influence of the extended family is much stronger in rural than in urban areas. The settlement of the rural areas tends to follow lineage and clan lines, and as a result, rural teens are more aware of intricate, extended family relationships. This knowledge of the elaborate kinship system helps the teen to identify with the family, lineage, clan, and community. Both the immediate and extended family, therefore, shapes the teen's worldview.

The conduct and reputation of one's family is important. Hard work, honesty, and good behavior are not only expected of all teens, but also cherished. Families strive to inculcate these values through informal education. Teens are expected to follow instructions given by their parents as well as their seniors. Any unbecoming conduct can be the subject of ridicule and condemnation by the parents and community. Shaking hands when greeting peers, washing hands before one starts eating, and complimenting people for services offered are considered important etiquette. It is considered rude and impolite to have eye contact with older people, particularly of the teens' parents' generation. Even shaking their hands is not acceptable. In a sense, seniority in age is highly respected and teenagers are admonished to avoid untoward conduct that may be interpreted as a sign of disrespect for their seniors. Riddles, myths, legends, and proverbs are used to remind teens of their obligation to respect their parents, seniors, and fellow peers.

All teens in rural areas are expected to participate in one way or another in producing food. The services tend to vary according to gender. Girls are supposed to do household chores such as fetching firewood, drawing water from the river, and cooking, as well as participating in petty trading in the many open-air markets that dot the countryside. Besides these chores, girls also babysit. Few rural families employ servants and household help. Because of the extended family, the household unit accommodates relatives. Such relatives are not paid for services they render, nor are they asked for rent. It is considered a reciprocal relationship, with one offering services in exchange for shelter and food.

While boys tend cattle, milk cows, plow, and clear farms, it is important to note that this division is not rigid. It is not uncommon to find boys performing tasks that are usually assigned to girls, particularly in families that do not have girls, or where they are still too young to undertake household chores. In sedentary societies, the school schedule determines when a teenager is supposed to perform an assigned task. By and large, teens that go to school usually perform the more demanding tasks of fetching fire-wood, tending cattle, and plowing during weekends. Those in boarding schools normally escape undertaking some of these tasks during the school year because of their absence from home.

The situation is rather different in the pastoral communities where Western education has not been entrenched. The division of labor tends to be rigid among the predominantly pastoral communities of northeast-ern Uganda, particularly the Karamojong. Some Karamojong boys consti-tute the warrior class, whose function is to defend the community and ensure that their livestock are not raided by neighboring communities in Uganda, or from across the border in Kenya. Security lapses coupled with the availability of guns to the citizenry have increased banditry in the northeastern border region of Uganda. As a result, the Karamojong of Uganda and the Pokot and Turkana communities of Kenya engage in ban-ditry and cattle raids. Teens enlist as warriors to defend their communities and to protect and replenish their herds.

The influence of the extended family in urban areas is rather minimal. Teens in urban areas, particularly from middle- and upper-income fami-lies, go to school. Upon graduation, they enter the job market as skilled or unskilled workers, depending on the number of years completed in school, their area of specialization, and the employment sector. Teens in urban areas tend to be more assertive than rural teens, and the traditional values of patriarchy are not held in high esteem. Also, teens in urban areas have more access to Western films and more exposure to pornography than their rural counterparts.

Because of the high cost of apartments, teens in urban areas tend to live with their parents well into their early adulthood years, while rural teenagers have to build their own cottages. However, the term "urban" masks some significant distinctions among various households. In the low-income areas within the towns, life is hard for most families. Some teens from low-income families find themselves caught in the vicious cycle of poverty. Under such circumstances, they rarely make it beyond primary school. Most of these school dropouts work in the informal sector industries. Others perform menial jobs. Girls are employed as housemaids.

TRADITIONAL AND NONTRADITIONAL FOOD DISHES

Ugandans have a wide array of traditional as well as nontraditional dishes. Traditional dishes include *matooke*, which is a staple made from bananas, sweet potatoes, corn (maize), and yams. *Matooke* is popular among the Baganda, for whom it is the main staple. It is served with various stews: beef, chicken, or fish. People do not use knives, forks, or spoons. Sweet potatoes are also an important staple. These can be boiled and eaten with porridge, or dried and ground into flour used to make a thick porridge, which is then eaten with the stews indicated above. Meanwhile, maize can be roasted and eaten, or dried and ground into flour and used in making a traditional cornbread, *ugali*, which is eaten with stew.

Unlike in the United States, where soda, wine, or beer is usually drunk with or immediately after the meal, the majority of Ugandans drink water, as beer or soda are too costly for some. Roasted beef is particularly popular and is served in many eateries frequented by the urban elite. In such eateries, a meal is eaten while the diners drink beer and discuss the latest social, political, and economic developments in the township. Rumor and gossip constitute a big part of these conversations.

Vegetables are an integral part of the diet. Peasants on their farms cultivate cabbages, collard greens, spinach, beans, and peas. Rural communities and the urban poor depend more on vegetables than on beef. The latter is expensive and most families cannot afford to buy meat on a regular basis. Vegetables are cheaper in rural than in urban areas. Fruits are also an important part of the general diet. Bananas, pineapples, oranges, and sugarcane are quite popular in urban and rural areas. Among the pastoral communities, cattle are the main source of food, providing them with beef, milk, and blood, the three most cherished foodstuffs. Pastoral communities also hunt wild game as a supplement.

Nontraditional dishes reflect the influence of the Asian and European communities. *Chapati*, which is made from wheat flour, is of Indian origin. French fries and hamburgers are now the meals of choice for many teenagers in urban areas. Chocolate and other candy are also popular among them. Most urban dwellers buy their foods from grocery stores or open-air markets, as well as from fast-food restaurants. Peasants in the rural areas produce their own food or buy from the local open-air markets.

Ugandans have two main meals a day, breakfast and dinner. Breakfast is eaten in the morning when teenagers are about to leave for school, and parents are getting ready to go to work. The breakfast menu comprises tea, bread, eggs, and fruit for the wealthy urban dwellers, while porridge or tea with boiled cassava, potatoes, or corn are popular among the low-income groups and peasants. Lunch is fairly light in urban and rural areas, because people are usually at their workplaces. A snack, porridge, or a packet of milk with bread suffices for lunch. Thus, dinner is the heaviest meal. As the entire family is usually at home, it is the main communal meal. Dinner is normally eaten between 6:00 and 7:00 P.M. because children are expected to go to bed early. Hence, children are fed first, and then the rest of the family eats. In rural areas, girls and boys eat separately. When a meal is prepared, an attempt is made to ensure that the amount is enough for everybody present as well as those who may drop in when people are eating. It is considered impolite to refuse to eat when you find people taking a meal. People have to share what is there, however little it is. A refusal can be interpreted to mean that one is greedy and would not like others to eat his food when they find him taking a meal. Joining together in a meal is a demonstration of good will and sociability.

Cooking is largely the preserve of women. In traditional society, a teenage boy who frequented the kitchen was scorned and became the subject of gossip and ridicule among his peers in the village. As a result, teenagers grew up with the notion that the kitchen is women's domain. Girls were trained in all aspects of cooking. Taking care of the husband and family meant being able to prepare good food and ensuring that everybody was satisfied. This view is still widely held by the majority of the population, including women. The situation is gradually changing because of the process of rural-to-urban migration, where men who either are single or have left their rural homes have no alternative but to prepare their own meals. Wealthy urban dwellers, however, invariably employ housemaids who do the cooking. The result is that girls from such households are rarely prepared for the cooking chores because the maid does most of the work.

An important aspect of the diet eaten by Ugandans is that obesity as a health problem is not a factor. This is because most Ugandans, both the rural farmers and urban workers, engage in work where they expend a lot of energy. Also, Ugandan teenagers are not preoccupied with physical exercises with a view toward weight reduction. At any rate, being slim creates the impression of one who does not eat well. All in all, Ugandans have a wide array of foods to choose from, although the choice is dependent on a number of factors: community, urbanization, level of income, and exposure to outside influences.

SCHOOLING

School is a very important institution in teens' lives. It is the means by which the majority of teenagers from humble origins make their way into the middle and upper income levels. Enrollment in schools has improved since the 1970s and 1980s, when insecurity and political instability engulfed almost the entire country. Uganda's formal educational system comprises primary school, secondary school, high school, and university. Students pay tuition and other fees that are determined by the Parents and Teachers Association. According to the 2000 UNESCO World Education Report, the number of students in school decreases at each level, with primary enrollment at 74 percent and secondary enrollment at 12 percent. The higher the level, the more selective the system becomes. Students have to compete at the end of every level to gain admission into the next. Students must take national and standardized examinations to qualify for admission to secondary school, high school, and university. The Uganda National Examination Council conducts the examinations. However, lack of tuition also contributes to the attrition rate. Children from poor families who cannot afford to pay school tuition are forced to leave school even if they earned good grades.

Gender bias is also a factor in the high attrition rate. There is favoritism shown for the education of boys. The patriarchal nature of societies encourages sending boys to school. When funds are scarce, families will send boys rather than girls to secondary and high schools. This preference is much higher among those who live in rural areas, where patriarchal views are still strong. Teen pregnancy contributes to the attrition rate among girls. Thus, there is an imbalance in the number of boys and girls attending schools, particularly in the postprimary levels. The level of teen literacy also reflects this gender imbalance. The 2000 UNESCO Report shows that while female youth literacy is 24 percent, the male youth literacy stands at 46 percent, which is almost double the female rate.

The Report further indicates that the Ugandan government spends 2.6 percent of the GDP on education. Much of what the government allocates for education is spent on teachers' compensation, which consumes nearly 70 percent. There are 35 pupils per teacher. While this is not high for a developing country, the critical issues are the availability of facilities, science equipment, and books for students. Only 30 percent of the total allocation is spent on the development of facilities and the purchase of equipment and books. There is stiff competition for the best schools in the country.

Besides public schools, Uganda has many private schools. Churches, foundations, and individual investors run the private schools. The schools charge high tuition that only those in the upper income level can afford. Because of the high tuition, private schools tend to have better instructional materials, smaller classes, and more motivated teachers.

While the Ministry of Education determines the curriculum, some private schools cater to international students and follow a curriculum that enables graduates to pursue higher education in Europe and the United States.

English is the medium of instruction in all public and private schools. The use of local dialects in lower grades is common in rural schools. While a few public high schools teach French and German, most private international schools invariably offer these languages in their curriculum. The subjects taught include mathematics, science, history, geography, religious studies, music, and fine art. In secondary and high schools, students study physics, biology, and chemistry as well.

Students in primary and secondary schools are expected to wear uniforms. The uniform code is often enforced during school hours. Most public primary schools are day schools, while most private primary schools are boarding schools. Most primary schools are mixed, catering to both boys and girls. The exceptions are the mission schools, which tend to be single-sex. Secondary schools can either be single-sex or mixed. The public universities are coeducational.

Students also engage in sports. Soccer is a very popular sport for boys, as are cricket, boxing, and rugby. Netball is the most popular sport among girls. Volleyball and athletics are also very popular for both sexes. The games are played after classes, usually after 3:00 P.M. Competitive athletes are required to report to school before classes for practice, and they can be asked to remain after classes. Those who go to day schools have to leave home very early to reach school in time for practice, or reach home late after a hectic day of practice. Competitions at the primary and high school levels are organized and winning teams are awarded trophies. Teams playing in the national leagues recruit some of their players from secondary- and high-school teams. Those who excel in the national leagues proceed to join the Uganda national team.

Music competitions are also quite popular. Primary and secondary music festivals take place at various levels: local, district, provincial, and national. As in the case of athletic competitions, winning teams are awarded trophies. Teachers whose choirs perform well are cited for recognition and sometimes promoted. Western, Oriental, and African music is sung in these festivals, reflecting the rich cultural diversity in the country. African songs and dances are very popular. There are many types of African songs, including ones for love and praise. Because of the AIDS pandemic, songs and plays have become quite popular in conveying messages to youth to beware the impact of the disease.

SOCIAL LIFE

Parents encourage teens to visit their relatives so they get to know one another. The visits enhance sociability among relatives. The visits are also encouraged because dating between relatives is strictly forbidden. Thus, such visits reduce the possibility of embarrassing dating between related teenagers. Dating before marriage is common. Muslims, however, are against dating and premarital sex. But teenagers do not always strictly follow this code.

There is no caste system in Uganda. Dating takes place within and across ethnic lines. However, income level is a significant factor, particularly if the difference is huge. Teenagers from extremely poor families have little chance of dating those from wealthy families and vice versa. Those from very poor families go to nonexclusive public schools and often drop out of school due to financial problems. They also live in poverty-stricken parts of the city, and rarely visit those affluent residential areas or social places that teens from rich neighborhoods frequent.

Public display of sexuality such as kissing in public, holding hands, or indecent dressing is frowned upon. It is considered impolite and shameful to display such manifestations of love and sexuality in public, particularly in the presence of parents-in-law. A young man must show the utmost respect for his mother-in-law. In traditional society, any physical contact such as shaking hands was forbidden by most communities. Although the situation is changing, the general respect between a boy and his potential parents-in-law is still maintained by most communities.

Teenagers find their suitors in schools, at dance parties, and by contact through sisters, cousins, aunts, or friends. Teenagers express their affection in love letters. Those who date socialize in many ways. The urban elite frequent movies theaters, disco dances, and even eat out. However, this is largely done discretely and without the knowledge of the parents. Girls often feign reasons to be out of the house for a couple of hours in order to visit a boyfriend. Excuses include going to visit an aunt or a schoolmate living in another part of the city. In rural areas, girls tend to be more open with their paternal aunts, with whom they discuss their love matters.

Dating does not necessarily translate into marriage, yet premarital sex is now much more common than in traditional society. This can partly be explained by the weakening of traditional society in the wake of such forces as urbanization and Westernization. Dating partners always take care not to have a child before marriage because abortion is unacceptable to most. Teenage motherhood, which occurs outside wedlock, brings shame to the parents of the girl and also reduces the attractiveness of the girl to a suitor. Nevertheless, teen pregnancies still occur and the girl's parents usually assume responsibility.

While prearranged marriages are becoming a thing of the past, there is always an attempt to find out about the family from which the bride or bridegroom hails. This is important because marriage between members of a clan is prohibited. Hence, it is not uncommon to find aunts and other relatives playing an important role in gathering such vital information, or recommending a girl or boy to the potential suitor. However, the final decision rests with the couple. But while dating is between the girl and the boy, the situation changes when the two get married. Once the marriage is complete, it is considered a family matter, because marriage is a way of perpetuating lineage, clan, and community. Any problems besetting the institution must be brought before the parents or close relatives, particularly in rural areas. Divorce is discouraged, although it is not outlawed. However, it is much harder in situations where the marriage has been blessed with children.

The way teenagers dress is a reflection of how Westernization has impacted Uganda. T-shirts, jeans, slacks, and suits are quite popular among teenagers. Names of international celebrities such as Michael Jordan and certain soccer stars are printed on T-shirts. The electronic and print media, international travel, and the movement of ideas via the Internet have coalesced to expose Ugandan teenagers to Western-style clothing. However, girls tend to be more conservative than boys in the way they dress. It is rare to see girls in trousers outside the urban centers. Some Muslim girls, though not all, wear the veil.

Ugandan teens. Courtesy of Catherine Agnes Nantongo.

RECREATION

Sports are one of the most important types of recreation. As indicated, sporting activities such as soccer, netball, and volleyball serve the purposes of recreation and competition as part of school activity. Outside the schools, soccer is the most popular sport in both rural and urban areas. Soccer in Uganda is a male sport and boys as young as 10 play the game. Teenagers who have dropped out of school and are interested in soccer join local clubs, which are sometimes patronized by local leaders or the local community. The clubs often get donations of uniforms, balls, or cash from companies that sponsor these activities as part of their marketing strategy. The clubs organize soccer competitions and some qualify to join the junior league. It is instructive that the government supports youth clubs because they constitute the pool from which national players are selected.

While soccer has nationwide support and clubs are found in urban and rural areas, netball, volleyball, tennis, rugby, and cricket draw a lot of support from the urban areas, where tournaments are organized by the respective clubs and sponsored by companies. Such tournaments are held on the weekends and attract large audiences, who pay to enter stadiums for these tournaments. The government actively supports games as a form of recreation.

In rural areas, the competitive throwing of sticks, teen wrestling, and the hunting of wild game are also popular forms of recreation. In traditional society, a good wrestler was admired and was considered the clan's hero. Hunting served the dual function of recreation and food gathering. Forces of modernization have undermined the significance of these recreational activities, but they still exist in rural areas.

Recreation in Uganda is seen as a form of relaxation, engagement in sport, and a socialization process among peers. It is not seen as a way of reducing weight or building muscles so that one can be perceived as fit. The fitness aspect of recreation is just beginning to be a factor among the urban elite, who frequent clubhouses and gyms equipped with modern exercise facilities.

ENTERTAINMENT

Music is an important form of entertainment. Besides music taught in schools as part of the extracurriculum, Ugandan teens have been heavily impacted by Western pop music. Hence, Ugandan towns have modern nightclubs, where disco dancing is part of teenage entertainment. Teens and their partners frequent discos, which are usually full on Fridays and

Saturdays. Teens go to these discos either accompanied or not. For those who are unaccompanied, it provides them with the opportunity to find suitors. It is considered impolite to dance with an accompanied girl.

Most teens own small pocket radios and audiocassettes which they often carry with them. For teens from upper income families in urban areas, international music is the preferred choice. The liberalization of the media has led to an increase in the number of radio stations, which now stands at 10. These stations offer a wide array of entertainment in the form of both local and international music. Plays are also shown on television, although these are mainly available in upper-income homes. For those in Kampala, the capital city, movie theaters offer another form of entertainment. Watching games, particularly on weekends, is also a popular form of entertainment. Teens flock to stadiums during soccer matches, which attract both sexes, although boys are the majority.

Though teens in rural areas have less access to movie theaters or nightclubs than their urban counterparts, rural teens are not immune from the international cultural influences that are prevalent in urban areas. The attempt to contain the spread of AIDS has resulted in films being shown in the rural areas by mobile theater units, which are mainly supported by nongovernmental organizations. While the films have a tone of somberness, they also carry a sense of humor. Hence, they serve the dual purpose of education and entertainment.

Some of the famous theater groups are Kampala Singers, Bakayimbira Dramactors, Kampala Amateur Dramatic Society, Black Pearls Ltd., Ndere Troupe, Ngoma Players, and the Planets. Kampala also houses famous galleries: Galrie de l'Alliance Francaise, Gallery Café, and Nomno Gallery. The famous Uganda National Museum is also located in Kampala. Thus, teenagers in Kampala have many forms of entertainment to choose from.

Dance parties patronized by teens are quite common in rural Uganda. The parties are common in December, particularly around Christmas. The music played in such parties is varied. Local music, music of other African countries—particularly Zaire—and Western music are played on such occasions. Local music groups include the Afrigo band and the Abayudaya Jews of Uganda. Ayub Ogada, Geoffrey Oryema, and Samite are some of the musicians who are popular among youth. What this shows is that the divide between urban and rural teenagers in the area of entertainment is not that great. The various radio stations have been quite instrumental in narrowing that gap.

Other forms of entertainment for rural teenagers include watching bullfighting and playing *kwesa*, a strategy game in which stones or beans are placed in pockets carved in a wooden board. Both girls and boys play *kwesa*. Also, verbal entertainment in the form of storytelling at night in the company of grandparents is an innovative way by which the old people tend to inculcate traditional values in teens. This is an advantage that rural teens have over their urban counterparts, who can only read some of these stories, sayings, and proverbs in books. The stories depict various themes in life: generosity, courage, leadership, kinship, respect for elders, moral uprightness, honesty, and hard work. The stories perform the dual functions of entertainment and education, which are equally important. Indeed, during national days, tournaments are organized to provide entertainment for the population. Such activities include music, dances, games, and plays. While the games inculcate the spirit of competition, the music and plays often evoke a spirit of patriotism and accomplishment.

RELIGIOUS PRACTICES AND CULTURAL CEREMONIES

Most Ugandans are Christians. They constitute 66 percent of the population, evenly divided between Protestant and Roman Catholic. The rest of the population is Muslim or holds indigenous beliefs, 16 percent and 18 percent respectively. The freedom of worship is entrenched in the constitution. As a result, these religions are found in every part of the country and attempt to influence the upbringing of their young followers. Churches run schools, training institutions, and social development and educational programs.

Both Roman Catholics and Protestants have pastoral programs to help their youth grow up as faithful members of the church. Because these two groups are closely tied to the Western educational system dating back to colonial times, the majority of the elite in Uganda went through schools that were patronized by these mission stations. Those who went to secular schools have a soft heart for these religious traditions because the institutions espoused more or less similar values to those found in the Christian tradition. As a result, teenagers from the elite closely identify with these Christian denominations. Through expansive social development programs such as relief work among the poor, many teenagers are associated with these mainstream churches. Some of them join seminaries to become priests. However, teenagers who go through the pastoral programs often partake of the sacraments offered by the church. Sunday is rest day and most of the teenagers flock to the church for prayer service. Easter and Christmas are the two most important days on the Christian calendar in Uganda.

For Muslims, Friday is the day of worship. They also observe noon prayers and participate in Islamic festivals including Ramadan. However, since Uganda is a secular state that is not inclined to any religion, Muslim students are free to attend the high school of their choice. Uganda does not have many high schools that are exclusively Muslim. Indeed, the best schools are private schools patronized by the mission stations or the few public schools run by the government. Islamic teenagers attend secular schools that are heavily Western in orientation. The result is the production of Muslim teenagers schooled in schools developed along the Western formal educational system. In a sense, there are no Christian Muslims, but there are Westernized Muslims.

Those who follow indigenous beliefs engage in customs and practices that reflect their worldview. In this regard, teenagers of parents who profess various indigenous religious beliefs are subjected to initiation rites, which tend to vary from one community to another. The rituals include naming ceremonies, recognition of the various developmental stages that one goes through from childhood to adulthood, and initiation into specific age-set systems. Communal feasts in which animals are slaughtered accompany the rituals. The name of the god is evoked and ancestors are called upon to be witnesses to these rituals, which are believed to ensure the moral stability and general prosperity of society.

As in the pastoral programs of the Christian churches, these cultural practices are significant because of the training the initiates go through. Girls are often advised by old women on what is expected of them as teenagers, as well as on their future roles as wives and mothers. Among the Baganda, for example, the term for marriage, *jangu enfumbire* (*come cook for me*), blended the qualities of being a wife, a good cook, and a responsible mother. In the same vein, the term signified the patriarchal nature of society and the division of labor based on gender. Despite the onset of a modern economy and Western influence, these views are still held dear by the society. Hence, the instructions provided to the initiates during training reflect and reinforce societal views.

Among the Karamojong, for example, the boys are initiated every three years, starting from the age of 19. Those initiated at the same time constitute an age-set. The age-set is identified by a name chosen by senior men. The names are associated with animals such as buffalo, leopard, and so forth. The group is identified by that name for purposes of warriorhood, seniority, and leadership. During the initiation ceremony, the group is schooled in the defense of the community, power and authority, religion, and service and discipline.

In examining these cultural practices it has to be emphasized that there is nothing unchristian about them. Indeed, it is not uncommon to find girls or boys who have undergone the traditional rituals but who also profess the Christian or Islamic faith. Some of these initiates go to secular or church schools. When sick, they go to hospitals whose healing practices are based on Western biomedicine. Even though each tradition has its unique attributes, the followers live in a nontheocratic society that fosters multiple solutions to the challenges that individuals face.

CONCLUSION

Ugandan teenagers have been impacted by a wide array of forces, including Westernization, education, and the media. The impact of these forces is more pronounced in the urban areas than in the countryside. Nevertheless, most teenagers generally have a better understanding of the world than many imagine. They have a sharp grasp of international events and issues ranging from national leaders and politics to economic and cultural trends. Yet despite those influences, Ugandan teens are proud of their country and optimistic about the future, despite the political turmoil of the 1970s and 1980s.

There is an ongoing cultural dialogue within Uganda in the wake of globalization. The divide between rural and urban is not that great because of the movement of ideas, people, and services between the two areas on the one hand, and the world on the other. While the erosion of traditional values is one of the major effects resulting from cultural encounters between Western and African cultures, it is important to note that through music, dances, dietary habits, and values, there is still an authenticity in what is Ugandan and African in the opening decade of this millennium.

RESOURCE GUIDE

Books

Behrend, Heike. *Alice Lakwena and the Holy Spirits: War in Northern Uganda.* Athens: Ohio University Press, 1999.
Kilbride, Philip, and Janet Kilbride. *Changing Family Life in East Africa: Women and Children at Risk.* University Park: Pennsylvania University Press, 1990.

Web Sites

http://www.africaguide.com/country/uganda
http://www.africanews.com/monitor
http://www.africaonline.com/site/uga/index
http://www.newafrica.com
http://www.unesco.org/education/information/wer

Chapter 14

ZAMBIA

Priscilla Muntemba Taylor and Scott Taylor

INTRODUCTION

The Republic of Zambia is a landlocked nation in the tropics of southern Africa. Distant from the Atlantic and Indian oceans, Zambia lies at the northern edge of the southern Africa region. Zambia borders seven other nations in the region, and thus shares many historical, cultural, and sometimes political ties with its neighbors. Known for its natural beauty, such as the magnificent Victoria Falls in the south or the country's astounding 19 national parks, many Zambians like to refer to their country as the "heart of Africa," a term that they feel describes both the country's location and its crescent-shaped (or, more imaginatively, heart-shaped) geography. At 290,724 square miles, the country is roughly the size of the state of Texas, yet its population is very small at just 10.3 million people.

However, despite its size, history, and natural wonders, Zambia is little known to most Westerners. Little wonder, as Zambia has not been a fixture in the headlines of the North American or European press. Western media attention tends to be drawn to crises in Africa, and Zambia is a peaceful and relatively uncontroversial place, from an international perspective. Notwithstanding its comparative obscurity, Zambia has a great deal to offer: the country is spacious, varied, and politically stable. The overwhelming majority of Zambia's population speak a language from the Bantu language group (one of several language families in Africa). Within the Bantu family, Zambians speak some 73 different dialects, many of which are themselves independent languages. In addition to its African population, Zambia is also home to small minorities of people of European and East Asian descent, many of whom have resided in the country for several generations. The majority of Zambians are Christians, with a minority of Muslims, Hindus, and those with indigenous beliefs comprising the remainder.

The Scottish explorer David Livingstone was among the first Europeans to travel extensively in the mid-nineteenth century through what is now Zambia. Subsequently, Zambia was under British control from 1890 until it gained its independence in October 1964. Given the country's long connection to Great Britain and the multiplicity of indigenous languages, English serves as both a lingua franca and the official language; most urban Zambians speak it fluently. Beginning in primary school, usually around age 8 or 10, many Zambian children are taught in English rather than their first tongue. Thus, although English is used far less frequently in the rural areas than in Zambia's cities, only in remote settlements would one encounter problems communicating in English.

Zambia's elevation on a plateau gives it a moderate climate, despite the fact that it is within tropical latitudes. There are two principal seasons: rainy from December to April, and dry from May to November, although Zambia's "winter" months from June to August can be quite cool. In most parts of the country, there is noticeable humidity only during the wet or rainy season. This comfortable, temperate climate is one of the reasons that British colonizers found Zambia such an inviting place to settle in the late nineteenth and early twentieth centuries: it reminded them of the climate in Europe! Although never numbering more than 300,000, Europeans came in significant waves to live in Zambia. Large-scale commercial farming, controlled exclusively by Europeans, was established in the mid-1920s. They also came to mine copper, which is plentiful in Zambia.[1]

One of Zambia's enduring assets is its natural beauty. Apart from Victoria Falls, the country is blessed with lakes, rivers, forests, and mountains of fantastic variety. Wildlife, too, is incredibly diverse. This, coupled with a rich cultural tradition, makes the country extremely attractive to both residents and foreign visitors alike.

Given this picture, it would seem as if Zambian teens would grow up in a kind of peaceful, temperate paradise: a land with both teeming cities and abundant exotic wildlife; a place that is home to the mighty Victoria Falls and is an increasingly popular destination for tourists from all over the world. Yet life can be very difficult in Zambia. Its natural resources (tapped and untapped) notwithstanding, Zambia is a very poor country, with a gross domestic product (GDP) per capita of barely $300 per year. In fact, the United Nations Development Programme's (UNDP) *World Development Report, 2001* ranks Zambia among the world's poorest countries. Zambia's ranking on the poverty index (number 143 out of 161 nations) includes the grim statistic that an estimated 63 percent of the population is living on $1 or less per day. The country has been hit hard by natural disasters (such as two severe droughts in the early 1990s), the AIDS crisis, a deteriorating infrastructure, and economic decline. According to the UNDP, Zambia's per-capita GDP fell by an average of 2.4 percent in the 1990s; as a result, the country's GDP per capita is worse than it was in 1975. Zambia has the dubious distinction of leading the world in this category.[2]

This situation stands in stark contrast to the heady days of the 1960s, when—with the country newly liberated from British domination—prices for Zambia's leading export, copper, were rising markedly, the economy was growing, and Zambians were filled with optimism about the future.

The 1990s, by contrast, represented a far harder time for teens to come of age in Zambia. The first decade of the twenty-first century promises only modest improvements, at best. Yes, life is difficult for many people in Zambia, teenagers included. Teens cannot help but be aware of the hardship, acute in some cases, in their own lives and in the lives of their countrymen. Yet the youth still try to find opportunities to dream and to enjoy life, despite the hardship. The biggest differences lie in urban versus rural households. While, clearly, poverty exists in both areas, urban teens are much more likely than their rural counterparts to have access to generally reliable public services, regular transportation, and educational opportunities. In the most remote areas of the country, scarcely touched by modern-day amenities, electricity and running water are luxuries that few enjoy. On the other hand, in major Zambian cities, like the capital, Lusaka, one is very likely to encounter teenagers similar to those from what we would call an upper-class family in the West. Their households sometimes boast multiple cars, a pool, a big house with a security gate, a maid, a gardener, and other domestic workers.

Thus, there is a great difference between rich and poor in Zambia. There are families where both parents own a car, and that can afford vacations to England, France, or the United States; then there are those that can barely have a proper meal every day. Some families live on one or two meals per day, and some students cannot afford to carry lunch to school—or to go to school at all.

TYPICAL DAY

The Zambian teenager's day starts much like that of his or her counterpart elsewhere in the world—that is, with school, although the number of students in school declined from nearly 100 percent in the 1980s to under 70 percent today, due to the introduction of school fees in the 1990s.[3] Teens attending school can be found at either a public school, funded by the government, or one that is privately run. Typically, these schools are open from 7:30 A.M. until 4:00 P.M. Like teens everywhere, Zambian teenagers get to school in a variety of ways, although it is worth noting that there is no such thing as a dedicated "school bus" in Zambia. Students may be driven to school by their parents or, in some particularly privileged cases, an assigned driver. Others use public transportation or hitchhike. In the cities, some schools may be a convenient walk from home. However, in rural areas, where private or public transportation may be irregular, students may walk for several kilometers in order to reach school. This places an extra burden on teenagers from impoverished rural areas; by the time they arrive at school in the morning, they may be already exhausted from the long trek.

In many schools, afternoon sports activities, which may last up to three hours, are scheduled once a week. Zambian students are involved in sports such as running, volleyball, netball (like basketball, but without the backboard), basketball, and tennis. "Football pitches" (soccer fields) are a ubiquitous feature of schools in Zambia, and soccer is one of the most popular sports in the country.

After school, many teens in Lusaka and other urban centers typically like to study, chat on the phone (if they have one), watch television, clean their rooms, go bike riding with friends, listen to music, and do their homework. Zambian teenagers, just like American teens, also enjoy going to shopping malls to hang out with friends. Again, life is different in rural areas, which tend to lack some of the amenities such as televisions, phones, and even reliable electricity. Nonetheless, although there are no Western-style shopping malls in rural Zambia, teenagers still like to relax, if possible, in the after-school hours. They may occupy their time by playing a game of soccer, sitting outside, or spending time talking with friends.

It is unusual for teenagers in Zambia to work outside of school, unless they are working for the family business, and even those are a select few. Among the 30 percent or more of students who were forced to leave school in the 1990s, work, perhaps on the family plot, is essential for survival. Many also have become hawkers of merchandise or even beggars in the urban centers.

Only a handful of enrolled teenage students work at places like gas stations or fast-food restaurants to make money for school supplies. Most teens of middle-class background look down their noses at such jobs, which they consider to be jobs for people who have not completed their

Farm workers with hoes. © David Tomley/CORBIS.

education. Teens depend on their parents and other relatives to support them through school.

Even in the poorer neighborhoods of Lusaka and other cities, many Zambian families have at least one worker to help with household chores. If a family is wealthy, they may have a full complement of domestic staff, including a house worker, cook, nanny, day guard, and evening guard. These workers are employed in such jobs because either they were unable to go to school due to financial difficulties, or they were unable to complete their education. It is common for houses in the capital city to have smaller quarters in the same yard where the domestics live so that they are available as needed after hours. This is actually a holdover from colonial days, when nearly all settlers employed Africans as domestic servants. Today, those old homes, now owned by other Zambians, still have these servant quarters, and domestic workers are still a part of the landscape. Because they live in such close proximity, in many cases Zambian teenagers may have spent much of their childhood with a particular domestic worker by the time they reach high-school age.

However, not all households can afford outside help, so the children must help out after school. It is worth noting here that gender roles tend to be clearly defined in the Zambian context. For example, until very recently boys were never expected to cook and clean around the house: girls assisted their mothers with cooking and cleaning chores, while boys worked in the yard. Recently, though, more parents are trying to groom their children, regardless of gender, to be more self-reliant and able to fend for themselves when they leave the household. One task common to both boys and girls is looking after their younger siblings.

FAMILY LIFE

Historically in Zambia, and throughout much of Africa, the family unit was much larger than the familiar Western nuclear family consisting solely of a mother, father, and children. Many Africans take a much broader, more encompassing interpretation of who is part of the immediate family. In fact, the term "extended family" is rarely used in Zambia because aunts and uncles are expected to play important roles, not only in their own children's lives, but also in those of their nieces and nephews. The same is true of grandparents and their grandchildren. (In many Zambian languages, one's cousins are referred to as siblings; uncles and aunts as parents, and so forth.) Therefore, it is fairly common, for instance, for an aunt or uncle to discipline a child. However, the maintenance of these traditional, close-knit family structures has been difficult in the modern economic and social structures that accompany city life. As a result, most of the urban families in Zambia are of the nuclear variety; few can afford to keep their extended families in the same household or vicinity as in outlying areas. Fortunately, in many cases, grandparents, aunts, uncles, and cousins live within the same city, or only a few hours distant. This makes it possible for families to visit one another with some regularity. However, there are also grandparents and others who live not in the central city, but in a far-flung village. While the cost and limited availability of transportation may make it difficult for teens to visit with these relatives, it is worth noting that parents are prone to pressuring their urban children to travel to visit grandparents, uncles, aunts, and so forth. In this way, an important connection to Zambian traditions, local languages, and cultural and family heritage is maintained.

Nonetheless, many Zambian teens have been brought up in urban homes where only English is spoken. This has already diminished certain connections to older relatives and to the past.

However, although the younger generations are becoming more "Americanized" in the conduct of their daily lives, Zambian parents tend to have more control over their teenage children's lives than in the United States. In fact, not even those children over the age of 18 are exempt; as long as they live in their parents' house, they have to abide by

their rules. Girls face even more parental supervision than boys, in part
because of cultural practices that constrain females of all ages. For example, if a teenage girl misbehaves and earns a bad reputation, her parents
will fear that she might not find anyone willing to marry her later in life
(and she might feel the same way). Because the expectation of marriage is
much stronger in Zambia (and Africa generally) than in the United
States, this is an important consideration, even for a teenager.

Since marriage is taken seriously, this affects dating behavior as well.
Whereas it might not be unusual for an American teenager to bring even
a casual date home to meet the parents, this is not permitted in Zambia.
Of course, parents might meet their teen's "friends" in other venues, but
neither girls nor boys may bring their *dates* home. Parents prefer not to see
too many girlfriends and boyfriends come and go. Serious relationships,
however, even at a young age, may prompt parents (especially of girls) to
ask questions about marriage.

It is very rare to find a household where only one parent works; the high
cost of living usually necessitates two incomes wherever possible. Importantly, more and more Zambian women have access to the same types of
jobs as their male counterparts. Indeed, it is not unusual to find Zambian
women occupying the highest positions in politics, commerce, and the
professions. Women own businesses and are executives in companies and
ministers in the government. Through these positions, and through a vibrant nongovernmental-organization community, women in Zambia
speak out increasingly for equal rights. Their recent success in these areas
represents an important break from the colonial- and postcolonial-era
norm of the African continent, where women have often been in subor-
dinate positions to men in politics and commerce.

Despite their advancement in society, women are still expected to cook,
clean, and make sure the family is intact, even after a full day at work.
Teenage girls are generally expected to assist. Conversely, the older men
usually go out to meet with friends for drinks after work, then go home ex-
pecting to find food ready for them. Although some mothers are attempting to educate their teenage sons to the contrary, it is not considered
"traditional" to find a man in the kitchen. However, since not all households are comprised of men who go out after work, some families do tend
to eat together at the same time, which is typically around 6:30 in the
evening.

Mothers are almost always home to eat evening meals with their
teenage children. Unlike in the United States, it is uncommon for women
to take on night jobs, unless they are in fields such as nursing. This is
partly due to limits on the availability of jobs (Zambia does not have a 24-

hour economy like the United States), partly due to safety concerns (the vast majority of nighttime jobs are as security guards), and partly because Zambian mothers prefer to be at home with their children in the evenings.

TRADITIONAL AND NONTRADITIONAL FOOD DISHES

Traditional foods in Zambia vary according to the different ethno-linguistic groups. However, one food staple, called *nshima,* is common to all groups. *Nshima* is made from ground corn, which is known in southern Africa as "mealie meal." It is prepared by mixing the mealie meal with hot water until it turns into a stiff dough. This dough is then eaten with what Zambians refer to in English as a relish, which can be anything from meat to vegetables to gravy.

Other common foods that fit within various ethnic traditions in Zambia include beans, pumpkins, cassava, dry and fresh fish, mushrooms, sweet potatoes, black peas, and okra. More exotic foods may include mice (eaten only in the eastern part of Zambia); a vegetarian dish called *chikanda,* which is widely referred to as "African polony" (baloney); caterpillars (eaten in the north); pumpkin and pumpkin seeds; and cassava leaves cooked with groundnuts. Those who own farms may rear chickens, ducks, goats, and, if possible, pigs and cows. Wild meat, such as impala and birds, and occasionally elephants, is hunted and killed by men and young boys. Nearly all the foods indicated here are eaten regularly, with the exception of pumpkin seeds and wild meat, which are prepared only on special occasions. Large farm animals, like cows and pigs, are slaughtered for very special occasions such as weddings or initiation ceremonies. Because large animals are expensive and cows represent an important source of both milk and manure for crops, they tend to be eaten less regularly by small farming families.

Owing to the abundance of lakes and rivers in Zambia, Zambians depend more on fish than on meat for their food. Every ethnic group has its own practice, some centuries old, of catching fish. The methods and instruments vary from the use of barriers across rivers to woven baskets, nets, barbed spears, and harpoons; even bows and arrows are used in some cases. Fish markets are popular, open-air displays where fishermen proudly display the catch of the day—and, of course, willingly negotiate their prices.

In urban areas, nearly all foods can be bought at a supermarket, and there are several large grocery chains in Zambia's major cities. Middle-class families who reside in cities like Lusaka tend to buy most of their goods at the supermarket, although most prefer to purchase vegetables at one of the city's many open-air marketplaces, where they are sold fresh. Most people prefer to go to the market because they are able to interact and negotiate with the sellers. For many years, urban markets have also offered those without education, particularly women, opportunities denied them elsewhere. For the poor, the markets also provide a place to buy small quantities of food available in the shops.

By and large, the traditional Zambian diet does not have ill effects on people's health. For example, except on some large commercial farms, fruits and vegetables are not grown using harmful pesticides, as they are in the developed world. Animals are raised free of the hormones and antibiotics common in American livestock. Given this balanced diet, health problems such as obesity and heart disease historically were rare in Zambia. However, the arrival of shopping malls and fast-food courts, with their special appeal to teenagers, has corresponded with an increasingly unhealthy urban population.

Breakfast is often bread or porridge and tea. A typical lunchtime meal for a teen might consist of *nshima* served with red meat or chicken and a vegetable. Given the time required to prepare meals, the high cost of food, and the inability to store "leftovers" for an extended period of time, the evening meal for the typical teen is usually the same as that eaten at lunch; wherever possible, families prepare sufficient quantities of food to last for the day. Traditionally, Zambians sat on the floor to eat and ate with their hands, but most families in urban households sit at a table in chairs and use knives and forks. Even the most Westernized families, however, still eat *nshima* with their hands (*nshima* tastes best when eaten with hands!).

The foods that teenagers find most appealing are *chikanda, nshima,* and vegetables with groundnuts. Unfortunately, parents are not able to prevent their children from eating nontraditional foods, especially if they spend their free time at the mall. Zambian teenagers, perhaps predictably, favor the same high-carbohydrate, high-fat foods that are popular among teens the world over, including pizza, rice, potatoes, macaroni and cheese, french fries (known as "chips" in Zambia), salami, sausages, lasagna, burgers, spaghetti, fish fingers, and meat pies. A number of fast-food places, including the American chain Subway, have opened up in Zambia in recent years, and many teenagers are developing a preference for nontraditional foods all the time. Increasingly, teenagers ask their parents to prepare nontraditional foods at home, or, if this is not possible, they go out with their friends to have it. Some teens do both: go out to eat fast food after school, but then head back home for a "proper meal" with the family.

Teenagers' eating habits, along with their diets, have worsened in recent years.

SCHOOLING

When Zambia gained its independence in October 1964, the country had fewer than one hundred university graduates, and fewer than a thousand men and women had completed a high school education. The president at the time, Kenneth Kaunda, stressed the importance of education for both men and women. President Kaunda and his government placed free universal education high on the list of national priorities, and women benefited from these policies as much as men. Zambia's literacy rates climbed markedly, along with primary school enrollments. The University of Zambia (UNZA) in Lusaka had only 312 students when it opened in 1966, yet by the 1980s UNZA's enrollment exceeded four thousand, and there were affiliated campuses in other parts of Zambia.

The success achieved early on was not maintained, however. When the country's economy began to decline sharply in the mid- to late 1970s, investment in social welfare needs declined. As a result, most of the public schools were not very well maintained, and the shortage of books, the lack of sports facilities, and even teachers' strikes (due to the government's nonpayment or underpayment of their salaries) became endemic. While a few government schools were well maintained, by the 1990s these had become increasingly rare. Not surprisingly, illiteracy rates today are higher among the 14–20 age group than among those aged 20–30, a trend that reflects educational declines in the 1990s.[4]

Catholic schools and other religious schools offer some alternatives to young people. In addition, some teens attend private schools, such as the International School of Lusaka (ISL), which is attended by foreign students as well. However, the facilities and resources at schools such as ISL come at a price; they charge tuition that few Zambians can afford, anywhere from $500 to $1,000 for a three-month period. While this is inexpensive by American private-school standards, in Zambia, where the per-capita income is just over $300 per year, it is out of reach for more than 90 percent of the populace. Finally, some teens prefer to go to boarding schools, which are usually government-run. This preference owes mostly to a desire to escape home every three months, although students are seldom prepared for the food at boarding school, which is notoriously badly prepared.

Zambian teenagers face ample testing in school. For example, special examinations must be passed to advance into grades 8 and 10. Near the end of one's high school career, in grade 12, another exam is required to qualify for entrance to the University of Zambia and the other major national university, Copperbelt University, located in the northern city of Ndola. Most teens do complete grade 12, but few of them manage to attend university. First, the university does not have the space to accommodate all those who desire to go, and second, many otherwise qualified students are unable to attend university because they cannot afford the tuition, notwithstanding the fact that the government pays 90 percent of the cost. Indeed, Zambia is a poor country, and families that rely on a single salary and/or a survival wage cannot afford luxuries like a university education for their children. As a result, some teenage graduates find work doing odd jobs or opt to attend one of Zambia's many vocational and technical schools to learn a trade such as accounting, furniture making, secretarial skills, and the like.

SOCIAL LIFE, RECREATION, AND ENTERTAINMENT

In Zambia, alcohol seems to carry the same mystique that it does elsewhere, including in Western countries. Alcohol experimentation is therefore widespread among teens, and occasionally, abuse occurs. The legal drinking age is supposed to be 21, but this is rarely enforced. Teenagers go out to a variety of clubs and are not asked to produce identification, even though every Zambian over the age of 16 should have a national identity card, known as the National Registration Card. Ironically, even the adult-oriented discos have no age restriction. In fact, few club owners are concerned about their patrons' age as long as they can afford to pay. Teenagers are known to spend money on alcohol and "clubbing," so if age limits were to be enforced regularly, most business owners would lose their business.

The access to bars and clubs can have serious consequences for youths, such as alcohol abuse and declining school attendance, and can lead to sexual promiscuity, unprotected sex (and hence the risk of AIDS), and drunk driving. Whereas only wealthy teenagers in the larger cities have access to their own cars, these relative few are often those seen in clubs. However, despite the fact that drunk driving is common among all age groups (there is no movement afoot to eradicate it), the police are more vigilant, paradoxically, when it comes to underage driving. In fact, the legal driving age of 18 is enforced fairly rigorously in an attempt to prevent teen accidents. Unfortunately, the bulk of Zambian police traffic enforcement takes place in the daylight hours!

Those who do not own cars rely on their friends or use cabs to go out at night. In contrast to the United States, teenagers in Zambia tend to be less fixated on driving as a way to improve their image and impress their friends. Indeed, a Zambian teenager is more popular when he or she can afford to buy drinks for his or her friends than when driving!

"Cultural globalization" has come to Africa in the form of American popular music, clothing, and iconography. Michael Jordan images and Nike T-shirts are a common sight around towns, for example, as are those bearing the logos of American sports teams. Even shopping habits have been altered by the influence of Western, particularly American, consumer culture. The opening of a large American-style shopping mall in Lusaka in 1999 instantly became a magnet for all residents of the city, especially teens. Characteristically American teen habits, such as hanging out at the mall with friends, partying, and at times, drinking, are now fairly commonplace.

Finally, since there is only one movie theater in regular operation, in Lusaka, most teens who have access to a VCR like to watch videos at home or with friends for entertainment. It should come as little surprise that the preferred videos are American-made.

RELIGIOUS PRACTICES AND CULTURAL CEREMONIES

Zambia is overwhelmingly Christian, though spread among various denominations. There are also a small number of Muslims and Hindus, populations that reside chiefly in the major cities. As is the case elsewhere, teenagers tend to embrace the religious traditions of their parents. Among the Jehovah's Witnesses, which is an active group in Zambia, for example, teenagers often take the lead in the house-to-house visits for which that denomination is famous the world over. In other denominations, many teenagers participate as members of their church's youth choir, and nearly every church has one. Singing and dancing are an important part of Zambian Christian ceremonies. Youth choirs of teens are not confined to the church building or Sunday performances, however. It is quite common, for example, for various youth choirs to perform for the president and visiting dignitaries at special functions.

As mentioned, religious schools are part of the fabric of the Zambian educational community. Students in religious schools, such as those run by the Catholic church or the Islamic faith, are open to nonpractitioners on a fee-paying basis. Students who don't share the faith of the school are expected to abide by Catholic rules and rites if the school is Catholic, Muslim rules and rites if the school is Islamic, and so forth. Notwithstanding the constitutional designation (effective beginning 1996) of

Zambia as "a Christian nation," government schools have no religious affiliation and therefore demand no religious compliance.

Traditional cultural practices also have a bearing on teenagers, though
the connection of the younger generations to these long-standing practices is perhaps more tenuous today. Different ethnic groups have different
traditions specific to teens. Most of these involve initiation rites that celebrate the acceptance of teenage boys and girls into adulthood.

In Zambia's Northwestern Province, for example, the *mukanda* ceremony is practiced; it aims at teaching boys how to look after their homes
when they become men. The overall program lasts between 6 and 12
months, and includes circumcision of the 13-year-old initiates.

The coming of age of teen girls is celebrated in virtually every ethnic
group in Zambia, and typically takes place around ages 12 to 13, after their
first menstruation. In most cases, this involves sequestering the girl or girls
away from others in the community, as is done with the males. Among the
Bemba, for example, the *ichisungu,* which literally means "reaching puberty," is only for a period of three days, and the girl (or girls) are accompanied only by a group of female elders chosen by the girl's mother. The
isolation can last for as little as a few days or as long as a month, such as
among the Lozi of Western Province (in contemporary times, this would
have to be scheduled during a school break). A common theme across
groups is preparing girls to become women, and eventually wives and
mothers. In the distant past, these roles might have been anticipated
shortly after the ceremony; in modern times, however, few marry before
their late teens or early twenties.

All of these various initiation ceremonies, practiced by many if not all
of Zambia's 73 ethnic groups, are a celebration. They mark, at least symbolically, the passage of a child into adulthood, even though his or her
teen years may just be starting! They also mark a happy time, in most cultures, that often involves dancing and much celebrating. However, each
of these traditions is also under threat in contemporary Zambia. They
face modifications and perhaps erosion or elimination in the face of a
cultural transformation in Zambia arising from more nuclear family
structures and the separation of families due to migration to the cities,
and rising identification with Western norms and practices. Indeed, with
the rise of Western cultural influences, many urban teens are more interested in Nike and fast foods than they are in traditional cultural practices
that may seem to them old-fashioned and remote. Sadly, however, many
young Zambians risk losing touch with their rich history and cultural traditions as a result.

CONCLUSION

Zambian teens have many of the same aspirations as their Western counterparts. They want to have a bright future that includes a family, education, security, and a comfortable quality of life. However, because Zambia is a poor country, not many of today's teenagers will have the opportunity to fulfill these very normal aspirations. As a result, some teenagers are forced to grow up quickly and confront a challenging and sometimes difficult existence from a very young age. Other teenagers tend to idolize and imitate the Western lifestyle and look down on their own as inferior. Many of these same middle-class Zambians, who have access to education, some wealth, and resources, will choose to emigrate rather than remain where they see few opportunities. This, of course, creates something of a vicious circle and a self-fulfilling prophecy, because if "the best and the brightest"—or at least those with the resources—leave Zambia, who will be left to build a better life for the future of the country? In both cases, many of the uniquely Zambian characteristics of teen life are withering away in the contemporary environment.

Nonetheless, despite the challenges, Zambian teens like to find ways to enjoy themselves. Where that enjoyment has extended into alcohol and/or drug use and abuse, and unprotected sex, that has created major challenges for the future. While many teens still remain optimistic, an increasing number lack real goals at all. It is unfair to point the blame at the teenagers themselves, however. Poverty, economic stagnation, and the high orphan rates created by the AIDS epidemic have combined to give rise to a generation, now teenagers, who have seen little but hardship in their lives. Those hardest hit include teens in the urban underclass and the rural poor from Zambia's remote rural regions.

The role of parents remains critical in Zambia, and this is where Zambian teenagers may have a genuine advantage over their Western counterparts. By custom and tradition, parents remain engaged in the activities of their children. Although teenagers anywhere don't like to be lorded over by their parents, in difficult times this is a real benefit to Zambian teens. This feature perhaps is also threatened, tragically, by rising AIDS rates within families, that have, in some instances, stripped children of one or both parents even before their teenage years.

Zambian teens are interested in the lives of other teenagers around the world. They would like to know more about their counterparts elsewhere, particularly those in the West. Part of this is outreach and curiosity; another part is rooted in a desire to engage in a sort of (harmless) "competition" of sorts, over the latest trends in clothing, music, and overall style.

However, while Zambian teenagers already know a great deal about their counterparts elsewhere—through TV, the media, and coverage of Western people and events in the news—they feel that teens in other countries, especially the United States, have not bothered to learn much about Zambia or its teen life. They are anxious, therefore, to put a more visible image of Zambia before the world stage. They hope that American teenagers will have the desire to learn as much about Zambia as Zambians have learned about the United States. Interaction between teenagers can result in a positive mutual exchange of ideas and in the sharing of cultural values and attributes, rather than the adoption of the habits of Americans (or Europeans) lock, stock, and barrel.

NOTES

1. Economist Intelligence Unit (EIU), *Country Profile, 2001/2002* (August 2001). London: Economist Intelligence Unit.
2. The World Bank. *World Development Report 2001*. New York: Oxford University Press.
3. EIU Country Profile, 2001/2002.
4. Ibid.

RESOURCE GUIDE

Books and Articles

Burnell, Peter. "The Party System and Party Politics in Zambia: Continuities Past, Present and Future." *African Affairs* 100, Issue 399 (April 2001): 239–63.
Hansen, Karen Tranberg. "Target Group Interventions among Youth in Zambia: Research Constructions and Social Life." *Anthropology in Action*, 10, 1 (2002): 34–41.
Ihonvbere, Julius O. *Economic Crisis, Civil Society, and Democratization: The Case of Zambia*. Trenton, N.J.: Africa World Press, 1996.
Serpell, Robert. *The Significance of Schooling: Life Journeys in an African Society*. New York: Cambridge University Press, 1993.

Web Sites

Central Statistical Office (CSO): http://www.finance.gov.zm/cso.htm
Chilongozi (safari and tour operator): http://www.chilongozi.com
Government of Zambia: http://www.state.gov.zm/index.html
The Post (Zambia's main independent newspaper): http://www.post.co.zm
The Zambia national Web page: http://www.zamnet.zm

Chapter 15

ZIMBABWE

Oyekan Owomoyela

INTRODUCTION

Zimbabwe is a landlocked tropical country in the heart of southern Africa. It is surrounded by Zambia in the north, Mozambique in the northeast and east, the Republic of South Africa in the south, and Botswana in the southwest and west. At a point in the northwest, a strip of the country projects between Zambia and Botswana to touch Namibia. During its modern history (since colonization), the country has changed its name several times; it started out as Southern Rhodesia, then became Rhodesia (when Northern Rhodesia became Zambia), later Zimbabwe Rhodesia, and finally Zimbabwe.

The country has an area of 390,759 square kilometers (about 150,873 square miles) and is divided into eight administrative provinces. Its capital is Harare (Salisbury until independence in 1980), the second-most important city being Bulawayo. The country's population of a little over 12 million people is more than 75 percent Shona; the second-largest African group is the Ndebele at something like 15 percent. The whites who once imposed their minority rule on the country now constitute an embattled barely 1 percent of the population.

The 1996 World Population Prospects put the Zimbabwean youth population at 20.6 percent of the total population (2,559,138 out of 12,423,000), with a median age of 17.8 years. The urban-rural breakdown of the youth figure for 1995 was 786,182 urban and 1,451,953 rural.

HISTORY

The name "Zimbabwe" is derived from the royal stone palaces (*dzimbawhe*) that the ancestors of the Shona constructed after they occupied the area sometime around the eleventh century. The largest of these palaces is the famous Great Zimbabwe, whose still-impressive ruins lie 27 kilometers (17 miles) east of present-day Masvingo in the Mtilikwe basin in the south-central part of the country. The kingdom's great wealth in gold began to attract European attention as early as the beginning of the sixteenth century, but Portuguese attempts to control the area were defeated during the seventeenth century. An influx of Nguni people fleeing from Chaka, the Zulu warrior-king, led to the establishment of an Ndebele kingdom alongside the Shona in the 1830s; today the Ndebele constitute the second-largest component of the country's population. Toward the end of the century, through the initiatives of the English adventurer Cecil John Rhodes, the area came under British control as Rhodesia. White settlers seeking gold arrived in large numbers, but they turned to farming on discovering that the precious commodity had long been depleted.

The shift to farming resulted in land and race policies that have bedeviled the country's history ever since. The settlers, who were always a small fraction of the total population, appropriated the best lands for large plantations and forced the indigenous population to the cramped, infertile remnant. Other settler policies forced Africans to work as virtual slaves for white farmers and in the mines. Moreover, like their white neighbors in South Africa to the south, the settlers adopted apartheid-like regulations that kept Africans out of the cities, except as pass-carrying menial workers.

African resistance to white takeover led to armed clashes as early as the 1890s. The first, known as the *chimurenga*, began in 1897 but was crushed the following year. The second, known as the second *chimurenga*, started in 1966 and eventually led to the country's attainment of independence with majority rule in 1980.

ECONOMY

Zimbabweans are mostly farmers. The white farmers run large plantations on which they grow tobacco, cotton, and maize for export, while African subsistence farmers cultivate maize, the staple food, on small plots. The country also produces minerals like gold, nickel, and asbestos.

The manufacturing sector received a boost after the international community imposed economic sanctions on the country in 1965 as a means of persuading the white minority government of Ian Smith to end its rebellious Unilateral Declaration of Independence, proclaimed earlier in the year. Owing to the country's adjustments in response, Zimbabwe had a well diversified economy at independence, which guaranteed it a degree of self-sufficiency. The economy has declined in recent years because of the flight of a sizeable percentage of the white population since independence. The first wave of emigrants fled just prior to independence, fearing possible reprisals by the new African rulers; after independence many more escaped in the face of the forced expropriation of their farms, coupled with sometimes deadly, government-instigated violence at the hands of so-called war veterans. Mismanagement and corruption were already aggravating the economic malaise when the most severe shock occurred: the government's ruinously expensive intervention in the power struggle in the Democratic Republic of the Congo in 1998. By 2001, massive layoffs in the farming sector had forced the country, which normally exported maize, to instead import as much as 600,000 tons of the staple. In addition to the problem of high unemployment, the country was, at the close of 2001, experiencing an inflation rate believed to be as high as 300 to 400 percent.

SOCIOECONOMIC CLASSES

Zimbabwe's society is diverse, incorporating several socioeconomic classes: upper, upper-middle, lower-middle, and low. Only a quarter of the population lives in cities, and most of these retain close connections with their extended families in the rural areas. The wealthiest people (the so-called chefs) and the professionals have largely taken over the positions, urban living quarters, and perks that the whites have vacated. They are highly Westernized, and their lifestyle emulates that of the people they have replaced.

TYPICAL DAY

Although there is a strong temptation to concentrate on what is customary in the urban areas when one discusses life in modern-day Zimbabwe, it is important to bear in mind that most Zimbabweans still live in the rural areas, and that even in the cities they are never too far from traditional life. The continuing sway toward the old ways results to some de-

Teens in Zimbabwe. Courtesy of Oyekan Owomoyela.

gree from colonial practices, which always sought to maintain visible markers of difference between white and black segments of the population, and which often ridiculed African attempts to emulate whites too closely. Discussion of the way youths spend their day must therefore include what is accepted in the rural areas as well as in the cities.

EMPLOYMENT

In 1992 youth represented 32.3 percent of the labor force, a figure that breaks down to 17.9 percent male and 14.5 percent female. The unemployment that has become rife in recent years owing to the collapsing economy makes those figures obsolete, though, since the youth population has been affected with the rest of the workers. Unemployed youth have been known to join unemployed adults in unconventional alternative employment as political thugs and ZANU-PF operatives, parading as war veterans in forceful takeovers of white-owned farms and violent attacks on the owners.

FAMILY LIFE

In rural areas, the extended family structure persists, with its associated living arrangement and habits. Age, kinship, and hereditary status undergird social relations; the older members of the community and family oversee the development of the younger ones, who in turn make themselves serviceable to their seniors. By contrast, the urban family unit is nuclear, and relations depend on socioeconomic status, with the Westernized professionals at the top of a hierarchical social pyramid. Youths in urban families generally have no responsibility for household chores, which are left to domestic servants, and they also lack the coaching and nurturing that their rural counterparts receive from their elders. Regular trips back to the village to spend time with relatives are a means of rectifying the disadvantage. In urban settings, youth patronize such social outlets as soccer clubs, youth clubs, church-based associations, workers' unions, and the like as substitutes for the age-based communal groups of the villages.

In both urban and rural settings, the traditional gender roles in family matters remain in effect. Even where the woman is a money-earning professional (as is often the case in the cities), she is still responsible for domestic matters, which might be only a matter of her supervising domestic workers and making decisions on household expenditures, and she does not consider it an imposition or exploitation to wait on her husband at mealtimes. Traditionally, neither did her adolescent daughter chafe at having to wait on her brother, but today's young women do not submit to that tradition without grumbling. The degree to which a young woman helps with household chores in the traditional scheme is evident in the explanation a father once offered for the *lobola* (bride price) a groom pays to his bride's parents at the time of their marriage: he characterized it as compensation to the bride's mother, who will be most affected by the loss of the help the young woman used to provide.

Courtesy is important, and relationships among family members as well as among community members as a whole are regulated by formalities. One of the basic rules is that younger people must always give due respect to their elders and superiors. Young people learn very early the formality of clapping their hands as a mark of respect when they greet their elders, or to express their appreciation for some favor they have received. They also learn to inquire about the health of the elders. They learn never to call their elders or superiors by their names. Likewise, traditionally a wife never addresses her husband by name; as soon as there is a child in the family she calls him (and refers to him as) the father of the child, for example Babawa Chido (Chido's Father). Modern couples observe the same code of etiquette (in public at least), referring to each other by their formal titles.

Traditional eating arrangements within the family observe and reinforce the order of precedence. Women serve the men and wait until they have finished eating before they sit down to their own meal. Generally, eating is communal but by age (or class) and gender. Grown men eat from communal bowls, as do grown women, and children eat together. Here again modernization has introduced changes, such that in modern households parents and children sit at table to eat together.

TRADITIONAL AND NONTRADITIONAL FOOD DISHES

Sadza, a stiff porridge made from maize, is a staple and may be eaten for breakfast, lunch, and dinner. Occasionally beans, black-eyed peas, and pumpkin serve as alternatives to maize. It is usual to accompany the *sadza* with vegetables, like pumpkin leaves, seasoned with peanut butter, fruits, nuts, and insects, which could be caterpillars, flying ants, or locusts caught when they swarm. These are boiled and dried in order to prolong their shelf life, and are used a little at a time. In more affluent homes some meat is an additional (or occasional) treat, perhaps chicken, goat, sheep, or cow. Less frequently, the meat might be crocodile, antelope, or, in places close to bodies of water, fish. Available fruits include baobab fruit, bananas, cucumbers, mangoes, papayas, pineapples, and tomatoes.

Beer brewed from millet or sorghum, and occasionally from corn or rice, is a prominent part of Zimbabwean social life, especially during festive and ritual occasions. European-style beer is also available in the cities, along with different soft drinks (sodas). Urban dwellers also have the option of going to restaurants and fast-food outlets for quick meals.

SCHOOLING

Before the arrival of the Europeans, the educational and socialization process started from a very early age, and it continued until initiation, when adolescents achieved full participatory membership in the community. It continues today in the rural areas, and its principal tenets are also part of the upbringing of youths even in urban settings. The process aims at imparting to youth the importance of acceptable behavior and its rules, and also some practical skills that enable them to sustain themselves and their dependents in the future. They learn, for example, the importance of such seemingly mundane social graces as respecting adults and deferring to them, always exchanging greetings with people they meet on the paths, even if they are complete strangers, and washing their hands before eating.

As in other African societies, young adults are responsible for imparting social and practical skills to their younger siblings and generally for looking out for them when their parents and other adults are absent, when they are either at work or at play. From the start, boys and girls receive a clear understanding of the different roles they will play in the community. Typically the young adults serve as role models for their siblings of the same sex, just as they look to older relatives of the same sex for guidance. In the case of boys, their grandfathers, fathers, and uncles are the ultimate teachers, the grandfathers being responsible for teaching them practical skills. The transfer of knowledge and skills takes place as boys watch their grandfathers, fathers, and uncles at their professions, or join their male siblings in herding livestock, working the farms, hunting bush rats, building huts and thatching them, or making simple cooking utensils.

As for the girls, they are responsible for looking after their younger siblings, male and female, while they themselves learn from their grandmothers, aunts, mothers, and older sisters. They also sometimes participate in herding livestock, and help in other household chores such as picking vegetables, edible mushrooms, and edible insects for the stew and condiments, and sweeping and polishing the floors of the huts. Quite often, a girl of 10 has enough cooking skills to take over the preparation of meals, and is responsible enough to care for younger children without requiring any supervision.

Youth are encouraged with specific inducements to develop different skills. These take the form of titles the society confers on those who excel in a particular pursuit, like hunting, weaving, farming, mediumship, playing the *mbira*, or healing. Thus, the master craftsman (weaver, builder, carver, and so forth) earns the title *mhidza*, the expert drummer is called a *maridzangoma*, while the expert *mbira* player is a *maridzambira*. Women who distinguish themselves in pottery and brewing receive the title *mhizhá* or *nyanzví*. The importance that attaches to the mastery of elegant speech is evident in the encouragement and opportunity youths receive to compose songs and poetic praises in honor of their own prowess (as wrestlers for example), or in celebrating the beauty of their sweethearts, and in the conferring of the honorific title *nyanduri* on those who distinguish themselves in the area.

The closest thing to a formal end of the traditional education process—what one might regard as the equivalent to modern graduation—is the initiation ceremony that in some of the country's ethnic subgroups marks the transition from juvenile to adult status. Children of the same sex and roughly the same age go through the rite of passage together, in age groups that become the bases for lifelong friendships and attachments. Traditionally, members maintain their associations for life, engaging in group projects together, going into battle as a regiment, and cooperating with one another in life crises. The initiation ceremony usually involves separation from the community for a period of days, during which the candidates receive concentrated instruction from designated teachers and are circumcised. After the rite the youths become adults for all practical purposes and are ready for marriage.

MODERN EDUCATION

Zimbabwe inherited two systems of education at independence in 1980: one was for Africans (blacks), and the other (which provided "high-quality" education) was for the rest—whites, coloreds, and Asians, who comprised less than 5 percent of the total population. The latter system

Zimbabwean students walking and biking to school.
© A. Lambert/Trip Archive.

was modeled after British and South African curricula, while the African system was designed to educate Africans in a way that would preclude their competing with whites socially, economically, or politically. After independence the new government revamped the systems, substituting a unified curriculum to educate all Zimbabweans in line with the needs of the society. Today education is compulsory for youths aged 7 to 15 years.

The 1982 syllabus emphasizes social studies, and is built on textbooks that promote Zimbabwean culture and stress group interdependence. It aims to produce useful and responsible citizenship, and gives priority to what the government describes as education for production—that is, education that teaches skills that have practical applications, rather than elitist (ivory-tower) education that has no utilitarian value. It also gives prominence to the heroic role of ZANU-PF freedom fighters in liberating the country from minority white rulers.

Apart from the government, different religious organizations—Roman Catholic, Anglican, and Methodist—operate their own schools (even up to the tertiary level) but receive nominal grants from the government at the primary and secondary levels. While the races are no longer segregated in Zimbabwean schools, the fees for most private institutions are prohibitively high for most African families. The government mandates school uniforms as a way of relieving some of the tensions that might result from the mix of students from widely different economic means. The uniforms are a device to protect less affluent students from complexes they might develop from seeing their more affluent schoolmates come to school in expensive attire day after day, when all they can afford is threadbare clothing. If a student happens to be unable to afford the school uniform, he or she is not prevented from attending school for that reason.

NATIONAL SERVICE

The government has adapted the National Service program in order to bolster the social relevance of the education and socialization youth receive. The minority regime of Ian Smith enacted the first National Service statute in 1976 in response to the intensification of the armed struggle for independence, and the statute was amended in 1979 on the eve of the country's independence. The original purpose of the program was to force recruitment into the armed forces, but with the de-emphasis on the military after independence, the program went into dormancy. In the mid-1990s the government began to look for ways of resuscitating the scheme, with economic rather than military objectives in view. The new aim is to create a cadre of disciplined youths with leadership and other useful skills; to promote unity among the country's populations through shared experiences; to create a citizenry that will assist the government in actualizing its policies; to promote selflessness, patriotism, community consciousness and a spirit of volunteerism; and to encourage a commitment to the preservation of the country's environment and natural resources.

Participants are university-bound students, high school graduates who cannot go further in their education, and school dropouts at all levels. The Service begins with some rudimentary military training designed to imbue the participants with a sense of discipline and leadership qualities; later they receive training in various disciplines, interspersed with work on community projects requiring such skills as plumbing, carpentry, and masonry. While in the past the government paid most of the educational expenses of students in tertiary institutions, it plans in the future, in response to the collapse of the economy, to require that students engage in a period of national service, as well as postgraduation service, in order to qualify for financial assistance.

Toward the end of 2001, a thousand students drawn from 10 provinces in the country inaugurated the restructured National Service program under the purview of the Ministry of Youth Development, Gender and Employment Creation. Their stint in Manicaland ended in January 2002. The governor of the province, in her address to the participants, described their mission as a third *chimurenga* designed to preserve Zimbabwe's cultural identity and reverse the trend that was making it difficult to distinguish between whites and Africans. Although the stated justification for the program is noble and worthwhile, developments suggest that it is only another tool the ruling party has found expedient for its political maneuvers. There is a widespread belief in the country that it is in fact a militia of ZANU-PF, a belief substantiated when on December 19, 2001, participants in the program in Harare besieged the suburb of Budiriro where they were supposed to be engaged in a cleanup. They instead attempted to force brooms on the residents and make them do the cleanup, and they roughed up those who resisted. The residents in the end chased them off with a barrage of stones. The youths' action came in the wake of Mugabe's call for them to wage war against the opposition Movement for Democratic Change.

PERSONAL CARE

Zimbabweans pay particular attention to grooming and personal care. Young people learn at an early age that they must start the day by washing themselves, and where a stream is nearby it becomes an attractive arena for swimming and frolicking with playmates. Adults also use such streams as convenient places to bathe instead of having water drawn from there and carried to the dwelling area. Because traditional propriety frowns on youth seeing adults naked, or men seeing women naked or vice versa, separate areas are usually set aside for the youth, the men, and the women.

The youth, especially the young women, continue the traditional practice of smearing the body with ointment to enhance its beauty, but they have replaced the traditional oil-and-soil mixture with modern manufactured substitutes. Among the most popular of these is the skin-lightening cream Ambi, whose attraction is explained by a somewhat widespread and (to many) embarrassing notion that a light-skinned complexion is more attractive than a dark one.

CLOTHING

Clothing habits have changed significantly as a result of contact with Europeans. Traditional clothing was sparse; women used to wear skimpy pieces of fabric (bark or cotton) or skin called *nhembe* for covering the genital area, supplementing them with coverings for the chest and the head. Both men and women used blankets to cover themselves during the cooler seasons. The missionaries, who controlled large land holdings in the early days of colonization, and who were therefore landlords to numerous Africans, converts and nonconverts alike, played a crucial role in forcing a change in dress habits, and today most people wear European-style clothes. In the urban areas and on the campuses of schools and colleges, the basic clothing is casual Western, but on more formal occasions young men wear ties and jackets, while young women wear dresses. Western influence is equally discernible in rural areas, where the traditional aprons have largely yielded to blouses and skirts or wrappers.

Young Zimbabweans rarely wear clothing that would be considered immodest, like skimpy shorts or tank tops that reveal inappropriate parts of their anatomy, although instances of provocative dressing do occur among urban teenagers. Whatever the style, cleanliness and neatness are the rule rather than the exception.

DATING

Traditional dating behavior among youth varies among the different ethnic groups and subgroups in the country. In some cases, a young man who is attracted to a young woman reveals his interest by seizing opportunities to speak with her, and she somehow lets him know if she reciprocates his interest—for example, by giving him an item of clothing belonging to her. The parents, especially hers, note the romance without interfering, unless there is some question about the suitor's character or family. In other cases, the young man secures the services of an intermediary, sometimes an older male relative and sometimes an age-mate. In all cases, though, the man takes the initiative.

In some groups little formality attaches to the process of getting married once both sides have come to an agreement. In matrilocal groups, the young man moves into the young woman's homestead, while in patrilocal ones the woman moves in with her husband. In some groups, though, formal steps are required for the marriage to be concluded. Sometimes the prospective groom and his family do a day's work on the farm of the father-in-law, who reciprocates with a feast in their honor, after which the young couple may set up house together.

Traditionally, dating was always done with marriage in view, unlike what is customary among youth today, who engage in casual relationships involving sex. In the traditional context, a bride who is found to be a virgin at marriage is a source of pride for her family; her grateful husband takes gifts to his parents-in-law to thank them for their virtuous upbringing of their daughter. A wife found not to be a virgin conversely brings disgrace on her family, and sometimes even demands by the husband for reparation, which might take the form of the wife's younger sister as another wife for the man. The extent to which youth behavior has changed in this regard is evident in the high incidence of teenage pregnancy in urban areas. Available statistics show that among sexually active unmarried teenage women, roughly two out of five become pregnant. Social prejudices make information about contraceptives and the contraceptive devices themselves inaccessible to the youth, and sex education is not a part of the curriculum in schools. While there is no law against giving contraceptives to youngsters, health personnel are reluctant to do so because it is a criminal offense for a man to have sexual relations with a woman under 16, although such encounters do happen.

A related problem is the spread of HIV/AIDS, which affects an estimated 25 percent of the population. UNICEF and the government of Zimbabwe collaborate on an HIV/AIDS Prevention and Education Program targeted specifically at youths. It includes an in-school campaign designed to offer students life-skill education and to train teachers for the same purpose. It uses the mass media (radio programs with assistance provided for script writing), drama, puppetry, songs, and interpersonal information.

These problems that derive from irresponsible sexual behavior are fed by a culture in which adolescent men think that their ego or their reputation among their peers is a function of their ability to "conquer" young girls, while the girls feel the need to be popular, a need they fear might be frustrated if they did not offer some sexual inducement to the boys to whom they are attracted.

RECREATION

Young Zimbabweans have always resorted to diversions to relieve the tedium and drudgery of daily life. Traditionally, herdboys engaged in trials of strength among themselves, and entered their herds and other animals in similar competitions, all the while declaiming poems as fighting boasts. Sometimes the boys themselves continue the contests by engaging in fights to settle the issue of who is the most valorous. Another form of pastime is the *zivara*, in which boys display their courage by dodging missiles (sticks and stones) thrown at them.

Another traditional pastime for the youth is the game of *nuri*, in which opposing teams attempt to impale a fast-moving root disk with wooden spears. The object is to nail the disk and lift it off the ground as proof of marksmanship. Another favorite is the board game *wari* (or *mwari*), which is played with an oblong wooden board with holes carved along both sides. Each of two opponents takes turns distributing seeds from the holes on his side of the board into the other holes according to a formula, with the object of capturing more seeds in the end than the opponent.

Young boys engage in fighting boasts as a means of winning favor from girls at the expense of rival suitors. They also compose *madétémbédzo* to celebrate the qualities of their girlfriends, and *madúnhúrirwá* to proclaim their own valor. While engaged in daily chores like herding cattle, boys also entertain themselves by playing the *chipendani*, a mouth-harp that consists of a bent supple stick whose ends are connected by a taut string. The player holds the instrument in his mouth and plucks the string with his fingers, modulating the tone by adjusting his mouth.

Girls for their part sing *jakwara* (work) songs to accompany such tasks as pounding grain and weeding the fields, and lullabies as they soothe and coddle babies. In the evenings, especially moonlit ones, they go with their playmates into the bush to sing, dance, and talk about boys. Evenings are also a good time for people of all ages and both genders to gather and tell folktales.

WORK CAMPS

Various other activities occur seasonally under the sponsorship of different organizations. The Zimbabwe YMCA Council sometimes sponsors International Youth Work Camps, which bring youths from inside and outside Africa together. Participants work on environmental projects, and engage in sports and Christian fellowship. The camps usually end with tours to sites like the Victoria Falls.

The National Book Council Youth Forum aims to help Zimbabwean youth become responsible adults by promoting a "vibrant reading culture" among them. It organizes its activities to coincide with the annual National Books Week and the Zimbabwe International Books Fair. The events it sponsors include book talks, meetings with authors, and sometimes an "Adopt a School—Give a Child a Book" campaign.

The country has a Ministry of Youth Development and a nongovernmental organization, the Zimbabwe National Youth Council, which is the coordinating body for youth organizations. It was established in 1983 and has a membership of 24 affiliated associations. Its function is "to coordinate and promote youth activities in Zimbabwe, to facilitate development of youth work, and to assist in employment creation for youth." This goal involves providing for representation of Zimbabwean youth in regional, national, and international youth activities and meetings. It is affiliated with the Southern African Development Coordination Conference and the Pan African Youth Movement.

The students' national coordinating council is the Zimbabwe National Students Union, with a membership of about five thousand university students. It works to represent the views of students on issues of national importance (education or peace and development, for example), and serves as a liaison with educational and political authorities. It sponsors seminars, conferences, study groups, exchanges, and meetings with authorities, and its members attend regional and international students' meetings.

In August 2001 two Zimbabwe upper high-school students were among 350 young people from around the world who participated in a 12-day Global Young Leaders Conference in the United States. It was sponsored by the Congressional Youth Leadership Council. Participants tackled issues including foreign aid, global warming, human rights, and tourism. One of the Zimbabwean participants demonstrated his independence of thought by voicing his concerns about the ongoing land problem in his country, stressing that "fast-track" land resettlement generates nothing but chaos, and that unless the land issue is confronted with deliberate planning, rather than opportunistically to gain votes for politicians, there will be no alleviation of the people's poverty.

ENTERTAINMENT

Outside the school orbit, urban youths take advantage of entertainment provided by nightclubs, such as concerts by popular bands and performers, both local and visiting. In addition to such concerts there are dances, often to music provided by disk jockeys at venues like Harare's the Sports Café and the Tube. These occasions often involve competitions among several DJs (some from neighboring South Africa) taking turns. Some of the clubs also have swimming pools where guests can swim during the day, or drink and eat "pub lunches" while watching the swimmers. Youths also engage in recreational and competitive sports such as athletics, basketball, cricket, soccer, swimming, tennis, and water polo. The competitions may be intraschool or interschool. Students engage in various social activities in school. Until recently the decisive missionary influence in education dictated that the songs students sang were Western or reflected Western values. Perhaps the best example of such music is *makwaya* (derived from the word "choir"), a combination of the African call-and-response style of singing and European harmonics. It was first developed in South Africa, from where it was imported into Zimbabwe. Another musical legacy of the European presence is gospel singing; it has produced several young stars, among them the 16-year-old high school girl Pergial Nare, who released her first album of gospel music in November 2001. Students also participate in clubs for such activities as dancing, public speaking, theater, bridge, darts, and chess. Some schools have well-equipped and quite competent jazz bands, *mbira* bands, and marimba orchestras. In some cases the band and orchestra members are drawn from several schools.

Interscholastic competitions in these activities in the context of festivals offer venues for students to demonstrate and hone their skills. The National Arts Council of Zimbabwe and the Zimbabwe Association of Theatre for Children and Young People organize district festivals featuring traditional ensemble performances (*mbira*, marimba) as well as drama, poetry, and gymnastics. These competitions are open to the public. Some schools also hold performances for the public outside the competitive scheme.

Typically, a school's cultural activities are designed to offer students opportunities to interact with their classmates and schoolmates, as well as with students from other schools. Students in all-boys schools sometimes join forces with those of all-girls schools for some cultural and recreational activities, because the authorities wish to offer them opportunities to develop the social skills they will need in the future.

RELIGIOUS PRACTICES AND CULTURAL CEREMONIES

The predominant religion in the country is Christianity, which commands the allegiance of an estimated 40 to 50 percent of the population. The Catholic Church is the largest single denomination, the others being Methodist, Anglican, Salvation Army, Seventh-Day Adventist, Dutch Reformed, Presbyterian, Congregational, Episcopalian, North American Apostolic (fundamentalist and charismatic), and African (Zimbabwe Assemblies of God and Vapostori). The Asian minority mainly practice either Islam or Hinduism, while the Jewish (Zionist) and Greek Orthodox communities also have their own religious institutions.

Indigenous Shona religion is monotheistic and centered around Mwari, the Supreme Being who created and rules the universe. The Ndebele know the same being as uMlimu. More immediate to the peoples' lives are the *mhondoro*, ancestral spirits who preside over the fortunes of the clan and the community. They are especially responsible for providing rain for the crops, and they punish offenses like incest and grievous antisocial behavior. Even closer to humans are the "spirit elders," the spirits of dead family members, known among the Shona as *vadzimu* and among the Ndebele as *amadhlozi*. Humans contact these supernatural figures through mediums (*svikiro*), typically during seances known as *bira*, during which the playing of *mbira* music, dancing, and beer drinking induce the medium to be possessed by the spirit.

CONCLUSION

Zimbabwean youths live in a world that is less secure than that of their American counterparts. Not only has their entire existence been in a context of political and social turbulence into which they are sometimes drawn willy-nilly, they also live with the constant awareness of the threat to their lives posed by the HIV/AIDS epidemic. What is more important, though, is that like their country, they are inheritors of a dual heritage: the traditional African one and the Western one that came with colonization. The Western component of the heritage is most evident in the urban areas and in the modern institutions, like the schools and the popular entertainment industry; but even here traditional elements find a place, sometimes as accents and sometimes as deliberate devices to emphasize the Africanness of the country. Consequently, while youth participate in the global trend towards Westernization, they maintain contact with their African cultural roots and retain significant elements of their traditional practices. A Zimbabwean youth suddenly transplanted to New York City will most likely be overwhelmed by the city's size and bustle, but not by its modern, Western amenities, with which he or she will be familiar, albeit on a smaller scale, from places like Harare and Bulawayo. An American youth visiting Harare would similarly see much that is familiar, if less grandiose and harried.

RESOURCE GUIDE

Books

Bechky, Allen. *Adventuring in Southern Africa*. San Francisco: Sierra Club Books, 1997.

Berliner, Paul F. *The Soul of Mbira: Music & Traditions of the Shona People of Zimbabwe*. Chicago: University of Chicago Press, 1993.

Cheney, Patricia. *The Land and People of Zimbabwe*. New York: J. B. Lippincott, 1990.

McCrea, Barbara, and Tony Pinchuck. *Zimbabwe and Botswana: The Rough Guide*. London: Rough Guides Ltd., 1996.

Myambo, Malissa Tandiwe. "Deciduous Gazettes." In *Opening Spaces: An Anthology of Contemporary African Women's Writing*, ed. Yvonne Vera. Oxford: Heinemann Educational Publishers/Baobab Books, 1999.

Nzenza-Shand, Sekai. *Songs to an African Sunset: A Zimbabwean Story*. Melbourne: Lonely Planet Publications, 1997.

Owomoyela, Oyekan. *Culture and Customs of Zimbabwe*. Westport, Conn.: Greenwood Press, 2002.

Rasmussen, R. Kent, and Steven C. Rubert. *Historical Dictionary of Zimbabwe*, 2nd ed. Metuchen, N. J.: Scarecrow, 1990.

Reynolds, Pamela. *Traditional Healers and Childhood in Zimbabwe*. Athens: Ohio University Press, 1996.

Swaney, Deanna. *Zimbabwe, Botswana and Namibia*. Hawthorn, Australia: Lonely Planet Publications, 1999.

Web Sites

Zimbabwean Music: http://www.dandemutande.com

http://www.africaonline.co.zw/

Mail and *Guardian* newspapers: http://www.mg.co/za/

National University of Science and Technology, Bulawayo: http://www.nust.ac.zw/

Prince Edward School, Harare: http://site.mweb.co.zw/peschool/
United Nations Youth Information Network: http://www.visionoffice.com/
    unyin/
The Daily News: http://www.dailynews.co.zw/
http://www.tourismzimbabwe.co.zw/

Other Information

Zimbabwe Tourism Office
Rockefeller Center, Suite 1905
New York, NY 10020
Tel.: (212) 332-1090

INDEX

ABOUT THE EDITOR AND CONTRIBUTORS

Toyin Falola is the Frances Higginbothom Nalle Centennial Professor in History at the University of Texas at Austin. He has written and edited numerous works on African history and Nigeria, including *The History of Nigeria* (Greenwood 1999), *Culture and Customs of Nigeria* (Greenwood 2000), *Culture and Customs of Ghana* (with Steven J. Salm) (Greenwood 2002), and *Key Events in African History* (Greenwood 2002).

Edmund Abaka is an assistant professor of history at the University of Miami, Florida. He is the author of a number of articles on African topics.

Mohamed Diriye Abdullahi is an independent researcher and language consultant. His interests include the languages, cultures, and history of the Horn of Africa. He is the author of *Customs and Cultures of Somalia* (Greenwood 2001).

Dorothy A. Akurang-Parry, a social activist concerned with problems facing Ghanaian teenagers, was educated in Ghana and Canada. Her research interest is in teen culture in Ghana.

Kwabena O. Akurang-Parry is an assistant professor of history at Shippensburg University, Shippensburg, Pennsylvania. His research interests include slavery and colonial rule in Ghana, the impact of abolition on gender and labor in colonial Ghana, the indigenous press in colonial West Africa, and colonial Ghana and the two world wars. His articles have appeared in many scholarly journals.

Nicodemus Fru Awasom was born in Cameroon and is a senior lecturer of history in the Faculty of Humanities and Social Sciences at the University of the Gambia, West Africa. His current research interests include constitutional political economy, intergroup relations, the Anglophone problem in Cameroon, and the Hausa-Fulani Muslim minorities in Cameroon's Western Grassfields. He has written several articles on Cameroon.

Ann Cooper is a graduate student at the University of Texas at Austin, focusing on West Africa and the Diaspora.

Ikechukwu Enwemnwa teaches at Shippensburg University in Pennsylvania. His general area of interest is teenage life and personality.

Ann Genova is a doctoral student at the University of Texas at Austin, specializing in postcolonial Nigerian history.

Christian Jennings is a doctoral student at the University of Texas at Austin, specializing in East African and environmental history.

John Mukum Mbaku is the Willard L. Eccles Professor of Economics and John S. Hinckley Fellow at Weber State University, Ogden, Utah. His present research interests are in public choice, constitutional political economy, trade integration, intergroup relations, and institutional reforms in Africa. He is the author of *Institutions and Reform in Africa: The Public Choice Perspective* (Praeger 1997), among other works.

George O. Ndege is an associate professor of history at Saint Louis University. He has written many articles and essays on various topics related to Kenya and Africa.

Oyekan Owomoyela is the Ryan Professor of African Literature at the University of Nebraska, Lincoln. He has published several books and articles on African literatures and cultures and is the author of *Culture and Customs of Zimbabwe* (Greenwood 2002).

Priscilla Muntemba Taylor, born in Zambia, is completing a degree in sociology at George Mason University and plans to work internationally in the field of women's rights and gender equality.

Scott Taylor is assistant professor of African studies at the School of Foreign Service of Georgetown University, Washington, D.C. He has written on African political economy and democracy.

Kirsten Walles is a doctoral student at the University of Texas at Austin, specializing in Islam in West Africa.

Jacqueline Woodfork has worked for many years as an administrator in the United States and Africa. She is an assistant professor of history at Loyola University, New Orleans, Louisiana, and she is writing a book on Senegal during World War II.